Specialized Courts
Dealing with Sex Delinquency

PATTERSON SMITH REPRINT SERIES IN
CRIMINOLOGY, LAW ENFORCEMENT, AND SOCIAL PROBLEMS

1. Lewis: *The Development of American Prisons and Prison Customs, 1776-1845*
2. Carpenter: *Reformatory Prison Discipline*
3. Brace: *The Dangerous Classes of New York*
4. Dix: *Remarks on Prisons and Prison Discipline in the United States*
5. Bruce *et al: The Workings of the Indeterminate-Sentence Law and the Parole System in Illinois*
6. Wickersham Commission: *Complete Reports, Including the Mooney-Billings Report.* 14 Vols.
7. Livingston: *Complete Works on Criminal Jurisprudence.* 2 Vols.
8. Cleveland Foundation: *Criminal Justice in Cleveland*
9. Illinois Association for Criminal Justice: *The Illinois Crime Survey*
10. Missouri Association for Criminal Justice: *The Missouri Crime Survey*
11. Aschaffenburg: *Crime and Its Repression*
12. Garofalo: *Criminology*
13. Gross: *Criminal Psychology*
14. Lombroso: *Crime, Its Causes and Remedies*
15. Saleilles: *The Individualization of Punishment*
16. Tarde: *Penal Philosophy*
17. McKelvey: *American Prisons*
18. Sanders: *Negro Child Welfare in North Carolina*
19. Pike: *A History of Crime in England.* 2 Vols.
20. Herring: *Welfare Work in Mill Villages*
21. Barnes: *The Evolution of Penology in Pennsylvania*
22. Puckett: *Folk Beliefs of the Southern Negro*
23. Fernald *et al: A Study of Women Delinquents in New York State*
24. Wines: *The State of the Prisons and of Child-Saving Institutions*
25. Raper: *The Tragedy of Lynching*
26. Thomas: *The Unadjusted Girl*
27. Jorns: *The Quakers as Pioneers in Social Work*
28. Owings: *Women Police*
29. Woolston: *Prostitution in the United States*
30. Flexner: *Prostitution in Europe*
31. Kelso: *The History of Public Poor Relief in Massachusetts: 1820-1920*
32. Spivak: *Georgia Nigger*
33. Earle: *Curious Punishments of Bygone Days*
34. Bonger: *Race and Crime*
35. Fishman: *Crucibles of Crime*
36. Brearley: *Homicide in the United States*
37. Graper: *American Police Administration*
38. Hichborn: *"The System"*
39. Steiner & Brown: *The North Carolina Chain Gang*
40. Cherrington: *The Evolution of Prohibition in the United States of America*
41. Colquhoun: *A Treatise on the Commerce and Police of the River Thames*
42. Colquhoun: *A Treatise on the Police of the Metropolis*
43. Abrahamsen: *Crime and the Human Mind*
44. Schneider: *The History of Public Welfare in New York State: 1609-1866*
45. Schneider & Deutsch: *The History of Public Welfare in New York State: 1867-1940*
46. Crapsey: *The Nether Side of New York*
47. Young: *Social Treatment in Probation and Delinquency*
48. Quinn: *Gambling and Gambling Devices*
49. McCord & McCord: *Origins of Crime*
50. Worthington & Topping: *Specialized Courts Dealing with Sex Delinquency*

PUBLICATION No. 50: PATTERSON SMITH REPRINT SERIES IN CRIMINOLOGY, LAW ENFORCEMENT, AND SOCIAL PROBLEMS

Specialized Courts Dealing with Sex Delinquency

A Study of the Procedure in Chicago, Boston, Philadelphia and New York

BY

GEORGE E. WORTHINGTON

Acting Director, Department of Legal Measures, American Social Hygiene Association, Member of Washington State and New York Bars

AND

RUTH TOPPING

Field Secretary, Bureau of Social Hygiene

Montclair, New Jersey

PATTERSON SMITH

1969

BOWLING GREEN STATE UNIVERSITY LIBRARY

Originally published 1925
Reprinted 1969 by
Patterson Smith Publishing Corporation
Montclair, New Jersey

SBN 87585-050-2

Library of Congress Catalog Card Number: 69-14954

343.53
W93w

466179

INTRODUCTION

PURPOSES AND METHODS OF THE STUDY

Many persons interested in problems of social hygiene have felt that in the courts dealing with sex offenders serious administrative inequalities often operate against women delinquents. Some learning of the provision for trial by jury of prostitutes in Chicago, believe this to be an important safeguard against sex discriminations. Indeed, at various times it has been publicly proposed that an effort be made in New York City to secure legislation to permit trial by jury in all classes of sex offenses.

The American Social Hygiene Association and the Bureau of Social Hygiene have been repeatedly appealed to for their views on this and other points connected with the courts dealing with sex delinquents. They finally decided to undertake jointly a study of the Morals Court of Chicago, with no preconceived findings to be reached and no propaganda to spread. It was their desire solely to ascertain the exact conditions and compare them with those obtaining in New York City. Later a study of the courts of Philadelphia and Boston was determined upon for comparative purposes.

Miss Topping was detailed by the Bureau of Social Hygiene to handle the social and statistical aspects of the survey, while Mr. Worthington of the American Social Hygiene Association undertook the study of the legal aspects.

Miss Topping spent a month in each city, following cases through the court, interviewing the Judges, probation officers and other court officials, visiting clinics and detention houses and institutions used by the court and collecting blanks, reports and all available literature.

Mr. Worthington paid several weeks' visit to each court, observing the court procedure from the bench, interview-

ing judges, court officials, district attorneys, etc., and recording the legal aspects of the surveys.

Following Chapter V, comparing the methods of each
court, the diagrams present to the eye the course which a case
takes in each court.

Comparatively few cities in the United States have separate courts for this special type of offense. In smaller cities
it is impracticable to maintain such independent courts. It
seemed possible, however, that to cities which contemplated
such an undertaking, a synthesis of what seemed to be the
best practice in each court, taking one feature from one court
and one from another, would be of value.

This synthesis Chapter VI attempts to make. Before publication it was submitted to specialists, including social
workers, health officers, probation officers, and judges. In
some instances their criticisms and suggestions have modified
the view originally presented. Special acknowledgment for
valuable criticisms is due to Chief Magistrate William
McAdoo, Magistrate Jean Norris, Miss Alice Smith, Mr. Fred-
erick H. Whitin, Miss Henrietta Additon, Mr. John Weston,
Mr. Charles Chute, Dr. William F. Snow.

The several chapters here presented appeared as articles
in the Journal of Social Hygiene, October 1921, January 1922,
April 1922, October 1922, June 1923 and June 1924.

While in some minor details there have been changes in the
court procedure since the studies were made, a later general
survey leads us to believe that in all important matters the
pictures presented are correct.

The demand for our reprints has been so great that the
supply is exhausted. Hence, we believe that their reproduc-
tion in this form will be of service.

We are indebted to Miss Mary A. Clark, statistician of the
American Social Hygiene Association for advice and help in
the preparation of tables.

KATHARINE BEMENT DAVIS

NEW YORK,
    January, 1925.

CONTENTS

CHAPTER IV

THE WOMEN'S DAY COURT OF MANHATTAN AND THE BRONX, NEW YORK CITY

CHAPTER V

SUMMARY AND COMPARATIVE STUDY OF THE SPECIAL COURTS IN CHICAGO, PHILADELPHIA, BOSTON, AND NEW YORK

CHAPTER VI

STANDARDS FOR A SOCIALIZED COURT FOR DEALING WITH SEX DELINQUENTS

LIST OF TABLES

CHAPTER I

THE MORALS COURT OF CHICAGO

CHAPTER II

THE MISDEMEANANTS' DIVISION OF THE PHILADELPHIA MUNICIPAL COURT

CHAPTER III

THE SECOND SESSIONS OF THE MUNICIPAL COURT
OF THE CITY OF BOSTON

CHAPTER IV

THE WOMEN'S DAY COURT OF MANHATTAN
AND THE BRONX, NEW YORK CITY

CHAPTER V

SUMMARY AND COMPARATIVE STUDY OF THE SPECIAL COURTS IN CHICAGO, PHILADELPHIA, BOSTON, AND NEW YORK

Specialized Courts
Dealing with Sex Delinquency

SPECIALIZED COURTS
DEALING WITH SEX DELINQUENCY

CHAPTER I

THE MORALS COURT OF CHICAGO

The Morals Court is a branch of the Chicago Municipal Court. The Municipal Court was created by an act of the Illinois Legislature in 1905.[1]

AUTHORITY AND JURISDICTION

The Municipal Court has jurisdiction of all misdemeanors;[2] quasi criminal actions,[3] such as violations of city ordinances; and also the functions of a magistrate, such as arraignments and proceedings for the prevention of the commission of crimes.[4]

The judges are elected for a term of six years, the qualifications providing that they shall be citizens of the state, at least thirty years old, and shall have engaged in the active practice of law or as a judge for at least five years next preceding their election.[1]

Appeals are taken directly either to the Supreme Court, or the Appellate Court under conditions hereinafter set forth.

Power is given the judges to create by order, branch courts

[1] Pars. 3313–3385, Illinois Statutes of 1913.
[2] Par. 3314, Subd. 3, Illinois Statutes of 1913.
[3] Par. 3314, Subd. 5, Illinois Statutes of 1913.
[4] Par. 3314, Subd. 6, Illinois Statutes of 1913.

3

from time to time, and under this authority, the Morals Court was created by Gen. Order No. 240 of April 3, 1913, of the Municipal Court, as amended Dec. 18, 1913, by G. O. No. 276. This order reads as follows:

It is hereby ordered, that there be and hereby is established a branch of this court before which all criminal and quasi-criminal cases of offenses of keeping, maintaining, leasing, and patronizing houses of ill fame and places for the practice of prostitution or lewdness, enticing female into or detaining female in a house of prostitution or other place where prostitution, fornication, or concubinage is practiced, inducing female to leave the state for the purpose of prostitution or fornication, open lewdness or other notorious act of public indecency tending to debauch the public morals, selling or dealing in obscene, immoral, or impure books, pictures or literature, and nightwalking, shall on and after April 7, 1913, be brought, tried and disposed of. The above shall include all criminal informations, complaints to hold to await the action of a grand jury and complaints for violation of ordinances. Said branch court shall be designated as Criminal Branch No. 2, and until further order herein shall be held in Court Room 1106 in the City Hall in the city of Chicago.

PURPOSES

The Morals Court was established at the request of the famous Chicago Vice Commission, which recommended such a court in order to put pressure on the city authorities and the State's Attorney to compel them to enforce the laws and wipe out the segregated vice district in Chicago. By bringing all such cases into one court, it was possible for the general public without much difficulty to observe in what manner the authorities enforced the law. . . . With all these cases in one court the activities of such persons can be controlled.

The activities of the police force are, of course, easily observed in such courts, and the social agencies of the city can better render personal service wherever such is required.[1]

The establishment of the Morals Court

" . . . followed as a natural sequence to the breaking up of the

---

[1] Chief Justice Harry Olson, "The Municipal Court of Chicago," an address delivered before the Ontario Bar Association, March 4, 1920, pp. 8–9.

segregated district, the judges having in mind that instead of that system of segregation which in the past was maintained to build up vice and destroy lives, they would segregate for the purpose of building up lives and destroying vice. As a result, Chicago may now boast of the fact that, instead of that segregated place where vice was cultivated and encouraged, and girls and women degraded and despoiled, it has a place for the gathering up of the unfortunate offenders; where those who desire to do better find friendly aid and encouragement; where the sick are ministered to, the vicious prosecuted and punished and where all the vile influences of the underworld are exposed to view—influences which, left unrestrained, soon gain a dominant power over the body politic." . . . When they were scattered among the other courts, "the unfortunate women were made the victims of unscrupulous bondsmen, shysters, panders, and fixers, who always abound in these courts, and whose manipulations it was impossible to observe or check because of the lack of administrative machinery, and because of the fact that the judges in these courts were being constantly changed and had no opportunity to become familiar with conditions beyond those appearing from the evidence in the case at bar. It requires considerable experience to deal properly with these cases and to acquire an understanding of them. Even the judge sitting constantly in the Morals Court finds difficulty in grasping the real situation. There is always present an undercurrent, which seldom shows itself above the surface. . . . This difficulty might be overcome by a judge sitting in this court permanently. . . . By maintaining this separate branch, . . . the defendants can be more or less protected from the operations of impostors; and, above all, we are given the opportunity of taking a glimpse at the social aspect of this morbid business and of ascertaining the physical, mental, and social condition of the individuals involved. . . . A trained judge becomes expert in determining what disposition should be made of each case in the light of all the bigger facts of which he becomes cognizant, which are necessary to a proper understanding of the problem, but are not presented to him from the witness-stand. He is also put in a position to call upon the many splendid social agencies for personal service whenever their aid is required." [1]

---

[1] Judge Harry M. Fisher, Tenth and Eleventh Annual Reports, Municipal Court of Chicago, 1915–1917, pp. 85–86.

To summarize, the purposes are: to reduce commercialized prostitution by a concentration of all prostitution and allied cases in one court, which would demonstrate the tremendous volume of the business of prostitution, and thereby result in arousing the public conscience; to check up the workings of the police in this particular field; to avoid waste of judicial power, save time, promote efficiency of administration, and lastly to deal more wisely with offenders and to marshal the social agencies organized for the assistance of such cases.

LAWS ENFORCED BY MORALS COURT

This report will be concerned more particularly with those phases of the court's activities which relate to prostitution either directly or indirectly. This, of course, is what the court is chiefly concerned with, although a few cases involving abduction, seduction, and obscene literature or pictures are also heard.

To shed light upon the jurisdiction as well as the limitations of the court in cases involving prostitution, it has been deemed wise to set forth the statutes and ordinances covering this subject.

Table 1 at the end of this chapter,[1] setting forth disposition of cases of sex offenders, during the first six months of 1920, classified by offense, shows that by far the greater number of cases brought into the Morals Court are for violations of city ordinances. The ordinances with which the Morals Court is concerned, are known as 2012, 2014, 2015, 2018, and 2019, of the Chicago Code of Ordinances of 1911, which ordinances read as follows:

2012. Disorderly Conduct—penalty. All persons who shall make, aid, countenance or assist in making any improper noise, riot, disturbance, breach of the peace or diversion tending to a breach of the peace within the limits of the city; all persons who shall collect in bodies or crowds for unlawful purposes, or for any purpose, to the annoyance or disturbance of other persons; all persons who are

---

[1] For discussion of all tables, see p. 66 ff.

idle or dissolute and go about begging; all persons who use or exercise any juggling or other unlawful games or plays; all persons who are found in houses of
ill-fame or gaming houses; all persons lodging in or found at any time in out-
houses, sheds, barns, stables or unoccupied buildings, or underneath sidewalks,
or lodging in the open air and not giving a good account of themselves; all persons
who shall wilfully assault another in said city, or be engaged in or aid or abet
in any fight, quarrel or other disturbance in said city; all persons who stand,
loiter, or stroll about in any place in said city waiting or seeking to obtain money
or other valuable thing from others by trick or fraud or to bid or assist therein;
all persons that shall engage in any fraudulent scheme, device or trick to obtain
money or other valuable thing in any place in said city, or who shall aid or abet
or in any manner be concerned therein; all touts, ropers, steerers, or cappers,
so-called, for any gambling room or house who shall ply or attempt to ply their
calling on any public street in said city; all persons found loitering about in any
hotel, block, bar-room, dramshop, gambling house, or disorderly house, or wandering about the streets either by night or day without any known lawful means of
support, or without being able to give a satisfactory account of themselves; all
persons who shall have or carry any pistol, knife, dirk, knuckles, slung-shot, or
other dangerous weapon concealed on or about their person; and all persons who
are known to be thieves, burglars, pickpockets, robbers or confidence men, either
by their own confession or otherwise, or by having been convicted of larceny,
burglary, or other crime against the laws of the State of Illinois, who are found
lounging in or prowling, or loitering around any steamboat landing, railroad depot,
banking institution, place of public amusement, auction room, hotel, store, shop,
thoroughfare, car, omnibus, public conveyance, public gathering, public assembly,
court room, public building, private dwelling-house, out-house, house of ill-fame,
gambling house, tippling shop, or any public place, and who are unable to give
a reasonable excuse for being so found, shall be deemed guilty of disorderly conduct, and upon conviction thereof shall be severally subject to a fine of not less
than one dollar nor more than two hundred dollars for each offense.

2014. Keeping house of ill-fame or assignation—penalty. No person shall
keep or maintain a house of ill-fame or assignation, or place for the practice of
fornication or prostitution or lewdness, under a penalty of not to exceed two
hundred dollars for every twenty-four hours such house or place shall be kept or
maintained for such purpose.

2015. Patrons or inmates of houses of ill-fame or assignation. No person
shall patronize, frequent, be found in or be an inmate of any house of ill-fame,
or assignation, or place for the practice of prostitution or lewdness, under a
penalty of not exceeding two hundred dollars for each offense.

2018. Night Walkers. Soliciting upon the streets or public places. All prostitutes, solicitors to prostitution, and all persons of evil fame or repute, plying
their vocations upon the streets, alleys, or public places in the city, are hereby
declared to be common nuisances, and shall be fined not to exceed one hundred
dollars for each offense.

2019. Public Nuisance. Every common, ill-governed or disorderly house, room
or other premises, kept for the encouragement of idleness, gaming, drinking,

fornication, or other misbehavior, is hereby declared to be a public nuisance, and the keeper and all persons connected with the maintenance thereof, and all persons patronizing or frequenting the same, shall be fined not exceeding two hundred dollars for each offense.

The state laws with which the court is particularly concerned are the following. Section 57a–1 of the Criminal Code, commonly known as the Kate Adams law:

Whoever is an inmate of a house of ill-fame or assignation or place for the practice of fornication or prostitution or lewdness, or who shall solicit to prostitution in any street, alley, park or other place in any city, village or incorporated town in this state, shall be fined not exceeding two hundred dollars, or imprisoned in the county jail or House of Correction for a period of not more than one (1) year, or both.

Section 57, keeping a disorderly house, patronizing, etc.:

Whoever keeps or maintains a house of ill-fame or place for the practice of prostitution or lewdness, or whoever patronizes the same, or lets any house, room or other premises for any such purpose or shall keep a common, ill-governed and disorderly house to the encouragement of idleness, gaming, drinking, fornication or other misbehavior, shall be fined not exceeding $200.

Section 57g, commonly known as the pandering law:

Any person who for procuring a female for a house of prostitution, or who by promises, threats, violence or by any device or scheme, shall cause, entice, persuade or encourage a female person to become an inmate of a house of prostitution, or shall procure a place as inmate in a house of prostitution for a female person, or any person who shall by promises, threats, violence or by any device or scheme, cause, induce, persuade or encourage an inmate of a house of prostitution to remain therein as such inmate, or any person who shall, by fraud or artifice, or by duress of person or goods, or by abuse of any position of confidence or authority, procure any female person to become an inmate of a house of ill-fame, or to enter any place in which prostitution is encouraged or allowed within this state, or to come into this state, or leave this state for the purpose of prostitution, or who shall procure any female person to become an inmate of a house of ill-fame within this state, or to come into this state, or leave this state for the purpose of prostitution, or who shall receive or give or agree to receive or give, any money or thing of value for procuring or attempting to procure, any female person to become an inmate of a house of ill-fame within this state, or to come into this state or leave this state for the purpose of prostitution, ''or any person who shall knowingly, without lawful consideration, take, accept, or receive money or thing of value from any female person from the earnings of her prostitution, or any person who shall directly or indirectly take, receive or accept money or other thing of value for providing, procuring or furnishing for another any person for the purpose of illicit sexual intercourse,'' shall be guilty of pandering, and upon conviction for an offense under this act, shall be punished by imprisonment in the County Jail or House of Correction for a period of not less than six months nor more than one year and by a fine of not less than $300 and not to exceed $1,000, and upon conviction for any subsequent offense under this act, shall be punished by imprisonment in the penitentiary for a period of not less than one year nor more than ten years.

Section 11, known as the Fornication and Adultery Law:

If any man and woman shall live together in an open state of adultery or fornication or adultery and fornication, every such person shall be fined not exceeding $500, or confined in the county jail not exceeding one year. For a second offense, such man or woman shall be severely punished twice as much as the former punishment, and for a third offense treble, and thus increasing the punishment for each succeeding offense. Provided, however, that it shall be in the power of the party or parties offending, to prevent or suspend the prosecution by their intermarriage, if such marriage can be legally solemnized, and upon the payment of the costs of such prosecution.

Section 270, known as the Vagrancy Law:

All persons who are idle and dissolute, and who go begging; all persons who use any juggling or other unlawful games or place; runaways; pilferers; confidence men; common drunkards; common night walkers; lewd, wanton and lascivious persons, in speech or behavior; common railers and brawlers; persons who are habitually neglectful of their employment or other calling, and do not lawfully provide for themselves, or for the support of their families; and all persons who are idle, dissolute, and who neglect all lawful business, and who habitually misspend their time frequenting houses of ill-fame, gaming houses or tippling shops; all persons lodging in or about in the night time in out-houses, sheds, barns, or in unoccupied buildings, or lodging in the open air, and not giving a good account of themselves, and all persons who are known to be thieves, burglars or pickpockets, either by their own confession or otherwise, or by having been convicted of larceny, burglary, or other crime against the laws of the state, punishable by imprisonment in the state prison, or in the house of correction of any city, and having no lawful means of support, who are habitually found prowling around any steamboat landing, railroad depot, banking institution, broker's office, place of public amusement, auction room, store, shop, or court, thoroughfare, car or omnibus, or at any public gathering or assembly or lounging about any court room, private dwelling houses, or out-houses, or are found in any house of ill-fame, gambling house, or tippling shop, shall be deemed to be and declared to be vagabonds.

Stats. 1913, 3737, Soliciting, by either male or female for prostitution.

If any one shall, through invitation or device, prevail upon any person to visit any room, building, booth, yard, garden, boat, or float kept for the purpose of gambling, or prostitution or fornication, he shall, on conviction thereof, for the first offense, be fined not less than $10 nor more than $100; second offense, $100 to $300, or six months in county jail.

It will be noted that in all of these ordinances and state laws, there is no provision for commitment except in the Kate Adams Law, the pandering law, and the fornication and adultery law. Only women offenders are punishable under the Kate Adams Law, the Supreme Court, in the case of *People against Rice, 277, Ill. 521,* having held that men cannot be inmates of a disorderly house.[1] It should be also noted that fornication and adultery are not offenses except where the parties live together in an open state of fornication or adultery; in other words, a single act of fornication or adultery does not constitute an offense. Table 1 at the end of this chapter contains a study of the records for a six-month period, which indicates the relative use of the foregoing laws and ordinances, as well as the disposition thereunder.

---

[1] "If the defendant is found guilty, the court may impose a fine; or (in the case of a female inmate of a house of prostitution, or one charged with soliciting on the street), it may, under Sec. 57a–1, Criminal Code, enacted in 1915, send her to the House of Correction for a period not exceeding one year, and impose a fine not exceeding $200. Formerly this Act was construed to apply to male inmates and to keepers; but our Supreme Court in the case of *People vs. Rice, 277, Ill. 521,* held this Act does not apply to male inmates, and, by the same reasoning, to keepers. By this holding, the real effectiveness of this statute is destroyed. Its effect is to enable the courts to deal out more severe punishment to those least deserving it, the unfortunate girls. The men who live upon them (unless they are guilty of pandering) . . . and the keepers, . . . who get more of the proceeds than the girls get, these may be fined not to exceed $200; whereas the girl may be sent to the House of Correction for one year, plus a $200 fine." Tenth and Eleventh Annual Report, Municipal Court of Chicago, 1915–1917, pp. 89–90.

This law was amended by the legislature in 1921. See Chapter 38, page 1195, Criminal Code of 1921, Section 57-A.

Another law with which the court is specially concerned is Paragraph 4, Section 6092, Laws of 1919, which provides that "when it appears to any judge or justice of the peace from the evidence or otherwise that any person coming before him on any criminal charge may be suffering from any communicable venereal disease, it shall be the duty of such judge or justice of the peace to refer such person to the direction of such hospital, sanitarium, or clinic, or to such other officer as shall be selected or appointed for the purpose of examining the accused person, and if such person be found to be suffering from any communicable venereal disease, he or she may by order of the court be sent for treatment to a hospital, sanitarium or clinic if any be available, and if necessary, be segregated for such terms as the court may impose at such hospital, sanitarium, or clinic." This law vests in the court duties that one ordinarily would expect to be exercised by a health department, and may explain some of the present procedure of the court.

PROCEDURE

The usual criminal procedure prevails of arrest, detention, and bail, complaint and trial. The class of cases tried before this Court does not require a grand jury indictment.

1. *Arrest.* Cases reach the Morals Court in two ways: first, upon the complaint of a citizen in which case a warrant is generally issued; and second, by police initiative, which may involve an arrest either with or without a warrant. There was at the time of the investigation no specially organized plain-clothes vice squad in Chicago. About five plain-clothes men operated directly under the general superintendent of police. In addition, there were two or three plain-clothes men in each police precinct who might be assigned to vice duties. The work of these men was limited largely to the detection and arrest of persons who solicit on the street for the purpose of prostitution,[1] rather than to the securing of evidence against

---

[1] See Case B, p. 22.

disorderly houses, hotels, apartments, etc. They also made occasional raids upon disorderly houses or hotels where a complaint had been entered. Practically no raids were being made, according to the best information available, except on places which had a general reputation for being disorderly, and where complaints of private individuals had been entered. Law enforcement authorities seemed to be unanimous in agreeing that the pseudo-respectable hotels and apartments were not being molested by the police. For this reason, the so-called better class of prostitutes and their customers were not passing through the machinery of the courts. This may account in part for the comparatively small number of bond forfeitures [1] during the six months' period.[2]

2. *Detention and Bail.* When a woman is arrested she is said by police headquarters officials to be detained for physical examination regardless of whether or not she can make bail. She is booked on an "open charge" and generally detained in one of the three detention houses over night. On the following morning, and before trial, she is taken to the Iroquois Hospital for examination.[3] In the case of the men who are arrested, provision is made for fixing immediate bail, and upon bail being made, the male defendant is released. Municipal Court Rules 24–30 contain the provision governing the acceptance of bail. The following is the rule for the acceptance of cash bail:

Rule 26. Any defendant arrested in any criminal case in which the Municipal Court has original jurisdiction, or in any quasi-criminal case, may, in lieu of giving bail for his appearance, deposit with the clerk or with any chief of

---

[1] See Table 5, fourth column, showing cash or surety bonds forfeited.

[2] "Not many prosperous looking prostitutes are brought in. Probably because of their relatively higher intellects, they are in a position to evade the authorities; although one is tempted to suspect that other influences contribute to their immunity." Tenth and Eleventh Annual Reports, Municipal Court of Chicago, 1915–1917, p. 85.

[3] Mr. Worthington noted that of the cases of women arraigned during the three days in which he was present at sessions of the court, all but four women had been examined previous to trial or arraignment.

police, captain of police, lieutenant of police, or desk sergeant of police, a sum of money, as follows:

For a violation of Section 2012 of the Chicago Code of 1911, $25 to $100.
For a violation of Section 2807 of the Chicago Code of 1911, $200.
For a violation of Section 1950 of the Chicago Code of 1911, $50 to $200.
For a violation of Section 2025 of the Chicago Code of 1911, $50 to $200.
For assault and battery, $25 to $100. In bastardy cases, $550.

In all other cases a sum equivalent to the maximum fine provided as a punishment for the offense. Unregistered bonds of the government of the United States and the city of Chicago may be deposited the same as money, such bonds being accepted at their par value with accrued interest. If any such bonds shall not be redeemed within thirty days after the accrual of liability growing out of a forfeiture or judgment against the defendant, the Clerk of the Court shall either turn said bond into the city treasury at its par value with accrued interest or shall sell it at private sale with or without notice at the current market price, rendering the surplus, if any, to the person that deposited said bond. (As amended by General Order No. 373, May 25, 1917.)

The judge then sitting in the Morals Court stated that in the case of a surety bail bond, the amount is customarily fixed at $400. Table 12, at the end of this chapter, shows the number and amount of cash bonds accepted in the Morals Court from January 1 to July 1, 1920. Only a partial list of bond forfeitures [1] for this period could be secured. This shows sixty-two forfeitures of cash bonds and two of surety bonds.

3. *Complaint and Trial.* According to the report of Judge Fisher, in virtually all cases coming before the Morals Court, complaint follows, rather than precedes, arrest. The offenders are apprehended on sight and brought before the court the next morning when a complaint is presented (upon application) for leave to file. Judge Fisher has the following to say

---

[1] A court attaché explained that the following was the procedure observed when a bond on which a third party was surety was forfeited: The bondsman appeared at an ex-parte hearing; the court was informed as to the nature of the evidence against the defendant, and the usual fine and costs assessed, which were paid by bondsman, whereupon he was released from obligations existing under his bond. In case of a cash deposit by a third person, he is returned the balance after the payment of fine and costs. The authors of this report did not personally observe such a proceeding.

about his practice in this respect, covering a period prior to December, 1917:

Great care should be exercised by the court in ascertaining whether the facts in the case justify filing a complaint. A guiding thought of the judge should be to prevent injustice. What greater wrong can be done a respectable woman than making a public record of immorality against her and forcing her to contest the charge in a public hearing, for when leave to file a complaint is given, a public trial must be had under the constitution and the laws of the state. It was, therefore, my practice to interrogate the complaining witness or officer in chambers in the presence of the state's attorney, the prosecuting attorney, defendant, and social worker on the application for leave to file a complaint. If no probable cause was shown, leave was, of course, refused. If the circumstances were such that justice would be better served by not prosecuting the complaint, the state's attorney or city prosecutor would, of his own motion or by the court's suggestion, withdraw the application for leave to file the complaint, even if a prima facie case were made out; thus the woman was saved the humiliation of a public trial and a permanent record.[1]

The practice observed at the time of the present investigation was for the clerk to have the complaint ready for the judge's signature upon the defendant's case being called. The judge thereupon signed it without any preliminary examination into the facts and then proceeded immediately with the trial or other disposition of the case. These complaints were said to have been drawn up by a police sergeant and needless to say advantage was not infrequently taken by the defendant of their many defects on a motion for a new trial or upon appeal. The procedure observed by the court in handling the cases was said to differ somewhat with the various judges. The judge sitting at the time of the investigation had a ruling that he would not split cases; that is, in case several people were brought in on a raid and one of them failed or refused to sign a jury waiver, all of the persons arrested at the same

---

[1] Tenth and Eleventh Annual Reports, Municipal Court of Chicago, 1915–1917, pp. 88–89.

time by the same officers, were sent to the Jury Branch, in spite of the fact that some of the defendants urged to be granted an immediate trial and disposition of their case. If any of the defendants in the case were women the court made the customary inquiry as to whether or not they had been physically examined. If any women had not been examined, the cases of all the defendants arrested with them were continued for ten days, so that the women might be examined and the laboratory reports received. In case it was stated that a woman had refused to be examined, the case was continued. Court attachés and health department representatives then had an opportunity to use their persuasive powers to get the woman to agree to such an examination. In the case of three women who came before the court, in which the statement was made that they had refused to submit to examination, one of the court attachés was overheard to say, "They'll give us a fight on it, but they will submit later on . . . "[1]

There was a conflict of opinion as to whether or not any of the men are examined. With the exception of a single case, no evidence could be found of the examination, treatment, or segregation of male defendants brought before the Morals Court, although provision is made by law[2] for the examination of persons charged with a criminal offense. The law further specifies, "If such person be found to be suffering from any communicable venereal disease, he or she may by order of the court be sent for treatment to a hospital, sanitarium, or clinic, etc." Searches were made of the court, probation, and institutional records for cases of this kind. Statements regarding the practice of the court and department of health in this regard were so conflicting as to form no basis for an accurate estimate of the number, if any, or disposition of the

---

[1] He further stated: "No bondsman will sign her bond unless the girl submits to the test," which was described as a "bit of coöperation" between the health department and the bondsmen.

[2] Paragraph 4, Section 6092, Illinois Laws of 1919, discussed on pp. 11 of this report.

cases. The one instance found was that of a young man twenty-two years old removed from the County Jail to the venereal disease ward of the County Hospital; the record showed that the boy had been serving a sentence imposed by the Morals Court.

As the defendants stepped up to the clerk's desk after their names had been called and they had been sworn in, a jury waiver was put before them accompanied by a muttered word from the clerk about signing which apparently conveyed little meaning to the defendant. If the defendant were represented by an attorney, he might advise her to sign the waiver, or if it seemed to be advantageous to have the case tried before the judge of the jury court, or if for any reason a jury trial were desired, the customary procedure was to refuse to sign the waiver, which automatically sent the case into the Jury Branch. This procedure was not infrequently taken advantage of by defendant's attorney to relieve him of any possible embarrassment which might arise from filing an affidavit of prejudice,[1] in case the judge might not be to his liking.

If the offense is a violation of a city ordinance, the prosecution is conducted by a deputy city prosecutor. If it is a violation of a state law, the deputy state's attorney prosecutes. The rules of evidence relating to civil cases govern in the case of a violation of a city ordinance, such a case being said to be construed in law as having the effect of a civil case, and, therefore, a preponderance of evidence is sufficient to sustain a conviction. In the offenses against state laws, however, it is necessary, under the rules of criminal evidence, to prove the case beyond a reasonable doubt. The judge stated that city cases may be dismissed by the city prosecutor without leave of court. State cases, however, cannot be dismissed

---

[1] The right to a change of venue in the Municipal Court is apparently unlimited as to the number of judges against which it might be directed. The case of *People vs. Ben Zellern* is reported in the Annual Report of the Chicago Committee of Fifteen for 1920 (p. 9) in which an affidavit was filed objecting to eighteen of the thirty-one judges, and a judge finally was assigned who was not objectionable to defendant.

by the state's attorney without the consent of a judge of the Municipal Court.

No court reporter is provided to take a stenographic record of the testimony or proceedings. This is a distinct disadvantage to the court as well as the parties, as the judge must rely wholly upon his memory to detect conflicting statements and evidence of perjury. The disadvantage to all concerned, in case of appeal, is apparent.

Finger-prints are not made of defendants appearing in the Morals Court, either before or after conviction, because of lack of statutory authority. The one accurate method for detecting recidivism adequately is therefore lacking.[1]

Probably the feature that most impresses the court visitor is the great number of cases that are continued. This is indicated to a certain extent by the third column of Table 5, which shows the number of continuances during the first six months of 1920, although one cannot determine from it how many cases these continuances represent, the number of times a single case may have been continued, nor the interval of time between continuances.[2] The day's docket may contain fifty or more cases, out of which during three days' observation, not

---

[1] The Cleveland Hospital and Health Survey (1920, p. 427) has the following to say in behalf of the finger-print system for this class of cases: "The finger-print system for convicted sex offenders is of the utmost value to the judge in his disposition of cases. Repeaters constantly give false names and often escape identification without such a system. As above indicated, the test of court treatment is the proportion of offenders who repeat. This test cannot be applied without an infallible system of identification. The finger-print system is the only one that is infallible. Constructively it enables the judge to determine, within five minutes after conviction of an offender, the probable value of probation, reformatory treatment, and the need for mental examination."

[2] In order to gain some definite knowledge of this practice, a study was made of the first one hundred women in 1920 whose cases had been continued one or more times. These one hundred cases are grouped in three tables at the end of this chapter, showing, respectively, the number of continuances in relation to final disposition (Table 8); the interval of time between appearance in Morals Court and final disposition (Table 9); and a third table showing the relation of number of convictions to intervals of time between first and final hearing (Table 10).

more than half a dozen cases a day were actually tried. In some continued cases the witnesses were not present although such witnesses were police officers. Some of these cases were dismissed and the defendants dicharged for want of prosecution. Several cases of violations of city ordinances were dismissed on motion of the city prosecutor who stated to the court that he did not believe the evidence he had was sufficient to convict. The state cases, however, which are prosecuted by the deputy state's attorney, were almost invariably tried. These were mostly fornication and adultery cases, with a few under the Kate Adams Law. Less than half a dozen cases a day are brought under the Kate Adams Law [1] which is the only law that provides for the commitment of prostitutes and night walkers, most of such cases being brought under Section 2018 of the city ordinance which provides by way of punishment, a maximum fine of $100 and no commitment. Exclusive of fornication and adultery, there is no ordinance or statute under which a man may be committed for any offense which involves prostitution, except pandering or white slavery. The keeper of a disorderly house is subject merely to a fine not exceeding $200, although his women inmates are subject to commitment. The Kate Adams Law which provides, among other things, for the punishment of inmates of houses of prostitution was held in the case of *People v. Rice,* 277 Illinois, 521, to apply only to the women. Consequently men cannot be convicted or committed under this law. The defendant in the case cited, was a clerk in a hotel which had the reputation of being disorderly. By this decision, keepers of bawdy-houses or pimps, who actually live in disorderly houses, if they are men, are not punishable under that law.

A number of cases were noted in which bonds were declared forfeited for non-appearance of defendants. In several instances the defendant called was a woman, and the health department representative was asked whether or not

---

[1] Since its amendment in 1921 the Kate Adams Law has been used more extensively in the cases of both women and men.

she had been examined. In a few cases the woman had been released on her own recognizance after examination. In two cases the results of the examination indicated that she was diseased. In these cases, capiases were issued for the rearrest of defendants. No instance of a capias issuing for the rearrest of a man was noted. The health department representative stated that a capias was issued only when examination revealed the defendant to be diseased. It was further noted that no inquiry was made as to whether or not the male defendants were diseased.

The observer is struck forcibly by the practice of long-time continuances.[1] The first continuance was customarily for ten days. This was the minimum time in which the report of the physical condition of the defendant was available to the court. If a defendant were reported infectious, it was customary to continue the case for a month. Further continuances were then granted at the request of the health department representative.

Table 10, at the end of this chapter, is illustrative. It is noteworthy that of the one hundred cases there shown only 11 per cent were tried without a continuance of more than ten days.

SPECIALIZATION

As indicated by the statement of Judge Fisher, quoted on page 5, the Morals Court is a specialized court more in name than in fact. Judge Fisher mentions the desirability of one judge being assigned to the court permanently. That this has not been done up to the time of the survey, is indicated by Table 7. This frequent change of judges renders it nearly impossible for any one judge to become expert in this class of cases. Furthermore, a considerable number of cases which should come before this court are not tried there due to a practice of filing affidavits for a change of venue against judges [2]

---

[1] See Note 2, page 17.
[2] See Note 1, page 16.

who are objectionable to the defendants and also due to the
practice of making frivolous jury demands. Under the existing procedure, because of rights existing under the Illinois
Constitution, a defendant is entitled in all cases to a jury trial
unless he signs a jury waiver. Failure to sign the jury waiver
results automatically in the granting to defendant of a jury
trial. When an experienced offender is brought before the
court or where the defendant is represented by crafty counsel,
the practice is to demand a jury if the judge sitting in the
Morals Court is objectionable to the defendant.[1] This automatically sends the case into the criminal jury branch, resulting, of course, in a delay.[2] Table 6, at the end of this chapter,
presents a study of court action on cases transferred from the
Morals Court to the Jury Branch, January 1 to June 30, 1920.
By the time the defendant's case is called in the Jury Court,
the objectionable judge may be gone from the Morals Court
and a new judge assigned there, in which case the defendant
may then sign a jury waiver and have a chance to be tried
before the judge in the Morals Court; or, as generally happens, the trial will be had before the judge of the Jury Branch
without a jury. An actual jury trial of a morals case is very
rare. Of the 93 who made jury demands during this period,
only five, or 5.3 per cent actually were tried by jury. Nor
are all morals cases in which a jury demand is made tried

---

[1] That the calculations of counsel and defendant miscarried somewhat during
the first six months of 1920 covered by our study is indicated by a comparison
of the percentage of convictions in the Morals Court with the percentage of convictions in cases transferred to the Jury Branch. These percentages stand as
follows:

	Men	Women	Total
Morals Court	25.1	20.1	22.9
Jury Branch	38.2	21.7	30.1

[2] The clerk states that the average period between appearance on charge and
trial by jury is about seven days. Between date of arraignment in Morals Court
and the call in the Jury Branch during the first six months of 1920, the average
length of time elapsing was 10 days; between date of arraignment in Morals
Court and final disposition in the Jury Branch, the average was 24 days.

in the Criminal Jury Court.[1] The calendar of this court is frequently so filled with other criminal cases that Morals Court cases requiring a jury trial occasionally have to be sent to other jury branches. Inasmuch as there are nine jury branches of the Municipal Court, it is possible for these cases to be scattered among nine different courts.

In order to give a concrete illustration of the way in which morals offenses were being handled at the time of the survey, the following record is given of cases, the trial of which was observed from a position beside the judge. These cover a four-day period in July, 1920.

ILLUSTRATIVE CASES

A. Couple taken in raid on disorderly hotel as a result of complaints by neighbors against house. Girl alleged she was a chambermaid and was charged with violation of Kate Adams Law (inmate). Girl had been physically examined and pronounced negative. Man charged with violation of city ordinance 2012 (disorderly conduct). Vice officers testified hotel was of known bad reputation and that previous convictions for prostitution had been obtained from the same address. Man admitted that he had gone to the same place once before "to get a woman"; that he had gone there again on the present occasion for the same purpose, and that the woman defendant had met him in the hall and taken him to her room for the purpose of prostitution, which purpose was accomplished. Officers corroborated this by testifying that defendants were in room together when they arrived. These allegations were denied by woman, who stated that in the course of her performance of the duties of chambermaid, she was engaged in cleaning up male defendant's room when the police entered. Her appearance in court would indicate that the occupation of chambermaid must be rather lucrative, inasmuch as she was expensively attired and had not spared the rouge in the

---

[1] Jury demands were made in 5847 Criminal Cases in the Municipal Court in 1919 automatically bringing that number into the Jury Branch. Of these, only 258 or 4.2 per cent took trial by jury after getting into the jury court. Of the Morals Cases during six months in 1920, 94.7 per cent did not take a jury trial after getting into the jury branch.

adornment of her face.   The fact that her physical condition was negative apparently weighed heavily in her favor, however, and she was acquitted.   Male defendant's admissions were accepted as a confession, and he was fined $1 and costs.

B. Three women charged with violation of ordinance 2018 for soliciting prostitution on the streets.   All three were eligible for trial, as examination had disclosed their physical condition to be negative in the matter of disease.   Officer testified he saw first woman addressing several men on the street after 10:30 in the evening; that he knew the woman to be a prostitute and that she had been arrested before.   Woman admitted that she had been arrested a few times before for solicitation, but stated that that was more than six months ago and that she was going straight now.   She said that she was employed to do housework two or three times a week at a place near where she was arrested and that on the evening in question she was going from this alleged place of employment to a "movie."   She furnished no corroboration as to her employment and also did not answer satisfactorily why she was going to a "movie" after 10:30 at night.   She was discharged with a word of warning to be careful in future.

The testimony of the officer as to the other two women, was that he had observed them walking back and forth on a corner where street-walkers usually solicit.   These two women tried to show in their defense as an alibi that one was on her way to visit the other. It happened that the judge lived near the address that the woman gave, so that he had judicial knowledge that she was giving a false address as there happened to be no such number in that block.   He asked the other woman how she was going to reach that address and she gave the name of a car line which she said she had taken, but which as a matter of fact did not run in that vicinity.   Because of these contradictions, the judge stated that their other testimony was discredited, and they were found guilty of soliciting on the streets. They were fined $3.00 with costs assessed at $2.00 ("three and two," in the language of the court).

C. Negro woman charged with violating city ordinance 2018.   Was arrested for soliciting on the street.   Had taken male customer to her room where they had been arrested.   Male defendant forfeited bail. No capias or bench warrant issued.   Arresting officers were asked what their evidence was.   Defendant offered no testimony.   Woman defendant had been at Lawndale Hospital under quarantine for a venereal disease for seven or eight weeks, and had been returned to court as non-infectious. The judge stated that inasmuch as she had been at the hospital so long she had been punished enough, and dismissed her case, saying to her as she left, "Go forth and sin no more."

D. Charge, fornication and adultery (statutory offense). Woman for fornication; man for adultery. Complainant, wife of male defendant. Woman defendant reported negative. The evidence showed that the male defendant had deserted his wife and had lived in an open state of adultery for thirty days with the woman defendant, during which time they had represented themselves as man and wife; that the female defendant knew her paramour to be a married man, and that she had described herself to the landlady and others as his wife. The judge sentenced the man to thirty days in the House of Correction and continued the case of the woman for a day, so that her social history might be secured to guide him in his disposition of her case.

E. Charge, fornication and adultery. Complaint by husband of woman defendant. Woman charged with adultery; man with fornication. Woman had been examined and found negative. Testimony was that defendants had left Chicago together and had cohabited for a week in Milwaukee until they were apprehended by the husband and Milwaukee police. Defendants dismissed, the court holding that the offense had been consummated outside the state, and was therefore not a violation of the Illinois laws.

F. Couple charged with fornication. Woman defendant a tiny Italian girl who appeared to be not more than fifteen, but who said she was nineteen. Man defendant a cripple who appeared in court on crutches. Girl defendant had been examined and found negative. Man defendant stated that he was employed at housework and was earning $12 a week. Charge admitted by both. He offered to marry girl defendant. Complaint had been made by mother of girl who stated that defendants had been living together for several days and she further stated that she very much objected to their getting married. The court continued the case for a few minutes and sent defendants into his chambers to be interviewed by woman bailiff to ascertain whether or not woman defendant was normal mentally and also to examine into the social history of defendants. (Apparently the proximity of the Psychopathic Laboratory was forgotten for the moment!) She returned in a few minutes, stating that she believed the girl to be normal mentally and gave her approval of the marriage, whereupon the court directed the defendants to withdraw to his chambers and be married by a Methodist minister who was present in court, and to report back after the wedding. One of the court attachés was sent down to the marriage license clerk to secure a license. In a short time the defendants reported back to the court that they had been married and their case was dismissed.

G. Three cases were called in which the women defendants had been released by the Health Department on their own recognizance after examination, and before the laboratory reports had been received. Defendants not being present in court, capiases were issued for the rearrest of the women. No bench warrants or capiases were issued for the missing men defendants. A statement was made that "it was dangerous -for diseased prostitutes to be at large." The officers who made the complaint said that they believed that the women in question had left town.

A half dozen other cases were called in which laboratory reports of the women defendants had not yet been received, whereupon the cases were continued, generally for ten days or two weeks.

H. In several cases, one or more of the women defendants were reported to have a venereal disease, in which event the case was postponed for several weeks, pending the defendant's return from the hospital.

I. For other cases observed, see pages 14–16, this report.

PHYSICAL ASPECTS OF THE COURT

The Morals Court is located on the tenth floor of the Municipal Building. Two side corridors, usually thronged with men and women having a direct or indirect interest in the cases, or with mere loiterers, lead to the entrance. Lawyers, bondsmen, and their clients may be heard transacting business and, the nature of the court being well known, a girl leaving the court room has little difficulty in making a date in these corridors. A court worker said that on a certain day she saw one girl solicit five men and another three. All took out notebooks and entered the dates. One of the girls was heard to call out: "Say, guy, do you want something easy?" No attendant or guard is stationed at the door to determine whether or not those who entered had business there.

The door of the court-room opens upon a space about twenty feet in width separating the bench from the seats at the rear of the room. The latter are occupied by defendants on bail, lawyers, witnesses, relatives, friends, or any who may care to hear the proceedings. Directly off the far side of the court-room are two small rooms. One of these has a telephone for general use, the other, about the size of a hall-bedroom, is used as a waiting-room for the girls and women brought to court each day from the detention houses or the County Jail. Two windows make the room light and airy. It is furnished with a long table, a few chairs, and a water-cooler. Three agate cups for common use hang near the latter. Ten to twenty girls may be locked in here at one time. As there is no toilet connected with the room,[1] the girls must rap on the door whenever they wish to use the public toilet for women around the corner from the court corridor. The woman bailiff or policewoman then unlocks the waiting-room door and leads the girls out past the persons on the benches at the rear of the room and through the crowded corridors between the court-room and the toilet. There she waits to conduct them all back to the waiting-room, where they are again locked in. Occasionally there has been a "break" for liberty, but no one has ever actually escaped.

The men's waiting-room is diagonally opposite that of the women's—a small, inside room without windows.

At the judge's right is a jury box, although jury cases are not heard in this court. Usually the seats are occupied by any interested spectators desirous of a closer view of the proceedings. On one occasion three girls, after their cases had been continued, ascended into the jury box in order to witness some of the other trials.

---

[1] A toilet and basin with running water have since been added.

The personnel of the Morals Court is comprised as follows:

1. Judge, elected for six years and assigned to the Morals Court by the Chief Justice of the Municipal Court.

2. Assistant State's Attorney, appointed by the State's Attorney.

3. Assistant City Prosecutor, appointed by the City Prosecutor.

4. Two men and one woman clerk, appointed by the Chief Clerk of the Municipal Court. The men perform the usual duties of a court clerk. The woman deputy acts as secretary of the Social Service Department. She endeavors to keep a card record of each woman arraigned in the Morals Court. She exercises also a sort of supervision over certain girls assigned to her by the judge and she may call in outside agencies to help in this work.

5. Two men and one woman bailiff, appointed by the Chief Bailiff of the Municipal Court.

6. A policewoman and a woman police-investigator, appointed by the Chief of Police.

7. A woman probation officer, assigned by the Chief of the Adult Probation Department.

8. A woman physician and a man psychiatrist, appointed by the Chief Justice of the Municipal Court. The physician examines cases referred to her by the Judge and treats hysteria or indisposition on the part of any woman detained in the court. A mental examination is given by the psychiatrist at the request of the Judge. Routine physical or mental examinations of all cases tried in this court are not made by these two officials.

9. A representative from the City Health Department, who reports to the court the results of the physical examination of women defendants.

SOCIAL SERVICE DEPARTMENT

In the fall of 1919 a Social Service Department was created in the Morals Court, under the control of the clerk of the Municipal Court. Mrs. Elizabeth M. Gardner was appointed secretary of this department by the clerk of the Municipal Court and is still serving. Her activities have been described under "Court Personnel," paragraph 4, p. 26, as well as in connection with the section on Records and Statistics, p. 58 ff.

It seems not unlikely that this department may have been an outgrowth of a discussion of "Social Service" by Judge Fisher in his report on the Morals Court,[1] especially in view of the fact that the establishment of such a department is one of his recommendations. He writes as follows:

I shall not attempt to name the numerous social service agencies entitled to credit for their unselfish labors in behalf of the unfortunate girls. These agencies work for the good they can accomplish and not for the credit they will get. But so important has their work become, that I am convinced that without their aid the court would in many cases be utterly helpless. The pity of it all is that a great community like ours should permit itself to accept aid, so absolutely necessary to the proper maintenance of its public institutions, from those who give it gratuitously, or from agencies supported by private contributions.

It was well enough for these private agencies to start the work, so as to demonstrate to the public its need and importance, but, that done, it becomes the duty of the community to assume the responsibility and relieve the private institutions to turn their attention to new fields of useful activity.

Can there be any reason why the city should be dependent upon any voluntary committee for information on vice conditions, or for the prosecution of serious offenders, or for the enforcement of the injunction and abatement laws, when the city is possessed of all the police and legal machinery necessary for the adequate performance of these important public functions? Yet without such voluntary help the work remains undone.

Or can any reason be assigned why the city should accept charitable contributions for the purpose of defraying the necessary expense of sending to her home some country girl who has suffered insult and degradation here? Still that is precisely what we are compelled to do in the Morals Court.

More than that, we are obliged to look to private agencies to take

---

[1] Tenth and Eleventh Annual Reports, Municipal Court of Chicago, 1915–1917, p. 91.

charge of girls in need of friendly guidance, to investigate cases for the court, to find employment for those in need of it. Even temporary shelter is not to be had for a girl unless it be provided by some charitable institution.

This Court should have a unified social service department for all its special branches, sufficiently equipped to render all personal service desired by the courts, and competent to make proper records, compile and analyze them. These special courts furnish abundant material for study, and the city ought to have the benefit of it.[1] The mere keeping of records result in little good, and often in harm. I stand firmly committed to the proposition that in cases where the charge is immoral conduct of a woman, all records of her case should be destroyed after the lapse of one year, unless she is in the mean time returned to the court. If our data were properly analyzed, and recorded, individual records with names could then be destroyed.

The value of a department such as Judge Fisher has outlined can be readily perceived. But where, as is the case, a department created presumably for these express purposes is practically ignored, defendants being assigned by the court first to one worker and then to another, all responsible to different departments of the Municipal Court and all burdened by other duties, it is apparent that only confusion can result. Certain essential facts (mostly unverified) in reference to each defendant are recorded. But as they are neither compiled nor analyzed, they afford no measure of achievement nor any basis for a social diagnosis.

DETENTION HOUSES

Prior to 1918 a woman arrested in Chicago was held in the nearest police station over night, being placed usually in the matron's quarters. In that year, however, three police stations, located in the northern, western, and southern sections of the city, respectively, were remodeled as places of detention for women. Arrested women now are taken to the

---

[1] Italics ours.

police station in the precinct where the arrest is made, booked, and then transferred to the nearest detention house. In the case of women arrested for sex offenses, the charge is left open on the books in order that all may be detained for examination at the Iroquois Hospital on the following morning. This avoids violation of the police regulations requiring all charges to be booked when known within twenty-four hours and at the same time makes it legally possible to hold the woman without bail. The next morning a woman matron from the detention house accompanies the girls on the wagon to the Iroquois Hospital and thence to the court where (in the case of the Morals Court) the woman bailiff locks them in the waiting-room.

Children (including boys under ten years of age) runaway girls, lost women, prostitutes, criminals, etc. are all held together in these three detention houses. As the women in each house are detained in one long room, serving as a dormitory, segregation is impossible. The matron said that one of the girls remarked: "What you don't know when you come in you know when you go out." Women arrested Saturday nights or before holidays are detained necessarily two or more nights in these houses. When a case is booked on an open charge, pending investigation, the girl may be detained as long as two weeks. The majority, however, spend but a single night here. Women whose cases are continued after their appearance in court and who do not furnish bail are detained in the County Jail with women serving sentence.

As the three detention houses are said to be practically alike, only one was inspected—Detention House No. 201, in the north end of the city. Here the girls are detained on the second floor in a long narrow room furnished with a double row of cots accommodating 25 or 30. In some small rooms to the side there are six basins with running water, one shower, and one toilet. Bed linen is changed only once a week regardless of the number of times the bed may change occupants. Two clean towels a day are furnished for common use. Individual cups, scalded each day by the "visiting" cook, hang in a somewhat jumbled mass near the water-cooler.

The girls are without occupation. They loll around on the beds at the far end of the room or sleep throughout the day. The girls frequently remark that they are glad of a chance to "rest up."

At one end of the room, near the door, are the matron's quarters—an office and a sitting-room. Three matrons working in eight-hour shifts are on duty. The one interviewed was formerly a trained nurse. A cook from the outside comes in and prepares meals for the girls on a two-burner gas range in the matron's office. The landing of an adjoining stairway serves as a scantily equipped kitchen and supply-room. The sanitary conditions were not of the best.

LAWNDALE HOSPITAL [1]

This hospital, an old building in the outskirts of the city, was first used for the treatment of venereally diseased women in June, 1918. Not being fire-proof, the doors and windows

---

[1] When a second investigation was made by the writers in 1922, it was noted that certain changes had been made: Venereally diseased women in need of hospitalization are now treated in the Lawndale Division of the Municipal Hospital for Contagious Diseases, having been transferred there in 1920 from an undesirable old building on the outskirts of the city. In that building, from which numerous escapes were made, the girls had little occupation and suitable grouping was impossible. In their present quarters on the top floor of one of the new buildings, conditions are vastly improved, both from a sanitary and a social viewpoint. Although no training is afforded, the girls are busily occupied in cleaning the dormitories; serving meals, doing all the kitchen work except cooking; making uniforms and throat swabs; ironing, mangling and sorting the laundry. Eight twelve-bed wards with glass partitions permit classification by disease and color, although during the day segregation is not attempted. A well-equipped recreation room opens on a covered roof, used in summer for outdoor exercise and games.

Patients may be released only upon order of the Commissioner of Health. Usually, they must show for gonorrhea, three consecutive negative smears taken every other day; and for syphilis, one negative Wassermann. When released as non-infectious, they are instructed to report to one of the free treatment stations maintained by the Chicago Department of Health. No follow-up system to insure reporting has, as yet, been developed.

are neither locked nor screened. Guards on constant duty are supposed to prevent escapes. During the first six months of the year there were about 25 escapes. It was said that most of the girls were brought back eventually. Frequently, however, they are not recovered until taken into court on a new charge.

There were 48 girls in the hospital on the day the institution was visited. Twelve of these were colored. During the first six months of the year the hospital cared for 274 women, all of whom came from the Morals Court, with two exceptions—one colored girl who went there voluntarily and one white girl transferred from the Chicago Home for Girls. The colored girl was pregnant as well as venereally diseased; and later she was to be sent to the County Hospital for confinement and then returned to Lawndale.

The hospital affords the girls no systematic instruction or occupation, aside from cleaning the dormitories and preparing meals. A number of girls were seen making throat swabs. No form of segregation exists.

When rendered non-infectious, the girl is returned to the Morals Court. Occasionally venereally diseased women sentenced to the House of Correction for larceny and other non-sex offenses, are still infectious at the expiration of their term. They are then transferred to Lawndale hospital for further treatment. These women, together with the few who enter the institution voluntarily, are discharged therefrom direct.

It was stated that there are six free clinics in Chicago for treatment of venereal diseases. A woman discharged from the hospital is given the address of the clinic nearest to her home in order that she may continue treatment until cured. No follow-up work is done, however, to see that the advice is followed.

PSYCHOPATHIC LABORATORY

A Psychopathic Laboratory was established as a part of the Municipal Court of Chicago on May 1, 1914. "Dr. William

J. Hickson, an American doctor, surgeon, and neurologist who had been trained in the psychopathic and neurological clinics of Bleuler in Zurich, Kraepelin in Munich, and Ziehen in Berlin, was chosen by the chief justice as director."[1]

Both the director of the Psychopathic Laboratory and the chief justice informed investigators that no routine mental examination is given to defendants appearing before the Morals Court. In fact, it was stated that only those who were believed by the judge or probation officer to be mentally deficient were sent to the laboratory.

The director of the laboratory informed us that he was not examining many Morals Court cases at the time of this survey, and that he had no new figures. He therefore referred us to his 1917 report.[2] Page 17 of this report contains the following statement: "We now submit the combined statistics of cases examined. . . . which embrace intensive individual, criminalistic, psychiatric, psychologic, neurologic, hereditary, anthropometric, and sociologic studies on 4486 cases, distributed as follows: Boys' Court, 2025; Domestic Relations, including Bastardy cases, 1275; *Morals Court, 947*; other criminal branches, 329. *A large proportion of the above were such clinically outspoken cases* [3] of defectiveness that our routine intensive and extensive examinations were unnecessary as far as reaching a diagnosis was concerned, but for statistical and research purposes, as well as on the grounds of thoroughness, we carried out the same systematic individualistic, intensive, and extensive studies on all, thus embracing both individualistic and general aims."

Dr. Hickson has the following to say about methods of approach.[4]

---

[1] Eighth and Ninth Annual Reports, Municipal Court of Chicago, 1913–1915.

[2] Report of Psychopathic Laboratory of the Municipal Court of Chicago, 1914–1917.

[3] The italics are ours.

[4] Report of Psychopathic Laboratory of the Municipal Court of Chicago, 1914–1917, pp. 28–29.

There are two methods of approach to mental diseases, the clinical and the psychological. In English-speaking countries the clinical method of approach dominates; on the continent the psychological method dominates. Both groups also rely on more or less extended periods of observation of their cases. This is true of cases of suspected feeble-mindedness as well as the psychoses.

In the feeble-minded field, Binet and Simon advanced the psychological procedure immeasurably when they contributed their positive, direct method of testing, thus doing away with the observation and field work system. They took psychological tests already in use in this field, worked up others, and combined these into definite, working, evaluated schemes which permitted securing a very definite evaluation of certain mental factors of cases within an hour, thus taking the tests directly to the case.

We have attempted to do the same for the psychoses and feel that this method will be as successful with them as it has turned out to be with the feeble-minded, and it will be only a question of time until the profession would as soon think of committing a case of mental disease to an observation hospital for days and weeks for diagnosis or differential diagnostic purposes as they would think of carrying on such a procedure with a case of scarlet fever or pneumonia, even though to-day some of our critics say it takes them weeks and even months to make a diagnosis of mental disease. That some of them, however, many of whom have little or no medical or psychiatric training, ever make a diagnosis is quite remarkable.

Cases of feeble-mindedness and psychopathy run true to form, and it is only necessary to analyze and know the kind and degree of defect to evaluate their past, present, and future behavior.

Just as Binet and Simon relied on tests that were already in use and combined these with others of their own which they worked up into groupings with a definite purpose, so we, too, have relied on many tests already in use in the psychiatric clinics and worked up others of our own, based on well-established existing principles, which enable us to get definite analyses of certain psychopathic and intelligence defects and their degrees, *thus enabling us to reach a diagnosis within an hour and allowing us not only to predict with practical approximation the future behavior of such cases, but also to know what their past has been like, and also the antecedent and ascendant hereditary possibilities.* As an example, we know that the average reckless gunman is a boy about the age of 19, with an intelligence level between 10.5 and 12.0 years, plus dementia praecox, etc.

This positive, direct method of mental diagnosis will revolutionize court procedure along these lines. It will add an important element of concreteness to the hypothetical question. The question will be put in some such form as this, "Given a man with such and such a mental make-up, under such and such conditions, what would happen?"

A finger-print system would seem an almost indispensable adjunct to the Morals Court, for the purpose of bringing to the attention of the judge the recidivists if the following statement of Dr. Hickson is true:[1]

In the matter of recidivism, the Morals Court cases take the lead over all others, which is quite natural since the majority of these girls are too feeble-minded or psychopathic to make a living legitimately, and they must ply their trade more or less in the open, while the boy delinquents, from the nature of their crimes, work surreptitiously. However, if this means of livelihood is taken away from them and none other provided, they will have to resort to other means, such as larceny, burglary, and the like. These girls are much greater prevaricators than the boys; in fact, there is no truth in them.

There are very few of the girls coming into the Morals Court who are actually first offenders. They have already begun their careers in their juvenile years. They show the same difficulties in school and environmental conflict, according to their nature, that the boys do. Parents come to court with their girls, and make the same complaints of incorrigibility that they do in the Boys Court with their sons. We are often asked as to why these girls appear so much younger than their years. This is no doubt due to the mental immaturity of such a high percentage of them. To the saying "every line a thought," we might add, "no thoughts, no lines." The masked faces of many of the praecox cases may also play a rôle here.

Again on page 96 he has the following to say:

It should be constantly borne in mind that we have no direct means of compiling number of arrests of Morals Court cases; but

---

[1] Report of Psychopathic Laboratory of the Municipal Court of Chicago, 1914–1917, p. 92.

we know from experience that they are practically all repeated offenders,[1] and practically none are first offenders. They show a much higher percentage of recidivism because they have to ply their calling more or less openly, as compared with the burglar, hold-up man, etc. Their returns are smaller, and they receive shorter sentences.

Dr. Hickson closes his report on the Morals Court cases with the following statement: [2]

Almost every means of an objective nature that could be speculated upon has been used for the suppression of vice; in later years such things, for instance, as imprisonment, fines, reformation, probation, parole, religion, big-sister movement, and all to no avail, no impression being made at all by any or all of these methods. Any well-regulated business would have long ago discarded such fruitless methods and struck out in new fields or in new ways after so much experimentation had been found wanting. Practically all thinking people who are interested in such public questions are growing impatient if not disgusted with the persistence any further along these lines.

The people attacking this problem should now realize, after their other unscientific methods have failed so ignominiously, that there is only one way to get at the root of any of these problems, and therefore the cure, which is going at it through scientific means and methods. The work of the Psychopathic Laboratory discloses the fact that a very high percentage of these girls are so mentally defective or psychopathic that there is no legitimate way open to them for making a living. This is an illustration of what scientific means can do for the elucidation of such problems. The final solution will require a thorough study of sex physiology, sex psychology, the relation of psychoses, neuroses, and alcoholic debauches, etc., to sex starvation, feeble-mindedness, dementia praecox, manic-depressive insanity especially; also of the sex instinct, which is the most primal instinct of all. We will have to have the assistance of the physician, the

---

[1] In this connection it may be interesting to examine Table 11 showing disposition in the Morals Court of 100 women arraigned, January 1 to June 30, 1920, who were known to have had two or more previous convictions.

[2] Report of Psychopathic Laboratory of the Municipal Court of Chicago, 1914–1917, p. 106.

neurologist, the psychiatrist, the sociologist, the statesman, etc., to help us.

We have noticed that as soon as any town within the radius of a couple of hundred miles or so of Chicago closes up its red-light district the girls begin to turn up in Chicago within a few days, showing that in closing up these districts we only spread these girls out over other parts of the same city or in other cities. Upon hearing this a man said, ''Let us close these districts all down at once all over the country.'' First, this would be impracticable; second, these girls would go round clandestinely; and third, a large number of them would be driven into other crimes, such as thieving, confidence games, shop-lifting, etc., for the large majority of them are feeble-minded, and psychopathic to such a degree that they cannot make a living.[1] Our problem will not be confined to the lower classes alone, for the sex instinct and the sex instinct on a psychotic basis manifests itself in all classes and in all walks of life.

There is no doubt that a routine mental examination of all sex delinquents would be invaluable, first to guide the judge in the kind of sentence to be imposed, and second, to guide the probation officer in the character of supervision given. Inasmuch as a routine test is not given at Chicago, it would seem that the psychopathic laboratory is of little value to the Morals Court, except perhaps for statistical purposes. Since most of the cases sent to it are so feeble-minded or insane as to be obvious to the judge, we fail to see what is gained by not sending such cases directly to a commission to pass on their mentality, for they must go to a commission eventually, even after examination by the laboratory, before they may be committed to an institution, either for the feeble-minded or the insane. Dr. Hickson's report, however, convinces us of the value and need of a routine examination.

---

[1] The investigators are unable to discover evidence to support this conclusion. It will be noted that Dr. Hickson states that he has not conducted a routine examination, even of Morals Court cases, that the large majority of his cases are obviously so deficient mentally, that it is apparent to a layman, viz., the judge. We know of no psychiatric or psychologic study that has been made of a true cross-section of all women following the occupation of prostitution. The need for such a study is apparent.

PROBATION

The Adult Probation Department serves all branches of the Municipal Court in which adults are tried.

Appointment of probation officers. Under the Illinois Statutes,

The circuit court of each of the several counties in this state may appoint a probation officer to act as such for and throughout the county in which he shall be appointed. The circuit court of any county may appoint such number of additional probation officers for such county as the court may deem to be necessary or advisable: *provided,* the number of probation officers to be appointed for any county shall in no event exceed one for every fifty thousand inhabitants or fraction thereof. . . .

In any city in this state having a population of seventy-five thousand or less inhabitants, as determined by the last preceding school census in which there has been or may hereafter be established a municipal or city court, such municipal or city court may appoint one probation officer for such municipal or city court in addition to those hereinbefore provided for. The other probation officers to which any county may be entitled as aforesaid, shall be equally apportioned between the county and the several cities, if any therein, that severally have a population of more than seventy-five thousand inhabitants.

Such probation officers so apportioned to such county shall be appointed by the circuit court of said county, and such probation officers so apportioned to such cities shall be appointed by the municipal or city courts in said several cities. The judges of the circuit court of any county and of the municipal or city courts therein established for cities having a population of more than fifty thousand inhabitants, shall meet as a unit body at such time as they deem proper, and at any such meeting may appoint a chief probation officer to act as such over all the probation officers appointed by any of said courts.

The Chief Probation Officer of the Adult Probation Department states in regard to this section:

The law as construed by the courts here gives the Municipal Court of Chicago, which is a city court having only jurisdiction within the city, the right to appoint all necessary probation officers and also our Circuit and Superior Courts the right to appoint a certain number of officers too.

We have construed the law so that the Municipal Court appoints one-half the officers and the Circuit and Superior Courts, jointly, the other half, and all three courts, the Chief.

Term of office and removal. "Said probation officers shall serve as such from the date of their appointment, shall be subject to the orders of the court appointing them, and removable in the discretion thereof by an order duly entered of record . . . " [1]

Special provisions are made for cities having a population between fifty and seventy-five thousand. The sections quoted, however, apply to Chicago.

Eligible for probation. Section 2 of the Adult Probation Laws provides as follows:

Any defendant, not previously convicted of a crime, greater than a misdemeanor, petit larceny and embezzlement excepted, who has entered a plea of guilty or has been found guilty of the verdict of a jury or by the finding of a court of violation of a municipal ordinance or of any criminal offense except murder, manslaughter, rape, kidnapping, willful and corrupt perjury or subornation of perjury, arson, larceny and embezzlement where the amount taken or converted exceeds two hundred dollars ($200) in value, incest, burglary of an inhabited dwelling house, conspiracy in any form or any of the acts made an offense under the election laws of this State, may, in the discretion of the judge hearing the case, after entry of judgment, and nothing remains to be done by the court except to pronounce sentence, be admitted to probation according to the provisions of this Act. . . .

Requirements for admission to probation.

Sec. 3. Before granting any request for admission to probation, the court shall require the probation officer to investigate accurately and promptly, the case of the defendant making such request, to ascertain his residence and occupation and whether or not he has been previously convicted of a crime or misdemeanor, or previously been placed on probation by any court; and the court may, in its discretion, require the probation officer to secure in addition, information concerning the personal characteristics, habits and associations of such defendant; the names, relationship, ages and conditions of those dependent upon him for support and education and such other facts as may aid the court as well in determining the propriety of probation, as in fixing the conditions thereof. . . .

Period of probation. If application for release of defendant on probation is granted, "the judge granting the same shall thereupon enter an order continuing the case for a period not exceeding six months in case of violation of a municipal ordinance and not exceeding one year in the case of other

---

[1] Illinois Adult Probation Laws in force July 1, 1915, Sec. 9. Published by Adult Probation Department, Court House, Chicago, Ill.

offenses and shall by such order fix and specify the terms and conditions of the probation of such defendant as herein provided.''

Conditions of probation.

Sec. 4. Release on probation shall be upon the following conditions:

(1) That the probationer shall not, during the term of his probation, violate any criminal law of the State of Illinois, or any ordinance of any municipality of the said State.

(2) That if convicted of a felony or misdemeanor, he shall not, during the term of his probation, leave the State without the consent of the Court which granted his application for probation.

(3) That he shall make a report once a month, or *as often as the court may direct,* of his whereabouts, conduct and employment, and furnish such other information relating to the conditions of his probation, as may from time to time be required by rule or order of court, to the probation officer under whose charge he has been placed, and shall appear in person before the court at such time as the court may direct or the rule of the court provide.

(4) That he shall enter into a bond or recognizance in such sum as the court may direct, with or without sureties, to perform the conditions imposed, which shall run to the People of the State of Illinois and may be sued on by any person thereunto authorized by the court for the use of the parties in interest as the same may appear.

And the court may impose any one or more of the following conditions:

(1) That he shall make restitution, *or reparation,* in whole or in part, immediately or within the period of probation to the person or persons injured or defrauded.

(2) That he shall make contribution from his earnings for the support of those dependent upon him, subject to the supervision of the court.

(3) That he shall pay any fine assessed against him as well as the costs of the proceedings, in such installments as the court may direct during the continuance of the probation period.[1]

Sec. 5. The court shall have discretionary power to remit such costs as may be imposed, or any portion thereof.

---

[1] The Chief Probation officer remarks in the Fourth Annual Report of the Adult Probation Department of Cook County, Illinois (Oct. 1, 1914—Sept. 30, 1915), in relation to this provision: ''When a defendant was convicted of an offense and a fine entered against him, and he was unable to pay, he was sent to the House of Correction to work it out at fifty cents or a dollar a day, while his family, in many instances, was compelled to seek charity for their support. Under paragraph three of section four of the new law, the Court has the power to admit the offender to probation and allow him to pay such fine in installments during the continuance of the probation period.''

Upon violation by the probationer of any of the conditions of probation, the same may be revoked and terminated and warrant issued for the arrest of the probationer.

Section 7 provides that,

Upon the termination of the probation period, the probation officer shall report to the court the conduct of the probationer during the period of his probation,[1] and the court may thereupon discharge the probationer from further supervision, or extend the probation period not to exceed six months in cases of a violation of the municipal ordinance and not to exceed one year in other offenses. . . .

Information furnished by the Department in its annual reports is more general than specific. Its Fourth Annual Report covering October 1, 1914 to September 30, 1915, contains only three tables giving statistics of sex offenses. These tables show respectively: "Number of Persons admitted to Probation for the Different Offenses during the Year," "Warrants issued from Jaunary 1, 1915 to October 1, 1915," and a third table without title or date, showing record and offenses of discharged probationers. Although the figures given in these tables relate to all classes of offense, only those pertaining to sex offenses are instanced below, except that for purposes of comparison the totals for all offenses are given. It will be noted that the tables bear little relation to one another, the probationers having been admitted to probation (probably) in the year of the report, whereas only a portion of those discharged had been admitted during the same year.

Table Showing the Number of Persons Admitted to Probation for the Different Offenses During the Year
(Possibly October 1, 1914 to September 30, 1915)[2]

Disorderly conduct[3]	847	Soliciting	15
Fornication	40	Patrons, disorderly house	26
Adultery	35	Keepers, disorderly house	1
Pandering	4	Inmates, disorderly house	4
		Total (sex offenses)	972
		Total (all offenses)	3629

[1] See tables on pp. 41, 42, 43, 47 and Table 13 at the end of this chapter.

[2] Fourth Annual Report of Adult Probation Department of Cook County, Ill., from October 1, 1914, to September 30, 1915. Sex offenses only are cited.

[3] Not limited to sex offenses.

Warrants issued from January 1, 1915, to October 1, 1915[1]

Violation Section 2012 (disorderly conduct)[2]................................ 67

Fornication........................ 2

Pandering........................ 1

Violation Section 2019 (Persons connected with nuisance)............ 4

Adultery.......................... 1

Violation Section 2018.............. 1
(Soliciting for prostitution)

Total (sex offenses)............... 76

Total (all offenses)...............526

Table (without title or date)
(Possibly October 1, 1914 to September 30, 1915)[1]

	Disorderly conduct[2]	Adultery	Soliciting	Inmates, disord. house	Patrons, disord. house	Fornication	Pandering
Improved............	850	44	65	29	8	37	1
Unimproved..........	228	9	74	23	9	13	1
In Pontiac or Penitentiary...............	2						
In House of Correction for violating probation...............	25	1	3	10		2	
In House of Correction for another offense..		1					
Died...............	1	1					
Totals............	1106	56	142	62	17	52	2

Total (sex offenses) 1437
Total (all offenses) 4551

[1] Fourth Annual Report of Adult Probation Department of Cook County, Ill., from October 1, 1914 to September 30, 1915. Sex offenses only are cited.

[2] Not limited to sex offenses.

In comparing the number of types of cases admitted to probation during the year under discussion (presumably October 1, 1914 to September 30, 1915) with the year preceding, the Chief Probation Officer remarks:

On the basis of the number of cases probationed for the whole year, burglary, receiving stolen property, obtaining money by false pretenses and violation of city ordinances, all show a large percentage of increase. Those offenses showing a decrease are: Contributing to dependency, contributing to delinquency, abandonment, soliciting, inmates of disorderly house, keeping a disorderly house, vagrancy, carrying concealed weapons; robbery and embezzlement. The first three offenses show a very large decrease and the last two a small decrease.

In view of these facts, it would seem that the Judges have been putting a much larger number of people on probation for offenses involving moral turpitude than for offenses related to the social evil. The natural inference would be that the Judges believe there is more chance of reforming persons convicted of larceny, burglary, receiving stolen property, and violation of city ordinances, than there is to mend the conduct of defendants in cases involving domestic infelicity or sex offenses.

The Fifth Annual Report, October 1, 1915 to September 30, 1916, contains two tables which show, respectively, the record of probationers discharged, tabulated according to offense, and a similar record in regard to women only. The former table relates apparently to men and women. In these tables, also, with the exception of totals for all offenses, only those figures which relate to sex offenses are presented.

Record of Probationers Discharged, Tabulated According to Offense
(Possibly October 1, 1915 to September 30, 1916)[1]

	Disorderly conduct[2]	Adultery	Soliciting	Inmates, disord. house	Patrons, disord. house	Fornication	Pandering
Satisfactory	480	30	12	31	....	34	4
Doubtful	48	....	3	3	....	3	....
Unsatisfactory	112	3	7	7	....	5	....
In House of Correction for violation	21	....	2	3	....	....	....
Died	1	....	....	....	....	....	....
Totals	662	33	24	44	....	42	4

Total (sex offenses)   809
Total (all offenses)   3197

[1] Fifth Annual Report of Adult Probation Department of Cook County, Ill., from October 1, 1915, to September 30, 1916. Sex offenses only are cited.

[2] Not limited to sex offenses.

The following table gives the results of cases of *women* discharged from probation during the *present year* (possibly October 1, 1915 to September 30, 1916) showing the number of those discharged as satisfactory, doubtful, unsatisfactory or in the House of Correction, for violation of probation or another offense committed, tabulated according to offenses.[1]

	Disorderly conduct[2]	Adultery	Soliciting	Inmates and patrons of disorderly house	Fornication	Pandering
Satisfactory..........	40	11	7	21	13	1
Doubtful.............	7	1	2	....	....	....
Unsatisfactory........	18	2	6	9	2	....
In House of Correction (One in County Jail)	6	....	2	4	....	....
Totals.............	71	14	17	34	15	1

Total (sex offenses) 152
Total (all offenses) 372

[2] Not limited to sex offenses.

The Fifth Annual Report furnishes also a special study of twenty-five Morals Court women:

Twenty-Five Morals Court Cases [1]

Heretofore we have stated that we didn't believe a girl should be admitted to probation from the Morals Court unless she particularly requested it. Our reason for that was because the expression of a desire to get the benefits of probation is an indication that she wishes to try and do better and does not fear supervision by the department.

As a rule, these girls dislike probation because it means that they will be followed up and the officer often finds that they are still in the same business. They hide from the officer so that it is impossible to help them get work in an honest employment. Besides that, they

[1] Fifth Annual Report of Adult Probation Department of Cook County, Ill., from October 1, 1915, to September 30, 1916. Sex offenses only are cited.

know that if they are brought into court for a violation of their probation, there is no chance for a jury trial with all the sentimental sympathy of that body. And the Judge may send them to the House of Correction for the original offense, without another trial.

If a girl is put on probation whether she wishes to or not, or if she is put on probation just to avoid payment of a fine, the effect is anything but good.

In all these cases, there should be a thorough investigation of the defendant made by a competent officer before probation and then if in the judgment of the Court there is a chance to improve her conduct, the Judge can with some prospect of benefit to the community, put the girl on probation.

We are giving here the results of an investigation of twenty-five Morals Court cases discharged from supervision by the department more than a year ago. These cases, like those of the Boys', Criminal and Domestic Relations Courts, are taken at random from our discharge files and a competent officer sent to look them up and report the result of her investigation.

The results given here to a person of little experience, appear to be startling. Yet when you take into consideration that there was no investigation prior to probation in any of these cases, it is not to be wondered at. If any investigation was made at all, it was only such as could be made by talking to the defendant and her friends at the time they were in court.

In fifteen of these cases, the officer has been unable to trace them.

Ten of the above fifteen cases we never were able to find *while on probation* because they gave false names and addresses.

In three, the relatives were found, but not the girl.

In three others, the friends of the girl say they believe her to have been married since she was on probation but could not tell us her married name or address or give us any clue by which we might locate her.

One woman has since served a sentence in the House of Good Shepherd for another offense, while her husband was in jail for pandering.

One reported to have been married but has lately left her husband and neither her mother nor her husband know where she is.

Another one reported married and gone to Pittsburgh.

One is dead.

In none of the twenty-five cases were we able to interview the girl, and the information obtained was from others. All of which confirms our judgment that it is absolutely necessary in *Morals Court probation cases* that a thorough investigation be made by a probation officer prior to probation, and that the defendant herself express a desire to be admitted to probation.

Since these cases were admitted to probation, a different system prevails and very few, if any, from the Morals Court are admitted to probation without a preliminary investigation.

The chief probation officer, in his Sixth Annual Report, October 1, 1916 to September 30, 1917, continues to emphasize the importance of an investigation in each case prior to probation, to ascertain the following facts about the probationer: (1) Residence; (2) Home surroundings; (3) Work record; (4) Criminal record, if any.

To further demonstrate the importance of this stipulation, a study was made of 2730 cases of men and women from all courts served (with the exception of the Domestic Relations Court), showing the number investigated prior to probation and the number not so investigated. The result revealed that:

The total number of investigated cases shows only 12 per cent discharged unsatisfactory, but those not investigated show 27 per cent unsatisfactory.

The previous years' study of 25 cases from the Morals Court would indicate that a far higher percentage of cases not investigated would appear as "unsatisfactory." In regard to the term "unsatisfactory," the report goes on to state:

Some persons have misunderstood our statistics, in that they have assumed that all the cases discharged as "unsatisfactory" are those having again violated the law. That is not true. Listed under that head are those who have committed another offense and have been punished—those who have failed to pay the full amount of their restitution—those having left the state without permission, and those having moved without leaving any trace, those having committed slight infractions of the law and been brought in by the officer, were discharged.

Again in the Seventh Annual Report (October 1, 1917, to September 30, 1918, the latest one available at the time of our investigation) the Chief Probation Officer finds it necessary to stress the importance of prior investigation:

In quite a number of cases the defendants failed to give their correct address and the probation officer is never able to locate them. This condition appeared in so many cases that it became necessary for the Department to have one man for the purpose of finding lost cases and cases of which we have never had the correct address. If the defendant is not found, the Department is powerless to supervise him and so far as any good results are concerned, he might just as well be discharged.

.   .   .   .   .   .

I am aware that the courts usually want to dispose of these cases at once and do not like to continue them too long to gather this information, but it is much better to take a little time to do the work well than to make a mistake and turn loose on the community people who should be sent to penal institutions.

.   .   .   .   .   .

A number of persons have been admitted to probation whose mentality is such that they are not responsible to God or man for their actions. Such cases are impossible and should never be placed on probation. There are some cases, however, that might be termed "borderline" cases which can be handled with fair results by the Department.

This report furnishes tables showing the number of men and women, respectively, admitted to probation and the record of women discharged. With the exception of totals for all offenses, the figures selected are for sex offenses only.

Table Showing Number of Men Admitted to Probation for Different Offenses During the Year
(Possibly October 1, 1917 to September 30, 1918)[1]

Disorderly conduct[2].................510
Keepers disorderly house............ 4
Inmates disorderly house........... 9

Adultery.......................... 14
Fornication....................... 23
Soliciting...... 2
Total (sex offenses) 562
Total (all offenses) 3284

Table Showing the Number of Women Admitted to Probation for Different Offenses During the Year
(Possibly October 1, 1917 to September 30, 1918)[1]

Disorderly conduct[2].................128
Fornication....................... 22
Soliciting........................ 27
Adultery.......................... 29

Patrons, disorderly house............ 4
Keepers disorderly house............ 10
Inmates disorderly house............ 24

Total (sex offenses)....................244
Total (all offenses).................638

[1] Seventh Annual Report of Adult Probation Department of Cook County, Ill., from October 1, 1917 to September 30 1918. Sex offenses only are cited.

[2] Not limited to sex offenses.

The following table gives the results of cases of women discharged from probation during the present year (possibly October 1, 1917 to September 30, 1918), showing the number of those discharged—satisfactory, doubtful, unsatisfactory; those in the House of Correction and Geneva for violation of

Table Showing Probation Results in Cases of Women Discharged as Shown by Records in the Adult Probation Department

Offense	Satisfactory	Doubtful	Unsatisfactory	House of Correction	Geneva
Adultery.....................	19	....	5	....	....
Fornication...................	19	1	7	2	1
Inmates disorderly house........	81	5	72	3	....
Soliciting....................	8	....	4	....	....
Totals.....................	127	6	88	5	1

Total (sex offenses) 227
Total (all offenses) 651

probation or a second offense committed, or died—tabulated according to offenses." [1]

Is respect to placing girls on probation without preliminary investigation, the Chief Probation Officer stated to investigator that there had been no change of policy. He said that certain girls are interviewed by one or more of the women officials of the court—all of whom accept the girls' uncorroborated story, not even verifying the address. One of these officials observed, "I always know when a girl is telling the truth." In a table furnished by the Probation Department concerning 16 men and 59 women on probation during the first six months of 1920, it is shown that the statements of six men and eight women were verified prior to their being placed on probation.

Although a woman probation officer is assigned to the Morals Court, she is seldom called upon to investigate cases, so does not remain continuously in the court. It still is no uncommon occurrence to find that the girl does not live at the address given. When a case is placed on probation the practice is to have the probation officer assigned to that court make out a history sheet "from information obtained from the clerk of the court, from the probationer, and from the Judge," to quote the chief probation officer.

A statement of the girl's physical and mental condition can be obtained from the Iroquois Hospital, the Psychopathic Laboratory or the court physician, upon request. When the history sheet is completed, it is presented to the Adult Probation Department which then assigns the girl to the woman probation officer in charge of the district where she claims to reside. This officer calls upon the girl once or twice a month, as it seems advisable, and the girl must report in person to this officer on a certain day each month, at the Adult Probation Department.

This Department is strongly opposed to the practice of

---

[1] Seventh Annual Report of Adult Probation Department of Cook County, Ill., from October 1, 1917, to September 30, 1918. Sex offenses only are cited.

continuing cases for a few weeks under the supervision of women officials of the court. No preliminary investigation is made and the women—confined by their regular court duties—can for the most part exercise very little real supervision over the girl. Furthermore, there is absence of any uniform or constructive policy in dealing with the girls. This is more readily apparent when one recalls the divided authority under which the women court officials operate. If at the end of the specified time the girl has "made good," the judge discharges her without pronouncing sentence. The case is entered on the docket, "discharged." It was impossible to learn how many girls had received this quasi type of suspended sentence as only one of the women officials keeps a record of girls placed in her care.

During the first six months of the year, 18 men and 69 women were placed on probation from the Morals Court (see Table 1 at the end of this chapter) and one man and three women of those transferred from Morals Court to the Jury Branch (see Table 6 at the end of this chapter). Of 100 women who were known to have had two previous arrests, fourteen were placed on probation; of those who were known to have had three previous arrests, seven were placed on probation; and of those who were known to have had five or more previous arrests, two were placed on probation (see Table 11 at the end of this chapter). The apparent discrepancy existing between the number of eighteen women given above and the total of twenty-three given in Table 11 is doubtless due to the impossibility of making a perfect check on recidivists in the absence of a finger-print system.

Judge Harry M. Fisher, who presided in the Morals Court for six consecutive months, 1916–1917, expresses what is alleged to be the general attitude among the judges regarding probation for sex offenders. In a review of the Morals Court in which he makes certain recommendations, he writes:

Can the benefits of the probation law be applied to defendants in the Morals Court with any degree of success? This question, unfortunately, must be answered in the negative. As stated before, three classes of offenders are brought before the court—the casual offender, the professional prostitute, and the keepers and panders.

As to those of the first class, probation is unquestionably advisable. If a girl is charged with her first offense, and her case appears hopeful to the court, the only sensible and effective thing to do is to give her a full and complete chance. She should be permitted to leave the court without any record, without further attachment to the court, without the need of reporting, or the danger of having an officer visit her home or place of employment. In that way alone she can forget her humiliation and the ordeal in connection with her arrest and trial. Moreover, there are always present those in the community whose business it seems to be to drive as many girls upon the street as they possibly can. The girl placed on probation in the Morals Court is in grave danger of having some one of these report the fact to her employer or her co-employees.

With reference to the second class, experience has taught us that probation has no restraining influence whatsoever. The object of the probation law is to place the offender on good behavior for a period of time. But since the offense is committed to obtain a livelihood, merely to place the girl on probation without finding means of support satisfactory to her is very clearly no remedy, and, in practice, has proved to be worse than useless. The only time the professional prostitute quits that life is when she sickens of it or when she gets married, which is the case of an astonishingly large number. But probation not only fails as a remedy, but often does real mischief. Many girls who have been placed on probation have been known to complain that some unscrupulous and vicious individual used that as an instrument for extortion. The argument used to intimidate her is that, now being on probation, if brought back to court she would not be entitled to a trial by jury, not to a change of venue from the judge who in the first instance found her guilty, and, having a previous record, it would unquestionably mean a jail sentence. Instances were reported where such girls sold jewelry or their valuable clothes to raise money to pay tribute to their persecutors.

The third class is never entitled to probation.

In isolated cases of weak-minded girls, who can keep up their spirits when constantly reinforced by a kind, sensible and encouraging probation officer, probation might be advisable, but these cases are rare.

The probation law, however, has a distinct value, even to the Morals Court. Under the provisions of the law, the court is empowered to investigate into the social condition of the defendant before judgment is entered. To this expedient the court should resort in every case where it might be of value. Under the strict rules of procedure and evidence, the court may not listen to anything except evidence adduced in open court by witnesses sworn to testify, but, after that hearing is concluded, the court may, under the probation law, have a proper investigation made. That investigation might prove that probation is inadvisable. But the court would, nevertheless, be placed in possession of facts, without which a proper judgment could not be arrived at.[1]

Table 13 at the end of this chapter, shows the status of 75 persons placed upon probation during the first six months of 1920. From the docket of the Morals Court and the Jury Branch of the Municipal Court, the names of 88 persons placed upon probation by these two courts were secured and sent to the Adult Probation Department for information. No reason was given for failure to supply information in regard to the other thirteen cases.

The data which follow relate also to the 75 probationers about whom information was secured, and shows whether probationer's story had been verified before trial, whether after being placed upon probation the probationer was found

	Was Story Verified Before Trial?		Was Correct Address Given?		In Court Again on a New Offense While on Probation	
	Yes	No	Yes	No	Yes	No
Men..........	6	10	15	1	1	15
Women........	8	51	49	10	5	54
Total.......	14	61	64	11	6	69

[1] Tenth and Eleventh Annual Reports, Municipal Court of Chicago, 1915–1917.

at the address given and whether the probationer had been arrested on a new charge during the period of probation.

HOUSE OF CORRECTION

The House of Correction, or Bridewell, as it is commonly called, is located a few blocks northwest of the Stockyards. The woman's department is housed in a twelve-year-old building. This is the only institution to which delinquent women in Chicago over eighteen years of age may be committed. (A bill for a state farm was passed by the Legislature but no appropriation made.)   Under the Illinois Statutes of 1917, Ch. 67, Sec. 12, provision is made for the establishment of a "House of Shelter" in connection with the House of Correction, "for the more complete reformation and education of females."   By this act any institution may be designated a "house of shelter" and the judge may recommend that the Superintendent of the House of Correction transfer a convicted woman to a designated private correctional institution. Also, the Superintendent of the House of Correction may in his discretion make transfers to other institutions.   Of the private institutions receiving delinquent women in the manner described, the House of the Good Shepherd, established "for the reformation and protection of delinquent white girls and women between the ages of ten and fifty," stands foremost. It has a capacity of 500.

The cell block at Bridewell is comprised of 198 outside cells arranged in three tiers.   Each cell contains a single bed and has running cold water and a toilet.

Sex offenders may be committed to the House of Correction for the following violations of state laws: Adultery, fornication, pandering, or, under the Kate Adams law, for soliciting or being an inmate of a house of ill-fame. No commitment penalty attaches to violations of city ordinances relating to sex offenses. If a person fined under these ordinances fails to pay the fine imposed she works it out in the

House of Correction at the rate of fifty cents a day. Unpaid fines imposed for violation of state laws are worked out at the rate of $1.50 per day.

During the first six months of the year, 118 women were received at Bridewell—a few on straight sentence, but by far the larger number for not paying their fine. On the day the institution was visited, the count was twenty-one— eighteen white and three colored. Prior to the last two years they frequently had up to 280 women.

Younger offenders are not separated from the older group nor are the colored women segregated from the white except in the shower-rooms, where they are not permitted to bathe at the same time. This room contains six showers placed in small compartments from which the shutters have been removed because the women had been found to engage in degenerate practices. A matron is stationed in the room while each group bathes.

Laundry work, cleaning, and sewing constitute the main activities. A few girls cook and wait on the table for the matrons, nurses, and doctors. The cooking for the women prisoners is done entirely by the men. About ninety women can work in the laundry at one time. Formerly there were enough inmates to do the necessary laundry work for police stations and other city institutions as well as for Bridewell. In those years about eighty women were occupied in the sewing room, where all the garments worn by the women as well as night and top shirts for the men were made on electrically-run machines. The men's mending was also done by the women. Now, however, there are not enough women to do the necessary laundry work and the sewing room is no longer used. The six women who were scrubbing and cleaning the central enclosure under the supervision of a matron, on the day the institution was visited, had been withdrawn from the laundry. The head matron pointed out the difficulty of attempting any kind of instruction or training with such a shifting population, especially in the case of girls working

out their fines, as these may be taken away the moment someone pays the balance.

The head matron stated the following to be the daily routine of the women:

6: 30	Rising bell; all wash, dress and clean their own cells.
7: 30	Breakfast; all proceed to dining room where they sit in rows at long benches under supervision. Conversation is prohibited. After break-fast the girls commence their duties. Two work in the office and do mending for inmates. One cooks and another waits on table for the staff. The others proceed to the laundry or do necessary cleaning.
11: 30	Dinner.
12– 1: 00	Recreation. (Women sent to small enclosure outdoors where they walk up and down or play ball.)
1– 4: 30	Work in laundry.
4: 30	Supper.
5– 7: 30	On recreation grounds.

The institution is open every day to visitors, but each girl
may receive only one visitor in thirty days. Former inmates
may not visit the prisoners.

Until the first of this year a representative of the Department of Public Welfare called every day to see if girls leaving
the institution were in need of clothing, money or aid of any
kind. This year, however, no appropriation was made for
the Department, so this oversight is no longer possible. The
institution does not coöperate with any private agencies in
relief work, follow-up or after-care for discharged persons.

COOK COUNTY JAIL

Women in the County Jail may be serving sentence or
awaiting trial. The three detention houses for women, as
stated, seldom keep them more than one night. After the girl
has been examined, if her case is adjourned and she fails to
make bail or is not sent to Lawndale Hospital for treatment,
she is transferred to the County Jail, where she mixes with
the persons imprisoned there for all kinds of violations of statutes and ordinances, the jail making no provision for segrega-

tion. The matron stated that the girls were detained some-times as long as four or five months. The women's section has accommodations for 54 inmates. Twenty-five were there the day the jail was visited. It was said to be seldom necessary to place more than one girl in a cell. Linen is changed regu-larly and fresh linen used for new arrivals.

The girls clean their own and jailers' quarters. Here they are said to have more "privileges" than in the House of Cor-rection. When the jail is short of workers it applies to the House of Correction for a transfer of the required number of inmates. Working hours are from 8 a.m. to 8 p.m.

Tuesdays and Fridays, between 1:30 and 2:30, visitors are allowed. At this hour on one of these days, the jail was visited. The visitors awaited the opening of the gate in an ante-room. Most of them crowded up the steps leading to it. When opened there was a stampede to the window where passes were issued. The visitors were then conducted to the sections where the persons they wished to see were confined. The inmates in each enclosure crowded forward to a screen of heavy, grayish, closely woven wire. The visitors ranged themselves opposite, behind another screen of the same sort. The two screens are about a foot apart. Two rows of people stood in this way, shouting their names back and forth to persons whose features were wholly indistinguishable. Forty persons simultaneously talking over a single wire would be as intelligible.

PREVENTIVE WORK

A number of private agencies and institutions in Chicago are carrying on remedial and preventive work for delinquent or predelinquent girls. Four of these are represented in the Morals Court. The Illinois Vigilance Association and the Chicago Law and Order League, represented jointly by the Rev. Alice Phillips Aldrich, who spends the day in court; the Woman's Protective Association, represented partly by Mrs. Aldrich and partly by Mrs. Anna Smith, a bailiff of the court;

and the Girls' Protective League, represented occasionally by one of its officials.

The judge refers to Mrs. Aldrich certain girls who need aid, advice or supervision. Mrs. Aldrich maintains no home for such girls. Some are placed in private institutions or restored to their relatives or friends. Efforts to secure employment are made when occasion arises. Sometimes Mrs. Aldrich is called upon to perform a marriage ceremony for one or more of the defendants.

At the time of visiting the court, two young girls whose names appeared on the docket but against whom no complaint had been filed, were brought before the judge. The arresting officer stated: "We have no evidence against these girls, but they were picked up in the course of a raid on a disorderly rooming-house." The girls said they came from North Dakota. The court asked "What shall I do with these two girls?" Mrs. Aldrich suggested: "I think they should be held until they can get out of the city; I think that I can raise the money by Saturday," (apparently funds from the Woman's Protective Association were not available for such cases) adding that she thought she knew of sources to which she could turn for it. The court said, "I have no jurisdiction to commit these girls to any place; I'll turn them over to you," indicating Mrs. Aldrich. Mrs. Aldrich stated that she did not know where to keep them. Turning to the girls she asked them if they would not rather stay at Lawndale Hospital than at the House of Correction, suggesting that it would be better for them. They agreed to this and promised to stay there voluntarily. It has been stated elsewhere that Lawndale is a detention hospital for venereally diseased convicted women, without provision for segregating offenders.

The Woman's Protective Association, having for its object "to follow cases of women offenders in the courts and to give protection, aid and friendly counsel," besides a general membership of 300 has delegates from sixteen prominent women's organizations of Chicago. Dues are one dollar a year. The

Association was founded in 1916. They now plan to have a personal representative in the court every day. Mrs. Smith acts as treasurer for a fund supplied by this Association. She may apply this where, in her discretion, it is needed, railroad fares representing the bulk of the expenditures, although occasional other uses are made of the money.

The work of the Girls' Protective League is directed by the local supervisor of the Interdepartmental Social Hygiene Board. Girls over eighteen years of age are referred to them by the Juvenile Protective Associations and other social agencies of the city. A number of their cases are received from the women's venereal disease ward of the Cook County Hospital. The League has its own corps of protective officers, who frequent parks, dance-halls, etc., especially on Friday and Saturday nights, watching couples and approaching any girls whose conduct seems to them questionable. Names and addresses of such girls are taken and reported to office headquarters weekly. Follow-up work is then done by workers specially assigned to such tasks. The League handled about 2600 cases during 1919 and 1920, when girls involved with soldiers and sailors were their chief concern, but it has not had so many since demobilization. In case of serious delinquency the girls are sometimes placed in private homes (small institutions). Others are sent back to their home towns where they are referred to proper agencies. In Chicago, the Girls' Protective League coöperates with numerous private organizations. Chief among these are: Salvation Army, Woman's Protective Association, Florence Crittenton Home (mainly for pregnant girls; capacity 22) Chicago Home for Girls (capacity 100), St. Margaret's Home (small home for Catholic girls), House of the Good Shepherd (capacity 500), Big Sisters (Catholic and Protestant), the Bureau of Personal Service (Jewish).

So far as remedial and corrective work for girls passing through the Morals Court is concerned, it did not appear that private agencies were making any scientific approach to the problem. It should be stated, however, that it is not possible to say to what extent coöperation on the part of such agencies is desired or made possible by the Court. Even numerically one cannot gauge the extent to which girls have been aided by these private groups month by month or year by year, as none of them keeps systematic records in regard to individuals assisted. Mrs. Smith, however, reports regularly to the Woman's Protective Association regarding expenditures on behalf of the girls.

RECORDS AND STATISTICS

Records. Consideration of three facts alone will show how seriously the value of the Morals Court records of individuals arraigned there is impaired:

1. No finger-prints, either before or after conviction, are taken.
2. Statements made by the individual are seldom checked up.
3. Sex, color, age or nativity are not specified on the docket.

The Secretary of the Social Service Department (a post held by a woman appointed by the Chief Clerk of the Municipal Court) [1] attempts to keep a card record of each girl or woman brought before the court. A copy of the card-form used stands below. Information called for by the starred items is copied from the Arrest Slip accompanying the complaint.

"Previous arrests" are noted in cases when the defendant is recognized and induced to reveal any alias. Again and again court clerks and officials asserted to investigator: "We know when they have been here before." The health department furnishes the social service secretary a daily report from which she can enter result of the Wassermann test or any statement regarding hospital or dispensary treatment

---

[1] This department has been fully described on pp. 26ff.

Morals Branch

Date...............192.... No.............

---

*Name...........................Height.......................
*Address.........................Weight
..................................Hair.......................
*Offense..........................Eyes.......................
....
Working..................Employment...........................
Previous Arrests.....,...
Previous Convictions......;.....................................
Age...
Race..
Birthplace..
     "   Father...
     "   Mother..
Father living.....................Mother Living................
Sisters...........................Brothers.....................
Married.........Single..........Divorced.........Widowed........
Children alive...................Dead...........
Grade in school...
Speak English...
Read   "   ....
Write   "   ....
How long in Chicago...
Age started prostitution......................................
Dispensary treatment..
Hospital care...
Psychopathic laboratory..,....................................
Physician's diagnosis......syphilis......gonorrhea......negative........

---

that may appear. The other facts, when supplied, are based upon the girl's unverified statements.

No corresponding record is kept of the men. Information concerning them can be secured from the docket, in respect only to docket number, name given, charge and disposition.

A word of explanation should be given in regard to the meaning of terms used under "disposition," whether in relation to men or women, as it will be necessary to bear that in mind in reviewing the tables at the end of this chapter.

One may be "discharged" because found not guilty; because of a faultily drawn complaint; for want of evidence in a case; because a short period of supervision (not on probation) presumably has terminated satisfactorily; because of being rendered non-infectious by treatment at Lawndale Hospital;[1] because of motion to vacate judgment,[2] or motion for new trial, or because reported feeble-minded by the Psychopathic Laboratory. Although some cases of *nolle prosequis* and non suits appear on the docket, many of these are entered as "dismissed for want of prosecution." An official of the Municipal Court writes: "To avoid public criticism it seems to be the policy of the state's attorney's office and also that of the city prosecutor's to have as few *nolle prosequis* and non suits entered on record as possible, and as a subterfuge they often suggest to the court that the suit be 'dismissed for want of prosecution.' " A continuance, besides indicating adjournment of a hearing may mean also that sentence is suspended for a brief period during which the girl is under a sort of supervision described elsewhere.[3] It may indicate also that a person is released on a personal recognizance bond.

It may be interesting to note in connection with the data supplied by the Morals Court, the minimum requirements for criminal court records set forth by the Committee on Statistics of Crime of the American Institute of Criminal Law and Criminology:[4]

---

[1] If women returned to the Morals Court after having been rendered non-infectious at Lawndale Hospital are, as was generally claimed, discharged by the Court, it appears that of the 687 women discharged during the first six months of 1920, 272, or 39.5 per cent, had first received treatment at Lawndale.

[2] While motions to vacate judgment or motions for new trial are entered on the docket, if sustained, the disposition is indicated as "discharged."

[3] See p. 26, par. 4; p. 48, par. 3.

[4] *Journal of Criminal Law and Criminology*, vol. 1, Sept. 1910, pp. 417–437.

What Criminal Court Records Should Show

(a) In Regard to the Criminal Process

1. Manner of commencing proceedings (by indictment, information presentment, inquisition, affidavit, complaint, etc., as the case may be).
2. Offense charged. 3. Date of offense, of indictment and of final disposition. 4. Pleas (guilty, nolo contendere, not guilty). If plea of guilty, then statement of precise offense which plea admits. 5. Disposition other than by trial or plea of guilty (indictment quashed, nolle prossed, demurrer sustained, dismissed, placed on file, etc.). 6. Mode of trial (by court or by jury). 7. Verdict (in case of guilty of lesser offense than originally charged, a statement of lesser offense). 8. Character of sentence (whether executed or suspended, etc.). 9. Appeal and result. 10. Institution to which sentenced. 11. Whether fine was paid. 12. Period of commitment for non-payment of fine.

(b) In Regard to Social Status of Defendant

1. Age. 2. Sex. 3. Color. 4. Race. 5. Birthplace. 6. Birthplace of parents. 7. Conjugal condition. 8. Education. 9. Occupation. 10. Citizenship. 11. Previous Convictions.

The police department keeps statistics showing the total number of arrests, arraignments and dispositions, by sex and offense, of persons arrested or arraigned in Chicago, but the court in which defendants are arraigned is not specified. Neither is it possible wholly to isolate sex offenses, because on their records "disorderly conduct" includes at least 23 other offenses, relating chiefly to disturbances of the peace. While a clerk of the Morals Court keeps a record of "cash bonds accepted," no record is kept of surety bonds or of releases on personal recognizance. The court papers indicate this in regard to each individual, but no summary is made. In certain cases warrants may be issued, but no record was available showing the number served. There are no statistics showing the number of bonds forfeited or the numbers of failures to appear on personal recognizance. The bond and recognizance papers are filed with the individual cases, the bonds being filed in the bond clerk's office on another floor in the building and the recognizances in the office of the chief justice.

Statistics. In attempting to form any accurate conception of the problems of the Morals Court or of the extent and nature of sex offenses in Chicago, as a whole, one is confronted with serious difficulties—many of them insurmountable.

Turning first of all to statistics published in Annual Reports of the Municipal Court we find in the first report of the Morals Branch,[1] under "Statistical Report of the Morals Court," the following statement:

Cases disposed of from April 7, 1913, to December 1, 1913............ 5005
From this number of cases we can give statistics of.................. 2938
The tables that follow are arranged by months, in respect to:
1. Number of cases, April-November, 5005
2. Color of defendants, June-November (of 2698)
3. Ages of defendants, June-November, in 3 to 4 year groups (of 2470)
4. Nationalities, June 28-November (of 2471)
5. Civil condition, June-November, married or single (of 2633), with an additional column of 28 "people" married in court
6. Offenses, June-November (of 2072)
7. Occupation, June-November (of 2657)
8. Placed on probation, April-November, 263. This is the only table showing disposition
9. Fines collected, April-November, $15,378

From the foregoing, it appears that the periods covered in the nine tables are not all uniform, three being for April through November, 1913; five for June through November; and one from June 28 through November.

At the beginning of the statistical report the statement is made in reference to the 2938 cases of whom statistics can be given that, "some defendants refused to give any information and others very little." Our own computation shows that the number of such defendants varies from 240 to 866.

---

[1] Seventh Annual Report, Municipal Court of Chicago, 1912–1913, p. 98.

In the Eighth and Ninth Annual Reports of the Municipal Court for the period December 1, 1913 to December 5, 1915, inclusive, a two and a quarter page statistical report of the Morals Branch is given.

These tables furnish a record of violation of laws and ordinances for the years 1914 and 1915, and disposition of cases appearing in those years.

One table furnishes a record of "cases disposed of" in 1914 and 1915, being in reality a record of violation of laws and ordinances, and a separate table shows dispositions made. The former table specifies 38 classifications of 25,006 violations with only 175 "*other cases.*" The latter, dealing with the same number of cases, specifies only four classifications. grouping 6339 as "other cases." These classifications deal only with sex offenses without, however indicating disposition of 484 cases of adultery and fornication, specified under "violations."

The three remaining tables relate to the number of "New Suits Filed," "Jury Trials," and the amount of "Fines Collected."

It will be noted that the only common and therefore comparable information set forth in the 1913 report and that for 1914-1915 is the total number of cases brought before the court and the amount of fines collected. As less than half of the 1913 cases are classified in respect to offenses, comparisons for the two succeeding years are impossible.

The next statistical report of the Morals Branch may be found in the Tenth and Eleventh Annual Reports of the Municipal Court for the period December 6, 1915 to December 2, 1917, inclusive. This comprises a table of "Cases Filed," grouped under "Felonies," "Misdemeanors," and "Quasi Criminal" for the respective years; "Cases Disposed of," similarly grouped and showing in addition the offense and disposition. Here one has a partial basis of comparison with the preceding period so far as offenses and dispositions are concerned.

No report of the Municipal Court has been published since 1917. It has been pointed out elsewhere that all cases heard in the Morals Court are not for sex offenses; nor are all sex offenses occurring in the City of Chicago heard in the Morals Court. A considerable number refuse to sign the jury waiver and so automatically are transferred to the Jury Branch. Such violations as take place in the 6th, 7th, 8th, 9th, and 10th precincts are heard at the South Chicago Station (8th precinct) as the precincts enumerated lie eight to twelve miles distant from the Morals Court. Furthermore in cases in which affidavits of prejudice are filed against any or all of the judges sitting in the criminal branches, the case may be assigned to any other of the judges in the civil branch. The 1917 report shows under the charge, "Keeping disorderly house" (to take but a single instance) 4518 cases heard in 17 different courts, as follows:

Branch No. 3	109	Maxwell St.	76
Boys' Court	18	Sheffield Ave.	3
Domestic Relations	3	Shakespeare Ave.	2
Jury Branch	1291	35th Street	206
Morals Branch	2585	Stock Yards	18
Harrison Street	84	Englewood	12
Desplaines Street	53	Hyde Park	13
E. Chicago Ave.	38	South Chicago	5
W. Chicago Ave.	2		

Still another fact must be taken into consideration: Whereas the term, "Disorderly conduct," as used in Morals Court cases refers chiefly to loiterers or inmates of houses of ill-fame, when used in relation to other courts, it may include (as in the police records) at least 23 other types of offense. The significance of this is more readily apparent when one bears in mind that of the eight charges of sex violation under which offenders may be brought into the Morals Court, the number of "disorderly conduct" cases tried in the Morals Court (Ord. 2012) stands second only to, "Keepers and Inmates of Disorderly Houses," (Ord. 2019).

Certain of the difficulties lying in the way of forming any accurate estimate of the nature and extent of sex offenses in Chicago may be summed up as follows:

1. Absence of finger-print system.
2. Failure to designate sex of the defendant.
3. Lack of comparable data:
   (a) In relation to individuals.
   (b) In relation to the criminal process.
   (c) In relation to periods of time.
4. Practice of hearing other than sex offenses in Morals Court.
5. Scattering of cases of sex offenses throughout other branches of the Municipal Court.
6. Inclusion of numerous other than sex offenses under term "Disorderly Conduct."

While the reports contain considerable information in regard to various aspects of the problem under consideration the data are so fragmentary and unrelated in character as to provide no adequate system of checks and balances looking toward the development of constructive policies in handling the delinquent woman.

For the reasons just set forth it became apparent at the time of our investigation that little insight into the procedure and workings of the Morals Court could be gained from the meager, fragmentary and by no means recent statistics available. Accordingly it was necessary to go direct to the 1920 docket of the Morals Court in order to abstract and compile essential data. This was made possible through the courtesy of the chief clerk of the Municipal Court and the kind assistance of his deputy, Mrs. Elizabeth M. Gardner, secretary of the Social Service Department of the Morals Court. Owing to the size of the docket and the limits of our time it was possible to cover only a six months' period—that of January 1 to June 30, 1920. Tables 1, 5, 6, 8 and 9 at the end of this chapter embody the result of our study of the docket.

DISCUSSION OF TABLES

Table 1 shows the final disposition of cases of sex offenders arraigned in the Morals Court during the first six months of 1920. These number 2207 of whom 1239 are men and 968 women. Of this number it will be noted that 312 men, or 25.1 per cent; and 195 women, or 20.1 per cent, were convicted—making total convictions of 507 or 22.9 per cent. Seven hundred and ninety-nine men and 687 women were discharged.[1] Perhaps most surprising of all the facts revealed by this table is the small number of commitments to an institution—nine men and five women—all sent to the House of Correction. This may be explained partly by the fact that Illinois has no state reformatory for women and partly by two facts mentioned elsewhere:

1. In the statutes and ordinances relating to sex offenses provision for commitment is made under the statutes only.
2. By far the greater number of cases brought into the Morals Court are for violations of city ordinances.

Table 5 presents a study of court action on cases appearing in the Morals Court during the period studied and shows in addition to final disposition other steps in the criminal process. An outstanding feature of this table is the number of continuances—2214 in the case of 1239 men; and 2441 in the case of 968 women. This has been more fully discussed on pages 17 ff.

Table 6, a study of court action on cases transferred from the Morals Court to the Jury Branch, January 1 to June 30, 1920,[2] shows a total of 93 cases—47 men and 46 women. Of these, two men and three women actually were tried by jury,

---

[1] In regard to the many implications of this term, see pp. 58–61.

[2] For the facts furnished in this table it was necessary to follow through from the docket of the Morals Court to the Jury Branch docket cases indicated to have been transferred to that branch.

all five being discharged. Other significant features of this table are pointed out on pages 19 ff.

Tables 8, 9 and 10, illustrative of the number and length of continuances through a study of 100 women whose cases were continued have been fully discussed on pages 17 ff.

From the Records Division of the Police Department we secured the data given in Tables 2 and 3 in regard to persons arrested for sex offenses in the entire city of Chicago. In Table 2 we have a comparison of arrests and convictions for the months, January, March and April, 1920. The figures for February had not been compiled by the division at the time of our inquiry, nor had the record been carried beyond April. Although these statistics cover only three of the six months covered in Table 1, it is nevertheless interesting to note how closely the percentage of convictions of arraigned persons in Table 1 corresponds to the percentage of convictions of arrested persons in Table 2, namely, of the men arraigned during the first six months of 1920, 25.1 per cent were convicted and of the men arrested during the three-month period, 27.6 per cent were convicted; of the women arraigned, 20.1 per cent were convicted and of the women arrested, 22.4 per cent; of the total arraigned, 22.9 per cent were convicted and of the total arrested, 26.8 per cent were convicted. Although neither table is wholly comparable with Table 1, each being for a different period of time and relating to the entire city, they form nevertheless a background for the facts enumerated in Table 1.

In the same way, Table 4, showing disposition of cases arraigned in the Morals Court for the four years 1916–1919, inclusive, affords some measure of activity in the Court and should be consulted in connection with Tables 1, 2 and 3.

Table 7 shows the names of judges who have presided in the Morals Court since its establishment and the approximate length of time each judge sat. There is no fixed system for returning to the Morals Branch, by rotation or otherwise, a judge who acquires experience in this class of cases.

Table 11 indicates disposition in the Morals Court of 100 women arraigned during the first six months of 1920 who were known to have had two or more previous convicitions. These deal with 100 consecutive cases taken by the secretary of the Social Service Department from the alphabetical card file kept by her of women and girls brought before the Morals Court. Of these, 54 were convicted on the new charge and disposed of as follows:

Probation 23
House of Correction................................. 4
Fined 27

The facts appearing in Table 12 were supplied by the court clerk from his record of cash bonds accepted during the first six months of 1920.

Table 13, showing record of 75 out of 88 persons placed upon probation during the first six months of 1920, is fully described on page 51.

APPEALS

As before stated, no provision is made for a court reporter to take stenographic notes of proceedings in the Morals Court. The necessity of this is apparent upon appeal. Appeals are taken directly from this court either to the Court of Appeals or to the Supreme Court. In other words, the appealed case is not retried before a higher court of original jurisdiction, but appeals are heard by an Appellate Court. This makes a written record particularly essential. As the record for appeal is made up at present, the attorneys and the court must come to an agreement on the facts. If the attorneys fail to stipulate what the facts are, it becomes necessary for the court to certify them from memory. The difficulty of this is apparent, in view of the number of cases heard daily and the failure of the judge to take notes in each case.

CONCLUSION

The foregoing report seeks merely to describe the structure, jurisdiction, and procedure—social as well as legal—of the Chicago Morals Court. Merits and defects have been commented upon only incidentally. In Chapter VI an attempt has been made to compare, analyze, and constructively criticize practices in the courts studied.

TABLE 1. FINAL DISPOSITION OF CASES OF SEX OFFENDERS ARRAIGNED IN MORALS COURT, CHICAGO, JANUARY 1 TO JUNE 30, 1920[1]

Ordinances		Total Arraigned	Transferred to Jury Branch	Nonsuit and Nolle Pros[4]	Dismissed, Want of Jurisdiction of Person	Dismissed, Want of Prosecution[4]	Discharged[4]	Convicted						
								Probation	Committed to House of Correction[7]	Fined[9]	Fined (Ex Parte)	Fine Reduced[10]	Total Convicted	Per Cent Convicted
Disorderly conduct (2012)	M	273	....	....	....	4	214	3	.....	48	2	2	55	20.1
	F	216	1	....	....	2	163	23	.....	20	5	2	50	23.1
Keeper disorderly house (2014)	M	16	3	1	2	1	5	....	.....	2	....	2	4	25
	F	10	2	....	....	....	8	....	.....	....	....	....	....	....
Patrons and inmates disorderly house (2015)	M	138	17	1	4	2	83	1	.....	28	1	1	31	22.4
	F	22	....	....	2	....	16	3	.....	1	....	....	4	18.1
Soliciting for prostitution (2018)	M	4	....	....	....	....	1	....	.....	3	....	....	3	75
	F	74	2	....	....	1	44	5	.....	15	5	2	27	36.4
Persons connected with public nuisance (2019)	M	696	18	....	26	....	458[5]	6	.....	179	7	2	194	27.8
	F	490	25	2	17	1	366[5]	20	.....	47	10	2	79	16.1
STATUTES[2]														
Adultery (Sec. 11, Crim. Code)	M	25	3	1	....	7	7[6]	3	3	1	....	....	7	28
	F	21	2	....	....	4	10	5	....	....	....	....	5	23.8
Fornication (Sec. 11, Crim. Code)	M	45	3	....	....	5	22[6]	5	3[8]	7	....	....	15	33.3
	F	29	4	1	....	3	12	5	1	3	....	....	9	31
Pandering (57-G)	M	18	3	2	....	1	9	....	3	....	....	....	3	16.6
	F	4	....	1	....	1	2	....	....	....	....	....	....	....
Inmates disorderly house or soliciting for prostitution[3] (57-A-1)	M	24	....	....	24	....	....	....	....	....	....	....	....	....
	F	102	10	....	5	....	66	8	4	9	....	....	21	20.5
Total	M	1239	47	5	56	20	799	18	9	268	10	7	312	25.1
	F	968	46	4	24	12	687	69	5	95	20	6	195	20.1
Grand Total		2207	93	9	80	32	1486	87	14	363	30	13	507	22.9

[1] For source of data, see p. 65.   [2] No charges during this period under State Law, Sec. 57, "Keeping and patronizing disorderly house or leasing place for that purpose."   [3] Commonly known as the Kate Adams Law.   [4] Re use of terms "non-suit," "nolle prosequis," "discharged," etc., see statement, p. 60.   [5] One discharged after June 30, 1920.   [6] Two have been detained one day and eight weeks, respectively, in the County Jail. The court, considering this the equivalent of serving time, discharged the defendants.   [7] These figures indicate direct commitment by the court and do not include cases sent to House of Correction for non-payment of fine.   [8] One committed after June 30, 1920.   [9] The docket does not specify whether fines were paid or worked out in the House of Correction.   [10] Frequently when motion to vacate judgment or motion for new trial was overruled, the fine was reduced or some lighter sentence imposed.

TABLE 2. COMPARISON OF ARRESTS AND CONVICTIONS OF SEX OFFENDERS FOR ENTIRE CITY OF CHICAGO FOR THE MONTHS OF JANUARY, MARCH, AND APRIL, 1920,[1] WITH PERCENTAGE OF CONVICTIONS

ORDINANCES		JANUARY, 1920		MARCH, 1920		APRIL, 1920		TOTAL		Per Cent of Convictions
		Arrests	Convictions	Arrests	Convictions	Arrests	Convictions	Arrests	Convictions	
Disorderly conduct[2] (2012)	M	1635	420	2022	633	1863	488	5520	1541	27.9
	F	226	41	291	72	245	55	762	168	22
Keeper disorderly house (2014)	M	2	.....	2	1	.....	.....	4	.....	.....
	F	3	.....	3	.....	.....	.....	6	2	50
Patrons and inmates of disorderly house (2015)	M	54	24	25	.....	11	4	90	28	31.1
	F	3	1	5	.....	.....	.....	8	1	12.5
Soliciting for prostitution (2018)	M	11	4	14	2	2	.....	2	.....	.....
	F	.....	.....	.....	.....	7	3	32	9	28.1
Persons connected with public nuisance (2019)	M	99	14	310	83	96	20	505	117	23.1
	F	59	12	115	13	52	26	226	51	22.5
STATUTES										
Adultery and fornication (Sec. 11, Crim. Code)	M	13	7	26	8	14	4	53	19	35.8
	F	15	4	20	9	9	3	44	16	36.3
Pandering (57-G)	M	4	1	1	.....	2	.....	7	1	14.2
	F	1	.....	1	.....	1	.....	3	.....	.....
Inmates disorderly house or soliciting for prostitution[3] (57-A-1)	M	.....	.....	.....	.....	.....	.....	.....	.....	.....
	F	30	6	21	3	12	3	63	12	19
Total	M	1807	467	2386	725	1988	516	6181	1708	27.6
	F	348	68	470	99	326	90	1144	257	22.4
Grand Total		2155	535	2856	824	2314	606	7325	1965	26.8

[1] Table furnished by Records Division, Police Department, Chicago. Convictions for February, May, and June were not completed at the time of our investigation.

[2] Includes all offenses under this ordinance, vid. p. 6-7.

[3] Commonly known as the Kate Adams Law.

TABLE 3. DISPOSITION OF CASES OF SEX OFFENDERS IN ALL COURTS OF CHICAGO, 1919[1]

ORDINANCES		Total	Bonds Forfeited	Peace Bonds	Discharged	Probation	House of Correction	County Jail	Other Institutions	Fined	Pending at end of Year	Total Convicted	Per Cent Convicted
Disorderly conduct[2] (2012)	M	31,173	34	73	22,989	569	8	......	......	7244	256	7821	25
	F	4,435	9	55	3,511	62	......	......	......	760	38	822	18.5
Keeper disorderly house (2014)	M	8	1	......	6	......	......	......	......	1	1	1	12.5
	F	11	1	......	5	1	......	......	......	2	2	3	27.2
Patrons and inmates disorderly house (2015)	M	120	......	......	91	......	......	......	......	17	12	17	14.1
	F	44	......	......	38	......	......	......	......	2	4	2	4.5
Soliciting for prostitution (2018)	M	29	......	......	16	2	1	......	......	10	......	13	44.8
	F	173	......	......	127	2	......	......	......	43	1	45	26
Persons connected with public nuisance (2019)	M	1,807	1	......	1,327	1	......	......	......	470	8	471	26
	F	1,123	4	......	800	14	......	......	1	283	21	298	26.5
STATUTES													
Adultery and fornication (Sec. 11, Crim. Code)	M	193	4	......	125	17	24	......	......	20	3	61	31.6
	F	167	3	......	120	22	6	1	......	11	4	40	23.9
Pandering (57-G)	M	39	3	......	22	5	7	1	......	......	1	13	33.3
	F	5	......	......	4	1	......	......	......	......	......	1	20
Inmates disorderly house or soliciting for prostitution[3] (57-A-1)	M	21	......	......	12	......	1	......	......	7	1	8	38
	F	344	7	......	235	9	13	......	1	75	4	98	28.4
Total	M	33,390	42	73	24,588	594	41	1	......	7769	282	8405	25.1
	F	6,302	24	55	4,840	111	19	1	2	1176	74	1309	20.7
Grand Total		39,692	66	128	29,428	705	60	2	2	8945	356	9714	24.4

1 Data furnished by Records Division, Police Department, Chicago.
2 Includes all offenses under this ordinance, vid. pp. 6-7.
3 Commonly known as the Kate Adams Law.

TABLE 4. DISPOSITION OF CASES ARRAINGED IN MORALS COURT FOR THE FOUR YEARS, 1916–1919 [1]

Years	Held in Criminal Court	Non-suit	Nolle Pros.	Dismissed, Want of Prosecution	Discharged	Probation	Committed to House of Correction [2]	Committed to County Jail	Fined
1916	16	68	12	303	3,402	159	838	12	1771
1917	7	17	10	181	3,749	289	791	3	2224
1918	8	44	6	194	3,586	176	623	7	1178
1919	12	10	8	296	2,977	119	172	3	913
Total	43	139	36	974	13,714	743	2424	25	6086 [3]

[1] Data furnished by Mr. Samuel P. Thrasher, Superintendent, Committee of Fifteen, Chicago.
[2] These figures include cases sent to House of Correction to work out fine.
[3] Grand totals cannot be figured for the reason given in the preceding footnote.

TABLE 5. STUDY OF COURT ACTION ON CASES ARRAIGNED IN MORALS COURT, JANUARY 1 TO JUNE 30, 1920 [1]

Ordinances	Sex	Total Arraigned	Transferred to Jury Branch	Continued [4]	Cash or Surety Bond Forfeited	Capias Issued	Motion to Set Aside Surety Bond Forfeiture Sustained [5]	Non-suit and Nolle Pros.	Dismissed, Want of Jurisdiction of Person	Dismissed, Want of Prosecution [4]	Discharged [4]	Probation	Committed to House of Correction [10]	Fined [9]	Fined (Ex Parte)	Motion to Vacate Judgment	Motion for New Trial Sustained	Fine Reduced [12]
Disorderly conduct (2012)	M	273		390	10	3	2			4	214	3		48	2	4		2
	F	216	1	403	9	12	3			2	163	23		20	5	11		2
Keeper disorderly house (2014)	M	16	3	22	1	1		1	2	1	5		3	2				2
	F	10	2	28							8							
Patrons and inmates disorderly house (2015)	M	138	17	255	6	1		1	4	2	83	1		28	1			
	F	22		66	1	2			2		16	3		1				
Soliciting for prostitution (2018)	M	4		4							1			3				
	F	74	2	159	2	5		2		1	44	5		15	5			2
Persons connected with public nuisance (2019)	M	696	18	1307	10	1			26		458[7]	6		179	7	8	1	2
	F	490	25	1289	9	10			17	1	366[7]	20		47	10	10	1	2
STATUTES [2]																		
Adultery (Sec. 11, Crim. Code)	M	25	3	71	1		1	1		7	7	3		1			1	
	F	21	2	75		1	1			4	10[8]	5						
Fornication (Sec. 11, Crim. Code)	M	45	3	114		2				5	22[8]	5	3[11]	7				
	F	29	4	90		2	2	1		3	12	5	1	3				
Pandering (57-G)	M	18	3	40	1			2		1	9		3					
	F	4		16		4		1		1	2							
Inmates disorderly house or soliciting for prostitution [3] (57-A-1)	M	24		11			1		24									
	F	102	10	315	14	4	1		5		66	8	4	9				
Total	M	1239	47	2214	29	8	8	5	56	20	799	18	9	268	10	12	3	7
	F	968	46	2441	35	40	12	4	24	12	687	69	5	95	20	21	5	6
Grand Total		2207	93	4655	64	48	20[6]	9	80	32	1486	87	14	363	30	33	8	13

1 In this table the defendant may appear in two or more columns. On June 30 there were 328 cases pending in the Morals Court, which, owing to limits of time, were not classified by offense. For source of data, see p. 65. 2 No charges during this period under state statute, Sec. 57, Keeping and patronizing, disorderly, house or leasing place for that purpose. 3 Commonly known as the Kate Adams Law. 4 Re use of terms, "Continued," "Discharged," etc., see statement, p. 60. 5 The docket for this period shows three cases of motion to set aside cash bond forfeiture made by three women defendants in their own behalf. A clerk of the court explained: "The cash bond is forfeited on a day when the defendant does not appear in court. He then comes in to court on a subsequent day and asks that the forfeiture be set aside." One of these women was cha'ged with fornication and the other two with violating the Kate Adams Law. In each instance the motion was granted and the defendants after a trial were discharged. 6 Three cases disposed of after June 30, 1920. 7 One discharged after June 30, 1920. 8 Two had been detained one day and eight weeks, respectively, in the County Jail. Considering this the equivalent of serving time, the court discharged them. 9 The docket does not specify whether fines were paid or worked out in the House of Correction. 10 These figures indicate direct commitment by the court and do not include cases sent to the House of Correction for non-payment of fine. 11 One committed after June 30, 1920. 12 Frequently when the motion to vacate judgment or motion for new trial was overruled, the fine was reduced or some lighter sentence imposed.

TABLE 6. COURT ACTION ON CASES TRANSFERRED FROM MORALS COURT TO JURY BRANCH, JANUARY 1 TO JUNE 30, 1920 [1]

ORDINANCES		Total	Transferred to Chief Justice	Cash Deposit Forfeited	Non-suit Nolle Pros.	Dismissed, Want of Prosecution	Discharged	CONVICTED			
								Probation	Fined	Fined (Ex Parte)	Total Convicted
Disorderly conduct (2012)	M	....	....	....	....	....	....	....	....	....	....
	F	1	....	....	....	....	....	1	....	....	1
Keeper disorderly house (2014)	M	3	1	....	....	....	2 [3]	....	....	....	....
	F	2	1	....	....	1	....	....	....	....	....
Patrons and inmates disorderly house (2015)	M	17	....	6	....	....	4 [3]	....	7	....	7
	F	....	....	....	....	....	....	....	....	....	....
Soliciting for prostitution (2018)	M	....	....	....	....	....	....	....	....	....	....
	F	2	....	....	....	1	1	....	....	....	....
Persons connected with public nuisance (2019)	M	18	1	1	1	5	1	....	8	1	9
	F	25	....	2	....	8	8 [4]	....	5	2	7
STATUTES											
Adultery (Sec. 11, Crim. Code)	M	3	1	....	....	....	2	....	....	....	....
	F	2	....	....	....	1	1	....	....	....	....
Fornication (Sec. 11, Crim. Code)	M	3	....	....	....	1	....	1	1	....	2
	F	4	....	....	1	....	3	....	....	....	....
Pandering (57-G)	M	3	2	....	....	....	1	....	....	....	....
	F	....	....	....	....	....	....	....	....	....	....
Inmates disorderly house or soliciting for prostitution [2] (57-A-1)	M	....	....	....	4	....	....	....	....	....	....
	F	10	....	1	....	1	2 [3]	2	....	....	2
Total	M	47	5	7	1	6	10	1	16	1	18
	F	46	1	3	5	12	15	3	5	2	10
Grand Total		93	6	10	6	18	25 [5]	4	21	3	28

[1] Cases shown on the docket of the Morals Court to have been transferred to Jury Branch of the Municipal Court were followed through on the docket of the latter court in order to ascertain action taken in each case.

[2] Commonly known as the Kate Adams Law.

[3] Of the total, one had jury trial.

[4] Of the total, two had jury trial.

[5] Total tried by jury, 5.

TABLE 7. JUDGES PRESIDING IN THE MORALS BRANCH OF THE MUNICIPAL COURT OF CHICAGO, APRIL, 1913, TO JULY, 1920 [1]

	1913	1914	1915	1916	1917	1918	1919	1920
January		Hopkins	Goodnow	Uhlir	Fisher	Uhlir Graham	Dolan	Sullivan
February		Hopkins	Goodnow	Uhlir	Fisher	Graham	Dolan Fisher	Sullivan
March		Hopkins	Goodnow Heap Hopkins	Uhlir	Fisher	Graham	Caverly Dolan Fisher Heap	Sullivan
April	Hopkins	Hopkins Goodnow	Heap Hopkins	Uhlir	Fisher Uhlir	Graham	Caverly Jarecki	Sullivan
May	Hopkins	Goodnow	Heap	Uhlir	Uhlir	Graham	Jarecki	Sullivan
June	Hopkins Sabath	Goodnow	Heap	Uhlir Wade	Uhlir	Graham	Jarecki Heap	Sullivan Donohoe Jarecki
July	Hopkins Martin Kearns Stewart	Goodnow	Heap	Wade	Uhlir	Graham	Heap	Heap
August	Stewart	Hopkins Goodnow	Robinson	Robinson	Robinson	Fisher	Prindiville Fisher Williams Orr	
September	Hopkins Stewart	Hopkins Goodnow	Uhlir	Wade Fisher	Uhlir Dolan	Cook	Fisher Sullivan	
October	Hopkins	Goodnow	Uhlir	Fisher	Uhlir	Cook	Sullivan	
November	Hopkins	Goodnow	Uhlir	Fisher	Uhlir	Cook	Sullivan	
December	Hopkins	Goodnow	Uhlir	Fisher	Uhlir	Dolan	Sullivan	

[1] Information furnished by chief clerk of the Municipal Court, Chicago.

TABLE 8. DISPOSITION OF ONE HUNDRED NEW CASES [1] (WOMEN) ARRAIGNED IN MORALS COURT, CHICAGO, JANUARY 1 TO JUNE 30, 1920, SHOWING NUMBER OF CONTINUANCES [2] PRECEDING FINAL DISPOSITION [3]

DISPOSITION	NUMBER OF CONTINUANCES							
	Total	1	2	3	4	5	6	7
Transferred to Jury Branch	3	1	1	......	......	1	......	.....
Continued	1	.....	......	......	......	......	......	1
Cash bond forfeited	3	2	......	1	......	......	......	......
Warrant issued	2	......	2	......	......	......	......	......
Dismissed, want of prosecution	1	......	1	......	......	......	......	......
Discharged	70	20 [4]	22	10	7	7 [5]	4	......
Probation	11	2	2	5	......	2	......	......
Committed to House of Correction	1	1	......	......	......	......	......	......
Fined	4	2	1	......	1	......	......	......
Ex parte fine	4	2	......	1	1	......	......	......
Total	100	30	29	17	9	10	4	1

[1] Cases not pending from 1919, not necessarily first offenders, but arraigned for the first time during period indicated.

[2] For relation of number of continuances of cases of 100 women to interval of time between first and final hearing, see Table 10.

[3] For source of data, see p. 65.

[4] Defendants married in two instances.

[5] Defendant married in one instance.

TABLE 9. DISPOSITION OF ONE HUNDRED NEW CASES [1] (WOMEN) ARRAIGNED JANUARY 1 TO JUNE 30, 1920, SHOWING INTERVAL OF TIME BETWEEN APPEARANCE IN MORALS COURT AND FINAL DISPOSITION [2] [3]

Disposition	Total	1–10 Days	11–20 Days	21–30 Days	31–40 Days	41–50 Days	51–60 Days	2–3 Months	3–5 Months or Over
Transferred to Jury Branch	3		2					1	
Continued	1								1
Cash bond forfeited	3	2				1			
Warrant issued	2				1	1			
Dismissed want of prosecution	1		1						
Discharged	70	8	18 [4]	8	8	9 [5]	3	11	5
Probation	11		1	3	1	1	1	3	1
Committed to House of Correction	1		1						
Fined	4			2		1		1	
Ex parte fine	4	1	1			1	1		
Total	100	11	24	13	10	14	5	16	7

[1] Cases not pending from 1919, not necessarily first offenders but arraigned for the first time during period indicated.
[2] For relation of number of continuances of cases of 100 women to interval of time between first and final hearing, see Table 10.
[3] For source of data, see p. 65.
[4] Defendants married in two instances.
[5] Defendant married in one instance.

TABLE 10. RELATION OF NUMBER OF CONTINUANCES OF CASES OF ONE HUNDRED WOMEN TO INTERVALS OF TIME BETWEEN FIRST AND FINAL HEARING [1]

TIME INTERVALS	NUMBER OF CONTINUANCES							
	1	2	3	4	5	6	7	Total
1–10 days	9	2	......	......	......	......	......	11
11–20 days	16	7	1	......	......	......	......	24
21–30 days	5	3	4	......	1	......	......	13
31–40 days	......	9	1	......	......	......	......	10
41–50 days	......	7	5	......	1	1	......	14
51–60 days	......	1	2	1	1	......	......	5
2–3 months	......	......	4	5	5	2	......	16
3–5 months or over	......	......	......	3	2	1	1	7
Total	30	29	17	9	10	4	1	100

[1] Based on Tables 8 and 9.

TABLE 11. DISPOSITION IN MORALS COURT OF 100 WOMEN [1] ARRAIGNED JANUARY 1 TO JUNE 30, 1920, WHO WERE KNOWN TO HAVE HAD TWO OR MORE PREVIOUS CONVICTIONS [2]

LATEST OFFENSE	TWO PREVIOUS CONVICTIONS								THREE PREVIOUS CONVICTIONS					FIVE OR MORE PREVIOUS CONVICTIONS		
	Total	Cash Bond For-feited	Warrant Issued	Non-suit	Dis-charged	Proba-tion	House of Correc-tion	Fined	Total	Warrant Issued	Dis-charged	Proba-tion	Fined	Total	Proba-tion	Fined
ORDINANCES																
Disorderly conduct (2012)	5	....	......	....	1	2	......	2	2	......	1	1	....	....	....	....
Soliciting for prostitution (2018)	2	1	......	....	......	1	......	....	....	......	......	......	....	....	....	....
Persons connected with public nuisance (2019)	35	4	13	1	12	5	......	....	16	6	1	4	5	2	1	1
STATUTES																
Adultery (Sec. 11, Crim. Code)	2	....	......	....	1	....	1	....	....	......	......	....	....	....	....	....
Fornication (Sec. 11, Crim. Code)	3	....	......	....	1	....	2	....	....	......	......	....	....	....	....	....
Inmates disorderly house or solicit-ing for prostitu-tion [4] (57-A-1)	27	....	1	....	2	6	1	17 [3]	5	1	......	2	2	1	1	.....
Total	74	5	14	1	17	14	4	19	23	7	2	7	7	3	2	1

[1] These are 100 consecutive cases taken by the secretary of the Social Service Department from the alphabetical card file kept by her of women and girls brought before the Morals Court. This card record is fully described on pp. 59 ff.

[2] Due to the lack of a finger-print system only known previous convictions can be cited; the women may actually have more convictions to their credit.

[3] Ten committed in default of payment.

[4] Commonly known as the Kate Adams Law.

TABLE 12. TABLE SHOWING NUMBER AND AMOUNT OF CASH BONDS ACCEPTED IN THE MORALS COURT, JANUARY 1 TO JULY 1, 1920 [1]

Amount	Men	Women
$10.00	5	....
14.00	1	....
15.00	9	....
20.00	5	1
25.00	201	62
30.00	10	....
35.00	2	....
40.00	4	2
50.00	133	108
70.00	1	....
75.00	6	1
100.00	28	10
150.00	1	1
160.00	1	....
200.00	10	3
206.00	1	....
210.00	1	....
250.00	1	1
400.00	1	....
500.00	....	1
Totals.........	421	190

Data upplied by Court Clerk from record of cash bonds accepted in Morals Court.

TABLE 13. STATUS OF 75 PERSONS, FROM TOTAL OF 88 PLACED UPON PROBATION FROM THE MORALS COURT OR THE JURY BRANCH DURING THE FIRST SIX MONTHS OF 1920, AS REPORTED BY THE ADULT PROBATION DEPARTMENT [1]

Conduct	Total		Disorderly Conduct		Patrons and Inmates Disorderly House		Soliciting		Persons Connected with Public Nuisance		Inmates Disorderly House or Soliciting for Prostitution		Fornication		Adultery		Not Given	
	M	F	M	F	M	F	M	F	M	F	M	F	M	F	M	F	M	F
Satisfactory	9	28		12	1	1		3	4	7		3	3	1		1		
Unsatisfactory	1	7		6		1		1	1							1	1	
Unsatisfactory— Warrant	1	8		1					1	5		1	1		1	1		
Still on probation (Conduct good)	2	8		2						2		1		2				
Still on probation · (Conduct not good)		1		1														
Still on probation [2]	3	7	1	1					1	1				2	1	3		
Total	16	59	1	23	1	2		4	7	15		5	4	5	2	5		1

[1] Table discussed on p. 51.
[2] No statement concerning conduct.

CHAPTER II

THE MISDEMEANANTS' DIVISION OF THE PHILADELPHIA MUNICIPAL COURT

The special court in Philadelphia which deals with cases involving sex delinquency, is known as the Misdemeanants' Division of the Municipal Court. This is the court which corresponds to the Chicago Morals Court.

JURISDICTION

The Municipal Court is a court of record created by an act of the General Assembly of the Commonwealth of Pennsylvania, approved July 12, 1913,[1] as amended by P. L. 1017, June 17, 1915, which gave it exclusive jurisdiction in juvenile cases, desertion and non-support of wife or children, abandoned and indigent parents; and limited jurisdiction in criminal[2] and civil cases.

The judges are elected by popular vote for a term of ten years, and receive a salary of $8,000.[3] At present there are nine[4] judges in the Municipal Court, one of whom is chosen

---

[1] P. L. 711.

[2] "Sec. 11. The said court shall have jurisdiction in all criminal actions and suits for penalties, except that it shall not have jurisdiction in the trial of indictments for arson, burglary, forgery, kidnapping, murder, voluntary manslaughter, perjury, rape, robbery, treason or misprision of treason, or for violation or conspiracy to violate the election or registration laws of this commonwealth, or for criminal libel, or for embezzlement by any public officer, or any offense involving breach of official duties by any public officer . . . The judges . . . shall be ex officio justices of the peace. . . . When defendants are bound over for trial . . . indictments may be presented before Grand Jury . . . which indictments may be tried either in existing courts, or in the Municipal Court."

[3] Act of July 21, 1919, P. L. 1065. The president judge receives $8,500.

[4] Increased to ten in 1922.

83

BOWLING GREEN STATE UNIVERSITY LIBRARY

by the Governor as president judge.   The court does not
meet in terms, but is required by law to be open at all times
for the transaction of business.   At present, it has the following divisions:

> The Domestic Relations Division
> The Criminal Division
> The Misdemeanants' Division
> The Juvenile Division
> The Civil Division

Judges are assigned to the various divisions by the president
judge.

The Misdemeanants' Division was created in 1915, after
the enactment by the General Assembly of the Act of June
17, 1915,[1] which gives the Municipal Court exclusive jurisdiction over disorderly street-walkers [2] and disorderly children,[3] between the ages of 16 and 21 years.   The designation,
"misdemeanants'," is not statutory.

The Misdemeanants' Division is the court's heritage from
the old Justice-of-the-Peace and Magistrates' Courts.   All
cases of sex delinquency which formerly could have been disposed of summarily by a magistrate, alderman, or justice of
the peace are disposed of summarily by this court.   Likewise,
all other cases of sex delinquency which require a jury trial
are given a preliminary hearing, and if the judge finds there
is probable cause to hold the defendant for trial, he is bound
over for the grand jury in the same procedure observed by a
magistrate.   No pleas are received, but upon admission of

---

[1] P. L. 1017.

[2] "In all proceedings concerning, or trials or charges brought against all persons, whether adults or minors, accused of disorderly street-walking."

[3] "In all proceedings concerning, or trials or charges brought against, all minors
between the ages of 16 and 21 years who shall disobey their parents' command,
or be found idle in the streets, and against all disorderly children."   Disorderly
children are defined as "all children not under the age of 16 years deserting their
homes without good and sufficient cause, or keeping company with dissolute or
vicious persons, against the lawful commands of their fathers, mothers, or guardians, or other person standing in the place of a parent."

guilt by defendant, sentence may be pronounced by the judge
—not in his capacity as a magistrate, but in his capacity as a
judge of the Municipal Court.

No jury-waiver system such as described in the section
relating to the Chicago Morals Court, exists. Indeed in the
formation of this court, much of the waste of the old common-
law system was retained. Thus, in cases requiring a jury
trial, a preliminary hearing is held before the Misdemeanants' Division. If probable cause is found, the defendant is
bound over for hearing by the grand jury. If the grand jury
returns a true bill, the defendant is tried on indictment before
a petit jury in the Criminal Division.[1] The hardship on witnesses in attending this multiplicity of hearings needs no
comment. A proposed remedy will be discussed in Chapter
VI. The vesting of exclusive jurisdiction in the Misdemeanants' Division of the cases referred to in notes 2 and 3
on page 84 is a departure from the old common-law system
of jurisprudence.

This court, which has become highly specialized, is housed
in a separate building at Twelfth and Wood Streets, which
building also contains medical and mental examination rooms,
fingerprint and identification bureau, and detention quarters
for women and girls, all of which is given special consideration in another part of this report.[2] The court sits three
days a week—Mondays, Wednesdays and Fridays, the sessions beginning at 10:30 in the morning and lasting for about
three hours.

It will be noted, that this court does not specialize on any
other kind of sex delinquency than that of street-walking,
and those offenses involving children between the ages of 16
and 21, over which this court is given exclusive jurisdiction.
All cases are tried in this court by the Judge without a jury.
Other offenses involving sex delinquency, as before stated,

---

[1] They may also be tried in the Court of Quarter Sessions as the District
Attorney may elect.

[2] Pages 97 ff.

have a preliminary hearing in this court by the judge sitting as a magistrate, and, if held, are bound over for trial before the Criminal Division or the Court of Quarter Sessions of the Peace. The latter are jury courts, and are not specialized.

For the purpose of the comparison with other courts, which will be made in Chapter V, a brief résumé of the Pennsylvania laws relating to sex delinquency is here given, with a statement as to the courts before which offenders are brought.

Curiously enough, the one sex offense over which the Misdemeanants' Division has exclusive jurisdiction, viz., streetwalkers, has no express definition in the laws of Pennsylvania, either statutory or common-law. The Municipal Court Act, above referred to, recognizes them as a distinct class of offenders. They are also mentioned in the statutes relating to the House of Correction,[1] which provide that streetwalkers, together with several other classes of offenders, may be committed to that institution as follows: From 3 months to 1 year for the first offense; from 9 months to 18 months for the second offense; from 18 months to 24 months for the third offense; and not more nor less than 24 months for the fourth and all subsequent offenses.

No mention of street-walkers can be found in the Pennsylvania decisions, but inasmuch as the common-law applies in that state in the absence of statute, the common-law definition is to be accepted.[2]

---

[1] Secs. 11967–11976 Penn. Statutes 1920.

[2] This does not seem to have been an offense at the English common law. The following two definitions are to be found in the decisions of Georgia and Michigan.

Pinkerton vs. Verberg, 7 L. R. A. 507 Mich. 1889. Street-walking is the offense of a common prostitute offering herself for sale upon the streets at unusual or unreasonable hours, endeavoring to induce men to follow her *for the purpose* of prostitution.

Gallaway vs. Mimms, Ga. 1908, 62 S. E. at 657. Street-walking—that is, the parading in the streets by lewd women, to the encouragement or advertisement of their means of livelihood.

In *Com. vs. Stalcup, 32, Lancaster Law Review 393, (Pa.),* it was held: ''An

The court, sitting as a magistrate tries summarily also, cases of disorderly conduct that involve sex delinquency.

According to Captain Lee, Chief of the Police Vice Squad, persons may be charged with disorderly conduct under the following circumstances.[1]

If she is a street-walker but we have not direct solicitation on her, but know her to be a woman of that type and I find her in conversation with four or five men, and she is seen on the way to a house of assignation, the man and woman are both arrested. By the man I show what her business is; I cannot charge her with being a disorderly street-walker, but charge her with disorderly conduct.[2]

Several convictions for disorderly conduct under circumstances similar to those enumerated by Captain Lee were observed and will be mentioned in the illustrative cases.

In the following offenses relating to sex delinquency, preliminary hearings only are held in the Misdemeanants' Division:

Adultery. Sec. 7670, Penn. Stats. 1920. Carnal connection by married person with someone other than his spouse, penalty fine not more than $500, or imprisonment not exceeding one year, or both.

Fornication. Sec. 7865, Penn. Stats. 1920. Carnal connection of unmarried persons—fine not exceeding $500.

Keeping a Bawdy House. Sec. 7708. Penn. Stats. 1920. If any person shall keep and maintain a common bawdy house, or place for the practice of fornication, or shall, knowingly, let or demise a house, or part thereof, to be so kept,

---

indictment alleging that the defendant 'openly and publicly, in and on a public highway, in the hearing of the citizens of the said Commonwealth, and to their manifest corruption and subversion, did solicit men for immoral purposes,' sets forth an offense which openly outrages decency and is injurious to the public morals and therefore constitutes a misdemeanor at common law, though not a public nuisance.''

[1] Interview with investigators, January 21, 1921.

[2] Disorderly conduct is not a statutory offense in Pennsylvania. It is defined as follows, in the Pennsylvania decision of *In re Alderman and Justices of the Peace, 2 Pars. Eq. Cas. 458, 464:* ''Lawless, contrary to the law; violating, or disposed to violate, law and good order; inclined to break loose from restraint; unruly; . . . all who violate the peace and good order of society, either as vagrants, disorderly persons, or for breach of the public peace.''

he or she shall be guilty of a misdemeanor, and on conviction be sentenced to pay a fine not exceeding $1000 and to undergo an imprisonment not exceeding two years (1860).

Frequenting a Bawdy House. Sec. 7709. Penn. Stats. 1920. If any male person having no apparent trade, occupation, or business, or being without any means of subsistence, shall stay, frequent or loiter in or about any bawdy house; or if any male person whatsoever shall ask for, demand, take or receive any money or other valuable thing, except in the course of lawful business, from the proprietors or inmate of any bawdy house; he shall be guilty of a misdemeanor, and, upon conviction thereof, shall be sentenced to undergo an imprisonment not exceeding three years and pay a fine not exceeding $1000, or either or both, at the discretion of the court.

Open Lewdness. Sec. 7908. If any person shall commit open lewdness, or any notorious act of public indecency, tending to debauch the morals or manners of the people . . . he shall be guilty of a misdemeanor . . . punishable by fine not exceeding $100, or imprisonment not exceeding one year, or both (1860).

Pandering. (1911) Sec. 7993. Punishable by imprisonment for not more than ten years at hard labor.

Placing wife in house of prostitution. (1911) Sec. 7994. Punishable by imprisonment for not more than ten years at hard labor.

Detention because of debt in house of prostitution. (1911) Sec. 7995. Punishable by imprisonment for not more than ten years at hard labor.

Receiving proceeds of prostitution. (1911) Sec. 7996. Punishable by imprisonment for not more than ten years at hard labor.

Transporting female for prostitution. (1911) Sec. 7997. Punishable by imprisonment for not more than ten years at hard labor.

Enticing into State for prostitution. (1909) Sec. 7999. Misdemeanor. Punishable by imprisonment for not more than five years or $500 fine.

The foregoing offenses are triable before a jury in either the Criminal Division or the Court of Quarter Sessions.

From the foregoing review of laws relating to chastity, it will be seen that the scope of the court's work is very limited as to sex delinquents. With the exception of children between the ages of 16 and 21 over whom the court may exercise full sway, practically the only class of sex delinquents with which the court may deal fully, are disorderly street-walkers and their customers. For these, the court has set up a very elaborate machinery which will be described in another part of the report. The pity of it is, that this machinery cannot be used for a larger number of the prostitutes of Philadelphia and their customers, because of inadequate vice-repressive legislation, and also because of the present limitation of the court's jurisdiction.

ARREST

The manner of bringing girls and women into court is described in the Sixth and Seventh Annual Reports of the Municipal Court as follows:

> Women and girls were brought into Court in several ways (1) arrests by the Vice Squad, police officers, officers of the United States Department of Justice, park guards, and the Sheriff; (2) complaints on the part of parents, relatives, or social agencies; and (3) by references of other officers or courts, such as the detective bureau, store detectives, the Juvenile and Domestic Relations Divisions of the Probation Department of the Municipal Court, and magistrates . . .[1]
>
> By far the largest number (42 per cent) of the cases brought in . . . were brought in by the Vice Squad, who are plain-clothes police officers working in pairs so that one may bear the other out as witness. Nearly two-thirds (64 per cent) of the women and girls brought in for disorderly street-walking were arrested by the Vice Squad. . . . The Vice Squad also made the largest number of arrests of women brought in for disorderly conduct (61 per cent), a misdemeanor in some ways closely allied to street-walking. In making the arrests for disorderly street-walking and soliciting, members of the Vice Squad exercise great care never to arrest a woman until she has indicated the house, or named a price or otherwise definitely committed herself, otherwise the case is discharged with the reprimand to the officer.[2]

Captain Lee, head of the Vice Squad, reported that arrests are generally made upon warrant, except in case of disorderly street-walking and disorderly conduct; the latter, because the offense is presumed to have taken place in the presence of the officer. It was observed that a case of being an inmate and keeper of a bawdy-house was dismissed by the judge where the arrests had been made without warrants—upon the theory that the illegal arrest had deprived the court of juris-

---

[1] Sixth Annual Report of the Municipal Court of Philadelphia, 1919, p. 125.
[2] Seventh Annual Report of the Municipal Court of Philadelphia, 1920, p. 125.

diction, even though the defendants were present in court. A contrary policy on the part of the police and the court is indicated by Table 9 of the 1920 report of the Women's Misdemeanants' Division of the Municipal Court of Philadelphia,[1] showing the manner of bringing cases into court and the nature of offenses committed; and Table 7 of the same report,[2] showing the disposition of all cases, classified by offense. This conflict was submitted to Captain Lee, over the telephone, and to officials of the court in person. Captain Lee said that the police report for 1920 showed that the police had made 224 arrests of inmates and frequenters and 103 arrests of keepers of disorderly bawdy houses. He stated that only "two or three" of these arrests had been made without warrant. Officials of the court corroborated the correctness of the statement of law above given, but in relation to the facts sent a telegram, of which a pertinent extract follows:

"Mr. Drown says some inaccuracies, also some questions of terminology . . ."

Immediately after arrest, all women defendants in sexual offenses in which the court has exclusive jurisdiction are taken to the Detention House at Twelfth and Wood Streets where they are slated, and given an opportunity to make bail. That few take advantage of this opportunity seems to be indicated by Table 15. Everyone interviewed was emphatic in denying that women defendants of this class were ever taken to the police station.

COURT PROCEDURE

The procedure in the Misdemeanants' Division is very much simplified. The trials are summary and conducted the

---

[1] See Table 28 at the end of this chapter, a reprint of Table 9 of the Municipal Court Report.

[2] See Table 6 at the end of this chapter which cites disposition of cases of sex delinquency only, the figures for such having been taken from the Municipal Court Report, 1920.

same as in a Magistrate's Court. Although the Municipal Courts Act [1] provides that the District Attorney shall prosecute the cases, this is not done, at present, in the Misdemeanants' Division. The absence of a trained lawyer for the prosecution places the state at a disadvantage, and the judge frequently has to fill in the gap by examining the witnesses. The trials are expeditious. As many as 40 cases were tried or given a preliminary hearing in the course of a half day. In fact the trials are so rapid, that it is sometimes difficult to distinguish a trial from a preliminary hearing.

Very few of the defendants are represented by counsel. Of the 100 or more cases observed in court, not more than three per cent had counsel. It is difficult to account for this unless the defendants who appear in this court are to a large extent impecunious. This may be true as to the street-walkers who number about 30 per cent [2] of all the defendants. About 30 per cent of all defendants are incorrigibles and runaways, the majority of whom are brought in upon complaint of parents or relatives. These cases are not very hotly contested. The defendants who are charged with keeping a bawdy house are more apt to have counsel, but inasmuch as only preliminary hearings of such cases are held in this court, counsel may not appear until they reach the Criminal Division. This dearth of counsel probably accounts for the fact that habeas corpus suits are practically unknown. It also explains, perhaps, why there appear to be no contests of the practice of finger - printing, physical examination, [3] etc., before trial, rather than after conviction. The court sits three times a week, on Mondays, Wednesdays, and Fridays. A history sheet of all the defendants is prepared by the probation de-

---

[1] Sec. 15716, Penn. Stats. 1920: "It shall be the duty of the District Attorney of said County to prosecute all cases in which prosecutions have been begun in the Municipal Court . . . or which are exclusively triable in the Municipal Court . . . or which the District Attorney elects to try in said Court."

[2] Sixth Annual Report of the Municipal Court of Philadelphia, 1919, p. 125.

[3] See Act of April 26, 1921.

partment, showing in the case of the women the following facts:

Number of case; name of defendant; charge; date of arrest; previous convictions, if any, with dates; whether or not venereally diseased; religion (as a guide in case of commitment to a private institution); whether living alone, with family, etc.; whether employed or not.

The object of this is to inform the judge, after conviction and before sentence, of certain extraneous facts regarding the defendant which will guide him to an intelligent disposition of the case. This is really in the hands of the judge *before* conviction rather than *after*. From observations spread over a period of half a dozen different days and of two different judges, there were no indications that the advance knowledge of these facts prejudiced the judge in any way. The practice, however, of thus making information available to the court *before* trial is objectionable from a constitutional standpoint. It opens the door to criticism of the fairness of decisions, regardless of how fair or just they may be. The practice, however, of placing such information before the judge *after* conviction and *before* sentence is highly commendable. It is the only practicable means by which the judge may secure such information as may permit him intelligently to dispose of the case. It was observed that the judge generally based his disposition of the case upon the facts thus submitted.

The procedure followed, stated briefly, is: Witnesses are sworn jointly; no formal pleas are received; police officer testifies as to facts which are corroborated by brother officer. This generally constitutes the state's case. The defendant then testifies herself, or her witnesses present their testimony. Rarely is defendant represented by counsel, and when not represented, she frequently is questioned by the judge, if she does not elect to testify. The court's decision is then rendered, and disposition is made.

ILLUSTRATIVE CASES

The following cases are illustrative, observed over a period of about six court-days, before two different judges:

M. W., colored. Charge—disorderly street-walker. Not represented by counsel. White vice squad officer testified that she solicited him from the porch of a house while he was in the street, for the purpose of prostitution; that he entered the house with her and she offered to commit prostitution for the sum of $1.50, whereupon he placed her under arrest, which she resisted. His testimony was not corroborated. She was questioned by the court and denied that she had solicited the officer, or offered to commit prostitution, but admitted that she resisted arrest. Her social history sheet showed no previous record and her medical examination showed her to be negative. She was convicted and given a sentence of 18 months in the House of Correction.

E. S., colored. Charge—disorderly street-walker. J. R., White, a man about fifty years old—charge, disorderly conduct. Neither represented by counsel. Colored vice squad officer testified that he observed E. S. accost J. R. on the street; that J. R. went with E. S. and he followed them; that he waited outside the house about fifteen minutes where they had entered and then entered and found them in bed together. Both were convicted. The history sheet of E. S. showed her to be negative and without a previous record. She was sentenced to six months in the House of Correction. J. R. said he was married, had three children and earned $22.50 a week in the shipyard. He was fined $10 and costs.

A. K. and C. H., white. Charged with being disorderly street-walkers, and J. W. and H. C., white, males charged with disorderly conduct. Not represented by counsel. Statement was made that the two women had not yet been physically examined and the case of the women was continued for two days, without bail, for examination. The two men were discharged without trial.

E. S., E. F., and M. T., all white, charged with being disorderly street-walkers. J. E., J. Y., and J. H., males, white, charged with disorderly conduct. Two vice squad officers testified that they saw them get out of an automobile and enter a rooming house together; that later they followed them into the rooming house, which they stated had a bad reputation. They found J. E. in bed with E. S. He was fined $10 and costs and the case of E. S. was continued for physical examination. J. Y. was found in bed with E. F. He was fined $10 and costs and the case of E. F. was continued for physical examination. J. H. and M. T. were found in a room together but fully dressed sitting on a bed. He had an empty suit case with him. Both were discharged although she had not yet been examined. J. E. and J. Y. were university students.

H. W., colored. Charge—disorderly street-walker. S. Y., white, charge disorderly conduct. Patrolman testified he observed H. W., whom he believed to be a common prostitute, accost S. Y. on the highway; that he followed them to a house which he entered a few moments later, finding them in bed together. H. W. did not testify and the man stated that he had gone there to get a drink. The woman ran a rooming house and had spent two years in the county prison for larceny. She was given three months in the House of Correction and the man fined $10, and costs.

N. W., white. Charge—disorderly street-walker. Vice squad officer testified that she solicited him on the street for the purpose of prostitution and that he had seen her at other times solicit other men. Preliminary investigation showed that she was living with a man to whom she was not married and that she was not employed. Medical examination showed her to be venereally diseased. She was given three months in the House of Correction.

M. B., white. Charge—disorderly conduct. Vice squad officers testified that they had seen her walking the streets before; that they saw her accost a man and that when they approached them the man escaped. History sheet showed the girl to be negative physically, but showed that she had previously been on probation from another court for larceny. Probation officers then got in touch with her family, who agreed to take her back to Massachusetts. She was therefore discharged on the condition that she return to her home.

A. R., white. Charged with frequenting disorderly house. Had already pleaded guilty and been given a sentence of six months in the House of Correction about a week before. She appeared in court with her father, who stated that he wished to take her home and her case was called up for re-hearing. In response to the plea of the father the court released her on probation on condition that she stay at home. She had no previous record and was not diseased.

E. G., white. Charged with disorderly street-walking. Admitted charge. Her record shows nine previous convictions. Also had record of being a drug addict, drugs being smuggled to her while she was at the Gynecean Hospital. Twice before committed to House of Correction and three times previously put upon probation. She was given a sentence of six months in the House of Correction.

E. C., colored. Charged with disorderly street-walking. Officer testified that she solicited him on the street and took him to a disorderly house where she offered to commit prostitution. Woman denied the claim and stated that she was being hounded by the officers. Her record showed nine previous convictions, two sentences to the House of Correction and four times placed on probation. Once she had been committed to the venereal ward of the Philadelphia Hospital. She had no work record. Her examination showed her negative. She was placed on probation for one year.

Twenty-seven other cases of disorderly street-walkers were observed, nine other cases in which the woman was charged with disorderly conduct, and twenty-three cases in which the man was charged with disorderly conduct. The enumeration of these cases would be very much of a repetition of the foregoing. An example or two of cases given preliminary hearing will be cited.

The most frequent cases of the kind are keeping a bawdy house and being an inmate or frequenter of a disorderly bawdy house:

A. E., white. Charge—keeping a bawdy house. Was married to a sailor who appeared in court with her. Had one child. Not represented by counsel. Officer testified that he had observed the place for about two years and that it had a bad reputation. A couple who had been arrested there at the same time as A. E. had been previously convicted of frequenting and being inmates of a disorderly bawdy house. During the course of the officer's testimony the fact appeared that he had made the arrest without a warrant. When the judge discovered this he severely reprimanded the officer for arresting without a warrant and discharged the defendant. This case indicates that jump raids [1] will not be countenanced in Philadelphia. Three sailors who had been arrested in the house of A. E. charged with frequenting a disorderly bawdy house, were discharged.

M. D., white. Charge—keeping a bawdy house. Represented by counsel. Police lieutenant testified that she had run a bawdy house to his knowledge for three years. On cross examination by the attorney for defense he stated that he had permitted it to run that length of time without taking action against it on the excuse that he was "waiting to get it right." The complainant in the present case, who was a university student, testified that he had visited the place three times, twice alone and each of the two previous times had had intercourse with P. G., an inmate of the house, and that after the second visit he had become infected with gonorrhea. He then had a warrant sworn out, and made a third visit with members of the vice squad. Two of the officers testified that the madam did not let them in at first, saying that she could not accommodate three· at once and that "they would have to go to another bawdy house." She let the student in, however, and they came back later. She permitted them also to enter, and they further testified that they heard her urge the student to hurry and go upstairs with P. G. The madam was bound over to the grand jury under a $1000 bond, and the girl inmate was bound over as an inmate under a $500 bond. Curiously enough the medical examination showed her to be not infected. The student was not arrested. The Court reprimanded him and said that he had as much of a right to punishment as the prostitute. The student claimed that he was taking treatment with his own doctor and was permitted to go with a word of advice by the Court.

Seven other cases were observed of the hearings for keeping disorderly houses or facts very much similar to those above stated. The cases of 16 persons charged with being inmates or frequenters of a disorderly bawdy house were observed. From the facts in the cases of the girls charged with being incorrigible or runaway children, it was apparent that the large majority were sex delinquents. The record of one girl arrested showed ten previous arrests for incorrigi-

---

[1] A jump raid is one in which a place is entered without a warrant and arrests are made on the theory that a crime is being committed.

bility and violating probation. Each re-arrest showed her to be re-infected with venereal disease although she had been held each time in the Gynecean Hospital until non-infectious. The case mentioned E. F., in the phase of this previous record, was discharged on the condition that she return to her mother in order to get married.

M. F., whose last charge had been that of disorderly street-walker, had a record of four previous arrests as being a runaway. She had been placed on probation each time. A preliminary investigation showed that she had had two recent abortions. She was found to be diseased and was committed to the Gynecean Hospital for treatment.

One young girl, M. N., had had two previous arrests for being a runaway. She had violated her probation each time and in her last arrest was taken in the company of one N. B., a boy about 21 years of age, who, she testified, had raped her just previous to the arrest. She became hysterical in court while she described the attack upon her. She was committed to the House of Good Shepherd much against her will, and N. B., who, she claimed, was guilty of rape, was held under a $300 bail on the charge of fornication and contributing to the delinquency of a ward of the Court.

One interesting case was observed in which the defendant, a colored woman, was charged with violating her probation, appeared in court with a perfectly white baby which she claimed was her own by a Jewish man who had made a cash settlement to be released from a bastardly prosecution. She was discharged upon her promise to join this man in Bethlehem.

PHYSICAL ASPECTS OF THE COURT AND DETENTION FACILITIES

Reference has been made to the building at Twelfth and Wood Streets and its special court for dealing with sex delinquents. While, as has been pointed out, the jurisdiction of the court itself is limited to certain classes of sex offense, the activities of departments housed in the same building extend to a far greater number, for women arrested on a charge of sex delinquency usually are taken at once to this building and slated. Those who do not succeed in making bail are detained in special quarters on the upper floors and on the following morning pass through a routine procedure of finger-printing, physical and mental examination, and investigation by a probation officer. Those released on bail report the next morning and undergo the same treatment.

Before entering into detail regarding the functions of these special departments, it may be well to describe their physical aspects: The building at Twelfth and Wood Streets, a remodeled, three-story stone schoolhouse, stands in the heart of the former red-light district. The Women's Misdemeanants' Division moved into this building in April, 1917. On the first floor are the court room, administrative, probation, and deputy sheriff's offices, and cells for men and women. Detention quarters for women 21 years old or over are provided on the second floor. Here also are the head matron's apartment, laboratory, and offices of the medical, psychological. identification, and clerical departments. The third floor is reserved as a place of detention for girls between the ages of 16 and 21. The basement of the building contains in addition to heating plant, etc., a laundry where the work is done by the girls awaiting trial.

Discussing the various features of the building in turn, it is noteworthy that admission to the court room is restricted to those having a direct interest in the proceedings. Mere onlookers are barred. Witnesses and persons on bail await the call of their cases in an ante-room. Those detained are brought down from the upper floors and seated in a lighted corridor at the rear of the court room. As their cases are called, a matron in charge turns them over to the tipstaff. Defendants and witnesses are then lined up before the judge at a distance of approximately twelve feet. In the intervening space sits a row of men, officials and clerks of the court, who face the defendants and witnesses. As the girls reply to questions and relate their stories, they must look across this battery of men's faces, in many instances undoubtedly a source of genuine embarrassment. A trained nurse is present

at all trials to quiet hysterical outbreaks. The whole procedure of the court is quiet, orderly, and businesslike.

Built into the court room and waiting rooms are a number
of tiny offices, one for each probation officer. Although small,
these offices at least insure privacy in interviews—a de-
sideratum too commonly overlooked.

Immediately adjoining the court room is the office of the
chief administrative of the Misdemeanants' Division. Just
beyond and adjoining his office is the office of the court representative and case supervisor. At the rear of the court
room is a large record room, where steel lock-files containing
full histories of every girl or woman brought to the court are
kept. Records of the men arraigned in this court are kept
at the Misdemeanants' Division for Men at 220 North 20th
Street. An elaborate card record and file index stand in this
room. Back of the record room is a corridor with four cells
for women. It was stated by the deputy sheriff, matron, and
others that these are used only in rare instances, sometimes
when drug addicts or others become violent. Girls are placed
in cells only on demand of the superintendent of the Detention
House. In the course of frequent visits to the court throughout a stay of several weeks, the investigator never saw them
occupied.

On a separate, non-communicating corridor are cells for
men. Men are not detained here over night, but are transferred from jails all over the city each morning. The deputy
sheriff, whose office is on this floor, locks several men in each
cell and releases them to the tipstaff as their cases are called.

The detention quarters for girls and women on the second
and third floors, deserve a special word, for here arrested
women may await trial in sunny and immaculately clean surroundings. The house accommodates about 50 women. The
older women, from 21 up, are confined to the second floor in
a 34 bed dormitory, large, light, and airy. Adjoining is a
lavatory with toilets, basins, and showers. Food, sent down
from the third floor, is served in an open space at one end

of the dormitory. At the other end, across a corridor, are
two isolation rooms for the use of girls in an infectious stage
of disease. The superintendent's strict adherence to schedule
insures sanitary conditions at all times. Not only are closets,
floors, and furniture cleaned regularly, but every Thursday
(as the writer frequently noted) the mattresses are vacuum-
cleaned and the beds sprayed. Linen is changed for each
new occupant and fresh nightgowns given the girls twice a
week, if they are detained that long. On entering the Detention House, the girl is stripped, given a shower, and her scalp
is cleansed. She then receives fresh house clothing, a complete change, with the exception of shoes and stockings. Her
own outer garments are hung in large paper "moth-bags"
and her underclothing sent to the basement laundry. When
a girl is found to be in an active state of disease, her clothing
is sterilized. Frequently certain preliminary examinations
are made by trained nurses when the girl is brought in during
the night. The chief object of these examinations is to detect
drug users in order that they may be ministered to promptly.
The girls, besides caring for their own floor, clean the down-
stairs offices under the supervision of a matron. They work
also in the laundry. These duties do not consume all their
time, however, and regular employment or recreation is not
provided.

The younger girls on the third floor, while accorded the
same routine treatment and given the same employment as
the women on the lower floor, enjoy more privileges and better accommodations. A large living and recreation room,
simply and attractively furnished in upholstered "mission"
style hardly suggests forcible detention. A reading table,
piano, victrola, large rug, and cheery skylight all contribute
to a homelike atmosphere. Opening into this room are five
small rooms, four of which are bedrooms containing three
beds each, the fifth serving as a sewing room. Across one of
the corridors is a seven-bed dormitory with three windows.
The girls on this floor have a private dining room with a some-

what formally set table. At one end of the floor is a kitchen where meals are prepared by a paid cook, a colored woman. Only rarely are detained girls allowed to help in preparing the food. The cook is assisted by a young white woman brought into court a few years ago and found to be feeble-minded. Work under constant supervision was recommended for her, but instead of committing her to one of the state institutions for the feeble-minded, she was detailed to the task of cook's assistant in the Detention House. Not only was her work highly praised by the matrons, but kitchen and equipment reflected constant care.

After 4:30, the girls may dance, sing, play games, or amuse themselves in other ways. The building has a roof-garden used by the second and third floor groups, each using opposite ends of the roof. Occasionally the older women are allowed to use the recreation room on the third floor, but always under supervision, and without being allowed to mingle with the younger women. In regard to the importance of segregating the younger girls from the "older and more hardened offenders," the superintendent seemed skeptical. If segregation is essential to safeguarding of morals, she feels the older women need to be saved from the younger rather than the reverse! The third floor group is taught hemming and crocheting. Although dresses, kimonos, under-garments, towels, wash cloths, and bed linen, etc., are made for house use, very little of the sewing is done by detained girls. One of the matrons, who also acts as sewing instructor, claims that the girls are there so short a time that it is hardly possible to train them properly and experience showed the wastefulness of entrusting to them material to be made up for use. Most of this sewing, therefore, is done by the in-structor and matrons.

The Detention House has a staff of 13 matrons working in eighteen-hour-shifts. Only two of these, the superintendent and her assistant, are resident. The superintendent's apart-ment is on the second floor and her assistant's on the third.

The superintendent estimates the daily average number of detained girls to be 45. The house does not take babies or girls under 16. The Travelers' Aid and other private agencies sometimes send girls there for "protection" or investigation.

On the day of our interview with the superintendent, February 3, 1921, there were 31 girls in the Detention House, 27 white and 4 colored.

On the second floor:

Protection. . .	3*
Violation of probation	6
Runaway.	1
Vagrancy.	1
Disorderly conduct.	3
Disorderly street-walking.	5
Total.	19

* One awaiting deportation by the Immigration Bureau.

On the third floor:

Protection.	5
Violation of probation	4
Runaway.	1
Incorrigible.	1
Runaway and incorrigible	1
Total.	12

As a rule, the superintendent stated, girls are detained only two or three days, although occasionally they may be kept for a longer period. She cited the case of one girl held as a witness since November 12, 1920. Sometimes, too, she explained, girls in need of hospital treatment might be held there and treated while awaiting a vacancy at the Gynecean Hospital. Of 635 cases admitted to the Detention House during the first three months of 1920, 30.3 per cent were disposed of within three days.

In certain cases, girls for whom the probation department is seeking work may remain until suitable employment is found. Girls detained but a single day usually are bail cases who did not succeed in making bail the night of arrest.

Table 15 at the end of this chapter compiled from the superintendent's record book shows the number of days each girl or woman admitted during the first three months [1] of 1920 remained in the Detention House. Of the 636 cases admitted, 87.6 per cent were detained ten days or less. Only 4.7 per cent were held more than 30 days. The same group is classified according to age and color in Table 14.

IDENTIFICATION BUREAU

The Finger-print Bureau of the Women's Misdemeanants' Division is said to make finger-prints of all arrested women brought to the Detention House who are 21 years of age or older, and to use its discretion in finger-printing those under 21. During the year 1920, of 1736 women arraigned in this Division, 1479 were finger-printed.[2] In our study of 50 cases placed upon probation during the first six months of 1920, it was found that 17 of that number, all under 21 years, were not finger-printed. These cases are more fully discussed on page 62. It will be noted that for the year 1920, only 14.8 per cent of the women arraigned in this court (for all offenses) were not finger-printed. Whereas, among the 50 sex offenders placed on probation, 34 per cent did not have their finger-prints taken. Of the 1479 women finger-printed, 695 were identified as old offenders. Copies of all finger-prints taken (except those of runaways) are sent to the Bureau of Police which in turn files, with the Identification Bureau of the Court, duplicates of all women's finger-prints.[3]

---

[1] In the time allotted, it was not possible to cover the six-month period.
[2] Seventh Annual Report of the Municipal Court of Philadelphia, 1920, p. 137.
[3] *Ibid.*

PHYSICAL EXAMINATION

Prior to 1917 only a limited number of women misdemeanants were examined physically. But with the occupancy of the building at 12th and Wood Streets in April, nearly every case coming before the court was given a routine physical examination. Although medical service was available in certain branches from the time the Municipal Court was established, no definite unified plan was worked out until 1917, when a group of prominent local physicians at the request of the president judge drew up a plan whereby persons appearing in court should be studied both physically and mentally, with the aim, as stated in the annual reports, of making diagnosis the basis of substantial justice. In Philadelphia, as elsewhere, the mobilization of the army served to emphasize the gravity of venereal disease as a public-health problem. The body of physicians called in consultation mapped out a plan of medical service extending to all divisions of the Municipal Court handling misdemeanants or criminals. To conduct this on the scale contemplated required a large staff of physicians and nurses. For the Misdemeanants' branch it provided first of all for a complete physical examination of women, before conviction, including the taking of smears and blood specimens. No legal authority could be found, either in the statutes or court-reports, for the practice of examining defendants physically before conviction. No record could be found of any contest of this procedure by writ of habeas corpus. Somewhat later, in October, 1918, the Gynecean Hospital, formerly a private sanatorium for women, receiving a state subsidy of from $25,000 to $50,000 annually, was reorganized to treat exclusively girls and women having venereal diseases. Owing to the influenza epidemic, however, it was not put to this use until the following January. It is stated in one of the annual reports of the Municipal Court:[1]

---

[1] Fifth Annual Report of the Municipal Court of Philadelphia, 1918, p. 3.

Not only has the Gynecean Hospital been a great factor in the social service division of the court, but by concentrating on a few phases of the venereal-disease problem, scientific progress has been made which will be presented when its value has been more fully demonstrated. Under the direction of Dr. Penrose, a system of tabulation of medical data has been established, which will doubtless yield some interesting facts concerning the medical diagnostic work of 1919.

This view was emphasized by the medical superintendent of the hospital who feels that the experience and observations of the medical department in treating diseased delinquent women will enable the court to make a definite scientific contribution in this field.

At the time of our study, two women physicians had offices in the Detention House, one who is also a psychologist, giving her entire time to the making of routine medical examinations of women brought there and to testing mentally cases referred to her by the psychiatrists. The other physician, in addition to making pelvic examinations of women brought to the Detention House and directing the taking of blood specimens and smears, acts as medical director of the Gynecean Hospital.

Usually within 24 hours of sending smears and blood specimens to the laboratories maintained by the Municipal Court, results are reported to the medical department and recorded on forms provided for each case. If the girl is found to have a venereal disease in an infectious stage, she is either committed at once to an institution, where she receives proper treatment, or sentence is deferred until she has been rendered non-infectious at the Gynecean Hospital. She is then returned to court to receive sentence on the charge lodged against her. She may be discharged outright, placed upon probation to report for medical treatment, or disposed of in some other way. The incidence of venereal disease among women arraigned in the Misdemeanants' Division during the first six months of 1920 is discussed on pages 140–141. Of the 455 women who were found to be infected with a venereal disease, 117 were committed to the Gynecean Hospital.[1] Information regarding the disposition of the remaining 338 diseased women was not readily available. A special report concerning 166 women and girls discharged from the Gynecean Hospital during the last six months of 1920, shows the following dispositions upon their return to the Misdemeanants' Division:

```
Detained at 12th and Wood Streets..............................   5
Referred to the Juvenile Branch................................   7
Returned to authorities in Lancaster, Pa.......................   1
Philadelphia General Hospital..................................   2
Returned to parents out-of town................................   2
Discharged.....................................................   2
Probation to leave town........................................  10
Probation continued............................................   1
Probation to report for medical treatment......................  71
Probation......................................................  42
Door of Hope...................................................   1
House of Correction............................................  11
House of Good Shepherd.........................................   8
Sleighton Farms................................................   2
State Reformatory for Women, Muncie............................   1
```

                                                               166

At the Gynecean Hospital, the infected girl receives regular treatment until the medical director pronounces her noninfectious, or until local lesions disappear. Before a case of gonorrhea may be discharged, the smear from the urethra and vagina, taken once every two weeks for three consecutive

---

[1] Table 37 at the end of this chapter shows the disposition of 1941 cases of women arraigned in the Misdemeanants' Division (for all offenses) during the year 1920 in relation to incidence of venereal disease. The Seventh Annual Report of the Municipal Court for 1920 contains on p. 129 the following statement regarding this table: "Of the 993 infected cases disposed of during the year, 32 per cent were committed to the House of Correction, 25.8 per cent were committed to the Gynecean Hospital, 15.1 per cent were placed on probation with medical supervision, 8.7 per cent were placed on probation, 7.8 per cent were discharged, and 10.7 per cent were disposed of in various other ways. It should be borne in mind in this connection, however, that there may be factors other than venereal-disease infection involved in individual cases which determine their disposition."

times, must be negative. At the end of this six-week period, gonococci may still be present in the cervix. In this case, she is returned to the court with the recommendation that she be placed upon probation to report for medical treatment at the State Dispensary.[1] To be discharged from the State Dispensary, the girl must show at least three consecutive negative smears taken two weeks apart. In cases of acute syphilis, five full-dosage injections of arseno-benzol or their equivalent, followed by a mercurial treatment, covering as many days as necessary, are required. Syphilitics are held in the hospital from five to six weeks. They must be rendered innocuous before discharged.

Frequently, continued treatment at the State Dispensary is ordered and made a condition in placing the girl on probation. The Dispensary is said to require two consecutive Wassermann negatives, taken a month apart, before discharge.

By permission of the medical director, we inspected the Gynecean Hospital, a remodeled, four-story private dwelling. The doors are locked and the windows barred because of many escapes during its early occupancy. One is impressed immediately by the absolute cleanliness of the building, and by its large, sunny rooms. The superintendent's office, the dining room, kitchen, and pantry are on the ground floor. The three upper floors contain each a fourteen-bed ward, and, in addition, three rooms with three beds each and one isolation room—the hospital accommodating 62 girls in all. On the day of our visit the count was 51. Syphilitics are usually confined to the fourth floor. Nurses' quarters, linen closets, etc., are on the second floor. A single room is provided for each nurse. On the same floor the girls have a recreation and living room. If space at the Gynecean is not available, the girl may be held temporarily at the House of Detention and receive treatment there or she may be sent to the Phila-

---

[1] Until July 1, 1920, the court had its own clinic, but from that time on it has been sending ambulatory cases to the State Dispensary.

delphia General Hospital under a detainer insuring her return to court at the completion of treatments. Pregnant girls are not detained at the Gynecean after the seventh month, but are also sent to the Philadelphia General Hospital under detainers. Colored girls are not admitted to the hospital. If a colored girl has a venereal disease in an infectious stage, she is usually committed to the House of Correction and treated there.

The hospital plant and the control of the patients are under the management of a nurse-superintendent. She employs seven maids who, in addition to their regular duties, supervise the laundry work and wait on the table. The medical director confines her supervision strictly to examination and treatment. She is assisted by two doctors and six trained nurses. The latter work in ten-hour shifts.

The patients are called at 6:30 daily and have breakfast at eight. They are taught the elementary principles of hygiene and sanitation and the nature of infection, with special reference to body sores. Instruction is given in sewing and fancy-work. They learn how to sterilize and repair rubber gloves and to assist the nurses in certain of their duties. They are required to make their own beds, clean floors, set table, and assist in cooking. Medication is administered daily.

The hospital receives patients from the Juvenile as well as from the Misdemeanants' Division. The superintendent frequently finds those from the former court more difficult to handle than the "hardened" prostitutes. According to her statement, older women often complain of "the lewdness of girls from the Juvenile Court." She claims to have many feeble-minded persons "who are not sufficiently deficient to commit."

Because of the practice of reporting for the fiscal rather than the calendar year, it was not possible to secure from the Gynecean Hospital a statement showing admissions and discharges for 1920 or for the first six months of that year. Figures for two other periods, however, show something of the volume of its work. In the Thirty-third Annual Report for the fiscal year ending May 31, 1920, the medical report contains the following statement:

Number of patients in hospital June 1, 1919................. 53
Number of patients admitted to hospital to May 31, 1920...... 316

                                                                369

For

Syphilis 30
Gonorrhea 242
Gonorrhea and syphilis................................... 96
No venereal disease...................................... 1

                                                                369

Average number of days in hospital of women with the following diseases:[1]
Syphilis .... 43 days
Gonorrhea .... 65 days
Gonorrhea and syphilis.............................. 44 days

[1] In the report on 166 cases already referred to, it was found that 123 women were infected with gonorrhea, 12 with syphilis, and 28 with gonorrhea and syphilis; the remaining three were free from infection. The average period of detention for cases of gonorrhea was 58 days; for syphilis, 35; and for gonorrhea and syphilis, 57. The record shows nine cases of gonorrhea detained from 70 to 80 days; seven from 81 to 90, and eleven from 91 to 161 days. Two cases of syphilis were detained 59 and 62 days, respectively. Those infected with both diseases show prolonged treatment, as follows: two, for 73 days; one, for 91; and one for 92 days; and one for 126, and one for 154 days.

In a similar report for January 1, 1920 to October 1, 1920, the hospital shows:

Number of patients in hospital, January 1, 1920.............. 59
Number admitted from January 1, 1920, to October 1, 1920.... 227

                                                                286

For

Syphilis 14
Syphilis and gonorrhea................................... 77
Chancroid and gonorrhea.................................. 1
Gonorrhea 192
No venereal disease...................................... 2

                                                                286

Reference has been made to the practice of placing upon probation to receive medical treatment girls who have a venereal disease in a non-infectious stage. For the purpose of supervising these girls more closely and of seeing that they take their treatments regularly, a trained nurse on the medical staff of the Misdemeanants' Division, with special experience in cases of venereal disease, received a special appointment for this work in November, 1920. The Medical Department furnishes her with the names of those required to report. On the day of our interview, the record showed that, commencing with November, 1920, 250 cases under her supervision were reporting. There were no figures showing the number who failed to report. Three times a week, this nurse checks her list [1] at the State Dispensary which she visits at the hours when the girls are most likely to report [2] in order that she may talk with them, keep them interested in their treatments and alive to the importance of continuing them. This nurse enters in her record the name, address, court number, and finally, the dispensary number of each girl required to report for treatment. The clinic nurse notes the date of each treatment given and the date when the girl is instructed to report again. This information is then sent to the court nurse and entered upon her book-record which, according to the plan at the time of our study, is eventually to be turned into an alphabetical card record in order to facilitate follow-up.

After describing the reorganization of the Gynecean Hospital the annual report [3] of the Municipal Court for 1918 states further:

At the same time, arrangement was made with the State Department of Health for the treatment of men found with venereal diseases. These men include those arraigned with street walkers in the Women's

---

[1] The Dispensary gives no certificates showing treatment has been taken or person has been cured.

[2] Wednesdays and Fridays, at one; Tuesdays, at seven.

[3] Fifth Annual Report of the Municipal Court of Philadelphia, 1918, p. 3.

Misdemeanants' Court and young men between the ages of 16 and 21. . . .

Apparently the opinion prevails among court officials interviewed early in 1920 that men known to have consorted with infectiously diseased prostitutes are given a physical examination and required to report regularly for treatment. This impression does not seem to be borne out, however, by figures secured from the Probation Department. These show that in the first six months of 1920, seven men were found to be diseased, of whom three reported for treatment. During the same period, 117 women were committed to the Gynecean Hospital because they had a venereal disease in an infectious stage. No records are available to indicate how many men are examined and no statement could be procured with reference thereto. It is evident, however, that a routine examination of male offenders is not being made.

MENTAL EXAMINATION

Toward the close of 1917, the court began to enlarge its facilities for mental examination. To this end it created a neuro-psychiatric division as a special branch of the medical department, placing it under the direction of Dr. Samuel Leopold who served as division psychiatrist in the United States Army and as chief medical examiner of the New York Guard at Camp Wadsworth. Dr. Leopold is assisted by two psychiatrists and a pyschologist, who, like himself, give part-time service to the Municipal Court, filling irregular assignments at the House of Detention in such a way that one or the other is on duty there each day. At present, they operate in the Men's, Women's and Juvenile Division of the Municipal Court, although Dr. Leopold plans to extend their activities to the Domestic Relations and Criminal Divisions.

At the time of our study this department was making about 400 mental examinations a month for the whole Municipal Court, whereas formerly the average was about 30 a month.

The Psychiatric Department aims to make a routine preliminary mental test of all cases brought to the Women's Misdemeanants' Court and to set aside for intensive mental study any who seem to require it. Occasionally, however, when girls are brought to the Detention House on a night preceding one of the court days (Mondays, Wednesdays, and Fridays) their cases may be called before the examination can be given. It is claimed by the director of this department that in the course of a fifteen-minute conversation with each girl he and his associates can pick out the feeble-minded, drug addict, psychopathic, psychoneurotic, etc. The girl is asked why she was arrested, at what grade she left school, whether she has been running around with boys, whether she has ever received treatment for nervousness in a hospital, whether she is subject to fits or spells, whether she is a drug user, and similar questions designed to draw her out in such a way as to indicate her mental trend—to show whether she talks connectedly and logically or whether she is excitable, emotional, etc. A stenographer who is present at these interviews takes down the girls' statements, although not strictly verbatim. At the close of the morning's interviews, the visiting psychiatrist dictates a summary of his estimate of the mental make-up and personality of each girl examined. If further investigation seems necessary, a psychiatrist other than the one conducting the preliminary inquiry is requested to make an intensive study and in certain instances a mental test by the court psychologist may be required.

According to a statement furnished by the director of this department, 785 girls and women received a preliminary psychiatric examination during the first six months of 1920. Of these, 246 were given the psychometric tests.

The director also stated that up to the time of our study, the chief function of the department had been to diagnose, to make recommendations for commitment, and to prevent certain unsuitable types from being placed on probation. While the existence of the department indicates that theoretically, at least, its value is recognized by officials of the court, there is little evidence in practice that weight is attached to its findings or recommendations. No separate study of the records of this department was made, but in reviewing the case histories of 50 probationers, attention was given to the psychiatrists' and psychologists' reports, which form a part of the defendant's record. The results of our examination of these mental histories are stated on pages 121–124, in the section relating to Probation.[1] Table 5 at the end of this chapter, shows the mental condition of women sex offenders arraigned in the Misdemeanants' Division during the first six months of 1920. This table is discussed on page 141. From Table 34 at the end of this chapter, it will be seen that of 1941 women's cases arraigned in the Misdemeanants' Division in 1920 (for all offenses), 1602 (82.5 per cent) were examined. Of these, 1040 (64.9 per cent) were reported normal.

After extended inquiry, through personal interviews and correspondence, it is impossible to state how many defendants arraigned in the Women's Misdemeanants' Division were pronounced mentally deficient and in need of custodial care. Nor could we learn for what number (if any) application for commitment to one of the state institutions for the feeble-minded was made and how many of these were admitted or declined. The opinion generally voiced by court officials was that such institutions had long waiting lists but no instances of rejected applications were cited. The chief physician of the State Institution for the Feeble-minded at Spring City, which cares for mental defectives from six years up, writes that the capacity of that institution is 1200, but for a long time they have been able to admit patients only as vacancies occur, and that they maintain an official waiting list from

---

[1] The relationship of the department to the court is also described in detail in connection with the discussion of the 50 cases.

which admissions are made. Pennsylvania Village for the Feeble-minded, a comparatively new institution at Laurelton, excludes "epileptics, bed-ridden cases, those suffering from active venereal disease, girls who are pregnant, violent or very troublesome cases, mental defectives of the real criminal type, colored girls, and those over 30 years of age."[1] As these are the only two institutions receiving feeble-minded persons in the eastern district of Pennsylvania, it is evident, in view of the limitations pointed out by their officials, that possible needs of the Women's Misdemeanants' Division can hardly be adequately met.

PROBATION

That the Probation Department constitutes a vital factor in the treatment of women misdemeanants in Philadelphia is evidenced in various ways. Its officers are said to interview every individual brought to the Detention House by the police or referred there by social agencies, and prior to any girl's arraignment in court, they attempt to verify her statements. It reviews and crystallizes the findings of all other departments connected with the court as a basis for its own recommendations to the judge. Its 24 officers and clerical workers, constituting 34.6 per cent of the entire personnel of the Women's Misdemeanants' Division,[2] far exceed in number

---

[1] Letter from superintendent of Pennsylvania Village.

[2] The personnel of the Women's Misdemeanants' Division at Twelfth and Wood Streets in January, 1920, was classifiable as follows:

Assignments	Executive	Clerical	Total
Probation Department	16	8	24
Medical Department	6	3	9
Neuro-psychiatric Department	3	1	4
Detention House	11	2	13
Bureau of Identification	1	1	2
Court-room	..	6	6
Deputy Sheriff's Office	5	4	9
Attached to Quarter Sessions Court	..	2	2
Total	42	27	69

those employed in any other single department of the Division. In the year 1920, 33 1-3 per cent of the 1941 cases of women and girls arraigned in this court (for all offenses), and 50 per cent of the 1292 convicted, were placed on probation.

In view of the wide divergence of opinion regarding the efficacy of probation as a remedial measure in dealing with adult offenders of this type, the extended use of the system in the Philadelphia court seemed to offer an exceptional opportunity for study. Because of the detailed case histories and reports kept by the Women's Misdemeanants' Division, it was apparent that definite data could be gathered not only relative to the social status and medical, court and other records of probationers, but specific information might be secured concerning the practices of the probation officers in regard to the frequency of their visits to the girls' homes or places of employment, the extent to which they were able to secure first-hand knowledge of their conduct, type of supervision and the nature of service rendered.

While recognizing certain inherent difficulties involved in any attempt to gauge the merits of probation as a means of reformation, and while experience would seem to indicate that women sex delinquents as a class possess certain characteristics that render them less responsive to ameliorating influence than other types of offenders, it appeared, nevertheless, not improbable that some estimate of the workings of the Philadelphia system of probation might be formed. In the last analysis, short of daily knowledge of the activities of a probationer, claims of reformation advanced by the officer must be discounted. Even if accepted at face value, they must be with the mental reservation that such is the girl's status to date. Needless to say, if the girls whose cases were studied could be followed up over a period of five, ten, twenty years, many revisions of judgment, upward or downward, would undoubtedly have to be made. At least a partial measure of their improvement would be whether they succeeded in keeping out of the local courts. If probationers join the ranks of recidivists, it is evident that for them the system was unavailing. Unfortunately, because of the conditions indicated, one may more justifiably dogmatize regarding failures than successes.

In view, therefore, of the importance of the subject itself and of the relatively large part that probation plays in the Women's Misdemeanants' Division of the Municipal Court, a rather full description of the procedure there will be given. Through the courtesy of the chief probation officer of the Municipal Court and of the administrator of the building at Twelfth and Wood Streets, we were afforded every facility that would make possible a close study of the practices of this Division. We were given not only free access to records but permitted to make transcripts of any available statistics or case histories. As the time was too short for studying the history of each case placed on probation during the six-month period under consideration, it was necessary to take a sample lot for analysis. It being generally conceded that ten per cent of the case histories of an organization should prove fairly indicative of its practices and achievements, transcripts of two sets of consecutive records were made, one of the first 25 cases placed on probation in 1920 and one of the last 25 for the period ending June 30, 1920. In this way allowance was made for possible seasonal influences upon conduct. These 50 cases form, in fact, 16.3 per cent of the 306 women sex offenders placed on probation during this period and 8.4 per cent of those placed on probation for the entire year, namely, 592 women sex offenders. The period covered extends from the date when probationer first became known to the court to the time of the completion of our study in February, 1921. In respect to certain facts noted elsewhere, the period was extended to October 1, 1921.

In the Municipal Court Act, Section 9, approved July 12, 1913, P. L. 711, as amended by Act of June 15, 1915, P. L. 988, provision is made for the appointment by the president

judge of a chief probation officer "and such additional probation officers as a majority of the judges may determine . . .
whose powers and duties shall be similar to those heretofore
appointed by the Court of Quarter Sessions of the Peace for
said county." Office is held at the pleasure of the president
judge.

With the exception of the Civil Division, the Probation
Department extends into all divisions of the Municipal Court.
The Probation Department of each division is under the direction of a probation officer in charge, who is responsible to
the chief probation officer of the Municipal Court. A routine
procedure of investigation and supervision is followed in
each division, except that in the Criminal Division no investigation is made until *after* conviction.

The Probation Department of the Women's Misdemeanants' Division comprises sixteen probation officers, two men
and fourteen women, assisted by a clerical staff of eight. One
of the men serves in the double capacity of administrative
head of the building at Twelfth and Wood Streets and probation officer of both the Men's and Women's Branches of the
Misdemeanants' Division. The other man probation officer
verifies marriages, takes charge of those leaving the city, acts
as custodian of effects of committed persons, keeps a record
of men's cases, and is said to see that men instructed to be
examined or to receive treatment for a venereal disease,
comply. This last point is discussed elsewhere. The fourteen
women probation officers are assigned as follows:

Court representative, who appears before the judge on each court
day to present any information regarding convicted women defendants that would aim in making suitable disposition of their cases. She
also presents to the judge a record sheet containing a summary of
defendant's social, medical, and court history.

Case supervisor, who takes complaints of parents or relatives regarding incorrigible or runaway girls, assigns cases to probation officers
and supervises case work of each officer. Once a month, she reviews
probation officers' reports noting how the cases have been handled—

whether statements are verified, important leads followed, and whether, on the whole, wisely handled. Suggestions or instructions respecting each case are written out and attached to the history sheet.

Four probation officers who investigate and supervise street-walkers.

Eight probation officers who investigate and supervise incorrigible and runaway girls.

Early every morning, the court representative transcribes from the arrest book kept by the deputy sheriff to "face sheets" (history blanks used by the Probation Department) particulars regarding women and girls brought to the Detention House the night before, showing name, address, charge, date, names of arresting officers, and a brief statement of the time, place, and circumstances of arrest. These face sheets are handed to the case supervisor who apportions them among the probation officers. Each officer then seeks to learn from the girls assigned to her, their social histories, noting down essential facts which she sets out to verify as soon as her interviews are completed. On one of the mornings when the writer was permitted to accompany a probation officer on her rounds, she made six calls—two for the purpose of verifying statements of arrested girls, and the others to learn something of probationers under her charge. In four cases, there was either no response to her ring or the girl apparently did not live at the address. At one of the addresses, the landlady of the house gave very little information regarding the girl arrested and pretended not to have a key to the room. It was evident that she was not wholly ignorant of the character of her lodgers and their friends. At the home of the sixth girl, the landlady said that she was still working in a laundry where, apparently, she had been employed for some time. When the probation officer finds that a girl has given incorrect information, she brings pressure to bear to make her tell the truth, saying that she will be detained until she does so. The facts finally ascertained, together with reports from the medical, neuro-psychiatric and finger-print departments, form the basis of a brief summary in respect to each arrested woman, which is presented to the judge by the court representative. These typewritten summaries state:

Number of case.
Name of defendant.
Charge.
Date of arrest.
Previous arraignments, if any.
Whether venereally diseased.
Religion (as a guide in case of commitment to a private institution).
Whether living with family.
Whether employed.

If the woman has been found mentally defective, that fact is said to be communicated verbally to the judge, as the result of the mental examination usually is not known in time to add to the history sheet.

Such, briefly, are the activities of the Probation Department prior to arraignment. Persons placed upon probation by the court are, in the case of runaways and incorrigibles, assigned to the probation officer of the district where the defendant resides.[1] Street-walkers or women convicted of disorderly conduct may be assigned to any one of four probation officers. It is not uncommon for a single officer to have more than 100 cases at a time under her supervision.

DISCUSSION OF PROBATION TABLES

In Tables 17 through 23, at the end of this chapter we have summarized the results of our study of the 50 probation cases referred to on a preceding page. Examining Table 17, a study

---

[1] The practice of the Probation Department in disposing of runaway and incorrigible girls without recourse to the court is fully described on p. 129.

of the social histories in relation to offense committed, we find the greatest number of probationers to have been arraigned for disorderly street walking or disorderly conduct—17 for the former and 13 for the latter offense. Five were brought in for violation of probation. The remaining 15 were charged with being incorrigibles, runaways, or inmates, keepers and frequenters of disorderly houses. Forty-three of the probationers are white and seven colored. Only five are of foreign birth. Fourteen are between 15 and 19 years of age; sixteen between 20 and 24; six between 30 and 39; and five are over 40. Twenty-one are single and 22 claim to be married. In three of these cases marriage was unverified and three were common-law marriages. Eight are widows, two being widows of common-law marriages. Nineteen are Roman Catholics, seventeen Protestants, three Hebrews, one Greek Catholic, two are not church members, and in eight cases the religion is not stated. Three never attended school; three progressed no farther than the third grade; six no farther than the fourth; one completed the fifth and thirteen stopped at the sixth. Eight completed the seventh; eleven the eighth; one the ninth. Two reached the first and second year of high school. In two instances the school grade completed is not given. Thirty probationers were living with their parents, husband, or other relatives at time of arrest. Three were keeping house; seven boarding; one lived at place of service; one with lover; and in two instances the manner of living is not recorded. The final section of the table relates to children of probationers. Twenty-five had no children; seven had from one to four legitimate children; eleven had children whose legitimacy was not established and seven had illegitimate children.

The number of arraignments prior and subsequent to the one in 1920 at which the 50 women were placed upon probation is indicated in Table 18. It will be seen that 28 probationers had never previously (so far as known) been arraigned in the Misdemeanants' Division; that 13 had been arraigned once before; six, twice; one, three times; one, four times, and one, ten times. The record of subsequent arraignments, up to October 1, 1921, shows that 32 probationers were not re-arraigned; 14 were re-arraigned once; two, twice; one, three times; and one, four times. A separate compilation shows nine probationers have had both previous and subsequent arraignments, as follows: four, one previous and one subsequent arraignment; one, one previous and two subsequent arraignments; one, one previous and four subsequent arraignments; one, two previous and one subsequent arraignment; one, three previous and one subsequent arraignment; and one, ten previous and one subsequent arraignment. Further light is thrown upon the practice of placing recidivists on probation by Tables 9 and 10 at the end of this chapter. These tables are fully discussed on pages 142–144.

Table 19, relating to incidence of venereal disease in the group, shows that 47 probationers were examined for one or both diseases. Of these, 25 were infected. In two cases the results of the examination were indecisive. It is noteworthy that of the 18 probationers discharged as satisfactory and not re-arrested, 14 were free from infection at the time of their examination and the four infected cases were not released from probation until they had been discharged from medical treatment. This bears out the claim of the probation department that freedom from venereal disease is a prime requisite in procuring discharge from probation, a policy and a practice that may fairly raise the query—is their probation a form of regulation?

Thirty-six of the 50 probationers received the routine preliminary mental examination fully described on page 112. An intelligence test was requested in 13 instances and given in eight. With respect to one of the 36 cases examined, the psychiatrist asked the privilege of a second examination two months later but this request was not complied with.

Of the 36 examined, eight show neurological examination negative or reveal no marked mental abnormality. Neurological examination is negative in regard to 10, four of these

being classed as evidencing poor judgment or being passive
and irresponsible; the remaining six are described as emo-
tionally unstable, as showing psychoneurotic tendencies, having low standards or subnormal. One girl is described as
hyperactive, talkative, self-satisfied, mildly psychotic, not
commitable; another, as suffering at present from anxiety
reaction owing to arrest which she states is without cause and
a third as indifferent, shows no emotional reaction to her present situation; history shows old drug habit; otherwise negative. Of the eight tested mentally by the psychologist, one
probationer received a favorable report on her mentality. The
other seven show the following I. Q's: 40, 45, 52, 62, 72, 76
and 86, respectively. In only three instances are reports of
psychiatrist or psychologist accompanied by recommendations and in only one of these are they specific rather than
general. For one girl, with an I. Q. of 72, charged with incorrigibility, the psychologist points out the need of "mental
stimulus and direction." She was seventeen years old, living with her parents, and free from disease. After eleven
months on probation she was discharged as satisfactory and
up to October 1, 1921, had not been re-arrested. Regarding
the other girl, with an I. Q. of 52 and also an incorrigible,
the psychologist remarks that she does not think her "capable
of adjusting herself to her environment without direction or
supervision." Re-examination within a year is recommended.
After nearly ten months on probation this girl was released
"because of lack of coöperation by father who had sought aid
of court and now blocked any supervision by department."
The third girl, 22 years old, convicted of disorderly conduct,
received careful study at the hands of the psychologist, who
fixes her mental age at 9.8, I. Q. 40. She then reports as
follows:

I am doubtful about M's mentality. I am inclined to believe her
feeble-minded, but hesitate to make a positive statement because she
has had so many handicaps. She tells me, for instance, that she was a

cripple until she was eleven years old and did not attend school until after that time. She states further that she has always been sickly. She has been known to the Medical Department at Twentieth and Summer Streets, from which Department I learn (by 'phone) that several diagnoses have been made concerning her physical condition. Her right lung was reported "affected" by one doctor; another diagnosed her a "neurasthenic"; another stated that she was "silly" and that no medical treatment would relieve her physical condition. She was discharged because of her utter lack of responsibility.

I find her reaction here typical of that of a feeble-minded person. Her attention is flighty, her reaction quick but senseless and irrelevant. She is extremely childish and talkative, keeps making all sorts of statements in her effort to impress me.

She is very nervous, appears unstable, and in my opinion irresponsible.

In justice to her, I think she should be

1. Built up physically in every way.

2. Trained mentally with the view of determining her ability.

3. Protected until we can make a definite report on her social responsibility based on actual experiment. Previous attempts to help her at home have failed. I therefore recommend that she be removed to some home or institution where the above suggestions can be carried out.

This report was made on January 9, 1920. Four days later, at trial, the judge placed the girl on probation and, apparently unaware of its existence, ordered that "a careful mental examination be made." The probation officer who interviewed girl at time of arrest notes: "This girl tells a very rambling story; is evidently nervous and seems low grade mentally." Despite her obvious mental deficiency, probation officer and judge both let this girl slip through the mill, although another department of the court had already diagnosed the case and made three constructive and what would seem wholly feasible recommendations. Beyond referring probationer to employment department, verifying her work record two months later, calling twice at her home, the second time finding no one in, it appears that nothing was done for this girl by her officer.

It is not even stated whether the job the girl had was secured through the employment department or through her own efforts. The probation officer's record is a lengthy statement of dates girl reports at office. On November 6, girl reported at office that she was living at home with parents. Apparently her statement was accepted without verification for on the same day she was released from probation by order of the judge. There would be little point in citing this case at length were it not for the fact that out of 50 cases, it is the only one for which definite recommendations were made, recommendations that either never reached the court or were disregarded. Taken in conjunction with the ignoring by the court of suggestions made by the Neuro-Psychiatric Department on behalf of the two other cases mentioned and the absence of suggestions or recommendations with regard to the remaining 33 cases examined, it would seem to imply that beyond diagnosis the department has little to offer or to indicate a lack of coördination between the Neuro-Psychiatric Department and the court.

It is noteworthy that 17 probationers of the 50 studied did not have their finger-prints taken. These all are 20 years of age or under. On each of these cases, the administrator of the Misdemeanants' Division noted: "Finger-prints not taken because of age and minor charge." The offenses for which the 17 were arraigned are as follows:

Disorderly Conduct	4
Violation of Probation	4
Incorrigibility	3
Runaway	2
Incorrigibility and runaway	2
Incorrigibility and disorderly conduct	1
Incorrigibility and violation of probation	1
	—
	17

The Philadelphia Court exercises over its probationers the type of supervision common elsewhere. The officers, after studying the girl's social history, seek to make desirable adjustments in her home and industrial life. Sometimes a change of environment is recommended. Suitable work is found through a special employment department serving the entire Municipal Court. Probationers are required to report at the Municipal Court usually once a week and officers are said to visit girl's home once a month or oftener—every week for a while and then every few weeks or every month or two. The probationer is required to report to her officer in person, although many, by special arrangement, are permitted to write every week or so.

From Tables 22 and 23, showing, respectively, the number of calls made by the probation officers at the girls' homes, the number of times probationers reported in person and by letter to the Probation Department during periods of probation varying from one week to 15 months, it will be noted that the officers called at the homes of 39 girls 110 times; that 35 girls reported to the Probation Department in person 236 times; and that 25 reported by letter 214 times. The case histories show only three instances of reporting by telephone.

Examining the tables more closely, we find in Table 22, that the homes of 11 girls were never visited; 15 homes were visited once; 10, twice; five, three times; one, four times; three, five times; one, six times; two, seven times; one, 10 times; and one, 11 times. Of the 39 homes visited, only nine received more than three calls, although 34 were on probation from 4 to 15 months. The administrative head of the Women's Misdemeanants' Division remarked in regard to visits to probationers' homes: "We do not believe in hounding a girl who is reporting regularly, and making her feel we lack confidence."

Table 20 correlates the number of calls made by probation officer at girl's home with the number of times she saw girl. Similarly, Table 21, correlates the number of calls with the number of times she saw relative or housekeeper. In 18 of the 39 cases where the home was visited, the probationer was not seen and in only five of these cases did the officer make more than two calls. The reports show that a relative or housekeeper was seen, even though girl was not at home, in 26 cases. Only eight girls were seen by the officer more than once in their homes. On the other hand, at 17 of the homes, relative or housekeeper was seen two or more times. It will be observed, by consulting Tables 20 and 22, that 29 of the 50 probationers were not seen at their homes by their officers.

Study of the case histories showed that six girls were called upon at their places of work and four were telephoned to there because the probation officer had been unable to see them in their homes. In addition to visits or telephone calls made with this object in view, the probation officers frequently telephoned to the girl's alleged place of employment for verification. Fifteen work records were verified, four could not be verified and in 31 instances, apparently no attempt at verification was made.

While less than half the probationers were seen at their homes, more than two thirds reported in person at the Detention House, as shown by Table 22. Reports of the probation officers do not state by whom the girl was interviewed in each case. Frequently, when the writer happened to be in the probation office at the time of such calls, she heard interviews somewhat as follows: "Are you working now?" or, "Are you behaving yourself?" (Incidentally negative replies to these queries were not made!) After one or two such questions, the date of girl's visit was noted on her card and returned to her, invariably with the admonition: "Now be a good girl." Of the 35 girls reporting in person, 21 did so more than twice, and 10, who were on probation six months or more, reported from 10 to 23 times.

It will be seen from Table 23, that 25 girls reported by letter. Of these, less than half wrote as many as three times, although some were on probation from six to fifteen months. There appears to be little relationship between the length of the probation period and the number of times a girl may write. Two girls, each on probation over a year, wrote only twice or three times. Two who wrote 16 times were on probation, one less than three months, and one over thirteen months. Instances could be multiplied.

Girls released from the Gynecean Hospital usually are required to report regularly to the State Dispensary for treatment, and are placed upon probation with that stipulation. The method of keeping a check on these girls is described fully in the section relating to Physical Examination.

"The term of probation may be indefinite as is often the case when medical attention is needed, or for a definite period, usually ranging from one to six months," according to the report of the Municipal Court for 1917,[1] but in practice it appears that the term of probation is not fixed in advance. It seems to vary from one month to two years or more, the period lengthening indefinitely in the case of girls requiring clinical treatment. Two court officials stated that an infected girl might be kept on probation two years or longer. The question of terminating probation is raised by the girl's officer who may recommend release when in her judgment supervision is no longer necessary. At that time, the girl's record is presented to the case supervisor, who stated to us that she considered first of all girl's physical condition with especial reference to whether free from venereal diseases. Next she reviewed girl's social history and conduct so far as known while on probation, giving particular consideration to her work record, general environment, and manner of living. Once a month, each probation officer sends to the case supervisor the names and records of girls whom she considers eligible for release. The supervisor, after examining these records, lists those whom she recommends for discharge. The list is sent to the Clerk of the Court, who prepares a transcript of each case for the judge's signature. These applications for release from probation are signed without further

---

[1] Fourth Annual Report of the Municipal Court of Philadelphia, 1917, p. 132.

court hearing. Power of discharge practically rests, therefore, with the case supervisor.

A girl may be charged with "violation of probation" for failing to observe conditions imposed at the time she is placed on probation, such as reporting for medical treatment, returning to her home, etc., or for committing a new offense. In any case, a bench warrant may be issued and the girl, if found, brought to court. Of 132 case of violation of probation disposed of at court hearings in 1920, five were discharged, 50 were again placed on probation, 45 were committed to correctional institutions, 27 committed to Gynecean Hospital and five disposed of in other ways.[1]

In order to present the most recent information available in regard to the other 50 cases studied, we asked the Probation Department in October, 1921, to advise us of the progress of each case up to that time and whether many of the girls had been brought into court since our data had been gathered. On October 1, 1921, therefore, the records of our 50 girls were as follows:

Discharged from probation as satisfactory and not re-arrested	18
Still on probation, not re-arrested	6
Discharged as unsatisfactory	1
Disappeared (no bench warrant issued)	1
Bench warrant issued, probationer not found	5
Re-arrested once	14
Re-arrested twice	2
Re-arrested three times	1
Re-arrested four times	1
Died	1
	50

Leaving out of consideration the six still on probation and the one who died, it appears that 18 of the probationers made good, so far as known, while 25 were known to be unsatisfactory.

---

[1] Seventh Annual Report of the Municipal Court of Philadelphia, 1920, Table 7, p. 154.

The status of the 18 probationers who were re-arrested was as follows on October 1. 1921:

Discharged from probation... 1
Discharged and taken home by husband........................... 1
Discharged because case could not be properly supervised out of city
    and state 1
Discharged by court on second re-arrest [1]........................ 2
Transferred from House of Correction to Home for Indigent (age 50) 1
Still on probation... 6
In Gynecean Hospital.. 1
Committed to House of Correction for three months in May, 1921.
    No further information.. 1
Bench warrant issued, probationer not found..................... 3
Sentence not stated... 1

                        —

                       18

[1] The records do not indicate whether discharge at time of third arraignment terminated probation previously imposed.

INCORRIGIBLES AND RUNAWAYS

In addition to its main task of making a preliminary investigation of all cases of women brought to the Misdemeanants' Division and of supervising such cases as may be placed upon probation, this Department has certain special functions in regard to three groups, namely: "Protection" Cases, Runaways, and Incorrigibles and those designated as "Incorrigible and Runaway." The three groups are variously termed "Friendly Service" or "Department" cases. Protection cases, as such, are never arraigned in court. A runaway or incorrigible girl is not brought before the court unless the efforts of the Probation Department prove unavailing. In this way, the "protection work" done by the Probation Department of the Municipal Court resembles that ordinarily carried on by women police in cities maintaining a Women's Police Bureau. Of 299 cases (25.6 per cent of the women and girls brought to the Misdemeanant's Division) adjusted in 1917 by the Probation Department without a court hearing,

266 were listed as incorrigible, runaway, or protection.[1]   In 1918, 288 cases (15 per cent), all incorrigible, runaway, and protection, were adjusted out of court.   Of these, 199 were brought to the Detention House on complaint of parent, relative, or guardian.   The remaining 29 were picked up by the police or referred by a social agency.[2]   In 1919, 224 (12.5 per cent) were adjusted without a court hearing.   Of these, 163 were incorrigible, runaway or protection cases.[3]   In 1920, 176 (39.5 per cent) were adjusted out of court.   The table which follows,[4] shows the total number of incorrigibles and runaways brought to the Detention House in 1920, and the number adjusted out of court:

	TOTAL CASES	ADJUSTED OUT OF COURT	
		Number	Per Cent
Incorrigible.	185	92	49.7
Incorrigible and Runaway.	70	22	31.4
Runaway.	190	62	32.6
Total.	445	176	39.5

Protection Cases

This group comprises girls who may voluntarily seek the aid and protection of the Probation Department, of which they frequently learn through welfare supervisors of department stores or factories; or girls who may be referred by such agencies as the Travelers' Aid, Society to Protect Children from Cruelty, and so forth.   These girls are not brought before the court but their problems are adjusted on a case-

---

[1] Fourth Annual Report of the Municipal Court of Philadelphia, 1917, p. 129.

[2] Fifth Annual Report of the Municipal Court of Philadelphia, 1918, pp. 152–153.

[3] Sixth Annual Report of the Municipal Court of Philadelphia, 1919, Table 8, pp. 150–151.   This number includes in addition to incorrigibles, runaway, and protection cases, thirteen girls brought in on other charges.

[4] Seventh Annual Report of the Municipal Court of Philadelphia, 1920, Table 3, p. 142.

work basis. It is said that finger-prints of these girls are not taken.

Runaways are brought to the Detention House chiefly by the Bureau of Missing Persons and the Travelers' Aid Society. Two special officers interview runaway girls, one, the case supervisor, handling Philadelphia girls exclusively, and the other Philadelphia, and out-of-town runaways.

In the case of out-of-town runaways, the probation officer communicates with the police and probation departments of the girl's home town, asking for a full investigation, and on the basis of the facts ascertained, seeks to make a suitable disposition of the case. An examination of many records of runaways showed uniformly prompt action in communicating with out-of-town agencies and authorities who could aid in locating girl. If it is found desirable to return the girl to her own town, it is usually arranged to have a probation officer there look after her. If necessary to take the runaway before the court, the Probation Department, through the court representative, presents the girl's social history precisely as it would in connection with girls or women arraigned on other charges. It is said to be customary to test runaway girls mentally and to give them a general medical examination. Only in rare instances, however, is a pelvic examination or blood test required. While finger-prints of runaways are sometimes taken, these are filed separately and do not become a part of the official court record unless the girls actually are arraigned in court.

Girls who have run away from their homes in Philadelphia are questioned by one of the two special probation officers referred to in the foregoing paragraph, or by the probation officer assigned to the district where the girl is said to reside. The district probation officer visits the girl's home and seeks in coöperation with her parents or guardian to make a satisfactory adjustment of the case, out of court if possible.

Incorrigible Girls

Charges of incorrigibility are brought as a rule by a girl's parent, relative or guardian. Such complainants are interviewed by two special probation officers handling runaway girls, who, on basis of facts furnished, fill out a face sheet calling for a detailed social history of the girl. As in the case of runaways, the district probation officer then makes an investigation.

The consent of the girl's parent or guardian to an informal "trial-probation" for at least a month is often asked. The district probation officer then handles the case precisely as she would if probation had been extended by a judge. Suitable employment and recreation are sought for the girl and supervision exercised over her. The probation officer is said to keep in touch with the home so as to know whether the girl's conduct shows improvement. With the incorrigibles as with the runaways, an attempt is made to forestall court action. If it is thought the girl may have exposed herself to the possibility of infection, the parent's consent to an examination at the Detention House is asked. It is said that incorrigible girls are seldom given mental or physical examinations unless placed before the court, nor are their fingerprints taken. Frequently, even when "trial-probation" has failed, the court will place the girl on probation and she will be assigned to the same probation officer who supervised her prior to arraignment.

Because of the interest attaching to any attempt to spare delinquent young women the stigma of a court record, the method of dealing with them in Philadelphia as a step in advance of probation, seemed to merit careful study. The complaint book of the Women's Misdemeanants' Division records 68 cases of incorrigibility for the first four months of 1920. The writer selected for study the first 30 consecutive cases handled as "friendly service" by the Probation Department. Probation officers were not interviewed regarding these cases and the writer's observations and conclusions are based, therefore, only on their written reports concerning each case. These indicate that parents and girls were interviewed, the stories of each apparently checked. Efforts on the part of the officer to counsel with the family and to reason with and admonish the girl, as occasion required, are a matter of record. But the officer's investigation is limited too frequently to family interviews. One is struck forcibly by total absence of comprehensive or significant data regarding the girl from a social, economic, physical, mental, or emotional standpoint, particularly in view of the court machinery available.

In twelve instances, the complaint was made by the mother, in ten by the father, in three by a sister, and in one by a brother. Two cases were referred by the Society to Protect Children from Cruelty, and two were reported by outsiders. Usually, three or four charges were made regarding the incorrigible. In 27 cases the girl was said to keep late hours or remain out all night; in 16 instances she was reported as "running around with sailors" or other strange men, soliciting on the streets or living with a lover. Frequently, also, the girl was accused of stealing or being impudent and beyond control. Twenty-six of the girls were white, three colored and the race of one was not stated. Twenty were 17 years old or under. Seven were examined physically and six mentally. Two were found to have syphilis. None was reported as deviating mentally from normal. At the completion of our study in February, 1921, the court records showed that five cases had been turned over to the court by the Probation Department, that 18 had been dropped by the Department, and that the remaining seven cases were still under supervision. The five arraigned in court had been first supervised by the Probation Department—one, ten days; one, 26 days; two, 50 days; and one, nearly four months. Those released by the Department were supervised for the following periods: seven, one to three months; four, three to six months; three, six to nine months; three, nine to eleven months; and one, over a year. Turning to the 18 cases closed by the Department without recourse to the court, it was found that seven were dropped because the family or referring agency reported improvement; five, because the girl married; one, because the girl was returned home in consequence of letter written to her aunt by the probation officer, although neither the girl nor aunt was interviewed; one, because of lack of coöperation on part of family; one, because girl could not be found; two were referred to other divisions of the court; one, an unmarried mother, was placed with her baby in a private institution. In three of the seven pending cases, improvement was reported by the family who asked that no further action be taken by the Probation Department; in two cases, the mother stated that girl was "scared" and doing better because she had been reported to the court, although in one instance the officer never saw the girl; in one instance the Juvenile Court asked the Misdemeanants' Division to drop the case because they had two boys in the same family and preferred to handle the entire problem; in the seventh pending case, the girl and her mother disappeared. The father, who lived elsewhere, said he had not seen them for a year. Of the five cases arraigned in court, one was discharged by the judge because of girl's willingness to marry; one was placed on probation and later sent with her baby to the Hebrew Sheltering Home; one, infected with syphilis, was committed to the Gynecean Hospital and later sent to the House of Good Shepherd where she was reported "doing well." Another girl (colored) with a 3+ Wassermann ("not in actively contagious stage") was "discharged to marry," the ceremony being performed at conclusion of hearing.

Obviously, sweeping conclusions cannot be drawn from so small a number of cases, particularly in view of the fact that finger-prints are not taken. From the foregoing, it appears that satisfactory adjustment without arraignment in court is claimed for 16 of the 30 incorrigibles.

EDUCATIONAL DEPARTMENT

A novel feature of the Municipal Court of Philadelphia is its Educational Department created for the purpose of analyzing the work of the court and coördinating its machinery in such a way that it would function expeditiously. In addition, the Department offers a course of lectures on topics bearing upon problems arising in the various divisions of the court. Through it, opportunity is afforded certain workers in each division to receive training at the Pennsylvania School for Social Work. The case supervisor in the Probation Department of the Women's Misdemeanants' Division completed the course in case work offered by that school. The Department maintains also a sociological library for the convenience of its workers. In 1919, it compiled a Social Service Directory of welfare agencies in Philadelphia. This has since been revised. In the report of this department for 1920 [1] it is stated that research studies have been made comprising an analysis of the salaries and duties of personnel in each division of the court. The report adds: "There is no standardized information in this country as to the cost of probation. We hope to be able to exchange information with other cities on this subject." The Department prepares charts and slides illustrative of its works and answers all inquiries concerning the court. Its aim is set forth in the concluding sentence of its report for 1920:

To study new and better methods of approach to our court problems; to develop new and better methods of work and technique, and to interpret them to the staff, to social workers and others, has been the aim of the department as the educational work has progressed during the year.

---

[1] Seventh Annual Report of the Municipal Court of Philadelphia, 1920, pp. 371–377.

CORRECTIONAL INSTITUTIONS

Women convicted in the Misdemeanants' Division may be committed to the following institutions:

>House of Correction.
>Sleighton Farm.
>State Industrial Home for Women.
>House of Good Shepherd.
>Door of Hope.

Commitments of women sex offenders to these institutions for the first six months of 1920 [1] and for the entire year [2] were as follows:

	First Six Months of 1920	1920
House of Correction..................	198	409
Sleighton Farm....	18	37
State Industrial Home for Women....	...	8
House of Good Shepherd...........	25	76
Door of Hope......................	5	10
	246	540

From these tabulations, it appears that the House of Correction received 80.4 per cent of commitments to penal institutions for the first six months of 1920 and 75.5 per cent for the entire year. The State Industrial Home for Women, a comparatively new institution, did not commence to receive commitments until November, 1920.

Owing to the relatively small number of commitments to reformatory institutions, public or private, these were not inspected. The writer was conducted hastily through the House of Correction at a time when the institution was said to be closed to visitors because of being painted. Opportunity to interview the superintendent of women was not afforded. Maximum sentence to this institution was said to

---

[1] Table 1, this chapter.
[2] Table 6, this chapter.

be two years and the minimum 30 days. From Table 2, at the end of this chapter, showing length of sentence to the House of Correction, it appears that three- and six-month terms are in the majority. Only one woman was committed for 30 days and only one for two years. One case apparently received a two and a half year sentence. Commitments to the other institutions are not for fixed terms.

RECORDS AND STATISTICS

The Municipal Court of Philadelphia maintains a statistical department which compiles from the court docket, case histories and other court records, information which it uses as the basis for numerous tables showing the volume of business handled by each division, nature of the civil or criminal process and the social status of the defendant. Statistics for the Women's Misdemeanants' Division are compiled chiefly from the case record filed for each defendant. This record comprises the following papers: Face Sheet, Medical Sheet, Mental Sheet, Report of Probation Officer, Correspondence. The manner of preserving and filing these records makes all information concerning each defendant very readily accessible. The papers specified are fastened securely together in a definite order and placed in separate folders for each case. These are filed numerically in steel lock-cabinets and indexed under every known name and alias. In the case of recidivists whose finger-prints are on file, the Bureau of Identification [1] furnishes the filing department with former names. Every morning a clerk from the Statistical Department copies from the face sheets the items which are to be tabulated. It was his practice at the time of our study to check the facts on the face sheet by the more accurate presentation in the body of the record, from which he secured also data not repeated on the face sheet, such as reports of the Medical and Neuro-Psychiatric Departments. While the Probation Department

---

[1] Discussed on p. 103.

aims to correct face sheets to correspond with verified facts, it frequently fails to do so. It was impossible to determine to what extent statements made by the defendant were verified. Considerable confusion arises also because of using (in practically all instances observed) but one face sheet for each defendant regardless of the number of times she is arraigned in court.

The Women's Department of the Misdemeanant Division uses a face sheet which calls for the following facts. This sheet measures 8¾ x 11¼ inches.

FACE

Case No.

Charge

Date of Arrest
By
Known to Other Division of Court
Case No.

Name
Maiden Name
Alias

Color or Race

Interviewed by
Date

Address
Floor
Kind of House
Time in House
Rent—Amt.   Per
Includes Board

Date of Birth
Age
Religion
Place of Birth
Native Language
Reads English
Writes English

Father—Place of Birth
            Native Language
Mother—Place of Birth
            Native Language

Time in Philadelphia
Marital Condition
Marriage—Date, Place, By Whom
Occupation—Industry   Eow.
Wage—Amt.   Per

Children
Ment. and Phys. Cond.
Date of Birth
Address
Father's Name
Address
Relationship to Woman
Separation or Death Date

Name of School Last Attended
School Grade Completed—Gr. or Div.
            Date Completed Grade
Age Left School
Age Began Work
Vocational Training

Lives with
Kinship
Address
Time Lived at This Address

Type of Dwelling
Number of Rooms
No. in Family—M.   F.
No. of Lodgers—M.   F.
Church
Denomination
Pastor or Priest
Address

Industry
Wage—Amt.   Per
Name of Employer
Kind of Business
Address
Period Worked Here—From   To
Occupation
Wage—Amt.   Per

Date of Arrival in U. S.
Name and Line of Steamer
Name Registered
Port of Entry
Received by
Address

Police Record
    Date of Hearing
    Charge
    Magistrate
    Disposition

Court History
Family and Relatives—Father   Mother
Kinship
Age
Address
Occupation

    Date of Hearing
    Charge
    Judge
    Disposition

OBVERSE

Institutional History
    Name of Institution
    Kind
    Age Placed
    By Whom
    Why
    Age Disch'd
    Provision for Placement

Sex History—First Intercourse
    Age
    With Whom
    Reason
    Marriage Promised
    Compensation Rec'd

       Prostitution
Age Entered
How Long
Continuous
Solicits Where
Hotels or Houses Frequented
House of Assignation
Call Flats

If Not Continuous, State Whether
      Married, Living with Parents, or
      Working
Earnings from Prostitution
    Amount Per Week
      Highest
      Lowest
      Week Prior to Arrest
    Disposition of Earnings
      To Lover, Husband, Parent, or Self
      If to Person Other Than Self, State
       All or Part
      Name and Address
      Length of Acquaintance
      Place of Birth
      Native Language

Girl's Reason for Entering Prostitution

Hair
Eyes
Weight
Height

Description

Not only are the records well preserved, but they are carefully and clearly typewritten with marginal headings. It is interesting also to note that this Division measures up to the standard set by the American Institute of Criminal Law and Criminology in regard to the minimum requirements for criminal court records,[1] in all save two particulars—citizenship and period of commitment for non-payment of fine.

DISCUSSION OF TABLES

Table 1 shows the disposition of cases of sex offenders arraigned in the Women's Misdemeanants' Division during the first six months of 1920. These number 1671 of whom 807 are men and 864 women. Of this number, it will be noted that 251 men, or 31.1 per cent, and 548 women, or 63.4 per cent, were convicted, making total convictions of 799, or 47.8 per cent. Four hundred and sixty-one men and 153 women were discharged. Twenty-six men and 241 women were committed to correctional institutions. In the case of women sent to Sleighton Farm or the House of Good Shepherd, the sentence was indeterminate, while commitments to the House of Correction and the County Prison were for fixed terms. The length of these terms, varying from five days to 32 months, is shown in Table 2. Of the 25 men committed to the House of Correction, nine received three-month, and thirteen, six-month sentences; of the 198 women committed to this institution, 87 received three-month, and 90, six-month sentences. Frequently, however, after serving a portion of their sentences, committed cases were sent to court for a rehearing and paroled by the judge for the balance of their term. Seventeen men and 306 women were placed upon probation. Two hundred and eight men and one woman were fined. The amounts are set forth in Table 3. In more than half of the cases, $10 or $15 fines were imposed.

The incidence of venereal disease among the women examined is indicated in Table 4. It will be noted that 44 of the

---

[1] Discussed in Chapter I, p. 61.

868 women arraigned (only 4 per cent) were not examined. Of the 824 examined, 455, or 55.2 per cent, were found to be infected—the highest percentage of disease occurring among the disorderly street-walkers and those keeping and maintaining disorderly houses—64.2 per cent of the former and 62.2 per cent of the latter being diseased.

A somewhat smaller number (740) were examined mentally, 85.2 per cent as contrasted with 96 per cent for venereal disease. The results of this study, shown in Table 5, indicate that 447, or 60.4 per cent were normal. Those deviating from normal are subdivided into seven groups, namely, retarded, border-line, moron, psychoses, psychoneuroses and neuroses, constitutional psychopathic inferiors, and epileptics. It will be noted that the great majority of cases deviating from normal are designated under a single head—constitutional psychopathic inferiors, numbering 221. These form 75.4 per cent of those deviating from normal.

Table 6, like Table 1, deals with the disposition of cases of sex offenders. The period covered, however, is for the entire year of 1920. It will be noted that the percentage of convictions for the longer period varies but slightly from the percentage for the six-month period.

Disposition of cases of sex offenders arraigned in the Criminal Division (Jury) of the Municipal Court is shown in Tables 7 and 8, for the first six months of 1920 and for the whole year, respectively. Comparing convictions of men and women, respectively, in this court with the convictions in the Misdemeanants' Division, it will be noted that the percentages for the two sexes are practically reversed:

CONVICTION OF SEX OFFENDERS, 1920

	Total Number Convicted				Per Cent Convicted			
	Women's Misdemeanants' Division		Criminal Division		Women's Misdemeanants' Division		Criminal Division	
	6 mos.	1 year	6 mos.	1 year	6 mos.	1 year	6 mos.	1 year
Male......	251	459	103	168	31.1	33.7	69.8	61.9
Female....	548	1132	7	12	63.4	63.	29.1	25.
Total....	799	1591	110	180	47.8	50.4	66.1	56.2

One element contributing largely to this result is the vigor with which the fornication and bastardy cases are prosecuted in behalf of unmarried mothers. The six-month period shows 81.2 per cent of convictions under this charge and for the year, 78.1 per cent, the number arraigned being 112 men for the six-month period and 192 men for the entire year.

Tables 9 and 10 deal with those women arraigned in the Misdemeanants' Division during the first three months of 1920 who had at any former time (so far as known) been placed upon probation. They numbered 123, or approximately one fourth of the total number of women arraigned in this period, and were tried on probation from one to six times. In Table 10, the relation is shown between the number of times the women had been placed upon probation and the number of times they had been arraigned on a new charge.

The extent to which arraignments (ranging from one to seven) out-number trial on probation is indicated in the following summary based on Table 10:

Of the 47 women placed on probation once, 44 were arraigned two or more times.
Of the 49 women placed on probation twice, 27 were arraigned three or more times.
Of the 19 women placed on probation three times, 14 were arraigned four or more times.
Of the 5 women placed on probation four times, 4 were arraigned five or more times.
Of the 2 women placed on probation five times, 2 were arraigned six or more times.

The one woman placed six times on probation was arraigned the same number of times. Stated in totals, of the 76 women placed upon probation two or more times, 54, or 71 per cent, were arraigned three or more times.

Table 9 presents an analysis of this group of 123 women, showing how frequently they had been placed upon probation prior to arraignment in the three-month period referred to and how often they were arraigned on a new charge subsequent to the last time placed upon probation in relation to the offense committed and the disposition made at time of court hearing in the first three months of 1920. While necessarily complex in its presentation, the table should repay a thoughtful examination. Dealing as it does, with only a limited number of cases, it nevertheless serves as a partial indication of what, on the surface at least, would appear to be a failure on the part of many probationers to realize the hopes entertained for them. One is struck perhaps first of all by the numerous subsequent arraignments of women to whom probation was repeatedly applied—that women to whom the clemency of the court was extended, once, twice, three, four, and five times, appeared before it again and again.

Of the 80 women who had been placed on probation once prior to 1920, only four succeeded in keeping out of the court thereafter; 17 were arraigned subsequently two or more times. Of 28 placed on probation twice, only one kept out of court; six were arraigned subsequently two or more times. The 12 who were placed on probation three times were all subsequently arraigned—nine, once; two, twice; and one, four times. One woman placed on probation four times was again arraigned subsequent to her fourth chance on probation. The two women tried five times on probation were arraigned subsequently—one, once; and one, twice. One naturally looks with interest to see in what manner these repeated offenders were disposed of at their latest hearing. Returning, therefore, to the first group, those formerly placed on probation once, we note that the ten credited with three or more subsequent arraignments were disposed of as follows: three were again placed on probation; one was committed to the Gynecean Hospital; six were sent to the House of Correction—two, for six months, one, for nine months, and three for a year. It is noteworthy that of the 123 women under consideration, 53, or 43 per cent, were again placed on probation.[1]

---

[1] That repeated arrests form no serious barrier to trial on probation is shown in the Seventh Annual Report of the Municipal Court of Philadelphia for 1920, where it is stated in the section on the Women's Misdemeanants' Division, p. 122,

Examining that portion of the table which shows the latest offenses on which the women were arraigned, it will be noted that next to Disorderly Street-Walking, Violation of Probation constitutes the chief offense—49 being arraigned on the former and 34, or 27.6 per cent of the entire 123, on the latter charge. Twenty-two of the women had been placed on probation once before and arraigned once since; one, twice before without a subsequent arraignment; and ten, twice before with one subsequent arraignment.

In the second group, those formerly placed on probation twice, the three credited with three or more subsequent arraignments were disposed of as follows: two were again placed on probation and one sentenced to the House of Correction for a year and a half. In the third, fourth, and fifth groups, those formerly placed on probation three, four or five times, it may be interesting to consider the disposition of the entire fifteen. Of the eleven credited with one subsequent arraignment, six were given still another chance; one was committed to the Gynecean Hospital; and four to the House of Correction—one for three months, two for six months, and one for two years. Of the three subsequently arraigned twice, one was placed on probation and one held in the House of Detention for treatment and one sent to the House of Correction for three months. The woman placed on probation three times before the 1920 conviction, and arraigned four times subsequent to that conviction, was committed to the Gynecean Hospital—a temporary disposition.

That continuing or adjourning cases is not a common practice in Philadelphia is shown by Table 11. The Statistician of the Municipal Court furnished the facts in this particular with reference to the first one hundred cases (women) dis-

---

that "of the 116 old offenders who had been arrested five or more times . . . 17 were placed on probation, 9 were placed on probation with medical supervision and one was placed on probation to leave town in care of individual." In other words, 23.2 per cent of those arrested five or more times were considered suitable types for probation.

posed of in the Misdemeanants' Division in 1920. It will be seen that only 22 cases were continued, 18 once and four twice. Of these, only five were continued beyond a week, one for eight, one for ten, one for 14, one for 58 and one for 63 days, respectively. Considering next the speed with which the entire 100 cases were disposed of, we find in Table 12, that 58 dispositions were made in three days, or less, and 32 in from four to seven days. The remaining ten cases were disposed of, seven within a month, and three within three months.

Tables 14 and 15, compiled by the writer from the record book kept by the superintendent of the Detention House, show age, color, and period of detention of cases admitted during the first three months of 1920. Of the 637 cases who entered during this period, 460 were white and 177 colored. Ages with respect to 18 cases are not stated. Two hundred and sixty-four (42.6 per cent) of the 619 whose ages are given, fall between 16 and 21 years. Eighty-three (13.4 per cent) are over 30. Of the 637 cases, 193 were detained three days or less. Three hundred and fifty-four (54 per cent) were held from four to ten days. Only 28 (4.4 per cent) were detained over a month.

With few exceptions, the same judges sit in rotation on the Misdemeanants' Division bench, and are thereby afforded an opportunity to acquaint themselves with the special problems which arise in this court. Such a system leads to specialization, and permits the judge to become expert in this particular field. (See Table 16.)

In Tables 17 through 23, we have presented the results of our study of 50 individuals placed upon probation during the first six months of 1920. The manner in which the records of these women were selected, together with summaries based upon our analysis of the material, is fully set forth in the section dealing with probation, pages 114–129.

Tables 24 through 45, at the end of this chapter, are reprinted (after renumbering) without change of type, from the Seventh Annual Report of the Municipal Court of Philadelphia, 1920, through the courtesy of the chief probation officer and the statistician of the court, and relate to cases heard in the Women's Misdemeanants' Division. Attention is called to the fact that Tables 24, 31, 32, 36, 41, and 43 relate to *individuals*. These tables deal with arraignments for all offenses heard in this court and should repay a careful examination, throwing light as they do on the business of the Division as a whole, and the status of all classes of defendants.

Special acknowledgments are due Mr. Frank S. Drown, the Court Statistician, for his unfailing courtesy in supplying us with statistics and any necessary information relating to them.

CONCLUSION

As in the case of the Chicago Morals Court, this report on Philadelphia has concerned itself with the structure and procedure of the Misdemeanants' Division, reserving for Chapter V comparisons, criticisms, or recommendations.

TABLES

TABLE 1. DISPOSITION OF CASES OF SEX OFFENDERS ARRAIGNED IN JUNE 30,

Offense		Total Arraigned	Discharged	Probation	Committed		Fine and Costs[3]	Other Disposition	Failed to Appear	Escaped
					Correctional institutions	Hospitals				
Disorderly street walking	M	1	1	....	....	....	....	....	....	....
	F	286	44	80	137	18	....	7	....	....
Disorderly conduct	M	325	152	10	11	...	128	23	....	1
	F	173	43	69	26	32	1	2	....	....
Frequenter or inmate disorderly house	M	387	264	5	7	...	74	23	14	....
	F	168	36	61	39	28	....	4	....	....
Keeping and maintaining disorderly house	M	68	34	2	2	...	3	27	....	....
	F	45	13	11	9	1	....	11	....	....
Pandering	M	5	....	....	3	...	....	2		
	F	...	....	....	...	...	....	...		
Fornication	M	5	3	....	...	...	....	2		
	F	...	....	....	...	...	....	...		
Fornication and disorderly conduct	M	1	1	....	...	...	....	...		
	F	...	....	....	...	...	....	...		
Adultery	M	1	....	....	...	...	....	1		
	F	...	....	....	...	...	....	...		
Male bawd	M	6	1	....	1	...	2	2		
	F	...	....	....	...	...	....	...		
Soliciting for immoral purposes	M	4	2	....	2	...	....	...		
	F	...	....	....	...	...	....	...		
Soliciting and disorderly conduct	M	3	2	....	...	...	1	...		
	F	...	....	....	...	...	....	...		
Incorrigibility[2]	M	...	...	...	...	...	....	...		
	F	94	5	49	10	29	....	1	....	....
Runaway[2]	M	...	...	...	...	...	....	...		
	F	63	8	25	10	21	....	1	....	....
Disorderly child	M	1	1	...	...	...	....	...		
	F	32	6	9	9	7	....	1		
Miscellaneous sex offenses	M	...	....	...	...	...	....	...		
	F	3	....	2	1	...	....	...		
TOTAL	M	807	461	17	26	...	208	80	14	1
	F	864	153	306	241	136	1	27	....	....
GRAND TOTAL		1671	614	323	267	136	209	107	14	1

[1] Table furnished by Statistician of Municipal Court. The following charges have been omitted because they are for other than sex offenses: drunkenness; illegal sale, purchase or possession of drugs; larceny; witness; protection and miscellaneous.

WOMEN'S MISDEMEANANTS' DIVISION, PHILADELPHIA, JANUARY 1 TO 1920 [1]

| NATURE OF DISPOSITION—DETAIL | | | | | | | | | | | | | | |
| COMMITTED TO CORRECTIONAL INSTITUTIONS | | | | COMMITTED TO OTHER INSTITUTIONS | | | | PROBATION | | | | | TOTAL NUMBER CONVICTED | PER CENT CONVICTED |
House of Correction [4]	County Prison [4]	House of Good Shepherd	Sleighton Farms	Gynecean Hospital	Philadelphia General Hospital	Door of Hope	Women's Misdemeanant's Division, House of Detention	Regular	Medical	To leave town	Continued Regular	Continued Medical		
131	...	5	1	15	2	...	1	42	30	6	1	1	217	75.8
10	1	...	...	...	...	...	...	9	...	1	...	...	149	45.8
19	...	4	3	30	2	...	...	44	17	3	3	2	96	55.4
7	...	...	...	...	...	...	...	5	...	...	...	...	86	22.2
34	...	3	2	24	4	...	...	37	18	1	5	...	100	59.5
2	...	...	...	...	...	...	...	1	...	1	...	...	7	10.2
8	...	1	...	1	...	...	...	3	7	...	1	...	20	44.4
3	...	...	...	...	...	...	...	...	...	...	...	...	3	60.
...	...	...	...	...	...	...	...	...	...	...	...	...	...	...
...	...	...	...	...	...	...	...	...	...	...	...	...	...	...
...	...	...	...	...	...	...	...	...	...	...	...	...	...	...
...	...	...	...	...	...	...	...	...	...	...	...	...	...	...
1	...	...	...	...	...	...	...	...	...	...	...	...	3	50.
...	...	...	...	...	...	...	...	...	...	...	...	...	...	...
2	...	...	...	...	...	...	...	...	...	...	...	...	2	50.
...	...	...	...	...	...	...	...	...	...	...	...	...	...	...
...	...	...	...	...	...	...	...	...	...	...	...	...	1	33.3
...	...	...	...	...	...	...	...	...	...	...	...	...	...	...
...	...	3	7	24	...	1	4	31	7	2	8	1	59	62.7
...	...	9	1	18	...	3	...	17	1	4	2	1	35	55.5
5	...	...	4	5	1	1	...	5	2	1	...	1	18	56.2
1	...	...	...	...	...	...	...	1	...	...	1	...	3	100.
25	1	...	...	...	...	...	...	15	...	2	...	...	251	31.1
198	...	25	18	117	9	5	5	180	82	17	21	6	548	63.4
223	1	25	18	117	9	5	5	195	82	19	21	6	799	47.8

[2] An incorrigible or runaway may or may not be a sex offender.
[3] For amount of fine see Table 3.
[4] For term of commitment see Table 2.

TABLE 2. LENGTH OF SENTENCE TO HOUSE OF CORRECTION OF SEX OFFENDERS COMMITTED JANUARY 1 TO JUNE 30, 1920 [1] [2] [3]

OFFENSE		TOTAL COMMITTED	1 MONTH	2 MONTHS	3 MONTHS	6 MONTHS	9 MONTHS	12 MONTHS	18 MONTHS	24 MONTHS	32 MONTHS	TERM NOT STATED
Disorderly street walking	M	...	...	...	...	...	...	...	...	...	...	...
	F	131	...	1	53	65	5	4	1	1	1	...
Disorderly conduct	M	10	1	...	5	3	...	1	...	...	...	...
	F	19	...	...	7	10	...	2	...	...	...	...
Frequenter or inmate disorderly house	M	7	...	...	1	5	...	1	...	...	...	...
	F	34	...	1	19	10	1	1	...	...	...	2
Keeping and maintaining disorderly house	M	2	...	...	...	2	...	...	...	...	...	...
	F	8	1	...	3	4	...	...	...	...	...	...
Pandering	M	3	...	...	2	1	...	...	...	...	...	...
	F	...	...	...	...	...	...	...	...	...	...	...
Male bawd	M	1	...	...	1	...	...	...	...	...	...	...
	F	...	...	...	...	...	...	...	...	...	...	...
Soliciting for immoral purposes	M	2	...	...	...	2	...	...	...	...	...	...
	F	...	...	...	...	...	...	...	...	...	...	...
Disorderly child	M	...	...	...	...	...	...	...	...	...	...	...
	F	5	...	...	4	1	...	...	...	...	...	...
Miscellaneous sex offenses	M	...	...	...	...	...	...	...	...	...	...	...
	F	1	...	...	1	...	...	...	...	...	...	...
TOTAL	M	25	1	...	9	13	...	2	...	...	...	...
	F	198	1	2	87	90	6	7	1	1	1	2
Grand Total		223	2	2	96	103	6	9	1	1	1	2

[1] Data supplied by Statistician of Municipal Court, Philadelphia.

[2] One man, found guilty of disorderly conduct, was committed to County Prison for five days.

[3] Women are also committed to Sleighton Farm and House of Good Shepherd, but on an indeterminate sentence.

TABLE 3. AMOUNT OF FINES IMPOSED IN CASES OF MEN SEX
OFFENDERS ARRAIGNED IN WOMEN'S MISDEMEANANT'S DIVISION,
PHILADELPHIA, JANUARY 1–JUNE 30, 1920 [1] [2]

OFFENSE	TOTAL NUMBER OF CASES	AMOUNT OF FINE[3]									
		$1.00	$5.00	$7.00	$7.50	$8.00	$10	$15	$20	$25	$50
Disorderly conduct	128	2	31	...	...	1	58	18	7	9	2
Frequenter or inmate disorderly house	74	...	13	3	2	...	35	16	1	4	...
Keeping and maintaining disorderly house	3	...	...	...	...	...	3	...	...	...	...
Male bawd	2	...	2	...	...	...	...	...	...	...	...
Soliciting and disorderly conduct	1	...	...	...	...	...	1	...	...	...	...
TOTAL	208	2	46	3	2	1	97	34	8	13	2

[1] Data furnished by Statistician of Municipal Court, Philadelphia.

[2] One woman was fined for disorderly conduct. Amount not stated. It is not the practice to fine women.

[3] Forty-three offenders paid costs as well as fines specified.

TABLE 4.   INCIDENCE OF VENEREAL DISEASE IN CASES OF WOMEN SEX OFFENDERS ARRAIGNED IN THE WOMEN'S MISDEMEANANTS' DIVISION, PHILADELPHIA, JANUARY 1 TO JUNE 30, 1920 [1]

OFFENSE	TOTAL ARRAIGNED [2]	TOTAL EXAMINED	INFECTED					NOT INFECTED	NOT EXAMINED OR RESULTS UNSATISFACTORY	
			Total	Per Cent of Total Examined	Gonorrhea	Syphilis	Gonorrhea and Syphilis		Number	Per Cent
Disorderly street walking	285	277	178	64.2	52	81	45	99	8	2.8
Disorderly conduct	174	166	81	48.7	34	23	24	85	8	4.5
Frequenter or inmate disorderly house	168	160	85	53.1	39	32	14	75	8	4.7
Keeping and maintaining disorderly house	51	45	28	62.2	9	11	8	17	6	11.7
Incorrigibility	70	66	33	50.	25	7	1	33	4	5.7
Runaway	64	58	24	41.3	15	4	5	34	6	9.3
Incorrigibility and runaway	23	23	11	47.8	7	3	1	12	...	...
Disorderly child	32	28	15	53.5	12	2	1	13	4	12.5
Miscellaneous sex offenses	1	1	...	...	...	...	...	1	...	...
TOTAL	868	824	455	55.2	193	163	99	369	44	4.

[1] Data furnished by Statistician of Municipal Court, Philadelphia.
[2] The discrepancies between these totals and the totals in Table 1 occur because of over-lapping in classification and differences in terminology.

TABLE 5. MENTAL CONDITION OF CASES OF WOMEN SEX OFFENDERS ARRAIGNED IN WOMEN'S MISDEMEANANTS' DIVISION, PHILADELPHIA, JANUARY 1 TO JUNE 30, 1920 [1]

OFFENSE	TOTAL ARRAIGNED [2]	TOTAL EXAMINED	NORMAL [3]		DEVIATING FROM NORMAL							NOT EXAMINED	
			Number	Per Cent	Retarded [4]	Border Line [5]	Moron [6]	Psychoses	Psychoneuroses and Neuroses	Constitutional Psychopathic Inferior	Epileptic	Number	Per Cent
Disorderly street walking	286	246	167	67.8	9	1	3	...	7	58	1	40	13.9
Disorderly conduct	173	149	85	57.	9	2	1	...	4	47	1	24	13.2
Frequenter or inmate disorderly house	183	130	93	71.5	...	...	1.	...	3	33	...	53	20.8
Keeping and maintaining disorderly house	36	35	24	68.5	...	...	...	...	2	8	...	1	2.7
Incorrigibility	71	66	28	42.4	8	...	...	1	2	28	...	5	7.
Runaway	63	61	27	44.2	3	4	...	...	1	26	...	2	3.1
Incorrigibility and runaway	23	22	10	45.4	2	1	1	...	1	7	...	1	4.3
Disorderly child	32	30	13	43.3	4	...	...	...	...	13	...	2	6.2
Miscellaneous sex offenses	1	1	...	...	...	...	...	...	...	1	...	...	...
TOTAL	868	740	447	60.4	35	8	6	1	20	221	2	128	14.7

[1] Data furnished by Statistician of Municipal Court, Philadelphia.

[2] The discrepancies between these totals and the totals in Table 1 occur because of over-lapping in classification and differences in terminology.

[3] This classification is based upon estimate formed by psychiatrist in 15- to 30-minute interviews with each girl or woman. This practice is fully described on p. 112.

[4] Includes individuals who are not feeble-minded, but who are retarded mentally in consequence of physical defects or poor environmental conditions, such as language defects, lack of opportunity, etc. (Statistician of Municipal Court).

[5] Probably feeble-minded, mental age above 145 months, I. Q. 75–89, (Statistician of Municipal Court).

[6] Mental age 84 to 144 months, I. Q. 50–74, (Statistician of Municipal Court).

TABLE 6. DISPOSITION OF CASES OF SEX OFFENDERS ARRAIGNED

OFFENSE		TOTAL ARRAINGED	DISCHARGED	PROBATION	COMMITTED Correctional institutions	COMMITTED Hospitals	FINE AND COSTS	OTHER DISPOSITIONS
Disorderly street walking	M	4	2	...	...	...	2	...
	F	566	75	149	283	49	...	10
Disorderly conduct	M	604	292	24	26	1	234	27
	F	309	65	121	59	56	1	7
Frequenter or inmate disorderly house	M	571	384	9	13	...	123	42
	F	327	99	87	85	42	2	12
Keeping and maintaining disorderly house	M	134	67	3	3	...	5	56
	F	95	39	14	13	5	...	24
Pandering	M	12	3	1	5	...	...	3
	F	...	...	...	...	...	...	...
Fornication	M	14	8	...	...	...	1	5
	F	...	...	...	...	...	...	...
Adultery	M	1	...	...	...	...	...	1
	F	...	...	...	...	...	...	...
Male bawd	M	12	2	1	3	...	2	4
	F	...	...	...	...	...	...	...
Soliciting for immoral purposes	M	9	5	...	2	...	2	...
	F	...	...	...	...	...	...	...
Incorrigibility[2]	M	...	...	...	...	...	...	...
	F	146	12	78	14	41	...	1
Runaway[2]	M	...	...	...	...	...	...	...
	F	129	14	57	16	38	...	4
Disorderly child	M	1	...	...	...	...	...	1
	F	76	6	34	15	19	...	2
Violation of probation								
Disorderly street walking	M	...	...	...	...	...	...	...
	F	27	2	9	10	4	...	2
Disorderly conduct	M	...	...	...	...	...	...	...
	F	15	...	6	7	2	...	...
Frequenter or inmate disorderly house	M	...	...	...	...	...	...	...
	F	6	...	3	2	1	...	...
Incorrigibility	M	...	...	...	...	...	...	...
	F	45	3	17	11	13	...	1
Runaway	M	...	...	...	...	...	...	...
	F	22	...	9	7	5	...	1
Miscellaneous sex offenses	M	...	...	...	...	...	...	...
	F	16	...	5	8	3	...	...
Miscellaneous sex offenses	M	...	...	...	...	...	...	...
	F	15	3	3	6	...	1	2
TOTAL	M	1362	763	38	52	1	369	139
	F	1794	318	592	536	278	4	66
GRAND TOTAL		3156	1081	630	588	279	373	205

[1] This table is based on Tables 7 and 32 in the report of the Women's Misdemeanants' Division of the Municipal Court, for 1920, omitting therefrom the following offenses: drunkenness; illegal sale, purchase or possession of drugs; larceny; witness; protection and miscellaneous. Certain classifications occurring in Table 1, covering dispositions of sex offenders during the first six months of 1920, are ommitted by the Statistican of the Municipal Court in the tabulations for the year. In

NATURE OF DISPOSITION—DETAIL

House of Correction	County Prison	House of Good Shepherd	Sleighton Farms	State Industrial Home for Women	Saint Joseph's Protectory	Gynecean Hospital	Philadelphia General Hospital	Door of Hope	Women's Misdemeanants Division, House of Detention	Regular	Medical	To leave town	Continued Regular	Continued Medical	Total Number Convicted	Per Cent Convicted
...	...	...	...	...	...	...	...	...	...	...	...	...	...	...	2	50.
263	...	18	2	2	...	42	5	....	2	80	52	10	4	3	432	76.3
25	1	...	...	...	...	...	1	....	...	24	...	...	...	...	284	47.
38	...	14	7	...	...	51	4	....	1	81	23	10	5	2	181	58.5
13	...	...	...	...	...	...	...	...	...	9	...	...	...	...	145	25.3
72	...	8	4	...	1	36	5	....	1	57	20	6	3	1	174	53.2
3	...	...	...	...	...	...	...	...	...	3	...	...	...	...	11	8.2
12	...	1	...	...	...	5	...	....	...	6	8	...	...	...	27	28.4
5	...	...	...	...	...	...	...	...	...	1	...	...	...	...	6	50.
...	...	...	...	...	...	...	...	...	...	...	...	...	...	...	...	...
...	...	...	...	...	...	...	...	...	...	...	...	...	...	...	1	12.5
...	...	...	...	...	...	...	...	...	...	...	...	...	...	...	...	...
...	...	...	...	...	...	...	...	...	...	...	...	...	...	...	...	...
...	...	...	...	...	...	...	...	...	...	...	...	...	...	...	...	...
3	...	...	...	...	...	...	...	...	...	1	...	...	...	...	6	50.
...	...	...	...	...	...	...	...	...	...	...	...	...	...	...	...	...
2	...	...	...	...	...	...	...	...	...	...	...	...	...	...	4	44.4
...	...	...	...	...	...	...	...	...	...	...	...	...	...	...	...	...
...	...	5	4	1	4	32	...	5	4	60	12	4	2	...	92	63.
1	...	13	2	...	...	34	...	3	1	44	1	11	1	...	73	56.5
7	...	1	6	...	1	17	1	1	...	25	5	1	2	1	49	64.4
6	...	3	1	...	...	4	...	....	...	2	4	....	3	...	19	70.
1	...	4	1	1	...	2	...	....	...	...	...	3	3	...	13	86.6
...	...	2	...	...	...	1	...	....	...	...	1	...	2	...	5	83.3
...	...	2	7	2	...	13	...	....	...	1	2	....	14	...	28	62.2
1	...	5	...	1	...	4	...	1	...	4	...	...	3	2	16	72.7
2	...	2	3	1	...	3	...	....	...	...	...	...	5	...	13	81.2
6	...	...	...	...	...	...	...	...	...	...	2	1	...	...	10	60.
51	1	...	...	...	...	...	1	...	...	38	...	...	...	...	459	33.7
409	...	76	37	8	6	244	15	10	9	360	133	43	47	9	1132	63.
460	1	76	37	8	6	244	16	10	9	398	133	43	47	9	1591	50.4

Table 1, 14 men are listed under the heading "Failed to appear," 1 under "Escaped," and 2 under "Probation to leave town." Apparently these men are grouped in other columns for the year.

[2] An incorrigible or runaway may or may not be a sex offender.

[3] These refer to cases "released on bail," "continued indefinitely," "transferred to Juvenile Division," etc.

TABLE 7. DISPOSITION OF CASES OF SEX OFFENDERS ARRAIGNED IN CRIMINAL DIVISION (JURY) OF MUNICIPAL COURT, PHILADELPHIA, JANUARY 1 TO JUNE 30, 1920 [1]

OFFENSE		TOTAL ARRAIGNED	TOTAL CONVICTED	PER CENT CONVICTED	DISCHARGED	NOLLE PROS.	RECOGNIZANCE FORFEITED	SUSPENDED SENTENCE	PROBATION	FINED [3]	COMMITTED TO HOUSE OF CORRECTION [4]	COMMITTED TO COUNTY PRISON [4]	EXPENSES [5]
Adultery	M	13	2	15.3	9	1	1	...	...	1	...	1	...
	F	9	2	22.2	5	2	...	...	1	1	...	...	...
Fornication	M	7	1	14.2	4	2	...	...	...	1	...	...	...
	F	2	...	...	2	...	...	...	...	...	...	...	...
Fornication and bastardy	M	112	91	81.2	20	1	...	3	...	...	...	...	88
	F	...	...	...	...	...	...	...	...	...	...	...	...
Keeper, inmate, or frequenter, bawdy house	M	36	9	25.	23	3	1	1	...	1	1	6	...
	F	13	5	38.5	7	1	...	2	2	...	...	1	...
Pandering	M	4	...	...	3	1	...	...	...	...	.	...	...
	F	...	...	...	...	...	...	...	...	...	...	...	...
TOTAL	M	172	103	69.8	59	8	2	4	...	3	1	7	88.
	F	24	7	29.1	14	3	...	2	3	1	...	1	...
GRAND TOTAL		196	110	66.1	73	11	2	6	3	4	1	8	88

[1] Compiled by investigator from Fee and Record book in District Attorney's office, Philadelphia.

[2] Not separately designated in record.

[3] A man and a woman were each fined $50 and costs and one man $10 and costs. Amounts of other fines not recorded.

[4] Terms usually a year in length. One man committed to House of Correction 3 months and another 18 months. Occasionally persons committed were fined in addition. Of the nine men committed to an instituiton, six were paroled after serving from one third to one half their sentences.

[5] Expenses represent a weekly sum, usually $3.00 to $4.00, which court orders defendant to pay to mother for 16 years. Lying-in expenses frequently are added to father's liability. Invariably the father is required to put up a $500 bond.

TABLE 8. DISPOSITION OF CASES OF SEX OFFENDERS ARRAIGNED IN CRIMINAL DIVISION (JURY), MUNICIPAL COURT, PHILADELPHIA, 1920 [1]

OFFENSE		TOTAL ARRAIGNED	TOTAL NUMBER CONVICTED	PER CENT CONVICTED	DISCHARGED	NOLLE PROS.	RECOGNIZANCE FORFEITED	SUSPENDED SENTENCE	PROBATION	FINED[3]	COMMITTED TO HOUSE OF CORRECTION[4]	COMMITTED TO COUNTY PRISON[4]	EXPENSES[5]
Adultery	M	15	2	13.3	11	1	1	...	...	1	...	1	...
	F	13	2	15.3	8	3	...	...	1	1	...	...	...
Fornication	M	9	2	22.2	4	3	...	...	1	1	...	...	...
	F	2	...	...	2	...	...	...	...	...	...	...	...
Fornication and bastardy	M	192	150	78.1	40	2	...	3	...	...	...	...	147
	F	...	...	...	...	...	...	...	...	...	...	...	...
Keeper, inmate or frequenter, bawdy house[2]	M	49	13	26.5	31	4	1	1	1	1	1	9	...
	F	33	10	30.3	21	2	...	3	5	...	...	2	...
Pandering	M	7	1	14.2	5	1	...	...	...	...	...	1	...
	F	...	...	...	...	...	...	...	...	...	...	...	...
TOTAL	M	272	168	61.9	91	11	2	4	2	3	1	11	147
	F	48	12	25.	31	5	...	3	6	1	...	2	...
GRAND TOTAL		320	180	56.2	122	16	2	7	8	4	1	13	147

[1] Compiled by investigator from Fee and Record book in District Attorney's office, Philadelphia.

[2] Not separately designated in record.

[3] A man and a woman were each fined $50 and costs, and one man $10 and costs. Amounts of other fines not recorded.

[4] Terms usually a year in length. One man committed to House of Correction 3 months and another 18 months. Occasionally persons committed were fined in addition. Of the twelve men committed to an institution, six were paroled after serving from one third to one half their sentences.

[5] Expenses represent a weekly sum, usually $3.00 to $4.00, which court orders defendant to pay to mother for 16 years. Lying-in expenses frequently are added to father's liability. Invariably the father is required to put up a $500 bond.

TABLE 9. ANALYSIS OF THE PREVIOUS COURT RECORDS OF WOMEN ARRAIGNED IN THE WOMEN'S MISDEMEANANTS' DIVISION IN THE FIRST THREE MONTHS OF 1920 WHO HAD EVER BEEN ON PROBATION

Number of Subsequent Arraignments in Relation to Number of Times Placed on Probation	Total	Disorderly Street Walking	Disorderly Conduct	Frequenter or Inmate Disorderly House	Keeping or Maintaining Disorderly House	Violation of Probation	Possessing or Suspected of Drugs	Incorrigibility	Runaway	Failed to Appear	Held for Criminal Court	Probation Discharged	Probation Continued	Probation Regular	Probation Medical	Probation To marry	Committed to Gynecean Hospital	Held in House of Detention for Treatment	House of Good Shepherd	Sleighton Farms	House of Correction 3 months	House of Correction 6 months	House of Correction 9 months	House of Correction 12 months	House of Correction 18 months	House of Correction 24 months
Once prior	**80**																									
0 subsequent arraignment	4	1	1					1	1			1							2	1						
1	59	21	5	5	3	22	3			1	1	1	10	8	5	2	11		3		6	7	2	1		
2	7	3	2	2										3	1		1				1	1	1	1		
3	8	2	1	5										1	1							1		3		
4	1	1												1												
5	1	1																				1				
Twice prior	**28**																									
0 subsequent arraignment	1	1											1													
1	21	9	1	1		10						1	4	4	1		2		3	2	2	2			1	
2	3	1	2									1		1						1						
3	1	1												1												
4	1	1												1												
5	1		1																							
Three times prior	**12**																									
1 subsequent arraignment	9	5	1	2		1							1	1	2		1	1			1	2				1
2	2	1	1	1										1			1									
4	1		1																							
Four times prior	**1**																									
1 subsequent arraignment	1					1								1												
Five times prior	**2**																									
1 subsequent arraignment	1	1												1							1					
2	1		1																							
Total	**123**	49	16	16	3	34	3	1	1	1	1	4	17	27	10	2	16	1	8	4	11	14	3	5	1	1

TABLE 10. RELATION BETWEEN NUMBER OF TIMES WOMEN ARRAIGNED
IN WOMEN'S MISDEMEANANTS' DIVISION IN FIRST THREE MONTHS
OF 1920 HAD BEEN PLACED UPON PROBATION AND THE NUMBER OF
TIMES THEY HAD EVER BEEN ARRAIGNED IN THIS DIVISION

NUMBER OF TIMES ON PROBATION	TOTAL NUMBER OF WOMEN	NUMBER OF TIMES ARRAIGNED ON A NEW CHARGE						
		1	2	3	4	5	6	7
1	47	3	30	6	3	1	4	...
2	49	...	22	17	5	4	1	...
3	19	...	...	5	8	2	2	2
4	5	...	...	...	1	2	2	...
5	2	...	...	...	...	...	1	1
6	1	...	...	...	...	...	1	...
TOTAL	123	3	52	28	17	9	11	3

TABLE 11. DISPOSITION OF FIRST ONE HUNDRED CASES (WOMEN)
ARRAIGNED IN 1920 IN THE WOMEN'S MISDEMEANANTS' DIVISION,
PHILADELPHIA, SHOWING NUMBER OF CONTINUANCES PRECEDING
FINAL DISPOSITION

DISPOSITION	TOTAL	NUMBER OF CONTINUANCES		
		No Continuances	Continued Once	Continued Twice
Discharged	7	5	2	...
$500 Bail for Court	1	1	...	...
Probation	34	25	8	1
Gynecean Hospital	19	16	2	1
Door of Hope	1	1	...	...
House of Good Shepherd	3	3	...	...
House of Correction	35	27	6	2
TOTAL	100	78	18	4

TABLE 12.   DISPOSITION OF FIRST ONE HUNDRED CASES (WOMEN) ARRAIGNED IN 1920 IN THE WOMEN'S MISDEMEANANTS' DIVISION, PHILADELPHIA, SHOWING INTERVAL OF TIME BETWEEN ARREST AND FINAL DISPOSITION

DISPOSITION	TOTAL	Less than 1 day	1 day	2 days	3 days	4 days	5 days	6 days	7 days	8 days	10 days	14 days	15 days	19 days	22 days	58 days	63 days	92 days
Discharged	7	...	1	2	3	...	...	...	1	...	...	...	...	...	...	...	...	...
$500 bail for court	1	...	...	...	1	...	...	...	...	...	...	...	...	...	...	...	...	...
Probation	34	1	...	7	7	7	1	2	5	...	...	...	1	1	1	...	...	1
Gynecean Hospital	19	2	2	2	4	3	...	...	4	2	...	...	...	...	...	...	...	...
Door of Hope	1	...	...	...	...	1	...	...	...	...	...	...	...	...	...	...	...	...
House of Good Shepherd	3	...	...	1	...	...	...	1	1	...	...	...	...	...	...	...	...	...
House of Correction	35	...	7	4	14	5	...	1	...	...	1	1	...	...	...	1	1	...
TOTAL	100	3	10	16	29	16	1	4	11	2	1	1	1	1	1	1	1	1

TABLE 13. RELATION OF NUMBER OF CONTINUANCES OF CASES OF TWENTY-TWO WOMEN TO INTERVALS OF TIME BETWEEN ARREST AND FINAL DISPOSITION [1]

TIME INTERVALS	TOTAL	NUMBER OF CONTINUANCES	
		1	2
2 days	2	2	...
3 days	8	8	...
4 days	4	4	...
6 days	1	1	...
7 days	2	1	1
8 days	1	...	1
10 days	1	1	...
14 days	1	...	1
58 days	1	1	...
63 days	1	...	1
TOTAL	22	18	4

[1] Based on Tables 11 and 12.

TABLE 14. AGE AND COLOR OF CASES HELD IN DETENTION HOUSE OF WOMEN'S MISDEMEANANTS' DIVISION, JANUARY 1 TO MARCH 31, 1920 [1]

AGE	TOTAL	WHITE	COLORED
16–21 years	264	210	54
22–25 "	178	108	70
26–30 "	94	63	31
31–35 "	33	23	10
36–40 "	35	29	6
41 up	15	9	6
Not given	18	18	...
TOTAL	637	460	177

[1] Compiled from Superintendent's record book.

TABLE 15.   LENGTH OF DETENTION OF CASES HELD IN WOMEN'S MIS-
DEMEANANTS' DIVISION. JANUARY 1 TO MARCH 31, 1920 [1]

NUMBER DAYS DETAINED[4]	TOTAL	WHITE	COLORED
1 day[3]	27	23	4
2 days	94	69	25
3 "	72	43	29
4 "	127	76	51
5 "	89	63	26
6–10 "	138	106	32
11–15 "	35	28	7
16–20 "	18	16	2
21–25 "	6	5	1
26–30 "	2	2	...
31–40 "	5	5	...
41–50 "	7	7	...
51–60 "	5	5	...
61–70 "	6	6	...
71–80 "	3	3	...
81–90 "	1	1	...
Not given	1	1	...
TOTAL	636[4]	459	177

[1] Compiled from Superintendent's record book.

[2] Day of admission and day of discharge counted as whole day.

[3] Usually bail cases.

[4] One white girl, not included in this list, was held five months and eighteen days.

TABLE 16. JUDGES PRESIDING IN WOMEN'S MISDEMEANANTS' DIVI-
SION, MUNICIPAL COURT OF PHILADELPHIA, 1917 TO 1920

	1917	1918	1919	1920
JANUARY	Gilpin	Gilpin Brown Brown Gilpin Gilpin Wheeler Brown Gilpin Gilpin Wheeler	Brown	Gorman
FEBRUARY	Gilpin	Wheeler Gilpin	Brown Bartlett McNichol Bartlett	Gorman Mac Neille Gorman
MARCH	Gilpin	Gorman Wheeler Cassidy	McNichol	Mac Neille
APRIL	Gilpin	Cassidy Cassidy Gilpin Gilpin Cassidy Cassidy Gilpin Gilpin Brown	McNichol Brown Gorman	Mac Neille
MAY	Gilpin Brown Gilpin Brown Gilpin	Gorman	Gorman	Mac Neille
JUNE	Gilpin	Gorman Brown Gorman	McNichol Bartlett McNichol Bartlett McNichol	Mac Neille Gorman
JULY	Gilpin Brown Gilpin	Gorman	McNichol Brown McNichol	Gorman
AUGUST	Gilpin Brown Gilpin	Gorman Mac Neille	Mac Neille	Gorman Cassidy
SEPTEMBER	Gilpin	Gorman	Mac Neille	Cassidy Mac Neille
OCTOBER	Wheeler	No court Oct. 2 to Nov. 8 (influenza epidemic)	Mac Neille	Mac Neille
NOVEMBER	Wheeler Gilpin Brown Gilpin	Brown	Mac Neille Bartlett Gorman	McNichol
DECEMBER	Brown Brown Gilpin Gilpin Brown Brown Gilpin Gilpin Brown Brown Gilpin Gilpin	Brown	Gorman	McNichol

TABLE 17. STUDY OF SOCIAL HISTORIES OF FIFTY WOMEN PLACED UPON PROBATION DURING THE FIRST SIX MONTHS OF 1920 [1]

OFFENSE	TOTAL NUMBER OF PROBATIONERS	COLOR AND NATIONALITY								AGE AT TIME OF ARREST						
		COLOR		NATIONALITY						15–19 YEARS	20–24 YEARS	25–29 YEARS	30–34 YEARS	35–39 YEARS	40–44 YEARS	Over 50 YEARS
		White	Col-ored	Ameri-can	Eng-lish	Irish	Italian	Polish Jewess	Hun-garian							
Disorderly street walking	17	12	5	14	1	1	.	...	1	1	5	5	1	1	3	1
Disorderly conduct	13	13	...	13	...	...	...	...	...	2	8	1	1	1	...	...
Violation of probation	5	4	1	4	...	...	1	...	...	4	...	...	...	...	...	...
Incorrigibility	3	3	...	3	...	...	...	...	...	2	1	1	...	...	...	...
Runaway	2	2	...	2	...	...	...	...	...	1	1	...	...	...	...	...
Incorrigibility and runaway	2	2	...	2	...	...	...	...	...	2	...	...	...	...	...	...
Inmates disorderly house	2	2	...	1	...	...	...	1	...	...	1	1	...	...	...	...
Keepers disorderly house	1	...	1	1	...	...	...	...	...	...	...	...	...	1	...	...
Frequenters disorderly house	1	1	...	1	...	...	...	...	...	...	...	1	...	...	...	...
Incorrigibility and violation of probation	1	1	...	1	...	...	...	...	...	1	...	...	...	...	...	...
Incorrigibility and disorderly conduct	1	1	...	1	...	...	...	...	...	1	...	...	...	1	...	...
Drunk and disorderly conduct	1	1	...	1	...	...	...	...	...	...	...	...	...	1	...	...
Contempt of court	1	1	...	1	...	...	...	...	...	...	...	...	...	...	1	...
TOTAL	50	43	7	45	1	1	1	1	1	14	16	9	2	4	4	1

[1] Based upon the study of fifty cases placed upon probation during this period. For discussion see pp. 114–129.

TABLE 17. STUDY OF SOCIAL HISTORIES OF FIFTY WOMEN PLACED UPON PROBATION DURING THE FIRST SIX MONTHS OF 1920—Continued

Offense	Total Number of Probationers	Civil Condition at Time of Arrest						Religion					
		Single	Married	Widow	Marriage Unverified	Common-Law Marriage	Widow of Common-Law Marriage	Roman Catholic	Protestant	Jewish	Greek Catholic	No Church	Not Stated
Disorderly street walking	17	4	6	3	1	1	2	3	8	...	1	...	5
Disorderly conduct	13	5	5	2	1	...	...	5	4	2	...	1	1
Violation of probation	5	4	...	1	...	...	...	4	1	...	...	1	...
Incorrigibility	3	3	...	...	...	...	...	2	1	...	...	...	...
Runaway	2	1	...	...	1	...	...	2	...	...	...	...	...
Incorrigibility and runaway	2	2	...	...	...	...	...	1	1	...	...	...	...
Inmates disorderly house	2	1	1	...	...	...	...	...	1	1	...	...	...
Keepers disorderly house	1	...	...	...	...	1	...	...	1	...	...	...	...
Frequenters disorderly house	1	...	1	...	...	...	...	...	...	...	...	...	1
Incorrigibility and violation of probation	1	1	...	...	...	...	...	...	1	...	...	...	...
Incorrigibility and disorderly conduct	1	...	1	...	...	...	...	1	...	...	...	...	...
Drunk and disorderly conduct	1	...	1	...	...	...	...	...	...	...	...	...	1
Contempt of court	1	...	...	...	...	1	...	1	...	...	...	...	...
TOTAL	50	21	15	6	3	3	2	19	17	3	1	2	8

TABLE 17. STUDY OF SOCIAL HISTORIES OF FIFTY WOMEN PLACED UPON PROBATION DURING THE FIRST SIX MONTHS OF 1920—Continued

Offense	Total Number of Probationers	Age at Leaving School								School Grade Completed										
		12 years	13 years	14 years	15 years	16 years	17 years	Never Attended School	Not Stated	Third Grade	Fourth Grade	Fifth Grade	Sixth Grade	Seventh Grade	Eighth Grade	Ninth Grade	First Year High School	Second Year High School	Never Attended School	Not Given
Disorderly street walking	17	3	4	3	2	4		1			3		5	3	3		1		1	1
Disorderly conduct	13			7	3	1	1	1		1	1		4	2	3	1			1	
Violation of probation	5			2	2	1						1	1	1	2					
Incorrigibility	3	1				2							1	1	1					
Runaway	2			1		1				1				1						
Incorrigibility and runaway	2			1		1				1					1					
Inmates disorderly house	2						1	1										1	1	
Keepers disorderly house	1					1									1					
Frequenters disorderly house	1			1									1							
Incorrigibility and violation of probation	1				1						1									
Incorrigibility and disorderly conduct	1								1		1									
Drunk and disorderly conduct	1			1																1
Contempt of court	1			1									1							
Total	50	4	4	17	8	11	2	3	1	3	6	1	13	8	11	1	1	1	3	2

TABLE 17. STUDY OF SOCIAL HISTORIES OF FIFTY WOMEN PLACED UPON PROBATION DURING THE FIRST SIX MONTHS OF 1920—Concluded

OFFENSE	TOTAL NUMBER OF PROBATIONERS	MANNER OF LIVING AT TIME OF ARREST								CHILDREN — LEGITIMACY AND NUMBER OF CHILDREN									
		With Parents	With Husband	With Relative	Keeping House	Boarding House	At Place of Employment	With Lover	Not Stated	None	Legitimate 1 child	Legitimate 2 children	Legitimate 3 children	Legitimate 4 children	Illegitimate 1 child	Illegitimate 2 children	Legitimacy not Established 1 child	Legitimacy not Established 2 children	Legitimacy not Established 3 children
Disorderly street walking	17	3	2	7		4			1	6	1	1	1	1	2		3	1	1
Disorderly conduct	13	5	1			6				6	1				1²		5		
Violation of probation	5	2		1	1	1		1		4					1				
Incorrigibility	3	3					1			2					1				
Runaway	2					1	1			1						1			
Incorrigibility and runaway	2	2								2									
Inmates disorderly house	2		1			1				1	1								
Keepers disorderly house	1				1					1									
Frequenters disorderly house	1				1								1						
Incorrigibility and violation of probation	1	1								1									
Incorrigibility and disorderly conduct	1	1								1									
Drunk and disorderly conduct	1		1						1						1³				
Contempt of court	1																1		
Total	50	17	5	8	3	13	1	1	2	25	3	1	2	1	6²	1	9	1	1

² One probationer had one illegitimate and two legitimate children.
³ One probationer had one illegitimate and six legitimate children.

TABLE 18. PREVIOUS AND SUBSEQUENT ARRAIGNMENTS

Offense	Total Number of Probationers	Number of Previous Arraignments						Number of Subsequent Arraignments in Women's Misdemeanants' Division up to October 1, 1921				
		0	1	2	3	4	10	0	1	2	3	4
Disorderly street walking	17	10	5	1	...	1	...	12	4	1	...	...
Disorderly conduct	13	9	1	2	...	...	1	9	3	...	1	...
Violation of probation	5	...	2	2	1	...	...	3	2	...	...	...
Incorrigibility	3	2	1	...	...	...	...	2	1	...	...	...
Runaway	2	2	...	...	...	...	...	1	...	1	...	...
Incorrigibility and runaway	2	2	...	...	...	...	...	2	...	...	...	...
Inmate disorderly house	2	...	2	...	...	...	...	2	...	...	...	...
Keeper disorderly house	1	...	...	1	...	...	...	...	1	...	...	...
Frequenter disorderly house	1	1	...	...	...	...	...	...	1	...	...	...
Incorrigibility and violation of probation	1	...	1	...	...	...	...	1	...	...	...	...
Incorrigibility and disorderly conduct	1	1	...	...	...	...	...	...	1	...	...	...
Drunk and disorderly conduct	1	...	1	...	...	...	...	...	...	...	...	1
Contempt of court	1	1	...	...	...	...	...	...	1	...	...	...
TOTAL	50	28	13	6	1	1	1	32	14	2	1	1

TABLE 19. INCIDENCE OF VENEREAL DISEASE AMONG FIFTY WOMEN PLACED UPON PROBATION DURING THE FIRST SIX MONTHS OF 1920 [1]

OFFENSE	TOTAL NUMBER PROBATIONERS	EXAMINED			RESULTS							
					INFECTED			NOT INFECTED			Inconclusive	Not examined
		For gonorrhea and syphilis	For gonorrhea only	For syphilis only	Both gonorrhea and syphilis	Gonorrhea only	Syphilis only	Of those examined for gonorrhea and syphilis	Of those examined for gonorrhea only	Of those examined for syphilis only		
Disorderly street walking	17	17	...	...	4	1	7	5	...	...	...	...
Disorderly conduct	13	11	...	2	...	1	3	5	...	2	2	...
Violation of probation	5	3	...	2	...	1	2	2	...	...	...	...
Incorrigibility	3	2	...	...	...	1	...	1	...	...	...	1
Runaway	2	2	...	...	1	...	...	1	...	...	...	...
Incorrigibility and runaway	2	1	1	...	...	...	...	1	1	...	...	...
Inmate disorderly house	2	1	...	...	1	...	...	...	...	...	...	1
Keeper disorderly house	1	1	...	...	...	1	...	...	...	...	...	...
Frequenter disorderly house	1	1	...	...	...	...	1	...	...	...	...	...
Incorrigibility and disorderly conduct	1	1	...	...	...	1	...	...	...	...	...	...
Incorrigibility and violation of probation	1	1	...	...	...	...	...	1	...	...	...	...
Drunk and disorderly conduct	1	...	...	...	...	...	...	...	...	...	...	1
Contempt of court	1	1	...	...	...	...	...	1	...	...	...	...
TOTAL	50	42	1	4	6	6	13	17	1	2	2	3

[1] See footnote to Table 17.

TABLE 20.   FREQUENCY OF CALLS AT HOME OF PROBATIONER IN RELA-
TION TO NUMBER OF TIMES FOUND AT HOME

NUMBER OF TIMES OFFICER FOUND PROBATIONER	TOTAL NUMBER OF PROBATIONERS	NUMBER OF CALLS MADE AT PROBATIONER'S HOME								
		1	2	3	4	5	6	7	10	11
0	18	8	5	2	...	1	...	1	1	...
1	13	7	4	...	1	...	...	1	...	...
2	5	...	...	3	...	2	...	...	...	...
3	3	...	1	...	...	...	1	...	...	1
TOTAL	39[1]	15	10	5	1	3	1	2	1	1

[1] Eleven homes were not called upon by probation officers.

TABLE 21. FREQUENCY OF CALLS AT HOME OF PROBATIONER IN RELATION TO NUMBER OF TIMES RELATIVE OR HOUSEKEEPER WAS FOUND AT HOME

NUMBER OF TIMES OFFICER FOUND RELATIVE OR HOUSEKEEPER	TOTAL NUMBER OF PROBATIONERS	NUMBER OF CALLS MADE AT PROBATIONER'S HOME								
		1	2	3	4	5	6	7	10	11
0	13	10	1	2	...	...	...	...	...	...
1	9	5	4	...	...	...	...	...	...	...
2	5	...	5	...	...	...	...	...	...	...
3	7	...	...	3	1	2	1	...	...	...
5	3	...	...	...	...	1	...	2	...	...
8	1	...	...	...	...	...	...	...	...	1
10	1	...	...	...	...	...	...	...	1	...
TOTAL	39[1]	15	10	5	1	3	1	2	1	1

[1] Eleven homes were not called upon by probation officers.

TABLE 22. FREQUENCY OF PROBATIONER'S REPORTING IN PERSON IN RELATION TO NUMBER OF CALLS MADE BY PROBATION OFFICER, AND TO LENGTH OF PROBATION

NUMBER OF MONTHS ON PROBATION	TOTAL NUMBER OF PROBATIONERS	NUMBER OF TIMES PROBATIONER REPORTED IN PERSON																		NUMBER OF CALLS MADE BY OFFICER AT PROBATIONER'S HOME									
		0	1	2	3	4	5	6	7	8	9	10	11	12	17	18	19	20	23	0	1	2	3	4	5	6	7	10	11
Up to 3 months	9	7	1		1															4¹	2	2	1						
4–6 months	14	3	1	7	1		1	1												2	5	3	2	1	1				
7–9 months	11	2	2	1		1		2	1						1	1				2	2	3			1	1	1		1
10–12 months	11	3			1	1	1			1	1	2	1							2	4	1			1	2	1		
13–15 months	5			2										1			1		1	1	2	1						1	
TOTAL	50	15	4	10	3	2	2	3	1	1	1	2	1	1	1	1	1		1	11	15	10	3	1	3	3	2	1	1

¹ One probationer was re-arrested on a new charge one week after being placed on probation.

TABLE 23. FREQUENCY OF PROBATIONER'S REPORTING BY LETTER IN RELATION TO LENGTH OF TIME ON PROBATION

NUMBER OF TIMES PROBATIONER REPORTED BY LETTER	TOTAL NUMBER OF PROBATIONERS	NUMBER OF MONTHS ON PROBATION				
		Up to 3	4–6	7–9	10–12	13–15
0	25	3	10	6	5	1
1	6	2	2	1	1	...
2	4	1	...	1	2	...
3	2	1	...	...	...	1
4	1	...	...	...	...	1
5	1	...	1	...	...	...
8	2	1	...	...	1	...
10	1	...	...	...	...	1
15	2	...	1	1	...	...
16	2	1	...	...	...	1
17	1	...	...	1	...	...
20	1	...	...	...	1	...
22	1	...	...	1	...	...
38	1	...	...	...	1	...
TOTAL	50	9	14	11	11	5

Note.—The tables following are reprinted without change of type from the Philadelphia Municipal Court Report for 1920, only the table numbers having been changed in order to follow the foregoing tables in proper sequence.

TABLE 24

COURT EXPERIENCE

Women and Girls (Separate Individuals) Before This Court for the First Time and First Arrest

Line No.	Court experience	Number of women and girls				
		Total	Disorderly street walking[3]	Inmate disorderly bawdy house[4]	Frequenting disorderly bawdy house	Disorderly child[5]
1	All individuals	1,736	489	147	39	69
2	Before this court for the first time	1,183	282	108	31	65
3	Never in any court before	1,054	257	100	30	52
4	With previous experience in other courts	129	25	8	1	13
5	Probation department, misdemeanants' division	1	—	—	—	1
6	Juvenile delinquent court	45	—	1	—	7
7	Juvenile dependent court	—	—	—	—	—
8	Domestic relations division	12	2	1	1	2
9	Criminal division	6	2	1	—	—
10	Magistrates court	39	13	4	—	1
11	Federal courts	2	—	—	—	—
12	Courts in other cities	16	1	—	—	1
13	Juvenile delinquent and dependent courts	1	—	—	—	1
14	Juvenile delinquent and domestic relations divisions	2	1	—	—	—
15	Juvenile delinquent and Federal courts	2	—	—	—	—
16	Juvenile delinquent and criminal divisions	1	—	—	—	—
17	Juvenile dependent and court in other city	1	—	—	—	—
18	Domestic relations division and magistrates' courts	1	—	1	—	—
19	With previous experience in this court	553	207	39	8	4
20	Never in any other court before	363	133	25	5	2
21	With previous experience in other courts	190	74	14	3	2
22	Juvenile delinquent court	29	1	2	—	2
23	Juvenile dependent court	1	1	—	—	—

See Philadelphia Municipal Court Report, 1920, footnotes on pp. 112–113.

TABLE 24

AND OFFENSE

With Previous Experience in This and Other Courts,[1] Classified by Offense Charged at in 1920[2]: 1920

Line No.	Number of women and girls									
	Keeping disorderly bawdy house[6]	Disorderly conduct[7]	Frequenting and inmate of disorderly house[8]	Drunk and disorderly	Drug cases[9]	Incorrigibility[10]	Runaway from home	Violating probation	Contempt of court	Other offenses[11]
1	88	282	125	46	32	139	125	84	7	64
2	61	205	102	26	7	128	113	1	—	54
3	53	186	94	22	7	107	94	—	—	52
4	8	19	8	4	—	21	19	1	—	2
5	—	—	—	—	—	—	—	—	—	—
6	—	4	4	—	—	16	11	1	—	1
7	—	—	—	—	—	—	—	—	—	—
8	1	4	1	—	—	—	—	—	—	—
9	—	1	—	—	—	2	—	—	—	—
10	5	6	1	3	—	—	—	—	—	—
11	1	—	1	—	—	—	—	—	—	—
12	1	3	1	—	—	—	8	—	—	1
13	—	—	—	—	—	—	—	—	—	—
14	—	—	—	—	—	1	—	—	—	—
15	—	1	—	1	—	—	—	—	—	—
16	—	—	—	—	—	1	—	—	—	—
17	—	—	—	—	—	1	—	—	—	—
18	—	—	—	—	—	—	—	—	—	—
19	27	77	23	20	25	11	12	83	7	10
20	15	53	18	8	12	9	9	63	5	6
21	12	24	5	12	13	-2	3	20	2	4
22	—	9	1	—	—	2	2	9	1	
23	—	—	—	—	—	—	—	—	—	—

TABLE 24—Concluded

COURT EXPERIENCE

Women and Girls (Separate Individuals) Before This Court for the First Time and First Arrest

Line No.	Court experience	Number of women and girls				
		Total	Disorderly street walking[3]	Inmate disorderly bawdy house[4]	Frequenting disorderly bawdy house	Disorderly child[5]
25	Domestic relations division	5	—	—	—	—
26	Criminal division	3	1	—	—	—
27	Magistrates' courts	144	69	11	3	—
28	Federal courts	4	2	1	—	—
29	Courts in other cities	2	—	—	—	—
30	Juvenile delinquent and domestic relations divisions	1	—	—	—	—
31	Juvenile dependent, domestic relations and criminal divisions	1	—	—	—	—

[1] Individuals in court more than once in 1920 have been classified according to court experience at time of first arrest in 1920.

[2] Individuals arrested in 1919 and not disposed of until 1920 have been classified according to offense charged in 1919. Individuals brought in for "violating probation" and "contempt of court" have been classified according to offense charged prior to "violating probation" and "contempt of court."

[3] Includes disorderly street walking, disorderly street walking and larceny, and disorderly street walking and possession of narcotic drugs.

[4] Includes inmate of disorderly bawdy house, and inmate of and frequenting disorderly bawdy house, and soliciting and inmate of disorderly bawdy house.

[5] Includes disorderly child and disorderly child and runaway.

TABLE 24—Concluded

AND OFFENSE—Concluded

With Previous Experience in This and Other Courts,[1] Classified by Offense Charged at in 1920[2]: **1920**—Concluded

Line No.	Number of women and girls									
	Keeping disorderly bawdy house[6]	Disorderly conduct[7]	Freing and and inmate of disorderly house[8]	Drunk and disorderly	Drug cases[9]	Incorrigibility[10]	Runaway from home	Violating probation	Contempt of court	Other offenses[11]
25	—	1	—	—	—	—	1	3	—	—
26	—	—	—	—	1	—	—	1	—	—
27	10	12	4	12	12	—	—	6	1	—
28	1	—	—	—	—	—	—	—	—	—
29	1	1	—	—	—	—	—	—	—	—
30	—	—	—	—	—	—	—	1	—	—
31	—	1	—	—	—	—	—	—	—	—

[6] Includes keeping disorderly bawdy house and keeping and maintaining disorderly bawdy house.

[7] Includes disorderly conduct and idle and disorderly.

[8] Includes frequenting disorderly house, inmate of disorderly house, and inmate of and frequenting disorderly house.

[9] Includes illegal sale or purchase of narcotic drugs, illegal possession of narcotic drugs.

[10] Includes incorrigibility, incorrigibility and runaway, and incorrigibility and larceny.

[11] Includes larceny, keeping disorderly house, vagrancy, runaway from institution, witness, material witnesses, protection, fornication, harboring minors for immoral purposes, and adultery.

TABLE 25

Time Between Disposition and Arrest on New Charge: Cases Concerning Women With
Between the Date of Last Previous Disposition and the Date Brought
Offenders at the Time

Line No.	Status at time brought in on new charge	Number of cases				
		Total	Months elapsed between last previous disposition and appearance in court on a new charge			
			Less than 1 month	1 month but less than 2	2 months but less than 3	3 months but less than 6
1	**Total (old offenders)** ------	**758**	**82**	**45**	**43**	**108**
2	**Released from the court's care**	**256**	**15**	**10**	**11**	**25**
3	Discharged after court hearing	87	7	8	5	7
4	Dropped by the probation department, never in court ---	10	5	—	—	1
5	Discharged from probation ---	6	1	—	1	—
6	Probation satisfactory ----	4	—	—	1	—
7	Absconded -----------------	1	1	—	—	—
8	Medical probation satisfactory -------------------	1	—	—	—	—
9	Discharged from hospital -----	4	—	—	—	—
10	Philadelphia General Hospital ---------------------	3	—	—	—	—
11	Gynecean Hospital ---------	1	—	—	—	—
12	Discharged from correctional institution -------------------	148	2	2	4	17
13	House of correction -------	146	2	2	4	17
14	County prison -------------	2	—	—	—	—
15	Fined -----------------------	1	—	—	1	—
16	**Pending disposition**----------	**28**	**6**	—·	**2**	**2**
17	Held under advisement --------	1	—	—	—	—
18	Continued until further notice	2	1	—	—	1
19	In house pending removal from city[1][2] ---------------------	1	—	—	1	—
20	On bail for further hearing----	1	—	—	—	—
21	Released under bail for criminal court[3] ------------------------	20	2	—	1	1
22	Failed to appear, bench warrant issued -------------------	3	3	—	—	—
23	**Under the court's care** ------	**474**	**61**	**35**	**30**	**81**
24	On probation[4] -----------------	343	40	24	24	66
25	Under supervision (informal) by probation department -----------------	13	5	—	1	4

TABLE 25

Previous Records in This Division, Classified by the Number of Months Elapsed in On a New Charge or for Violating Probation, by the Status of the of Arrest: **1920**

Line No.	Number of cases							
	Months elapsed between last previous disposition and appearance in court on a new charge							
	6 months but less than 9	9 months but less than 12	12 months but less than 18	18 months but less than 24	2 years but less than 3	3 years but less than 4	4 years but less than 5	5 years and over
1	124	89	72	70	73	28	22	2
2	39	29	26	26	42	19	12	2
3	8	9	2	8	11	12	9	1
4	—	1	—	—	—	2	1	—
5	2	—	—	—	1	—	1	—
6	1	—	—	—	1	—	1	—
7	—	—	—	—	—	—	—	—
8	1	—	—	—	—	—	—	—
9	—	—	2	—	1	1	—	—
10	—	—	1	—	1	1	—	—
11	—	—	1	—	—	—	—	—
12	29	19	22	18	29	4	1	1
13	29	19	22	18	29	3	—	1
14	—	—	—	—	—	1	1	—
15	—	—	—	—	—	—	—	—
16	2	3	2	8	2	—	1	—
17	—	1	—	—	—	—	—	—
18	—	—	—	—	—	—	—	—
19	—	—	—	—	—	—	—	—
20	1	—	—	—	—	—	—	—
21	1	2	2	8	2	—	1	—
22	—	—	—	—	—	—	—	—
23	83	57	44	36	29	9	9	—
24	53	45	29	28	20	7	7	—
25	1	—	—	1	1	—	—	—

TABLE 25—Concluded

Time Between Disposition and Arrest on New Charge: Cases Concerning Women With
Between the Date of Last Previous Disposition and the Date Brought
Offenders at the Time

Line No.	Status at time brought in on new charge	Number of cases				
		Total	Months elapsed between last previous disposition and appearance in court on a new charge			
			Less than 1 month	1 month but less than 2	2 months but less than 3	3 months but less than 6
26	On probation	224	23	17	15	35
27	On medical probation without treatment at Gynecean Hospital	33	3	4	2	4
28	On medical probation following treatment at Gynecean Hospital	71	9	3	6	23
29	Released from institution on probation	1	—	—	—	—
30	Released from Philadelphia General Hospital, insane department, on probation	1	—	—	—	—
31	On parole	101	7	7	5	11
32	From County Prison	1	—	—	—	—
33	From House of Correction	53	2	2	4	6
34	From House of Good Shepherd	35	4	3	1	4
35	From Sleighton Farm	11	1	2	—	1
36	From St. Joseph's Protectory	1	—	—	—	—
37	In institution[1]	14	9	1	—	3
38	Gynecean Hospital[1]	10	8	1	—	1
39	House of detention[1][2]	1	—	—	—	—
40	Philadelphia General Hospital[1]	1	1	—	—	—
41	Door of Hope[1]	1	—	—	—	1
42	House of Good Shepherd[1]	1	—	—	—	1
43	Escaped	16	5	3	1	1
44	From Gynecean Hospital	1	—	1	—	—
45	From Philadelphia General Hospital	1	—	1	—	—
46	From sheriff	1	—	1	—	—
47	From other institutions	13	5	—	1	1

[1] Brought into court for contempt of court.

[2] Women's misdemeanants' house of detention.

[3] This was the status so far as the misdemeanants' division was concerned.
This court has no record of the disposition of these cases in the criminal court.

TABLE 25—Concluded

Previous Records in This Division, Classified by the Number of Months Elapsed in On a New Charge or for Violating Probation, by the Status of the of Arrest: 1920—Concluded

	Number of cases							
	Months elapsed between last previous disposition and appearance in court on a new charge							
Line No.	6 months but less than 9	9 months but less than 12	12 months but less than 18	18 months but less than 24	2 years but less than 3	3 years but less than 4	4 years but less than 5	5 years and over
26	32	27	20	25	17	7	6	—
27	6	10	2	—	1	—	1	—
28	13	7	7	2	1	—	—	—
29	—	1	—	—	—	—	—	—
30	1	—	—	—	—	—	—	—
31	27	11	14	7	8	2	2	—
32	—	—	—	—	—	—	1	—
33	19	6	8	3	3	—	—	—
34	8	4	4	4	1	1	1	—
35	—	1	1	—	4	1	—	—
36	—	—	1	—	—	—	—	—
37	1	—	—	—	—	—	—	—
38	—	—	—	—	—	—	—	—
39	1	—	—	—	—	—	—	—
40	—	—	—	—	—	—	—	—
41	—	—	—	—	—	—	—	—
42	—	—	—	—	—	—	—	—
43	2	1	1	1	1	—	—	—
44	—	—	—	—	—	—	—	—
45	—	—	—	—	—	—	—	—
46	—	—	—	—	—	—	—	—
47	2	1	1	1	1	—	—	—

[4] It is probable that a number of these women and girls had absconded or had been discharged from probation.

TABLE 26

DISPOSITION AND

Cases Disposed of at Court Hearings, Classified by Nature of Disposition and

Line No.	Disposition	Number of cases				
				Old offenders		
		Total	First offenders	Total	Number of times arrested	
					2 times	3 times
1	Total	1,941	1,183	758	362	181
2	Discharged	339	276	63	37	13
3	Outright	299	246	53	31	12
4	To marry	18	13	5	4	—
5	To leave town in care of individual	11	8	3	2	—
6	In care of individual	9	7	2	—	1
7	To leave district	2	2	—	—	—
8	Probation	647	436	211	114	45
9	Regular	398	310	88	48	17
10	With medical supervision	142	82	60	30	14
11	To leave town in care of individual	49	42	7	3	—
12	Probation continued	58	2	56	33	14
13	Regular	49	2	47	30	10
14	With medical supervision	9	—	9	3	4
15	Held in women's misdemeanants' house of detention for treatment	9	7	2	1	1
16	Committed to Gynecean Hospital	258	165	93	59	23
17	Committed to correctional institution	587	231	356	135	95
18	House of Correction	452	181	271	97	72
19	House of Good Shepherd	83	30	53	26	14
20	Sleighton Farm	38	13	25	10	8
21	State Industrial Home for Women	8	2	6	1	1
22	St. Joseph's Protectory	6	5	1	1	—
23	Committed to other institutions	26	16	10	5	2
24	Philadelphia General Hospital	15	8	7	4	2
25	Door of Hope	10	8	2	1	—
26	St. Vincent's Home	1	—	1	—	—
27	Held under bail for criminal court	46	34	12	5	1
28	Continued indefinitely	15	10	5	2	1
29	Transferred to juvenile division	7	6	1	1	—
30	Fine and costs	4	2	2	1	—
31	All others	3	—	3	2	—

TABLE 26

TIMES ARRESTED

Number of Times Arrested and Brought in Before This Division: 1920

Line No.	Number of cases							
	Old offenders							
	Number of times arrested							
	4 times	5 times	6 times	7 times	8 times	9 times	10 times	11 times
1	99	47	36	14	9	6	2	2
2	6	3	1	2	—	1	—	—
3	5	3	1	—	—	1	—	—
4	—	—	—	1	—	—	—	—
5	1	—	—	—	—	—	—	—
6	—	—	—	1	—	—	—	—
7	—	—	—	—	—	—	—	—
8	25	15	8	1	1	1	—	1
9	12	7	3	—	—	1	—	—
10	8	5	1	—	1	—	—	1
11	3	—	1	—	—	—	—	—
12	2	3	3	1	—	—	—	—
13	1	3	2	1	—	—	—	—
14	1	—	1	—	—	—	—	—
15	—	—	—	—	—	—	—	—
16	2	4	3	1	—	1	—	—
17	59	22	22	9	8	3	2	1
18	46	19	19	8	7	1	2	—
19	7	1	2	1	—	1	—	1
20	4	1	1	—	1	—	—	—
21	2	1	—	—	—	1	—	—
22	—	—	—	—	—	—	—	—
23	—	2	1	—	—	—	—	—
24	—	1	—	—	—	—	—	—
25	—	1	—	—	—	—	—	—
26	—	—	1	—	—	—	—	—
27	5	—	—	1	—	—	—	—
28	1	1	—	—	—	—	—	—
29	—	—	—	—	—	—	—	—
30	—	—	1	—	—	—	—	—
31	1	—	—	—	—	—	—	—

TABLE 27

DISPOSITION AND STATUS

Cases Disposed of at Court Hearings, Classified by

Line No.	Status at time of arrest	Number of cases				
				Placed on probation or probation continued		
		Total	Dis-charged	Regular	With medical super-vision	To leave town
1	Total	1,941	339	447	151	49
2	First offenders	1,183	276	312	82	42
3	Old offenders	758	63	135	69	7
4	Released from court's care	256	29	48	18	3
5	Discharged after court hearing	87	14	21	8	2
6	Dropped by probation department, never in court	10	—	6	—	—
7	Discharged from probation	6	2	1	—	—
8	Probation satisfactory	4	2	1	—	—
9	Absconded	1	—	—	—	—
10	Medical probation satisfactory	1	—	—	—	—
11	Discharged from hospital	4	—	1	1	—
12	Philadelphia General Hospital	3	—	1	1	—
13	Gynecean Hospital	1	—	—	—	—
14	Discharged from correctional institution	148	12	19	9	1
15	House of correction	146	12	19	9	1
16	County prison	2	—	—	—	—
17	Fined	1	1	—	—	—
18	Pending disposition	28	5	3	2	—
19	Held under advisement	1	1	—	—	—
20	Continued until further notice	2	—	—	—	—
21	In house pending removal from city[1][2]	1	—	—	—	—
22	On bail for further hearing	1	—	—	—	—
23	Held under bail for criminal court[3]	20	4	2	2	—
24	Failed to appear, bench warrant issued	3	—	1	—	—
25	Under the court's care	474	29	84	49	4
26	On probation[4]	343	21	69	38	2
27	Under supervision (informal) by probation department	13	2	2	3	—

TABLE 27

AT TIME OF ARREST

Disposition and Status at Time of Arrest: 1920

Line No.	Number of cases									
	Committed to correctional institutions					Committed to other institutions				
	House of Correction	House of Good Shepherd	Sleighton Farm	State Industrial Home for Women	St. Joseph's Protectory	Gynecean Hospital	Philadelphia General Hospital	Door of Hope	Held under bail for criminal court	All others
1	452	83	38	8	6	258	15	10	46	39
2	181	30	13	2	5	165	8	8	34	25
3	271	53	25	6	1	93	7	2	12	14
4	120	11	3	1	—	13	2	—	5	3
5	25	3	1	—	—	7	1	—	3	2
6	1	2	—	—	—	1	—	—	—	—
7	1	—	1	—	—	—	—	—	—	1
8	1	—	—	—	—	—	—	—	—	—
9	—	—	—	—	—	—	—	—	—	1
10	—	—	1	—	—	—	—	—	—	—
11	1	—	1	—	—	—	—	—	—	—
12	1	—	—	—	—	—	—	—	—	—
13	—	—	1	—	—	—	—	—	—	—
14	92	6	—	1	—	5	1	—	2	—
15	90	6	—	1	—	5	1	—	2	—
16	2	—	—	—	—	—	—	—	—	—
17	—	—	—	—	—	—	—	—	—	—
18	10	3	—	—	—	2	—	—	3	—
19	—	—	—	—	—	—	—	—	—	—
20	1	—	—	—	—	—	—	—	1	—
21	—	1	—	—	—	—	—	—	—	—
22	—	1	—	—	—	—	—	—	—	—
23	8	1	—	—	—	1	—	—	2	—
24	1	—	—	—	—	1	—	—	—	—
25	141	39	22	5	1	78	5	2	4	11
26	88	26	16	4	1	65	2	2	3	6
27	1	—	1	—	—	4	—	—	—	—

TABLE 27—Concluded

DISPOSITION AND STATUS

Cases Disposed of at Court Hearings, Classified by

Line No.	Status at time of arrest	Number of cases				
		Total	Discharged	Placed on probation or probation continued		
				Regular	With medical supervision	To leave town
28	On probation	224	17	50	13	2
29	On medical probation without treatment at Gynecean Hospital	33	—	•	13	—
30	On medical probation following treatment at Gynecean Hospital	71	2	16	9	—
31	Released from institution on probation	1	—	1	—	—
32	Released from Philadelphia General Hospital, insane department, on probation	1	—	—	—	—
33	On parole	101	8	12	4	1
34	From County Prison	1	—	—	1	—
35	From House of Correction	53	4	8	3	—
36	From House of Good Shepherd	35	3	2	—	1
37	From Sleighton Farm	11	1	1	—	—
38	From St. Joseph's Protectory	1	—	1	—	—
39	In institutions[1]	14	—	2	3	1
40	Gynecean Hospital[1]	10	—	1	2	1
41	House of Detention[1][2]	1	—	—	1	—
42	Philadelphia General Hospital[1]	1	—	—	—	—
43	Door of Hope[1]	1	—	—	—	—
44	House of Good Shepherd[1]	1	—	1	—	—
45	Escaped	16	—	1	4	—
46	From Gynecean Hospital	1	—	—	1	—
47	From Philadelphia General Hospital	1	—	—	—	—
48	From sheriff	1	—	—	—	—
49	From other institutions	13	—	1	3	—

[1] Brought into court for contempt of court.
[2] Women's misdemeanants' house of detention.
[3] This was the status so far as the misdemeanants' division was concerned. This court has no record of the disposition of these cases in the criminal court.

TABLE 27—Concluded

AT TIME OF ARREST—Concluded

Disposition and Status at Time of Arrest: **1920**—Concluded

| | Number of cases | | | | | | | | | |
| | Committed to correctional institutions | | | | | Committed to other institutions | | | | |
Line No.	of House Correction	House of Good Shepherd	Sleighton Farm	State Industrial Home for Women	St. Joseph's Protectory	Gynecean Hospital	Philadelphia General Hospital	Door of Hope	Held under bail for criminal court	All others
28	67	20	9	2	1	36	—	1	2	4
29	13	—	2	—	—	3	1	—	1	—
30	7	6	4	2	—	22	—	1	—	2
31	—	—	—	—	—	—	—	—	—	—
32	—	—	—	—	—	—	1	—	—	—
33	39	13	5	1	—	11	2	—	1	4
34	—	—	—	—	—	—	—	—	—	—
35	31	1	1	—	—	3	1	—	1	—
36	7	11	—	—	—	6	1	—	—	4
37	1	1	4	1	—	2	—	—	—	—
38	—	—	—	—	—	—	—	—	—	—
39	6	—	—	—	—	1	—	—	—	1
40	6	—	—	—	—	—	—	—	—	—
41	—	—	—	—	—	—	—	—	—	—
42	—	—	—	—	—	1	—	—	—	—
43	—	—	—	—	—	—	—	—	—	1
44	—	—	—	—	—	—	—	—	—	—
45	8	—	1	—	—	1	1	—	—	—
46	—	—	—	—	—	—	—	—	—	—
47	1	—	—	—	—	—	—	—	—	—
48	1	—	—	—	—	—	—	—	—	—
49	6	—	1	—	—	1	1	—	—	—

[4] It is probable that a number of these women and girls had absconded or had been discharged from probation.

TABLE 28

MANNER OF BRINGING

Cases Disposed of at·Court Hearings, Classified by Officials or Others

Line No.	Offense charged	Total	Arrests					
			Total	Vice squad	Police officer	Park guard	Detective bureau	Store detective
1	All offenses.........	1,941	1,625	828	675	42	28	30
2	Sex offenses	942	930	528	380	18	—	—
3	Disorderly street walking ----------------	566	560	367	190	1	—	—
4	Inmate of disorderly bawdy house ---------	157	156	63	91	—	—	—
5	Frequenting disorderly bawdy house --------	41	39	16	23	—	—	—
6	Disorderly child -------	76	76	28	31	17	—	—
7	Keeping disorderly bawdy house -------	95	94	53	41	—	—	—
8	Other sex offenses -----	7	5	1	4	—	—	—
9	Disorderly conduct -------	306	295	188	86	17	3	—
10	Frequenting and inmate of disorderly house ----	127	125	45	79	—	1	—
11	Drunkenness --------------	51	47	22	22	2	—	—
12	Illegal selling, buying, or possession of narcotic drugs -------------------	36	35	23	12	—	—	—
13	Incorrigibility -------------	144	35	6	18	1	—	7
14	Runaway -------------------	128	92	9	55	3	17	1
15	Violating probation -------	132	14	1	2	—	5	—
16	Sex offenses -----------	43	5	1	1	—	2	—
17	Disorderly street walking -----------	27	3	1	1	—	—	—
18	Other sex offenses..	16	2	—	—	—	2	—
19	Disorderly conduct ----	15	1	—	—	—	1	—
20	Frequenting and inmate of disorderly house...	6	5	—	—	—	—	—
21	Drunkenness -------------	1	—	—	—	—	—	—
22	Incorrigibility ----------	45	2	—	—	—	2	—
23	Runaway -----------,----	22	1	—	1	—	—	—
24	Contempt of court -------	17	4	1	3	—	—	—
25	Sex offenses -----------	8	2	1	1	—	—	—
26	Disorderly conduct ----	3	1	—	1	—	—	—
27	Frequenting and inmate of disorderly house..	2	1	—	1	—	—	—
28	Illegal selling, buying or possession of narcotic drugs ----------------	1	—	—	—	—	—	—
29	Incorrigibility ----------	2	—	—	—	—	—	—
30	Runaway ----------------	1	—	—	—	—	—	—
31	Other offenses -------------	58	48	5	18	1	2	22
32	Larceny -----------------	24	24	—	1	—	1	22
33	Witness ----------------	9	7	—	5	1	1	—
34	Protection -------------	7	1	—	1	—	—	—
35	All others -------------	18	16	5	11	—	—	—

TABLE 28

CASES INTO COURT

and Manner of Bringing Cases in Court, by Offense Charged: 1920

Line No.	Other	Arrests-on warrants				Complaints				All other
		Total	Sheriff	Police officer	Other	Total	Parent	Sheriff	Other	
1	22	209	169	19	21	73	37	12	24	34
2	4	10	6	2	2	1	—	—	1	1
3	2	5	3	1	1	—	—	—	—	1
4	2	—	—	—	—	1	—	—	1	—
5	—	2	1	1	—	—	—	—	—	—
6	—	—	—	—	—	—	—	—	—	—
7	—	1	1	—	—	—	—	—	—	—
8	—	2	1	—	1	—	—	—	—	—
9	1	7	7	—	—	1	—	—	1	3
10	—	1	—	1	—	1	—	—	1	—
11	1	1	1	—	—	3	—	1	2	—
12	—	—	—	—	—	—	—	—	—	1
13	3	58	48	6	4	44	28	5	11	7
14	7	13	8	2	3	14	5	6	3	9
15	6	109	95	6	8	3	2	—	1	6
16	1	38	32	2	4	—	—	—	—	—
17	1	24	20	1	3	—	—	—	—	—
18	—	14	12	1	1	—	—	—	—	—
19	—	12	8	2	2	1	1	—	—	1
20	5	—	—	—	—	—	—	—	—	1
21	—	1	1	—	—	—	—	—	—	—
22	—	39	36	2	1	1	1	—	—	3
23	—	19	18	—	1	1	—	—	1	1
24	—	9	4	1	4	2	—	—	2	2
25	—	5	1	—	4	—	—	—	—	1
26	—	2	1	1	—	—	—	—	—	—
27	—	—	—	—	—	1	—	—	1	—
28	—	—	—	—	—	1	—	—	1	—
29	—	1	1	—	—	—	—	—	—	1
30	—	1	1	—	—	—	—	—	—	—
31	—	1	—	1	—	4	2	—	2	5
32	—	—	—	—	—	—	—	—	—	—
33	—	1	—	1	—	1	—	—	1	—
34	—	—	—	—	—	2	1	—	1	4
35	—	—	—	—	—	1	1	—	—	1

TABLE 29

COLOR AND OFFENSE

Cases Disposed of At Court Hearings and Adjusted Without Court Hearings, Classified by Offense Charged and Color: 1920

Offense charged	Number of cases					
	Disposed of at court hearing			Adjusted without court hearing		
	Total	White	Negro	Total	White	Negro
All offenses	**1,941**	**1,375**	**566**	**253**	**226**	**27**
Sex offenses	942	536	406	6	5	1
Disorderly street walking	566	282	284	2	2	—
Inmate of disorderly bawdy house	157	98	59	1	1	—
Frequenting disorderly bawdy house	41	25	16	—	—	—
Disorderly child	76	62	14	2	2	—
Keeping disorderly bawdy house	95	66	29	—	—	—
Other sex offenses	7	3	4	1	—	1
Disorderly conduct	306	269	37	14	12	2
Frequenting and inmate of disorderly house	127	77	50	—	—	—
Drunkenness	51	50	1	—	—	—
Illegal sale, purchase or possession of narcotic drugs	36	23	13	1	1	—
Incorrigibility	144	119	25	114	97	17
Runaway	128	120	8	62	60	2
Violating probation	132	121	11	6	6	—
Sex offenses	43	37	6	1	1	—
Disorderly street walking	27	22	5	1	1	—
Other sex offenses	16	15	1	—	—	—
Disorderly conduct	15	13	2	1	1	—
Frequenting and inmate of disorderly house	6	6	—	—	—	—
Drunkenness	1	1	—	—	—	—
Incorrigibility	45	42	3	3	3	—
Runaway	22	22	—	—	—	—
Larceny	—	—	—	1	1	—
Contempt of court	17	13	4	—	—	—
Sex offenses	8	5	3	—	—	—
Disorderly conduct	3	3	—	—	—	—
Frequenting and inmate of disorderly house	2	2	—	—	—	—
Illegal possession of narcotic drugs	1	1	—	—	—	—
Incorrigibility	2	1	1	—	—	—
Runaway	1	1	—	—	—	—
Other offenses	58	47	11	50	45	5
Larceny	24	21	3	4	3	1
Witnesses	9	8	1	2	2	—
Protection	7	7	—	38	34	4
All others	18	11	7	6	6	—

TABLE 30

Color of First Offenders and Old Offenders: Cases Disposed of At Court Hearings, Classified by First Offenders and Old Offenders, Offense and Color: 1920

Offense charged	Number of cases						
	Total	First offenders			Old offenders		
		Total	White	Negro	Total	White	Negro
All offenses	**1,941**	**1,183**	**815**	**368**	**758**	**560**	**198**
Sex offenses	942	553	303	250	389	233	156
Disorderly street walking	566	282	125	157	284	157	127
Inmate of disorderly bawdy house	157	108	63	45	49	35	14
Frequenting disorderly bawdy house	41	31	19	12	10	6	4
Disorderly child	76	65	52	13	11	10	1
Keeping disorderly bawdy house	95	61	41	20	34	25	9
Other sex offenses	7	6	3	3	1	—	1
Disorderly conduct	306	204	177	27	102	92	10
Frequenting and inmate of disorderly house	127	102	58	44	25	19	6
Drunkenness	51	26	25	1	25	25	-
Illegal sale, purchase, or possession of narcotic drugs	36	7	4	3	29	19	10
Incorrigibility	144	130	106	24	14	13	1
Runaway	128	111	103	8	17	17	
Violating probation	132	2	1	1	130	119	11
Sex offenses	43	—	—	—	43	37	6
Disorderly street walking	27	—	—	—	27	22	5
Other sex offenses	16	—	—	—	16	15	1
Disorderly conduct	15	1	—	1	14	12	2
Frequenting and inmate of disorderly house	6	—	—	—	6	6	—
Drunkenness	1	—	—	—	1	1	—
Incorrigibility	45	—	—	—	45	42	3
Runaway	22	1	1		21	21	—
Contempt of court	17	—	—	—	17	14	3
Sex offenses	8	—	—	—	8	5	3
Disorderly street walking	4	—	—	—	4	2	2
Other sex offenses	4	—	—	—	4	3	1
Disorderly conduct	3	—	—	—	3	3	—
Frequenting and inmate of disorderly house	2	—	—	—	2	2	—
Illegal possession of narcotic drugs	1	—	—	—	1	1	—
Incorrigibility	2	—	—	—	2	2	—
Runaway	1	—	—	—	1	1	—
Other offenses	58	48	38	10	10	9	1
Larceny	24	21	18	3	3	3	—
Witness	9	8	7	1	1	1	—
Protection	7	6	6	—	1	1	—
All others	18	13	7	6	5	4	1

TABLE 31

AGE

Women and Girls Disposed of At Court Hearings, Classified by Age of First Offenders and Old Offenders:1 920

Age	Number of women and girls					
	Total		First offenders		Old offenders	
	Number	Per cent. distribu- tion	Number	Per cent. distribu- tion	Number	Per cent. distribu- tion
All ages......	1,736	100.0	1,183	100.0	553	100.0
Under 21 years ..	641	36.9	497	42.0	144	26.0
Under 16 years¹ .	3	.2	3	.3	—	—
16 years ..	135	7.8	121	10.2	14	2.5
17 years ..	140	8.1	114	9.6	26	4.7
18 years ..	132	7.6	104	8.8	28	5.1
19 years ..	106	6.1	77	6.5	29	5.2
20 years ...	125	7.2	78	6.6	47	8.5
21 to 24 years ..	376	21.7	269	22.7	107	19.3
25 to 29 years ..	346	19.9	189	16.0	157	28.4
30 to 34 years ..	165	9.5	101	8.5	64	11.6
35 to 39 years ..	94	5.4	59	5.0	35	6.3
40 to 44 years ..	58	3.3	36	3.0	22	4.0
45 to 49 years ..	28	1.6	18	1.5	10	1.8
50 to 54 years ..	20	1.2	8	.7	12	2.2
55 to 59 years ..	3	.2	1	.1	2	.4
60 to 64 years ..	4	.2	4	.3	—	—
70 to 74 years ..	1	.1	1	.1	—	—

¹ Evidence of the correct age of these 3 girls could not be obtained until after the court hearings.

TABLE 32

AGE AND COLOR

Women and Girls Disposed of At Court Hearings Classified by First Offenders and Old Offenders, Age, and Color: 1920

Age	Number of women and girls								
	Total			White			Negro		
	Total	First of-fenders	Old of-fenders	Total	First of-fenders	Old of-fenders	Total	First of-fenders	Old of-fenders
All ages	1,736	1,183	553	1,217	814	403	519	369	150
Under 21 years..	641	497	144	504	381	123	137	116	21
Under 16 years..	3	3	—	3	3	—	—	—	—
16 years..	135	121	14	111	99	12	24	22	2
17 years..	140	114	26	123	99	24	17	15	2
18 years..	132	104	28	105	78	27	27	26	1
19 years..	106	77	29	77	52	25	29	25	4
20 years..	125	78	47	85	50	35	40	28	12
21 to 24 years..	376	269	107	226	162	64	150	107	43
25 to 29 years..	346	189	157	220	119	101	126	70	56
30 to 34 years..	165	101	64	116	66	50	49	35	14
35 to 39 years..	94	59	35	65	38	27	29	21	8
40 to 44 years..	58	36	22	38	22	16	20	14	6
45 to 49 years..	28	18	10	22	13	9	6	5	1
50 to 54 years..	20	8	12	20	8	12	—	—	—
55 to 59 years..	3	1	2	2	1	1	1	—	1
60 to 64 years..	4	4	—	4	4	—	—	—	—
70 to 74 years..	1	1	—	—	—	—	1	1	—.

TABLE 33

AGE AND

Cases Disposed of At Court Hearings, Classified by

Line No.	Offense charged	Number of cases							
		All ages	Under 21 years						
			Total	Under 16 years	16 years	17 years	18 years	19 years	20 years
1	All offenses	1,941	721	9	143	163	154	116	136
2	Sex offenses	942	182	3	22	38	36	30	53
3	Disorderly street walking	566	67	1	—	4	6	20	36
4	Inmate of disorderly bawdy house	157	33	—	5	7	9	3	9
5	Frequenting disorderly bawdy house	41	3	—	—	—	2	—	1
6	Disorderly child	76	76	2	17	27	19	7	4
7	Keeping disorderly bawdy house	95	3	—	—	—	—	—	3
8	Other sex offenses	7	—	—	—	—	—	—	—
9	Disorderly conduct	306	101	2	10	16	14	30	29
10	Frequenting and inmate of disorderly house	127	36	1	3	4	15	5	8
11	Drunkenness	51	7	—	—	2	3	1	1
12	Illegal sale, purchase, or possession of drugs	36	—	—	—	—	—	—	—
13	Incorrigibility	144	142	1	55	37	19	16	14
14	Runaway	128	125	2	36	42	30	6	9
15	Violating probation	132	89	—	15	16	28	18	12
16	Sex offenses	43	14	—	1	4	4	2	3
17	Disorderly street walking	27	4	—	1	—	—	—	3
18	Other sex offenses	16	10	—	—	4	4	2	—
19	Disorderly conduct	15	5	—	1	—	1	2	1
20	Frequenting and inmate of disorderly house	6	5	—	1	—	2	1	1
21	Drunkenness	1	—	—	—	—	—	—	—
22	Incorrigibility	45	45	—	5	8	15	11	6
23	Runaway	22	20	—	7	4	6	2	1
24	Contempt of court	17	9	—	—	2	2	—	5
25	Sex offenses	8	5	—	—	1	1	—	3
26	Disorderly conduct	3	1	—	—	—	—	—	1
27	Frequenting and inmate of disorderly house	2	1	—	—	—	—	—	1
28	Illegal sale, purchase or possession of drugs	1	—	—	—	—	—	—	—
29	Incorrigibility	2	1	—	—	1	—	—	—
30	Runaway	1	1	—	—	—	1	—	—
31	Other offenses	58	30	—	2	6	7	10	5
32	Larceny	24	15	—	1	2	3	6	3
33	Witness	9	5	—	—	3	—	2	—
34	Protection	7	6	—	1	1	2	1	1
35	All others	18	4	—	—	—	2	1	1

TABLE 33

OFFENSE

Offense Charged and Age of Offender: **1920**

Line No.	Number of cases									
		21 years and over								
	Total	21 to 24 years	25 to 29 years	30 to 34 years	35 to 39 years	40 to 44 years	45 to 49 years	50 to 54 years	55 to 59 years	60 yrs. and over
1	1,220	417	386	177	106	65	32	28	4	5
2	760	242	243	120	68	38	23	17	4	5
3	499	172	162	82	41	19	9	13	1	—
4	124	45	39	21	8	3	4	2	1	1
5	38	13	12	6	3	—	4	—	—	—
6	—	—	—	—	—	—	—	—	—	—
7	92	9	29	10	15	15	6	2	2	—
8	7	3	1	1	1	1	—	—	—	—
9	205	89	58	25	15	12	4	2	—	—
10	91	39	33	7	8	3	—	1	—	—
11	44	3	9	9	9	5	4	5	—	—
12	36	4	19	9	1	2	1	—	—	—
13	2	2	—	—	—	—	—	—	—	—
14	3	3	—	—	—	—	—	—	—	—
15	43	15	17	3	4	3	—	1	—	—
16	29	7	12	3	4	2	—	1	—	—
17	23	5	9	3	3	2	—	1	—	—
18	6	2	3	—	1	—	—	—	—	—
19	10	5	4	—	—	1	—	—	—	—
20	1	1	—	—	—	—	—	—	—	—
21	1	—	1	—	—	—	—	—	—	—
22	—	—	—	—	—	—	—	—	—	—
23	2	2	—	—	—	—	—	—	—	—
24	8	3	2	—	—	2	—	1	—	—
25	3	1	—	—	—	1	—	1	—	—
26	2	—	1	—	—	1	—	—	—	—
27	1	1	—	—	—	—	—	—	—	—
28	1	—	1	—	—	—	—	—	—	—
29	1	1	—	—	—	—	—	—	—	—
30	—	—	—	—	—	—	—	—	—	—
31	28	17	5	4	1	—	—	1	—	—
32	9	7	1	1	—	—	—	—	—	—
33	4	4	—	—	—	—	—	—	—	—
34	1	1	—	—	—	—	—	—	—	—
35	14	5	4	3	1	—	—	1	—	—

TABLE 34

MENTAL CONDITION

Cases Disposed of at Court Hearings,

Line No.	Offense charged	Number of cases		Examined	
		Total	Not examined	Total	Normal
1	**All offenses**	**1,941**	**339**	**1,602**	**1,040**
2	Sex offenses	942	206	736	529
3	Disorderly street walking	566	88	478	347
4	Inmate of disorderly bawdy house	157	47	108	84
5	Frequenting disorderly bawdy house	41	19	22	18
6	Disorderly child	76	11	65	33
7	Keeping disorderly bawdy house	95	39	56	45
8	Other sex offenses	7	2	5	2
9	Disorderly conduct	306	45	261	164
10	Frequenting and inmate of disorderly house	127	21	106	74
11	Drunkenness	51	12	39	28
12	Illegal selling, buying, or possession of narcotic drugs	36	10	26	20
13	Incorrigibility	144	14	130	65
14	Runaway	128	10	118	65
15	Violating probation	132	7	125	56
16	Sex offenses	43	1	42	22
17	Disorderly street walking	27	1	26	17
18	Other sex offenses	16	—	16	5
19	Disorderly conduct	15	3	12	6
20	Frequenting and inmate of disorderly house	6	—	6	3
21	Drunkenness	1	—	1	—
22	Incorrigibility	5	3	42	18
23	Runaway	22	—	22	7
24	Contempt of court	17	2	15	7
25	Sex offenses	8	1	7	2
26	Disorderly conduct	3	1	2	—
27	Frequenting and inmate of disorderly house	2	—	2	2
28	Illegal selling,, buying or possession of narcotic drugs	1	—	1	1
29	Incorrigibility	2	—	2	2
30	Runaway	1	—	1	—
31	Other offenses	58	11	47	30
32	Larceny	24	3	21	16
33	Witnesses	9	2	7	4
34	Protection	7	2	5	2
35	All others	18	4	14	8

TABLE 34

AND OFFENSE

Classified by Mental Condition and Offense Charged: 1920

Line No.	Number of cases						
	Examined						
	Retarded	Border line	Moron	Psychoses	Psycho-neuroses	Psycho-pathic personality	Epileptic
1	112	27	24	3	30	359	7
2	35	6	6	—	12	141	5
3	17	2	5	—	10	93	4
4	4	1	1	—	1	16	1
5	—	—	—	—	—	4	—
6	12	2	—	—	—	18	—
7	—	—	—	—	1	10	—
8	2	1	—	—	—	—	—
9	23	5	6	1	2	59	1
10	3	1	2	—	3	23	—
11	2	1	—	—	—	8	—
12	—	—	—	1	1	4	—
13	18	4	5	—	4	33	1
14	14	4	5	—	3	27	—
15	9	4	—	—	4	52	—
16	2	1	—	—	1	16	—
17	1	—	—	—	—	8	—
18	1	1	—	—	1	8	—
19	2	—	—	—	1	3	—
20	—	—	—	—	1	2	—
21	—	—	—	—	—	1	—
22	2	—	—	—	1	21	—
23	3	3	—	—	—	9	—
24	1	1	—	—	1	5	—
25	1	—	—	—	—	4	—
26	—	—	—	—	1	1	—
27	—	—	—	—	—	—	—
28	—	—	—	—	—	—	—
29	—	—	—	—	—	—	—
30	—	1	—	—	—	—	—
31	7	2	—	1	—	7	—
32	3	—	—	—	—	2	—
33	1	1	—	—	—	1	—
34	1	—	—	—	—	2	—
35	2	1	—	1	—	2	—

TABLE 35

MENTAL CONDITION AND COLOR

Cases Disposed of At Court Hearings, Classified by Mental Condition and Color: 1920

Mental condition	Number of cases						
	Total	White			Negro		
		Total	First offenders	Old offenders	Total	First offenders	Old offenders
All conditions ..	1,941	1,375	815	560	566	368	198
Examined.......	1,602	1,136	655	481	466	285	181
Normal	1,040	680	425	255	360	231	129
Retarded	112	94	61	33	18	10	8
Border line	27	27	18	9	—	—	—
Moron	24	16	11	5	8	5	3
Psychoses	3	2	2	—	1	1	—
Psychoneuroses and neuroses	30	25	15	10	5	3	2
Constitutional psychopathic inferior	359	286	123	163	73	34	39
Epileptic	7	6	—	6	1	1	—
Not examined	339	239	160	79	100	83	17

TABLE 36

MENTAL CONDITION AND AGE

Women and Girls Disposed of At Court Hearings, Classified by Mental Condition and Age: 1920

Mental condition	Number of women and girls			
	Total	Age		
		Under 21 years	21 to 44 years	45 years and over
Total	1,736	641	1,039	56
Examined	1,417	576	808	33
Normal	941	339	574	28
Retarded	98	57	41	—
Border line	23	16	7	—
Moron	21	12	9	—
Psychoses	3	—	3	—
Psychoneuroses	27	9	16	2
Constitutional psychopathic inferior	300	142	155	3
Epileptic	4	1	3	—
Not examined	319	65	231	23

TABLE 37

VENEREAL DISEASE

Cases Disposed of At Court Hearings, Classified by Venereal

Line No.	Venereal disease	Number of cases					
		All offenses	Disorderly street walking	Inmate of disorderly bawdy house	Frequenting disorderly bawdy house	Disorderly child	Keeping disorderly bawdy house
1	Total	1,941	566	157	41	76	95
2	Examined	1,852	558	145	40	67	86
3	Not infected	859	209	67	19	29	46
4	Infected	993	349	78	21	38	40
5	Gonorrhea	467	129	42	9	25	17
6	Syphilis	319	140	27	8	9	10
7	Active	214	92	16	5	7	9
8	1 plus	3	3	—	—	—	—
9	2 plus	24	11	1	—	—	—
10	3 plus	26	11	1	1	1	—
11	4 plus	157	66	13	3	6	8
12	Not reported	4	1	1	1	—	1
13	Not active	105	48	11	3	2	1
14	1 plus	3	2	—	—	—	—
15	2 plus	7	4	—	—	—	—
16	3 plus	14	7	2	—	—	—
17	4 plus	75	33	8	3	2	1
18	Not reported	6	2	1	—	—	—
19	Gonorrhea and syphilis	207	80	9	4	4	13
20	Syphilis active	166	60	7	3	3	11
21	1 plus	2	—	—	1	—	—
22	2 plus	21	7	1	—	—	—
23	3 plus	24	11	—	—	1	—
24	4 plus	94	37	6	1	—	10
25	Not reported	25	5	—	1	2	1
26	Syphilis not active	41	20	2	1	1	2
27	3 plus	7	2	—	—	—	—
28	4 plus	22	12	1	1	—	2
29	Not reported	12	6	1	—	1	—
30	Not examined or results unsatisfactory	89	8	12	1	9	9

TABLE 37

AND OFFENSE

Disease and Offense Charged: **1920**

Line No.		Number of cases								
	Disorderly conduct	·Frequenting and inmate of disorderly house	Drunkenness	Illegal sale, purchase or possession of narcotic drugs·	Incorrigibility	Runaway	Violating probation	Contempt of court	Other offenses
1	306	127	51	36	144	128	132	17	65
2	294	111	51	35	135	119	132	17	62
3	148	59	31	11	71	68	66	5	30
4	146	52	20	24	64	51	66	12	32
5	71	24	8	8	46	32	34	6	16
6	40	18	6	10	13	6	17	3	12
7	26	16	3	6	10	5	10	2	7
8	—	—	—	—	—	—	—	—	—
9	7	2	—	—	2	—	—	1	—
10	4	1	—	—	3	2	2	—	—
11	15	13	3	6	5	3	8	1	7
12	—	—	—	—	—	—	—	—	—
13	14	2	3	4	3	1	7	1	5
14	—	—	1	—	—	—	—	—	—
15	2	—	—	1	—	—	—	—	—
16	1	—	—	1	1	—	2	—	—
17	10	2	2	2	1	1	5	1	4
18	1	—	—	—	1	—	—	—	1
19	35	10	6	6	5	13	15	3	4
20	30	10	6	5	4	10	11	2	4
21	—	—	—	—	—	1	—	—	—
22	7	1	—	2	—	1	1	1	—
23	3	3	1	—	1	1	1	—	2
24	18	6	2	2	1	5	4	1	1
25	2	—	3	1	2	2	5	—	1
26	5	—	—	1	1	3	4	1	—
27	1	—	—	—	—	1	3	—	—
28	2	—	—	1	1	1	—	1	—
29	2	—	—	—	—	1	1	—	—
30	12	16	—	1	9	9	—	—	3

TABLE 38

VENEREAL

Cases Disposed of At Court Hearings, Classified by Venereal Disease at

Line No.	Venereal disease at next to last appearance in court	Number of cases and venereal disease at last appearance in court			
		Total	Not examined or results not satisfactory	Examined	
				Total	Not infected
1	Total	1,941	89	1,852	859
2	Examined	753	1	752	307
3	Not infected	342	—	342	207
4	Infected	411	1	410	100
5	Gonorrhea	143	—	143	43
6	Syphilis	134	1	133	28
7	Active	127	1	126	26
8	Not active	7	—	7	2
9	Gonorrhea and syphilis	134	—	134	29
10	Syphilis active	134	—	134	29
11	Syphilis not active	—	—	—	—
12	First offenders	[1]1,188	88	1,100	552

[1] Includes 1,183 first offenders and 5 old offenders.

TABLE 38

DISEASE

Last Appearance in Court and Next to Last Appearance in Court: 1920

Line No.	Number of cases and venereal diseases at last appearance in court							
			Examined					
			Infected					
	Total	Gon-orrhea	Syphilis			Gonorrhea and Syphilis		
			Total	Active	Not active	Total	Syphilis active	Syphilis not active
1	993	467	319	214	105	207	166	41
2	445	199	141	81	60	105	95	10
3	135	84	26	18	8	25	21	4
4	310	115	115	63	52	80	74	6
5	100	76	9	7	2	15	12	3
6	105	13	66	29	37	26	25	1
7	100	12	62	29	33	26	25	1
8	5	1	4	—	4	—	—	—
9	105	26	40	27	13	39	37	2
10	105	26	40	27	13	39	37	2
11	—	—	—	—	—	—	—	—
12	548	268	178	133	45	102	71	31

TABLE 39

VENEREAL DISEASE,

Cases Disposed of At Court Hearings, Classified by

Line No.	Venereal disease	Number of cases				
		Total	Dis-charged	Placed on probation or probation continued		
				Regular	With medical super-vision	To leave town
1	Total	1,941	339	447	151	49
2	Examined	1,852	284	428	150	48
3	Not infected	859	207	342	—	38
4	Infected	993	77	86	150	10
5	Gonorrhea	467	33	24	51	6
6	Syphilis	319	37	42	83	3
7	Active	214	22	22	60	2
8	1 plus	3	—	—	2	—
9	2 plus	24	1	4	5	—
10	3 plus	26	2	2	13	1
11	4 plus	157	17	16	40	1
12	Not reported	4	2	—	—	—
13	Not active	105	15	20	23	1
14	1 plus	3	—	2	1	—
15	2 plus	7	1	1	1	—
16	3 plus	14	3	2	4	—
17	4 plus	75	10	13	17	1
18	Not reported	6	1	2	—	—
19	Gonorrhea and syphilis	207	7	20	16	1
20	Syphilis active	166	6	14	11	1
21	1 plus	2	—	—	—	1
22	2 plus	21	2	3	4	—
23	3 plus	24	1	—	—	—
24	4 plus	94	2	4	7	—
25	Not reported	25	1	7	—	—
26	Syphilis not active	41	1	6	5	—
27	3 plus	7	—	—	—	—
28	4 plus	22	1	3	5	—
29	Not reported	12	—	3	—	—
30	Not examined or results unsatisfactory	89	55	19	1	1

TABLE 39

AND DISPOSITION

Venereal Disease and Nature of Disposition: 1920

Line No.	Number of cases									
	Committed to correctional institutions					Committed to other institutions			Held under bail for criminal court	All others
	House of Correction	House of Good Shepherd	Sleighton Farm	State Industrial Home for Women	St. Joseph's Protectory	Gynecean Hospital	Philadelphia General Hospital	Door of Hope		
1	452	83	38	8	6	258	15	10	46	39
2	447	81	38	8	5	258	14	9	44	38
3	129	53	13	6	4	2	5	7	34	19
4	318	28	25	2	1	256	9	2	10	19
5	127	4	17	2	—	186	4	1	2	10
6	106	17	5	—	1	11	2	—	7	5
7	72	12	2	—	1	10	2	—	5	4
8	1	—	—	—	—	—	—	—	—	—
9	9	2	—	—	—	—	1	—	—	2
10	5	—	—	—	—	3	—	—	—	—
11	56	10	2	—	1	7	1	—	4	2
12	1	—	—	—	—	—	—	—	1	—
13	34	5	3	—	—	1	—	—	2	1
14	—	—	—	—	—	—	—	—	—	—
15	3	1	—	—	—	—	—	—	—	—
16	3	—	2	—	—	—	—	—	—	—
17	26	3	1	—	—	1	—	—	2	1
18	2	1	—	—	—	—	—	—	—	—
19	85	7	3	—	—	59	3	1	1	4
20	70	6	3	—	—	49	2	1	1	2
21	—	—	—	—	—	1	—	—	—	—
22	9	—	—	—	—	2	1	—	—	—
23	13	—	—	—	—	10	—	—	—	—
24	40	3	—	—	—	35	1	—	1	1
25	8	3	3	—	—	1	—	1	—	1
26	15	1	—	—	—	10	1	—	—	2
27	3	1	—	—	—	3	—	—	—	—
28	7	—	—	—	—	4	1	—	—	—
29	5	—	—	—	—	3	—	—	—	1
30	5	2	—	—	1	—	1	1	2	1

TABLE 40

VENEREAL DISEASE AND COLOR

Cases Disposed of at Court Hearings, Classified by Venereal Disease at Time of
First Arrest in 1920 and color: 1920

Venereal disease and Wasserman reaction in syphilis cases	Number of cases						
	Total	White			Negro		
		Total	First offenders	Old offenders	Total	First offenders	Old offenders
Total	1,941	1,375	815	560	566	368	198
Examined	1,852	1,299	739	560	553	355	198
Not infected	859	631	395	236	228	156	72
Infected	993	668	344	324	325	199	126
Gonorrhea	467	356	191	165	111	78	33
Syphilis	319	178	92	86	141	85	56
Active	214	126	73	53	88	60	28
1 plus	3	2	1	1	1	—	1
2 plus	24	13	6	7	11	7	4
3 plus	26	17	11	6	9	5	4
4 plus	157	91	53	38	66	47	19
Not reported ---	4	3	2	1	1	1	—
Not active ---	105	52	19	33	53	25	28
1 plus	3	3	—	3	—	—	—
2 plus	17	2	2	—	5	—	5
3 plus	14	9	3	6	5	1	4
4 plus	75	35	11	24	40	21	19
Not reported ---	6	3	3	—	3	3	—
Gonorrhea and syphilis	207	134	61	73	73	36	37
Syphilis active.	166	109	43	66	57	26	31
1 plus	2	2	1	1	—	—	—
2 plus	21	14	6	8	7	3	4
3 plus	24	15	6	9	9	7	2
4 plus	94	60	29	31	34	16	18
Not reported ---	25	18	1	17	7	—	7
Syphilis not active	41	25	18	7	16	10	0
3 plus	7	3	2	1	4	—	4
4 plus	22	14	10	4	8	6	2
Not reported ---	12	8	6	2	4	4	—
Not examined or results unsatisfactory	89	76	76	—	13	13	—

TABLE 41

VENEREAL DISEASE AND AGE

Women and Girls Disposed of At Court Hearings, Classified by Venereal Disease and Age: 1920

Venereal disease	Number of women and girls							
	Total	Under 21 years	21 to 24 years	25 to 29 years	30 to 34 years	35 to 39 years	40 to 44 years	45 years and over
Total	1,736	641	376	346	165	94	58	56
Not examined	103	55	13	14	10	5	3	3
Examined	1,633	586	363	332	155	89	55	53
Not infected	776	307	157	142	70	44	33	23
Infected	857	279	206	190	85	45	22	30
Infected	857	279	206	190	85	45	22	30
Gonorrhea	404	160	89	81	35	17	7	15
Syphilis	294	77	67	71	39	21	9	10
Active	202	63	49	49	19	12	5	5
1 plus	2	—	2	—	—	—	—	—
2 plus	24	8	4	4	3	4	1	—
3 plus	22	11	2	5	2	—	1	1
4 plus	146	38	40	40	14	8	2	4
Not specified	8	6	1	—	—	—	1	—
Not active	92	14	18	22	20	9	4	5
1 plus	2	—	—	—	1	1	—	—
2 plus	6	1	1	1	2	1	—	—
3 plus	11	2	4	3	1	1	—	—
4 plus	67	10	12	17	15	5	4	4
Not specified	6	1	1	1	1	1	—	1
Gonorrhea and syphilis	159	42	50	38	11	7	6	5
With syphilis active	125	32	42	30	8	6	4	3
2 plus	17	5	4	6	1	—	1	—
3 plus	21	9	8	3	1	—	—	—
4 plus	84	16	29	21	6	6	3	3
Not specified	1	1	—	—	—	—	—	—
With syphilis not active	34	10	8	8	3	1	2	2
3 plus	3	1	—	2	—	—	—	—
4 plus	21	6	4	5	1	1	2	2
Not specified	10	3	4	1	2	—	—	—

TABLE 42

VENEREAL DISEASE AND

Cases Disposed of At Court Hearings, Classified by Mental Condition

Line No.	Venereal disease and Wasserman reaction in syphilis cases	Number of cases			
				Examined	
		Total	Not examined	Total	Normal
1	Total	1,941	339	1,602	1,040
2	Examined	1,852	294	1,558	1,005
3	Not infected	859	140	719	469
4	Infected	993	154	839	536
5	Gonorrhea	467	51	416	260
6	Syphilis	319	64	255	172
7	Active	214	35	179	119
8	1 plus	3	1	2	2
9	2 plus	24	3	21	15
10	3 plus	26	3	23	16
11	4 plus	157	25	132	86
12	Not reported	4	3	1	—
13	Not active	105	29	76	53
14	1 plus	3	1	2	—
15	2 plus	7	2	5	4
16	3 plus	14	6	8	3
17	4 plus	75	17	58	43
18	Not reported	6	3	3	3
19	Gonorrhea and syphilis	207	39	168	104
20	Syphilis active	166	28	138	78
21	1 plus	2	1	1	1
22	2 plus	21	3	18	9
23	3 plus	24	3	21	13
24	4 plus	94	16	78	48
25	Not reported	25	5	20	7
26	Syphilis not active	41	11	30	26
27	3 plus	7	2	5	3
28	4 plus	22	7	15	14
29	Not reported	12	2	10	9
30	Not examined or results unsatisfactory	89	45	44	35

TABLE 42

MENTAL CONDITION

and Venereal Disease At First Arrest in 1920: **1920**

Line No.		Number of cases					
		Examined					
	Retarded	Border line	Moron	Psychoses	Psycho-neuroses and neuroses	Constitutional psychopathic inferior	Epileptic
1	112	27	24	3	30	359	7
2	110	27	24	3	30	352	7
3	55	13	11	2	11	157	1
4	55	14	13	1	19	195	6
5	30	10	8	—	5	101	2
6	12	3	4	1	8	54	1
7	6	1	3	1	6	42	1
8	—	—	—	—	—	—	—
9	—	1	1	—	—	4	—
10	2	—	—	—	—	4	1
11	3	—	2	1	6	34	—
12	1	—	—	—	—	—	—
13	6	2	1	—	2	12	—
14	—	—	—	—	—	2	—
15	—	—	—	—	—	1	—
16	2	—	—	—	—	3	—
17	4	2	1	—	2	6	—
18	—	—	—	—	—	—	—
19	13	1	1	—	6	40	3
20	12	1	1	—	6	37	3
21	—	—	—	—	—	—	—
22	—	—	—	—	1	7	1
23	8	—	—	—	—	4	1
24	6	—	1	—	5	17	1
25	3	1	—	—	—	9	—
26	1	—	—	—	—	3	—
27	1	—	—	—	—	1	—
28	—	—	—	—	—	1	—
29	—	—	—	—	—	1	—
30	2	—	—	—	—	7	—

TABLE 43

DISPOSITION IN

Cases Involving Women and Girls Under the Court's Care Brought in for Rehearing,
Rehearing:

Line No.	Disposition after rehearing	Number of cases					
			Status at time of rehearing				
					Paroled from		Held under bail for criminal court
		Total	On probation	On medical probation	House of Correction	House of Good Shepherd	
1	All dispositions	559	38	17	3	3	5
2	Discharged	60	4	6	1	—	2
3	Outright	48	4	6	1	—	2
4	To leave town in care of individual	8	—	—	—	—	—
5	To marry	3	—	—	—	—	—
6	In care of individual	1	—	—	—	—	—
7	Probation or parole	382	11	8	1	2	2
8	Regular	197	—	2	—	—	2
9	With medical supervision	161	3	—	—	—	—
10	To leave town in care of individual	7	1	—	—	—	—
11	Probation or parole continued—regular	11	7	—	1	2	—
12	Probation or parole continued with medical supervision	6	—	6	—	—	—
13	Committed or remanded to hospitals	24	1	—	—	—	—
14	Gynecean Hospital	8	1	—	—	—	—
15	Philadelphia General Hospital	7	—	—	—	—	—
16	House of Detention[1]	9	—	—	—	—	—
17	Committed or remanded to correctional institutions	66	4	1	1	—	1
18	House of Correction	38	1	—	—	—	1
19	House of Good Shepherd	13	3	1	1	—	—
20	Sleighton Farm	9	—	—	—	—	—
21	State Industrial Home for Women	1	—	—	—	—	—
22	All others	27	18	2	—	1	—

[1] Women's Misdemeanants' House of Detention.

TABLE 43

REHEARING CASES

Classified by Status at Time of Rehearing and Nature of Disposition After 1920

Line No.		Number of cases						
		Status at time of rehearing						
	In House of Correction	In House of Good Shepherd	In Sleighton Farm	In Gynecean Hospital	Held in house[1] for treatment	In Philadelphia General Hospital	In Door of Hope	All other
1	167	74	13	192	18	8	5	16
2	34	4	—	6	1	1	—	1
3	28	2	—	2	1	1	—	1
4	4	2	—	2	—	—	—	—
5	2	—	—	1	—	—	—	—
6	—	—	—	1	—	—	—	—
7	109	54	8	153	13	5	3	13
8	99	51	8	20	2	1	3	9
9	10	1	—	131	9	4	—	3
10	—	2	—	2	2	—	—	—
11	—	—	—	—	—	—	—	1
12	—	—	—	—	—	—	—	—
13	3	—	1	15	3	1	—	—
14	2	—	—	5	—	—	—	—
15	1	—	1	3	1	1	—	—
16	—	—	—	7	2	—	—	—
17	21	13	4	17	1	—	1	2
18	21	5	—	8	1	—	1	—
19	—	6	—	7	—	—	—	—
20	—	2	4	1	—	—	—	2
21	—	—	—	1	—	—	—	—
22	—	3	—	1	—	1	1	—

TABLE 44

OFFENSE AND

Complaint Cases Adjusted by Probation Department Without

Line No	Offense charged	Number of cases					
		Total	Nature of adjustment				
			Adjusted by field worker	Placed under supervision	Committed to		Held for guardian
					Gynecean Hospital	Philadelphia General Hospital	
1	All offenses	253	38	60	9	8	30
2	Sex offenses	6	—	—	—	—	2
3	Disorderly street walking	2	—	—	—	—	2
4	Inmate of disorderly bawdy house	1	—	—	—	—	—
5	Disorderly child	2	—	—	—	—	—
6	Other sex offenses	1	—	—	—	—	—
7	Disorderly conduct	14	2	1	1	1	—
8	Illegal possession of drugs	1	—	—	—	1	—
9	Incorrigibility	114	23	43	1	2	1
10	Runaway	62	5	6	4	1	18
11	Violating probation	6	1	1	2	1	1
12	Disorderly street walking	1	—	—	—	1	—
13	Disorderly conduct	1	1	—	—	—	—
14	Incorrigibility	3	—	—	2	—	1
15	Larceny	1	—	1	—	—	—
16	Other offenses	50	7	9	1	2	8
17	Larceny	4	—	—	—	—	—
18	Witness	2	—	1	—	—	—
19	Protection	38	7	8	1	1	3
20	All others	6	—	—	—	1	5

[1] Not included in total number of cases adjusted.

TABLE 44

DISPOSITION

Court Hearing, Classified by Offense and Nature of Adjustment:

Line No.	Number of cases							
	Nature of adjustment							
	Discharged			Returned to authorities in other city	Referred to other divisions	Referred to outside agencies	Dropped	Complaint—girl not brought in—warrant issued[1]
	Outright	In care of individual	To leave town with relative					
1	5	10	9	1	13	9	61	1
2	—	1	—	—	2	1	—	—
3	—	—	—	—	—	—	—	—
4	—	1	—	—	—	—	—	—
5	—	—	—	—	1	1	—	—
6	—	—	—	—	1	—	—	—
7	2	—	1	—	1	1	4	1
8	—	—	—	—	—	—	—	—
9	2	1	—	—	5	1	35	—
10	1	8	5	1	1	2	10	—
11	—	—	—	—	—	—	—	—
12	—	—	—	—	—	—	—	—
13	—	—	—	—	—	—	—	—
14	—	—	—	—	—	—	—	—
15	—	—	—	—	—	—	—	—
16	—	—	3	—	4	4	12	—
17	—	—	2	—	1	—	1	—
18	—	—	1	—	—	—	—	—
19	—	—	—	—	3	4	11	—
20	—	—	—	—	—	—	—	—

TABLE 45

DRUG USERS

Women and Girls Disposed of at Court Hearings, Classified by Use of Drugs and Old
and New Offenders: 1920

Use of drugs	Women and girls					
	Total		First offenders		Old offenders	
	Number	Per cent. distribu- tion	Number	Per cent. distribu- tion	Number	Per cent. distribu- tion
All women and girls	1,736	100.0	1,183	100.0	553	100.0
Do not use drugs	1,626	93.7	1,137	96.1	489	88.4
Drug users	110	6.3	46	3.9	64	11.6
Kind of drug used not reported	11	.6	7	.6	4	.7
Heroin	73	4.2	24	2.0	49	8.9
Morphin	20	1.2	10	.8	10	1.8
Cocain	4	.2	3	.3	1	.2
Opium	2	.1	2	.2	—	—

CHAPTER III

THE SECOND SESSIONS OF THE MUNICIPAL COURT OF THE CITY OF BOSTON

The branch of the Municipal Court of the City of Boston which hears cases of sex delinquency is known as the Second Sessions. This is not a specialized court, in that besides hearing all cases in which one of the defendants is a woman, it also tries many other kinds of misdemeanors and violations of municipal ordinances regardless of the sex of the defendant. An observation of eight sessions revealed that the offenses ranged all the way from walking on the grass in the park to selling decayed meat, and from violating traffic ordinances to selling bananas without a license. This court, while not specialized within the strict meaning of the term, corresponds, nevertheless, to the courts studied in Chicago and Philadelphia.

JURISDICTION

The Municipal Court of the City of Boston, sometimes called the Central Court, was created by Act of the Legislature in 1866, succeeding the Police Court of Boston.[1] This court, in turn, was "an outgrowth and modification of the old justice of the peace system." The Municipal Court sits in the Suffolk County Court House and its jurisdiction embraces wards six, seven, eight, nine, ten, eleven, twelve, sixteen, seventeen, and eighteen. This area includes all of the old City of Boston, containing practically all of the more important hotels and lodging houses, the business district, and a large

---

[1] Report of Commission of Legislature on the Inferior Courts of Suffolk County, 1912, p. 5.

portion of the residential district. In greater Boston, there are other district courts of concurrent jurisdiction, viz: Brighton, Charlestown, Dorchester, East Boston, Roxbury, South Boston, West Roxbury, and Chelsea. The present study, however, will be limited to the Central Court.

The Municipal Court has original criminal jurisdiction of all misdemeanors except conspiracies and libels, and of all felonies which are punishable by imprisonment in the state prison for not more than five years.[1] In 1906, the Boston Juvenile Court with jurisdiction of offenses involving children under the age of seventeen was created.

The Second and Final Report of the Judicature Commission, 1921, says:

The word "inferior" often used as to these courts is a purely technical term when properly used, but is apt to have an unfortunate significance in the minds of many people. The courts are not "inferior" in importance in any sense whatever. They are in many ways the most important courts in the Commonwealth because of the fact that they represent the administration of justice in Massachusetts to the minds of more people than any other courts.

The Municipal Court of the City of Boston, because of its position as the central court in the largest city of the state, . . . forms a class by itself, and has been so dealt with by the legislature. There are normally . . . 60,000 criminal entries in this court annually. The administrative experiments, which have been tried in this court with the authority of the legislature, particularly under the act of 1912, have brought it into a position as a modern court with reasonable equipment and opportunities for service, so that it is capable of still further development in its usefulness whenever the legislature considers it advisable to take the necessary steps.

The Second Sessions, with which the present study is concerned, hears cases of persons seventeen years of age and over, including all cases in which the defendant is a woman. There are nine justices of the Central Court, including the

---

[1] Report of the Commission of Legislature on the Inferior Courts of Suffolk County, 1912, p. 6.

chief justice, and, in addition, there are four special justices. The chief justice does not sit regularly in any session and the other justices rotate between different sessions throughout the year. Under this arrangement the judge is changed in the Second Sessions approximately every seven weeks. There are twenty-six probation officers attached to the Central Court, three of whom (one man and two women) are assigned to the Second Sessions.

Trial by jury is not provided in the laws establishing the Municipal Court of Boston, neither does the trial of a criminal case in that court constitute a waiver to the constitutional right of trial by jury, under the present law. Appeal lies in all criminal cases as a matter of course. Appealed cases automatically go to the Superior Court where the case is tried de novo [1] before a jury, without reference to the prior trial in the court below. The following quotation from the Final Report of the Judicature Commission [2] gives a true picture of what happens in cases appealed from the Municipal Court:

The present number of terms (was) provided for several years ago, since which time criminal business of the county has increased tremendously, approximately 300 per cent. In 1919 two or three special sittings have been had, but even then entirely inadequate to help out the situation. At the beginning of each regular sitting we have approximately 500 cases. Jury sittings are of three weeks' duration, fifteen days in all. We cannot try over one case every day,

---

[1] ''The present method of de novo retrial of facts is fast becoming obsolete; it is a survival of the justice of the peace . . . courts, which are themselves largely of the past; through the ease with which the lower court judgments may be vacated, it precludes respect for the court which enters them; it conduces to lax work of bench and bar; it consumes in legal expense an undue proportion of the amount in dispute, in a class of cases least able to bear such expense; it tends to increase the so-called gambling element of litigation, and there are not wanting evidences that it is fostering a tendency at the second trial to make the evidence fit the needs of the case; in a word, it is a direct encouragement of perjury.'' Report of the Commission of Legislature on the Inferior Courts of Suffolk County, 1912, pp. 12–13.

[2] Loc. cit., pp. 91–93.

on an average. This means that substantially 485 must be disposed of in some manner other than trial. This of necessity means filing as disposition, and unwarranted leniency in many cases, a situation we are practically forced into.[1]   The pressure of business is so great that cases cannot be as fully examined by either the district attorney or the court as is desirable.

At present long gaps between March and June and September sittings mean big volume of grand jury work in June and September. Decision in the case of Commonwealth vs. Harris, requiring separate examination of witnesses, makes the work extremely cumbersome. Tremendous increase in automobile cases, transfers of bastardy cases to criminal court, extradition in non-support cases, and cases coming to us through newly created statutes, such as Fire Prevention Bureau, etc., has given criminal courts a large amount of new work.

I cannot too strongly inveigh against the present state of affairs in the administration of the criminal law. . . . The tremendous pressure of business does make it impossible to handle cases as they should be handled. The government is practically at the mercy of such defendants as are represented by counsel, who know very well that if they advise their clients to insist on a plea of not guilty and a trial they can clog the meager term of court to the point where the district attorney will himself cry for mercy. That the district attorney may take them at their word now and then, and make them try or plead, is so much of an uncertainty that it fails to daunt them.

Consequently the district attorney and his assistants call in police officers and government witnesses and get their stories. Then defendants' counsel are heard, and then, unless a trial is absolutely unescapable, a crime is disposed of by agreement between counsel, and the judge is asked to rubber-stamp the agreement with his O. K. If there is the slightest doubt that he will do so the case goes off the list to await the time when a judge will be presiding who is not likely to be so independent. This course is not strictly defensible, but it gets its modicum of excuse from the desire that an agreement made by attorneys be carried out—an idea that has some force, although such agreements are always made with an expressed or implied condition that they are subject to sanction of the court. The judge has,

---

[1] Table 19, at the end of this chapter, shows that nearly one third of the appealed cases of sex offenders in the year 1920 received this type of disposition.

of course, the power to upset any agreed disposition that comes before him, and to make his own full and independent investigation into the case and to use his own judgment, but if he does so he uses up much precious time and embarrasses the district attorney exceedingly. Any judge who has had experience with the administration of the criminal law is likely to follow unhesitatingly the recommendations of a district attorney, whose judgment he trusts, but he is put in an embarrassing position if things have happened which shake his confidence in the district attorney, and I doubt if in any case a judge feels any satisfaction in taking the responsibility for the product of the judgment of somebody else.   It must irk to be a rubber-stamp.

While the district attorney is by force of his powers and duties invested with a certain amount of quasi-judicial discretion, I cannot believe that he was ever intended to have or that he ought to have judicial powers beyond his power to nolle pros., and yet, in the practical working out of the present situation, he does, in effect, exercise the power of the judge without having the judge's responsibility.

Another bad feature of the situation is that in the process of trading between the district attorney and the defendant's counsel the district attorney too frequently has to barter a part or the whole of a well-merited sentence imposed by the lower court.   In spite of the fact that now and then the sentence of the lower court reveals the knowledge of the lower court judge that his disposition of the case will be made the subject of barter in the Superior Court, I believe that the great majority of the lower court judges in . . . County disregard that knowledge and are utterly conscientious in trying to deal with each case on its own merits.   My own judgment, formed after careful examination in many cases, has convinced me of this, and that their sentences were just. . . . A lower court judge may well feel that his careful work on a case is no more than a sigh in a gale.

In a large majority of appeal cases defendants have counsels.   A bunch of ten gamesters are fined $10 each in the lower court.   Five have no lawyers and pay their fines and thereby get criminal records. The other five have lawyers upon whose advice an appeal is taken. Then the district attorney is given an option to try the gamesters before a jury, or to take pleas of nolo and put the cases on file, the defendants escaping a criminal record.   As against this trivial matter, there are cases of rape, robbery, burglary, aggravated assaults, and other serious crimes which must be tried.   With a limited opportunity for trial, still further limited by the time that must be given to jail delivery, the district attorney takes the serious cases to try and contents himself with the offered disposition of the gaming cases. Then the young gamesters go back to their dice, rail at their five companions who now are marked with criminal records, and thumb their noses at the chagrined police.

The above statements apply with equal force to the Boston Municipal Court as well as to the district courts. They point out very clearly the weak link in the judicial system. This puts the judge at a most decided disadvantage, as well as the probation officer. The judge, knowing that the defendant, particularly if he or she is represented by an attorney, is almost sure to appeal from his decision, and that because of the reasons above stated the defendant may never receive any punishment whatsoever, because of a nolle pros, or a plea of nolo which will result in the case being placed on file by the district attorney, is fairly certain to decide that the lesser of two evils will be either to put the defendant on probation or to mete out a sentence and suspend it, placing the defendant on probation for a period of from three months to two years, with the implied understanding that the defendant will waive his appeal. This procedure results in the placing upon probation of many persons who are not proper subjects for probation. One case particularly was noted of a female pickpocket, who had been arrested thirty-one times previously and had served penitentiary sentences in other states, who was given a suspended sentence and placed on probation for a year and a half. It is obvious that the task of the probation officer is well nigh hopeless in such a case.

A study of the appealed cases over a period of one year substantiates the foregoing quotations from the report of the Judicature Commission. Table 19, at the end of this chapter, of appealed cases for this period shows very few cases that were actually tried in the Superior Court, the majority being nolle prossed or placed on file under conditions which indicate a bargaining between the district attorney and defendant.

As before stated, the court is not at all specialized as to the kind of cases tried. All cases of sex delinquency, however, are brought before it. The laws relating to sex delinquency are, in Massachusetts, designated "Laws against Chastity." The laws creating offenses of this kind over which the court has jurisdiction are as follows:

Massachusetts General Laws, 1920, Chapter 272

Sec. 2.   Fraudulently and deceitfully enticing or taking away a woman or girl for prostitution or unlawful sexual intercourse, or aiding or assisting therein. (Three years in jail or $1000 or both.)

Sec. 4.   Age of consent (18) (man only guilty).   (Three years in jail or $1000 or both.)

Sec. 5.   Intercourse with idiot.   (Same as 4.)

Sec. 6.   Owner or keeper of place who permits female to resort there for unlawful sexual intercourse.   (Same as 4.)

Sec. 7.   Whoever, knowing female to be a prostitute, shall share in proceeds of prostitution.   (One year in House of Correction or $1000 or both.)

Sec. 8.   Soliciting for prostitute.   (House of Correction, one year, or $500 or both.)

Sec. 12.   Procuring female for house of prostitution.   ($100 or $500 or three months–two years.   Employment office sending girl to house of prostitution, $50–$200.)

Sec. 13.   Detaining or aiding in detaining in house prostitution.   (One–two and one-half years in House of Correction or $100–$500.)

Sec. 14.   Adultery.   (Two years in jail or $500.)

Sec. 16.   Lewd and lascivious cohabitation by man and woman not married to each other or man and woman guilty of open and gross lewdness and lascivious behavior.   (Two years in jail or $300.)

Sec. 18.   Fornication.   (Three months or $30.)

Sec. 24.   Keeper disorderly house.   (Two years.)

Sec. 25.   Restaurant of café proprietor who keeps enclosed booths or stalls. ($50–$500 or two months or both.)

Sec. 26.   Whoever, for the purpose of immoral solicitation or immoral bargaining shall resort to any café, restaurant, saloon or other place where food or drink is sold or served to be consumed on premises, and whoever shall resort to any such place for the purpose of, in any manner, inducing another person to engage in immoral conduct, and whoever, being in or about such place, shall engage in any such acts.   ($25–$500 or one year or both.)

Sec. 53.   Common night-walkers, both male and female . . . persons who with offensive or disorderly acts or language accost or annoy in public places persons of the opposite sex . . . lewd, wanton, and lascivious persons in speech or behavior . . . idle and disorderly persons . . . those persons who neglect all lawful business and habitually misspend their time by frequenting houses of ill-fame . . . (Reformatory or $20 or six months in House of Correction.)

Sec. 62. Night-walker, twice before convicted. (House of Correction, two and one-half years.)

Sec. 66. Vagrants. Persons wandering abroad and visiting houses of ill-fame and not giving a good account of themselves. (Reformatory or six months in House of Correction.)

Chapter 140

Sec. 26. Lodging-house or innkeeper, who knowingly permits premises to be used for purpose of immoral solicitation, immoral bargaining, or immoral conduct. ($500–$1000 or six months–one year or both.)

Sec. 27. Failing to keep proper register; falsely registering name or address of self or other occupant of room. ($100–$500 or three months or both.) Or failure to register.

Chapter 139

Sec. 4. Every building, part of building, tenement, or place used for prostitution, assignation, or lewdness and every place where such acts occur, is a nuisance.

Sec. 5. Keepers of such a nuisance. ($100–$1000 and three months–three years.)

Sec. 20. Whoever knowingly lets premises for purposes of prostitution, assignation or lewdness or knowingly permits premises to be used for such purposes, or after notice of such use omits to eject persons, etc., therefrom. ($50–$100 and three months—one year.)

In every one of the foregoing cases, the defendant is entitled to a trial by jury, and a demand for a jury will entitle the defendant to a trial de novo in the Superior Court. The nature of the trial in the Municipal Court depends upon the judge who happens to be sitting on the bench at the time. One judge was observed to hold a formal trial, with witnesses testifying from the witness stand. Another judge called the defendant and witnesses to the bench, where the trial could not be heard, even from the lawyers' benches inside the railing. His trials were very informal. In no case was there a State's Attorney to prosecute. Occasionally the prosecution was conducted by an experienced police officer. The judge almost invariably assisted in the direct and cross-examination. No stenographic report of the proceedings is taken. At the time this study was made, the police department was still new, most of the members having served not more than a year, due to the disruption of the department caused by the police strike of the previous year. It was claimed by the superintendent of police and others that the reason for the small number of cases involving sex delinquency was that the new policemen had not yet become well enough acquainted with the haunts of the prostitute to make many arrests.[1] Be that as it may, not more than a dozen cases of this nature came before the court in a period of eight days, and only two or three of these cases were actually tried. The case of one street-walker was continued, and another pleaded guilty, with the understanding that the record would show "found guilty." She was placed on probation for a year under a suspended sentence. There was no record against her under the name given, in the probation files, but she appeared to be a hardened prostitute of several years' experience. The others were fornication cases, which appeared to be cases of private immorality rather than prostitution. Some of these were continued, and the others pleaded guilty and were placed on probation.

The court docket for the first six months of 1920 shows the following number of arraignments for sex delinquency:

Idle and disorderly..	58
Common night-walker	24
Violating True Name Law.....................................	83
Keeping a disorderly house...................................	2
Common nuisance, house of ill-fame...........................	18
Permitting place to be used for immoral purpose.................	6
Adultery	45
Fornication	158
Lewd and lascivious cohabitation..............................	105
Accosting person opposite sex (mashing).......................	13
Living off earnings of prostitute..............................	2

---

[1] Because of the possibility that conditions during the first six months might not be representative, this study was made to cover the entire year, divided, however, into half-year periods so that data for the first six months might be comparable with facts gathered in Chicago and Philadelphia for the same time. A comparison, however, of arraignments in the first and second half of the year, compiled from the docket, shows 504 in the former and 531 in the latter.

The first two violations are undoubtedly made up of prostitutes, as may be also a part of the next. Those charged with fornication may also include a number of promiscuous persons. A fair estimate of the number of prostitutes passing through the court machinery during this period would probably be about one hundred. It would therefore seem that the study was conducted at a time when conditions were practically normal. Table I, at the end of this Chapter, shows the dispositions of the foregoing cases.

Neither the laws of Massachusetts nor the regulations of the health department provide for the examination or quarantine of persons infected with venereal diseases. From a legal standpoint, therefore, the court is not concerned with the physical condition of defendants as is the case in the other courts studied. Defendants convicted in this court are not finger-printed.

ILLUSTRATIVE CASES

The following cases are illustrative:

S., white. Charge—common night-walker, arraigned and case continued at request of defendant's attorney; bail fixed at $300, furnished immediately, thus preventing probation officers from getting in touch with defendant.

G. and F., white. Charge—lewd and lascivious cohabitation; pleaded guilty; continued one week for sentence because of possibility that they might marry; returned the next day with wedding certificate, and sentence suspended.

B. and B., white. Charge—fornication; case continued week; from story given probation officer, woman was high-school teacher and man was her fiancé; they admitted charge and were placed on probation for six months.

Colored couple. Charge—adultery; pleaded guilty; she was given sentence of three months in common jail and he the same in the House of Correction; they waived their right of appeal, however, and accepted probation for three months. Their lawyer said to them audibly as they left the bench, "Now don't get caught for three months.'' The inference being that if they did they would have to serve out their sentence.

White couple. Charge—lewd and lascivious cohabitation; pleaded guilty; their history showed that they had lived together for eight years; case continued for ten days for probation officers to investigate practicability of marriage, defendants being released on their own recognizance.

I., white. Charge—idle and disorderly; continued at request of defendant's attorney; defendant had been arrested in disorderly house, and investigator was informed that the foregoing is the usual charge for such an inmate.

The other cases observed are set forth in the text of the report.

PHYSICAL ASPECTS OF THE COURT AND DETENTION FACILITIES

The Second Sessions of the Municipal Court of the City of Boston occupies a large room on the main floor of the Court House at Pemberton Square. On the corridor leading to it are the court-rooms of the First Sessions and the Domestic Relations Division of the Municipal Court. During sessions of these three courts the corridor is congested. The public is freely admitted to the Second Sessions and its numerous long benches are invariably crowded with spectators. A central enclosure directly opposite the judge is reserved for the lawyers appearing in connection with the cases. On the left side of the room are two wooden docks for men and women defendants, respectively, who have been detained in jail awaiting trial. While seated within these docks, the defendants are not visible from the court-room. When one of the defendants is called, he stands up in the dock facing the judge. Bail cases await trial in the court-room. When called they stand in front of the judge, a little to the right, complainants or witnesses a little to the left, and the lawyer within the enclosure directly in front of the judge. Defendants, complainants and witnesses are sworn usually by the court clerk; in his absence, by the judge.

The court-room personnel comprises the judge, clerk, attendant, one man and two women probation officers.

A double row of feebly lighted, wretchedly ventilated cells in the basement of the courthouse constitutes Boston's Detention House for Women. Although the Municipal Court of Boston has jurisdiction only over those persons arrested within Central Boston, the House of Detention is used for all women arrested (and not bailed) from the outlying districts of East Boston, South Boston, Charlestown, Roxbury, West Roxbury, Brighton, Chelsea, and Dorchester, after they have been booked at the local police station. If, on arraignment in court a case is continued, the woman is transferred to the Suffolk County Jail on Charles Street until the date set. Accommodations are in every respect better. Cells in the courthouse comprise three tiers, but only the lowest one is in general use. On one morning when the writer visited the Detention House six arrested women were there—two in one cell, three in another, and one woman in delirium tremens in a third cell. When the probation officer was asked why more women than one were placed in a cell when several cells were unoccupied, she answered, "Oh, the girls like company."

The cells are equipped with bunks for one or more occupants. Shortly after eight on the morning of our visit, an officer removed two women who had been arrested for drunkenness in Charlestown the night before and took them to the Charlestown Court for trial.

At eight o'clock every morning, one of the two women court probation officers interviews at the Detention House those brought in during the night. Twice the writer was permitted to accompany one of these officers in order to observe the procedure in regard to detained women. The probation officer first examined a sheet prepared by the matron, showing name, offense, date of arrest, age, and place of employment of each person brought in during the night. The probation officer transcribed these facts on yellow cards, one for each case. With these cards in hand she proceeded to interrogate each girl, asking her if she had ever been arrested before, something of her family history, whether married, if so, whether living with husband, husband's work and place of business. On completing her rounds the probation officer consults the court card file for the purpose of identifying, if possible, any case with a previous record. Such statements as can be verified within a short time are then turned over to the probation officer in whose district the girl was arrested. When this additional information is available the court probation officer signs a statement in respect to each case to the effect that she has investigated and found facts therein stated to be true. In addition, she fills out a slip showing docket number of case, name, date placed on probation (if previously a probation case), date of expiration of probation, and date of surrender.[1] This slip, with the matron's statement, is sent to the court clerk.

At trial, the judge has before him the arresting officer's complaint and bail papers (if a bail case), but no social history or record of previous court history.

PROBATION

The Probation Department of the Municipal Court of the City of Boston serves the three Criminal Sessions of that court and its court of Domestic Relations. Men's cases are heard in the First Sessions; women's, or men's and women's jointly, in the Second Sessions; and overflow cases from both in the Third Sessions. The Domestic Relations Court, in addition to the usual type of case heard in such courts, has jurisdiction also over bastardy cases and cases of incorrigible and runaway girls between the ages of seventeen and twenty-one. The Department investigates, also, certain cases brought before the Probate Court.

Probation officers are appointed by the chief justice of

---

[1] Regarding practice of ''surrender,'' see pp. 232–233.

the Municipal Court of the City of Boston, with the concurrence of the associate justices, and hold office at the pleasure of the court. They are organized as follows:

One administrator, designated Chief Probation Officer.
First deputy, supervising sixteen probation officers—fifteen men and one woman.
Second deputy (a woman) supervising eight women.
Director of the Medical Department, assisted by a woman physician serving part time.

The sixteen probation officers working under the direction of the First Deputy are assigned as follows:

Two general supervisors.
Two officers stationed in the court to make preliminary investigation of criminal cases (men) only, one assigned to the First and one to the Second Sessions.
One investigator of cases brought before the Domestic Relations Court (men).
Eight investigators and supervisors of men brought in on a charge of drunkenness. At present, however, because of the falling off in number of this type of case, these eight men handle those brought in on other charges as well.
One officer who prepares and presents cases in court (men's). This officer, who is an attorney, assists any probationer in need of legal aid. His services may be required in cases of ejectment, industrial accident, extortion, divorce suit, or other legal difficulty—civil or criminal.
One officer who collects fines or money paid in restitution.
A woman probation officer who handles women in agreement cases, looks after the interests of mothers and children in separation cases, investigates complainant's story in bastardy cases, hears and seeks to adjust cases of incorrigible and runaway girls, without court action, and supervises such girls if, in the event of court action, they are placed upon probation.

The eight women serving under the direction of the Second Deputy are assigned as follows:

Two officers stationed in the court to interview all arrested women before trial.
One officer to find employment for women.
Five investigators and supervisors.

The chief justice of the Municipal Court stated to the writer that he has aimed, in selecting probation officers, to appoint persons who have had special training which would be of value in their work, in addition to the general knowledge requisite for the proper discharge of their duties. Thus, three men and three women officers are graduates of a law school and four of this number are members of the bar. Their professional training enables them to render legal assistance to probationers when necessary. In the same way, a physician, who is also a psychiatrist, was added to the staff of the probation department when the need of examining certain defendants mentally became apparent.

At least seven distinct lines of activity are carried on by the Probation Department:

1. Investigation of arrested persons.
2. Adjusting domestic difficulties:
   (a) Marital.
   (b) Incorrigible and runaway children.
3. Instituting proceedings to establish paternity in bastardy cases.
4. Investigation of Probate Court cases:
   (a) Separation.
   (b) Guardianship.
   (c) Petition.
5. Supervision and aid of persons placed on probation.
   (a) Social.
   (b) Economic.
   (c) Medical.
   (d) Legal.
6. Medical service—physical and mental examination of selected persons.
7. Writing and filing of court and social history of each case brought to trial.

As this study is concerned chiefly with methods of handling sex offenders in morals courts, only certain of the items enumerated will be discussed in detail.

Investigation of arrested women: This function of the Probation Department has been fully described in the section relating to the Detention House, pages 226–227.

Supervision and aid of persons placed on probation: A woman convicted of an offense against chastity may be placed upon probation, with or without a suspended sentence, but always for a fixed period of time, which may be extended,[1] however, at the discretion of the Probation Department.

---

[1] For extensions of probation, see Table 14, column 4, and Table 15 at the end of this chapter.

If placed upon probation under a suspended sentence she may appeal only at the time sentence is imposed, for if she should violate the conditions of probation, the suspension of sentence could be revoked and the sentence executed without power of appeal. Of 56 women receiving this type of probation during the first six months of 1920, 15 were re-arrested for violation of probation, but the suspended sentence was imposed in the case of only six.[1]

If the probation is accepted without appeal, it may be of two types, "inside" and "outside." Inside probation is applied to those girls who, in the judgment of the Probation Department, need closer supervision than can be exercised by a single probation officer when the girl is at large. Two private institutions are used for this purpose, the House of Good Shepherd (Catholic) and Welcome House. The court cannot commit girls to these homes, but their agreement to spend a specified time (varying from one month to one year) within them is made a condition of their probation. The girl signs a card reading as follows:

Boston................19......
I, ...
do hereby agree to go to

....
to remain for.....................................
or until further order from court.

....
Witness ....

The reverse of the card states:

Municipal Court, Boston................19......
....
was placed on probation until................19....
with the permission of Court at her own request to
go to (House of Good Shepherd or Welcome House).
Probation Officer.

---

[1] Of the remaining nine, one was dismissed from probation and the probation period of the other eight extended. in two instances. twice.

A girl placed upon inside probation cannot be released without the consent of the judge who sentenced her. Of 228 girls placed upon probation in 1920, 70[1] were "committed" to private institutions in the sense indicated in the foregoing.

A girl to whom outside probation is applied, is assigned to the probation officer in whose district she resides. This officer is said to study her special needs in order to meet them as far as may be possible. She is said to visit her from time to time (at least once a month), to observe her manner of living, to learn if she is regularly employed and where, and to study her habits, recreation, etc. Probationers are not permitted to call at the probation office until the day their probation expires, unless in special need of advice or assistance. Girls who are visited by probation officers are not required to write except to notify of change of address. Each girl is given, when placed upon probation, a printed card reading in part as follows:

> To ....
> Believing that you will profit by the leniency of the Court, you are placed on probation until nine o'clock ...., 19...., on which date you must appear or you will be defaulted and the Probation Officer will report to the Court about your case . . .

On Wednesday morning of every week, girls whose terms of probation expire on that day, report at the office of the second deputy probation officer for a review and final disposition of their cases. A list of these girls is given the second deputy, together with the report of each girl's probation officer, including the officer's recommendation on the case. A separate folder is provided for each probationer which contains all data relative to her case. With this information in hand, the deputy then interviews each girl. She may either have the case dismissed, or, upon written consent of the defendant, have it continued, as the circumstances seem to require. Either course may be followed without consulting

---

[1] Figures supplied by Chief Probation Officer.

the judge. For disposition of women placed upon probation in 1920, see Table 14, at the end of this chapter. If probation is extended, the girl signs a written consent. The Commissioner of Probation estimates that about 25 per cent of all cases placed on probation from the Municipal Court during the year are extended. His estimate is borne out by Table 15, showing 58 extensions out of 205 cases placed on probation during the first six months of 1920. In determining proper disposition of the case, the deputy is said to take into consideration the following points, among others: probation officer's recommendations; girl's work record; statement of police officers to whom girl is known; reports of relatives or friends.

If the girl fails to report on the Wednesday specified, she is "defaulted" and then notified that she must call. "Default" as used by the Probation Department indicates failure to appear at expiration of probation period. A probation or police officer may serve judge's warrant. "Violation of Probation" refers to the violation of any condition imposed by the judge or Probation Department. It may refer also to any misconduct on part of probationer causing arrest.

If a probationer is brought in on a new charge before expiration of probation, she is arraigned before the judge. If she is arraigned in court on the new charge, the probation officer is said to "surrender" her, and the clerk, instead of specifying the actual offense committed, merely writes "surrendered" on the docket. When her case is heard there are two charges against her so far as the Probation Department is concerned. Usually, in the event of a new charge being brought, the probation officer awaits conviction on the new charge before surrendering her on the old. If surrendered, the judge makes disposition according to the history and needs of the case, and recommendation of the probation officer. Usually he files the less serious charge and sentences on the graver one. If second offense is same as first, usually the new charge is filed and sentence made on the first charge.

Probation may be extended or a more severe penalty inflicted. The girl is invariably surrendered for repetition of offense or commitment of an analogous offense. Practice varies widely, however, according to individual cases. Probation Department records show 43 women's cases surrendered during the first six months of 1920. Of these, 36 were again placed upon probation and seven sentenced to a penal institution. During the entire year, 88 women's cases were surrendered, of whom 64 again received probation and 19, a sentence to a penal institution. Five were dismissed or placed on file. Only 16 per cent in one instance and 13 per cent in the other received a more severe penalty for violating their probation, and the record does not state in how many instances appeal from the severer penalty was made. Probation officers in Massachusetts have the usual powers of arrest within the state.

Each woman probation officer carries about 125 cases at one time. Each man probation officer carries nearly 200 cases at one time.

In the year 1920, 33.4 per cent of the 463 men's cases arraigned in this court (for sex offenses) and 39.2 per cent of the 397 convicted, were placed on probation. The percentage of women's cases so disposed of runs higher, 39.8 per cent of the 572 arraigned and 50.5 per cent of the 451 convicted having received probation.[1]

Of the 155 men's cases placed upon probation in 1920, 75 (48.3 per cent) were dismissed from probation, presumably as satisfactory, at the expiration of their term. Of the 228 women probationers, 70 (30.7 per cent) were so dismissed.[2] Six men and 25 women were surrendered.[3] Thirty-six men (23.2 per cent) and 65 women (28.5 per cent) defaulted, i.e., failed to report at the probation office as required on date of

---

[1] For all dispositions see Tables 1 and 5, at the end of this chapter.

[2] For dispositions at expiration of probation in relation to offense, see Table 14, at the end of this chapter.

[3] This term explained on p. 232.

expiration of probation. Probation was extended in the case of 27 men and 50 women.

DISCUSSION OF PROBATION TABLES

Tables 22 through 26 at the end of this chapter show the results of our study of 50 cases placed upon probation during the year 1920. Through the courtesy of the Chief Probation Officer, we were given free access to records and allowed to make transcripts of case histories. In order to avoid selection of cases and at the same time not to limit the study to any special season of the year, four groups of cases were chosen as follows: The first 15 cases placed upon probation in 1920; the last ten in June; the first 15 in July; and the last ten in December. These 50 cases constitute 21.9 per cent of the 228 women's cases placed upon probation in 1920, and should prove fairly representative, therefore, of the work of the department.

Examining Table 22, a study of the social histories in relation to offense committed—we find that 38 were convicted for offense involving private immorality: adultery, fornication, lewd and lascivious cohabitation; and the remaining twelve for commercialized forms of prostitution: keeping houses of ill-fame, violating the True Name Law, common night-walker. Forty-four of the probationers are white and six, colored. Thirty are American born. Six, at time of arrest, were between 18 and 19 years of age; 17, between 20 and 24; eight, between 25 and 29; 11, between 30 and 40; and two, over 45. Fifteen claim they are single and 28 that they are married; six that they are widowed; civil state of one is not given. Manner of living at time of arrest is not stated with respect to six. Five are said to have been living with their parents; five, with husband; one, with relative; eight, keeping house; six, in hotel or rooming house; and nine, with lover. Twenty-eight had no children; 15 had from one to three legitimate children; and five had each one illegitimate child; legitimacy of children of two probationers was not established. The Boston records contain no reference to age or grade of leaving school. Statements regarding religion are too inadequate to tabulate.

The number of arraignments prior and subsequent to the one in 1920 when the 50 women were placed on probation is indicated in Table 23. It must be borne in mind, however, that these represent only *known* arraignments. For in the absence of a finger-printing system, court and probation officers have only their memories to rely upon when the girl gives a new alias. The Probation Department claims that 36 of these probationers were first offenders; six had been previously arraigned from one to three times; one, four times; two, five times; one, 10; one, 13; one, 14; one, 17, and one 22 times. Forty are said to have had no subsequent court record up to October 1, 1921. Four have one subsequent arraignment; three, two; one, three; one, four; and one five subsequent arraignments. A separate compilation shows that five probationers have had both previous and subsequent arraignments: one had one previous and one subsequent; one, four previous and one subsequent; one, thirteen previous and four subsequent; one, ten previous and five subsequent; and one, twenty-two previous and three subsequent arraignments. The three latter were 43, 44, and 33 years old, respectively. It is noteworthy that these five women, who, with a single exception, were known to be repeated offenders and past an age where it was probable that they could benefit by probation, were nevertheless placed on probation under a suspended sentence. And although all were surrendered within periods varying from six weeks to four months, in no instance was the suspended sentence imposed. Neither is it recorded that any of these women was visited in her home. An officer called upon one at her place of employment. Four were given a physical examination. The one, age 44, with a record of 13 previous arrests, was found to be infected with syphilis and gonorrhea.

As no routine physical or mental examination of all convicted persons is made, information regarding the condition
of these 50 probationers is necessarily incomplete.   The
records show that nineteen were examined physically, two of
whom were found to be infected with gonorrhea and one with
gonorrhea and syphilis.   Five probationers, three of whom
were single, one married and one a widow, were pregnant.   The
records show but one mental examination, the result of which
is reported as follows: "Drug user; girl not psychotic or
feeble-minded but has superficial and inferior character
make-up."

From Tables 24 and 25, showing respectively, the number
of calls made by officers at the girls' homes and the number
of times probationers reported by letter, it will be seen that
the officers called at the homes of 29 probationers 106 times,
and that 18 girls reported by letter 57 times although this is
not required unless girl changes her address.   Examining the
tables more closely, we find that the homes of 21 probationers
were not visited, but of this number one was referred to
another department of the court, four returned to their home
towns and four were placed in a private institution on "inside" probation.   The records of two probationers could not
be found.

Of the 29 homes visited, only 11 were called upon more
than three times, although 27 were on probation from four to
12 months.   Table 24 correlates number of calls made with
the number of times probationer, relative, or housekeeper
was found at home.   In 11 of the 29 homes visited, the probationer was not seen.   Only thirteen girls were seen by the
officer more than once, in their homes.   It appears, therefore,
from Table 24 that only 18 girls were seen by the officer in
their homes.   Ten girls were called upon once by the officer
at their place of employment; and two girls, twice.   The
records show that 20 probationers called from one to six
times at the Probation Department before the expiration of
their period.   With the exception of five cases, probation was

for six months; one was for three weeks; one, for seven months; and three, for one year. Four probationers received "inside" probation at the House of Good Shepherd. The six probationers who were surrendered before the expiration of their term were again placed on probation by the court, three being sent to the House of Good Shepherd on "inside" probation.

In order to make the Boston records comparable with those of Philadelphia, the Probation Department was asked to advise us of the progress of each case up to October 1, 1921. On that day the records of the 50 girls were as follows:

```
Dismissed from probation and not re-arrested, so far as known......  24
Still on probation and not re-arrested, so far as known.............   3
Defaulted and warrants issued—probationer not found..............  13
Re-arrested once, so far as known...............................   5
Re-arrested twice, so far as known..............................   2
Re-arrested three times, so far as known,.......................   2
Re-arrested four times, so far as known.........................   1
                                                                 ——
                                                                 50
```

The status of the ten probationers who were re-arrested was as follows on October 1, 1921:

```
Dismissed from probation.......................................   1
Still on probation.............................................   2
Committed to State Farm on August 1, 1921—no further informa-
    tion ......................................................   1
Defaulted and warrant issued—probationer not found.............   6
                                                                 ——
                                                                 10
```

MEDICAL DEPARTMENT

The Medical Department, theoretically a part of the Pro-. bation Department, is said by the chief justice of the Municipal Court to be the only full-time, permanent medical department attached to a court in the State of Massachusetts. The chief justice views the establishment of a medical department in the light of pioneer work and he believes that emphasis should be placed upon mental rather than upon physical examination; that education of the public and the court officials as to the value of such work by means of printed literature and lectures should constitute a definite function of the department. To this end, he said, numerous pamphlets have been prepared by the present medical director and by his predecessor.

In regard to the physical examination of women, the chief justice believes that the practice should be followed only to a limited extent; that in no case should compulsion be employed. It is his belief that any attempt at routine compulsory examination even of convicted women would arouse strenuous opposition. While the value of mental examination is stressed by the chief justice and by the medical director, no routine mental examination of all cases arraigned in court is made. Certain cases are referred by the judge or probation officer, although no precise basis for the selection was apparent.

The medical director stated to the writer that he interviews as many defendants as possible in the Domestic Relations Division and Criminal Sessions of the Municipal Court, besides examining more thoroughly those cases who seem to be distinctly abnormal mentally. He holds that most delinquents (sexual offenders included) are constitutionally inferior, whether or not their inferiority manifests itself in character defect only, or in low intelligence. He believes that from the point of view of behavior the present tendency is to lay too much stress on feeble-mindedness as such, if by that is meant low intelligence, measured by psychological tests, and that one of the reasons why feeble-mindedness is so frequent among delinquents studied is that the more intelligent are more likely to escape arrest. He stated that less than six commitments a year of feeble-minded persons found in the Second Sessions Court are made.

Examinations for venereal disease in 1920 numbered 284 men and women. Of these, 45 (15.4 per cent) showed positive Wassermann reactions and 10 (3.5 per cent) showed smears positive for the gonococcus. The director did not state how many of these cases were men and how many women, but added that "very few" men were examined.

PENAL INSTITUTIONS

Convicted sex offenders may be committed by the Municipal Court to the following institutions: Common Jail, House of Correction, State Farm, Reformatory for Women. Commitments for the first six months of 1920 and for the entire year were as follows:

	Jan. to June, 1920		Year of 1920	
	Men	Women	Men	Women
Common Jail	5	33	11	73
House of Correction	14	17	41	18
State Farm	..	1	..	1
Reformatory for Women	..	8	..	12
	19	59	52	104

Of the 19 men sentenced to a penal institution in the first six months of 1920, 17 appealed; and of the 59 women so sentenced, 58 appealed. In the year 1920, 46 men and 101 women appealed their cases. In other words, during the first six months of 1920, 96.1 per cent of those sentenced to a term in a penal institution appealed; and for the year, 94.2 per cent appealed. Following these appeals through to the Superior Court it was found that sentence to a penal institution was meted out to but one man and two women in the six months' period [1] and to two men and five women in the whole year.[2] No woman was sentenced in the Superior Court to the State Farm or to the Reformatory for Women.

RECORDS AND STATISTICS

The Municipal Court of the City of Boston has published but one annual report since its inception. This was issued in

---

[1] See Table 17, at the end of this chapter.
[2] See Table 19, at the end of this chapter.

1915. Statistics of arrests and criminal prosecutions of men
and women are contained in the Annual Reports of the
Bureau of Prisons of Massachusetts. Only broad classifications are employed, however: offenses against the person;
offenses against property; offenses against public order;
drunkenness and "other" offenses. In order to secure information relating to sex offenses only, it was necessary to
compile our data direct from the docket, where the particular offense is specified in each case. The docket of the
Municipal Court, Second Sessions, records the number of the
case, name of defendant, offense, plea, date of arraignment,
number of continuances, amount of bail, name of person putting up bail, judgment, disposition, length of term (if imprisoned), whether case appealed, amount of bail required
by the Superior Court, and whether secured. Each reap-
pearance in court of cases on probation is recorded under the
original docket number, with nature of disposition. Where
two defendants are arraigned on the same charge, as frequently occurs in the case of a man and woman arrested together, the court record with respect to each is given under
one number in such a way that it is often difficult to determine
which defendant is referred to, as the name is not always
written opposite each item of information.

The Probation Department keeps a monthly record, showing the number of cases placed on probation, the number of
surrenders and defaults, as well as other information. The
surrenders and defaults may be and usually are of cases
placed on probation at some previous time. In this way, the
department can furnish no figures showing, in respect to the
number placed on probation within a given period, how many
were dismissed, how many defaulted or were surrendered,
etc. In other words, it is not in a position to measure accurately, its progress for a given period. Such information
could be compiled from the court docket, as was done by the
writer in connection with this study, but it is not the practice
of the department to make such compilations. Each proba-

tioner's case is filed in a separate folder containing a court card showing name, aliases (if any), docket and file numbers, birthplace, occupation, and court history; a blue sheet recording the results of the probation officer's investigation and summary of trial, a probation card with write-up of case, record of calls made, action taken, summary of correspondence, etc. Reports from the Medical Department are filed in probationer's folder. Folders are filed numerically in wooden cabinets.

DISCUSSION OF TABLES

Facts compiled from the docket have been summarized in Tables 1 through 21 in two periods, one covering the first six months of 1920 and one, the entire year. The reason for this is given on page 223, footnote 1. Data compiled from probation and court records of 50 probationers are set forth in Tables 22 through 26.

Discussing these tables ad seriatim, we find in Table 1 that 504 sex offenders (218 men and 286 women) were arraigned in the Second Sessions during the first six months of 1920. Of this number it will be noted that 190 men, or 87.1 per cent, and 231 women, or 80.7 per cent, were convicted, making total convictions of 421, or 83.3 per cent. This relatively high percentage of convictions is invalidated by the numerous appeals from serious penalties. Twenty-three men and 63 women, 12.6 per cent and 27.2 per cent respectively, of those convicted carried their cases to the Superior Court. When it is remembered that convictions include those placed on file and those placed on probation, from which sentences appeals naturally are not taken, it will be seen that the real significance of the situation is not revealed. A sounder basis for judgment is offered by Table 2, showing appeals in relation to disposition. Of those fined, 16 per cent appealed; *of those committed to penal institutions, 97 per cent appealed.* Their fate in the higher court is discussed farther on in connection with Tables 17 and 18.

Forty-five men and 13 women were fined during the six-months period, in amounts ranging from $5 to $500, according to Table 3. The usual sum was found to be $10, 33 men and 10 women being fined this amount. Ten persons appealed from these fines and all escaped paying them by having their cases nolle prossed or placed on file in the district attorney's office.[1]   Table 4 shows the length of the sentences to the House of Correction and common jail. Only three out of 19 men and four out of 50 women received sentences to these institutions of more than six months; 12 men and 35 women were given terms of three months or less. Yet 17 of the men and all of the women appealed. All but three (two men and one woman) escaped a penal sentence in the Superior Court; eight were fined; the others defaulted or were nolle prossed or placed on file by the district attorney, with the exception of two pending cases and three whose disposition was not recorded. The nine women committed by the Municipal Court to the State Farm and State Reformatory for Women carried their cases to the higher court where two defaulted on the date set for their trial; four were nolle prossed or filed by the district attorney; and three were placed on probation.

Table 6, like Table 1, deals with the disposition of cases of sex offenders. The period covered, however, is for the entire year of 1920. It will be noted that the percentage of convictions and appeals from sentences varies but slightly from the corresponding percentage for the six-month period. Of the 147 men and women who appealed from penal sentences, all but seven escaped such a sentence in the Superior Court. Of the remainder, only 34 received a sentence of any sort, 14 being fined and 20 placed on probation.[2]

---

[1] See Table 18, at the end of this chapter.

[2] In order to learn something of the effects of probation in the Superior Court, a study was made of the first ten cases placed upon probation by the court, in 1920. It was found that on July 1, 1921, one was reporting by letter from out of town; one, living in Boston, was writing and calling regularly; one, needing medical treatment, was not reporting; one had been re-arrested once; and the whereabouts of six were unknown. Four of these cases had a previous

From Table 7, showing pleas in relation to offense during the first six months of 1920, it will be seen that 178 pleaded guilty on arraignment and 297, not guilty. Of the latter, 245, or 82.4 per cent, were found guilty.

That continuing or adjourning cases is a somewhat common practice in Boston is indicated by Table 8, which shows that 74 out of 100 cases were continued from one to six times. Only 16 of these cases, however, were continued more than twice. No case was extended beyond 33 days, as evidenced by Table 9. Of the 74 cases, 45 were disposed of within a week.

Tables 11, 12, and 13 deal with Bail Forfeitures in the Municipal Court. The docket records 57 such forfeitures in the year 1920 (Table 12), 13 of cash bail in amounts of $20, $25, and $50; 33 of real estate where surety was pledged in amounts ranging from $100 to $500; and eight of personal recognizance bonds. Recovery in the case of real estate forfeitures was sought in 32 instances. Following these cases in which bail was estreated through to the Superior Court, where such suits are heard, it was found that suit was discontinued in 14 cases on payment of trifling sums running from $20 to $35. The other 18 cases were still pending on July 1, 1921. In no case was the amount of the bond collected in the Superior Court.

Table 14 shows disposition of men and women probationers, placed on probation in 1920, at the expiration of their terms. This has been discussed on pages 233–234, in the section dealing with probation. Table 15, dealing with extensions on probation, is discussed on page 232. Table 16 sets forth the nature of judicial assignments.

Table 17 shows that out of a total of 86 sex cases appealed to the Superior Court from January 1 to June 30, 1920, ap-

---

court history in the Municipal Court, not counting the conviction which was appealed. Two were convicted twice; one, four times; one, five times in the Municipal Court and once in the Superior Court, for assault and battery with intent to kill.

parently not more than 22 ultimately came to trial. It must be clearly understood that convictions had already been had in the Municipal Court in the whole 86 cases. Some way was found, however, to defeat justice in the remaining 58, or 74 per cent of the total. This was accomplished in various ways, as shown by Table 18: five defaulted; four were unknown; two were still pending; the balance, 53, or 61 per cent of the total, were disposed of by some action of the district attorney, either by nolle prossing or placing on file.

The same ratio for the twelve-months period of 1920 holds good as that of the six-months period. (Table 19, this chapter.)   Out of a total of 167 appealed cases, only 46, or 27 per cent, were disposed of by the court as a possible result of a trial (whether these were actually tried or entered pleas, does not appear). Two, given as "Discharged," are not included in the 27 per cent inasmuch as nothing appeared on the docket to indicate whether the discharge was granted because of a legal technicality or as a result of a trial, or for failure to prosecute, etc. Nine defaulted, 11 are marked "Unknown," and five are still pending. This leaves 94, or 56 per cent, which were disposed of via the district attorney's office-route. If the lower court were correct in its judgment of conviction, 121 or 72 per cent defeated justice by the simple expedient of demanding a trial de novo.

Tables 18 and 20, at the end of this chapter, illustrate to what extent the dispositions of the court below were .overturned by this means. *These tables further indicate the futility of establishing a specialized branch in the Boston Municipal Court, until the fundamental question of the trial de novo has been settled.*

It will be seen in Tables 21 that 50 per cent of the 58 men who appealed their cases in 1920, and 76 per cent of the 109 women, were out on bail while awaiting disposition at the hands of the district attorney in the Superior Court.

Tables 22 through 26 have been fully discussed in the section on probation, pages 234–237.

Many references have been made in this report to the means possible to defeat justice by resorting to the trial de novo. The innocent and unoffending-appearing title of "appeal" is given to this procedure in the official records. The procedure is not an appeal as that term is commonly understood. The decision of the lower court is not reviewed by a higher court, as is done in the case of an appeal, in the commonly accepted usage of that term. The only formality required is the giving of notice within the statutory period and the filing of a bond. Should the case ultimately come to trial in the Superior Court, a new trial would be had without any reference whatsoever to what transpired in the lower court. Some interesting deductions may be made from Table 1, which give the percentage of the appeals to those convicted in the lower court. This shows that the persons who are taking the most advantage of this loophole in the machinery of justice, are those engaged in commercialized prostitution—a few figures will illustrate. Of the keepers of houses of ill-fame (nuisance), 57.1 per cent of the females, and 66.6 per cent of the males, appealed. Of the persons permitting premises to be used for immoral purposes, 100 per cent appealed. Of the common night-walkers, 73.6 per cent appealed. Of the idle and disorderly (prostitutes), 51.5 per cent appealed. Of those deriving support from the earnings of prostitutes (pimps), 100 per cent appealed.

However, of those convicted of offenses involving private immorality, such as fornication, adultery, and lewd and lascivious cohabitation, only a small proportion appealed. Inasmuch as many more females than males appealed, in the case of fornication and adultery, it might be inferred that many of those who did appeal were prostitutes who had been apprehended under these charges. Those identified with commercialized prostitution are very loath to accept probation. They regard any kind of supervision as an interference with their business. They therefore seldom bargain with the court and agree to accept a suspended sentence with probation as the price of waiving their rights to appeal. Rather, they take chances on the trial de novo, as they can always make bond. Their chances for ultimate freedom by this means are three to one. Even if they should ultimately lose out, and are really tried and convicted in the Superior Court, they still have a chance of being placed on probation. That many of them are, is indicated in Tables 17 and 18 at the end of this chapter. Practically the same ratio holds for the year period, as is shown in Tables 19 and 20.

It will be noted that the percentage of those convicted runs very high (Tables 1 and 5, this chapter). This heading does not differentiate between those found guilty. It was noted by Mr. Worthington in the trials observed that frequently defendants represented by counsel asked that the record show that they had been found guilty even when they pleaded guilty.[1] This was no doubt done to preserve their right to appeal, in case that course should later be determined upon. (Whether the size of defendant's pocket-book had any influence upon the subsequent decision to appeal was not ascertainable.)

Of the dispositions, it will be noted that probation, either straight or suspended sentence, predominates. This is largely due to the bargaining to prevent appeal, previously referred to. Many defendants are thus thrust upon the probation officer, with little reference as to whether or not that person may benefit by probation. Such a practice must render the task of the probation officer nearly hopeless. Very few women are sent to the State Reformatory, as indicated both by the six-months and twelve-months tables. There ought to be much the same ratio of defendants who should be amenable to reform, as those who are amenable to probation; therefore, if defendants who are placed on probation had received a scientific disposition of their cases, there should have also

---

[1] For pleas in relation to offense and conviction, see Table 7, at the end of this chapter.

been a large number committed to reformatories. The great difference between the figures for those committed to the reformatories and those placed on probation indicates that these sentences must have been rendered without much reference to the kind of treatment the individual case demanded.

TABLE 1. DISPOSITION OF CASES OF SEX OFFENDERS ARRAIGNED IN JANUARY 1 TO

Offense		Total Arraigned	Defaulted[2]	Jurisdiction Declined	Dismissed for Want of Prosecution	Discharged	Placed on File[3]	Fined[4]
Adultery	M	25	...	1	...	...	3	...
	F	20	...	...	...	...	...	...
Fornication	M	77	2	...	...	2	8	26
	F	81	8	...	...	3	9	10
Lewd and lascivious co-habitation	M	46	2	...	1	7	6	...
	F	49	2	...	1	5	5	...
Nuisance—house of ill-fame	M	8	...	...	...	2	...	2
	F	8	...	...	...	1	...	...
House of ill-fame	M	1	...	...	...	1	...	...
	F	1	...	...	...	...	...	...
Disorderly house	M	...	...	...	...	...	...	...
	F	2	1	...	...	...	1	...
Permitting premises to be used for immoral purposes	M	4	...	...	...	2	...	2
	F	2	...	...	...	1	...	...
Violating True Name Law	M	43	1	...	...	2	20	16
	F	40	...	...	...	2	18	2
Common night walker	M	...	...	...	...	...	...	...
	F	24	2	...	...	3	1	...
Idle and disorderly	M	...	...	...	...	...	...	...
	F	58	4	2	1	18	4	1
Accosting and annoying person of opposite sex	M	13	...	...	...	4	4	...
	F	...	...	...	...	...	...	...
Deriving support from the earnings of a prostitute	M	1	...	...	...	...	...	...
	F	1	...	...	...	...	...	...
TOTAL	M	218	5	1	1	20	41	46
	F	286	17	2	2	33	38	13
GRAND TOTAL		504	22	3	3	53	79	59

[1] Compiled from docket of Municipal Court of the City of Boston, Second Sessions, 1920. This table is discussed on pp. 241, 244–247.

[2] For amount of bail forfeitures, see Table 11.

[3] These defendants either plead guilty or were found guilty but no sentence was imposed.

[4] For amount of fine, see Table 3.

THE MUNICIPAL COURT OF THE CITY OF BOSTON, SECOND SESSIONS, JUNE 30, 1920.[1]

| CONVICTED | | | | | | | SUMMARY OF CONVICTIONS AND APPEALS | | | |
| PROBATION | | COMMITTED TO PENAL INSTITUTIONS | | | | | | | | |
Straight	Suspended Sentence	Common Jail[5]	House of Correction[6]	State Farm[6]	Reformatory for Women[6]	Un-known	Total Convicted	Per Cent Convicted	Total Appealed[7]	Per Cent Appealed of Those Convicted
5	13	1	1	...	...	1	23	92.	2	8.6
5	11	2	1	...	...	1	19	95.	3	15.7
23	11	2	3	...	...	...	73	94.8	5	6.8
24	13	7	6	...	1	...	70	86.4	15	21.4
13	12	1	4	...	...	...	36	78.2	5	13.8
20	10	3	1	...	2	...	41	83.6	6	14.6
1	...	...	3	...	...	...	6	75.	4	66.6
...	3	3	1	...	...	...	7	87.5	4	57.1
...	1	...	...	...	...	...	1	100.	...	...
...	...	...	...	...	...	...	1	50.	...	...
...	1	...	...	...	...	...	2	50.	2	100.
...	...	...	...	...	...	...	1	50.	...	...
3	1	...	...	...	...	...	40	93.	2	5.
11	6	...	1	...	...	...	38	95.	3	7.8
1	3	10	...	1	3	...	19	79.1	14	73.6
4	8	7	7	...	2	...	33	56.8	17	51.5
1	1	1	2	...	...	...	9	69.2	2	22.2
...	...	...	...	...	...	...	...	...	...	...
...	...	...	1	...	...	...	1	100.	1	100.
...	...	1	...	...	...	...	1	100.	1	100.
46	38	5	14	...	...	1	190	87.1	23	12.6
65	56	33	17	1	8	1	231	80.7	63	27.2
111	94	38	31	1	8	2	421	83.3	86	20.4

[5] For length of term see Table 4.
[6] Sentence indeterminate.
[7] For comparison of convictions and appeals in relation to offense, see Table 2. For disposition of appealed cases in Superior Court, see Table 17. For correlation of disposition in Municipal Court and Superior Court, see Table 18.

TABLE 2. CONVICTIONS AND APPEALS IN RELATION TO OFFENSES AND
CITY OF BOSTON, JANUARY

OFFENSE		TOTAL		PLACED ON FILE		FINED	
		Convicted	Appealed[2]	Convicted	Appealed	Convicted	Appealed
Adultery	M	23	2	3	...	...	...
	F	19	3	...	...	...	...
Fornication	M	73	5	8	...	26	1
	F	70	15	9	...	10	1
Lewd and lascivious cohabitation	M	36	5	6	...	...	...
	F	41	6	5	...	...	...
Nuisance—house of ill-fame	M	6	4	...	...	2	...
	F	7	4	...	...	...	...
House of ill-fame	M	...	...	...	...	...	...
	F	1	...	...	...	...	...
Disorderly house	M	...	...	...	...	...	...
	F	1	...	1	...	...	...
Permitting premises to be used for immoral purposes	M	2	2	...	...	2	2
	F	1	...	...	...	...	...
Violating True Name Law	M	40	2	20	...	16	2
	F	38	3	18	...	2	2
Common night-walker	M	...	...	...	...	...	...
	F	19	14	1	...	...	...
Idle and disorderly	M	...	...	...	...	...	...
	F	33	17	4	...	1	1
Accosting and annoying person of opposite sex	M	9	2	4	...	...	...
	F	...	...	...	...	...	...
Deriving support from the earnings of a prostitute	M	1	1	...	...	...	...
	F	1	1	...	...	...	...
TOTAL	M	190	23	41	...	46	5
	F	231	63	38	...	13	4
GRAND TOTAL		421	86	79	...	59	9

[1] Compiled from docket of Municipal Court of the City of Boston, Second Sessions, 1920. For discussion of this table, see p. 241.

DISPOSITION OF CASES ARRAIGNED IN THE MUNICIPAL COURT OF THE
1 TO JUNE 30, 1920 [1]

| PROBATION | | | | COMMON JAIL | | HOUSE OF CORRECTION | | STATE FARM | | REFORMATORY FOR WOMEN | | PERCENTAGES | |
| Straight | | Suspended Sentence | | | | | | | | | | | |
Convicted	Appealed	Convicted	Appealed	Convicted	Appealed	Convicted	Appealed	Convicted	Appealed	Convicted	Appealed	Convicted (Of those arraigned)	Appealed (Of those convicted)
5	...	13	...	1	1	1	1	...	...	...	...	92.	8.6
5	...	11	...	2	2	1	1	...	...	...	...	95.	15.7
23	...	11	...	2	1	3	3	...	...	...	...	94.8	6.8
24	...	13	...	7	7	6	6	...	...	1	1	86.4	21.4
13	...	12	...	1	1	4	4	...	...	2	2	78.2	13.8
20	...	10	...	3	3	1	1	...	...	2	2	83.6	14.6
1	...	...	...	...	...	3	3	...	...	...	...	75.	66.6
...	...	3	...	3	3	1	1	...	...	...	...	87.5	57.1
...	...	...	...	...	...	1	...	...	...	...	...	100.	...
...	...	1	...	...	...	...	...	...	...	...	...		
...	...	...	...	...	...	...	...	...	...	...	...	50.	...
...	...	...	...	...	...	...	...	...	...	...	...		
...	...	...	...	...	...	...	...	...	...	...	...	50.	100
...	...	1	...	...	...	...	...	...	...	...	...	50.	...
3	...	1	...	...	...	...	...	...	...	...	...	93.	5.
11	...	6	...	...	...	1	1	...	...	...	...	95.	7.8
1	...	3	...	10	10	...	...	1	1	3	3	79.1	73.6
4	...	8	...	7	7	7	7	...	...	2	2	56.8	51.5
1	...	1	...	1	...	2	2	...	...	...	...	69.2	22.2
...	...	...	...	...	...	...	...	...	...	...	...		
...	...	...	...	...	...	1	1	...	...	...	...	100.	100.
...	...	...	...	1	1	...	...	...	...	...	...	100.	100.
46	...	38	...	5	3	14	14	...	1	...	...	87.1	12.6
65	...	56	...	33	33	17	17	1	1	8	8	80.7	27.2
111	...	94	...	38	36	31	31	1	1	8	8	83.3	20.4

[2] For disposition of appealed cases in Superior Court, see Table 17. For correlation of disposition in Municipal Court and Superior Court, see Table 18.

TABLE 3.   AMOUNT OF FINES IMPOSED IN CASES OF SEX OFFENDERS
ARRAIGNED IN THE MUNICIPAL COURT OF THE CITY OF BOSTON,
SECOND SESSIONS, JANUARY 1 TO JUNE 30, 1920 [1]

OFFENSE		TOTAL NUMBER OF CASES	AMOUNT OF FINES				
			$5	$10	$20	$100	$500
Fornication	M	26	4	20	2	...	...
	F	10	2	8	...	...	...
Nuisance—house of ill-fame	M	2	...	...	...	2	...
	F	...	...	...	...	...	...
Permitting premises to be used for immoral purposes	M	2	...	...	...	...	2
	F	...	...	...	...	...	...
Violating True Name Law	M	16	...	13	1	2	...
	F	2	...	1	...	...	...
Idle and disorderly	M	...	...	...	...	...	...
	F	1	...	1	...	...	...
TOTAL	M	46	4	33	3	4	2
	F	13	2	10	...	1	...
GRAND TOTAL		59	6	43	3	5	2

[1] Compiled from docket of Municipal Court of the City of Boston, Second Sessions, 1920.   For discussion of this table, see p. 241.

[2] For number of fines appealed, see Table 2, column 6; and for correlations of disposition by fine in Municipal Court with disposition in Superior Court, see Table 18.

TABLE 4. LENGTH OF SENTENCE TO HOUSE OF CORRECTION AND COMMON JAIL OF SEX OFFENDERS COMMITTED BY THE MUNICIPAL COURT OF THE CITY OF BOSTON, SECOND SESSIONS, JANUARY 1 TO JUNE 30, 1920

Offense		Total Committed	LENGTH OF COMMITMENT														
			HOUSE OF CORRECTION									COMMON JAIL					
			1 mo.	2 mos.	3 mos.	4 mos.	6 mos.	8 mos.	12 mos.	15 mos.	10 das.	1 mo.	2 mos.	3 mos.	4 mos.	6 mos.	12 mos.
Adultery	M	2	...	...	...	...	1	...	...	...	...	...	...	...	...	...	1
	F	3	...	...	...	...	...	1	...	...	...	...	...	...	...	...	2
Fornication	M	5	1	...	2	...	...	...	...	...	...	1	...	1	...	...	...
	F	13	2	4	...	...	...	...	...	...	...	4	1	2	...	...	...
Lewd and lascivious cohabitation	M	5	...	...	3	...	1	...	...	...	...	...	...	...	...	...	1
	F	4	...	...	...	...	...	...	...	...	1	...	...	2	...	1	...
Nuisance—house of ill-fame	M	3	...	...	2	...	1	...	...	...	...	...	...	...	...	...	...
	F	4	...	...	1	...	...	...	...	...	...	...	...	2	...	1	...
Violating True Name Law	M	...	...	...	...	...	...	...	...	...	...	...	...	...	...	...	...
	F	1	1	...	...	...	...	...	...	...	...	...	...	...	...	...	...
Common night-walker	M	...	...	...	...	...	...	...	...	...	...	...	...	...	...	...	...
	F	10	...	...	...	...	...	...	...	...	...	...	...	...	7	3	...
Idle and disorderly	M	...	...	...	...	...	...	...	...	...	...	...	...	...	...	...	...
	F	14	...	...	2	4	1	...	...	...	...	...	...	2	5	...	...
Accosting and annoying person of opposite sex	M	3	...	1	...	...	1	...	...	...	...	...	1	...	...	...	...
	F	...	...	...	...	...	...	...	...	...	...	...	...	...	...	...	...
Deriving support from the earnings of a prostitute	M	1	...	...	...	...	...	...	1	...	...	...	...	...	...	...	...
	F	1	...	...	...	...	...	...	...	...	...	...	...	...	...	1	...
TOTAL	M	19	1	1	7	...	4	...	1	...	1	1	1	...	...	...	2
	F	50	3	4	3	4	1	1	...	1	...	4	3	18	3	3	2
GRAND TOTAL		69	4	5	10	4	5	1	1	1	1	5	4	18	3	3	4

[1] Compiled from docket of Municipal Court of the City of Boston, Second Sessions, 1920. For discussion of this table, see pp. 241–242.

[2] For appeals from sentences to these two institutions, see Table 2, columns 11 and 13; and for correlation of disposition by sentence to penal institutions with disposition in Superior Court, see Table 18.

TABLE 5. DISPOSITION OF CASES OF 'SEX OFFENDERS ARRAIGNED IN THE

Offense		Total Arraigned	Defaulted[2]	Jurisdiction Declined	Dismissed for Want of Prosecution	Dismissed on Motion of Attorney for Defendant	Discharged
Adultery	M	39	...	1	...	...	2
	F	31	...	...	...	...	1
Fornication	M	157	8	...	...	...	6
	F	164	19	...	...	...	6
Lewd and lascivious cohabitation	M	103	5	...	1	...	9
	F	102	7	1	1	...	8
Nuisance—house of ill-fame	M	13	...	...	...	...	4
	F	24	2	...	...	...	3
House of ill-fame	M	2	...	...	...	...	1
	F	2	...	...	...	...	...
Disorderly house	M	4	...	...	...	...	2
	F	6	2	...	...	...	1
Permitting premises to be used for immoral purposes	M	4	...	...	...	...	2
	F	2	...	...	...	...	1
Violating True Name Law	M	86	1	...	...	...	8
	F	80	...	...	1	...	11
Common night-walker	M	...	...	...	...	...	...
	F	62	5	...	...	1	8
Idle and disorderly	M	...	...	...	...	...	...
	F	97	8	4	2	...	27
Accosting and annoying person of opposite sex	M	51	...	...	4	...	9
	F	1	...	...	...	...	1
Deriving support from earnings of a prostitute	M	3	...	...	...	...	...
	F	1	...	...	...	...	...
Soliciting for a prostitute	M	1	...	...	...	...	...
	F	...	...	...	...	...	...
Total	M	463	14	1	5	...	43
	F	572	43	5	4	1	67
Grand Total		1035	57	6	9	1	110

[1] Compiled from docket of Municipal Court of the City of Boston, Second Sessions, 1920. This table is discussed on pp. 217, 243.|

[2] For amount of bail forfeitures, see Table 12.

[3] These defendants either plead guilty or were found guilty but no sentence was imposed.

For disposition at expiration of probation, see Table 14.

MUNICIPAL COURT OF THE CITY OF BOSTON, SECOND SESSIONS, 1920 [1]

		CONVICTED									SUMMARY OF CONVICTIONS AND APPEALS			
		Probation[4]		Committed to Penal Institution						Total Convicted	Per Cent Convicted	Total Appealed[7]	Per Cent Appealed of those Convicted
Placed on File[3]	Fined[4]	Straight	Suspended Sentence	Common Jail[5]	House of Correction[5]	State Farm[6]	Reformatory for Women[6]	Pending	Unknow				
4	...	8	19	1	3	...	...	...	1	35	87.1	4	11.4
1	...	6	17	4	1	...	...	...	1	29	93.5	5	17.2
16	69	33	14	4	7	...	...	...	...	143	91.	12	14.3
24	23	45	22	18	6	...	1	...	...	139	84.7	23	16.5
18	2	20	34	3	10	...	...	1	...	87	84.4	12	13.7
12	...	32	31	6	2	...	2	...	...	85	83.3	10	11.7
...	2	2	1	...	4	...	...	...	...	8	61.5	5	62.5
1	2	3	6	6	1	...	...	...	...	19	79.1	8	42.1
...	1	...	...	...	...	...	...	...	...	1	50.	1	100.
1	...	...	1	...	...	...	...	...	...	2	100.	...	...
...	1	...	1	...	...	...	...	...	...	2	50.	...	...
2	1	...	...	...	...	...	...	...	...	3	50.	1	33.3
...	2	...	...	...	...	...	...	...	...	2	50..	2	100.
...	...	...	1	...	...	...	...	...	...	1	50.	...	...
38	25	13	1	...	...	...	...	...	...	77	88.3	3	7.6
32	5	23	6	1	1	...	...	...	...	68	85.	6	8.8
6	1	3	8	23	...	1	6	...	...	48	77.4	30	62.5
7	1	12	12	14	7	...	3	...	...	56	57.7	25	44.6
7	6	7	2	2	14	...	...	...	...	38	74.5	16	42.1
...	...	...	...	...	...	...	...	...	...	...	...	...	...
...	...	...	...	1	2	...	...	...	...	3	100.	2	66.6
...	...	...	...	1	...	...	...	...	...	1	100.	1	100.
...	...	...	...	...	1	...	...	...	...	1	100.	1	100.
...	...	...	...	...	...	...	...	...	...	...	...	...	...
83	108	83	72	11	41	...	...	1	1	397	85.5	58	14.6
86	33	124	104	73	18	1	12	...	1	451	78.8	109	24.1
169	141	207	176	84	59	1	12	1	2	848	81.8	167	19.7

[5] The tabulation of amounts of fines and length of commitment term for the first six months of the year were considered sufficiently illustrative of the practice in Boston. See Tables 3 and 4.

[6] Sentence indeterminate.

[7] For comparison of sentences and appeals in relation of offense, see Table 6. For disposition of appealed cases in Superior Court, see Table 19. For correlation of disposition in Municipal Court and Superior Court, see Table 20.

TABLE 6. CONVICTIONS AND APPEALS ·IN RELATION TO OFFENSE AND
CITY OF BOSTON,

OFFENSE		TOTALS		PLACED ON FILE		FINED	
		Convicted	Appealed[2]	Convicted	Appealed	Convicted	Appealed
Adultery	M	35	4	4	...	...	...
	F	29	5	1	...	...	...
Fornication	M	143	12	16	...	69	2
	F	139	23	24	...	23	1
Lewd and lascivious cohabitation	M	87	12	18	...	2	...
	F	85	10	12	...	...	...
Nuisance—house of ill-fame	M	8	5	...	...	2	...
	F	19	8	1	...	2	1
House of ill-fame	M	1	1	...	...	1	1
	F	2	...	1	...	...	...
Disorderly house	M	2	...	...	...	1	...
	F	3	1	2	...	1	1
Persons permitting premises to be used for immoral purposes	M	2	2	...	...	2	2
	F	1	...	...	...	...	...
Violating True Name Law	M	77	3	38	...	25	3
	F	68	6	32	...	5	4
Common night-walkers	M	...	...	...	...	...	...
	F	48	30	6	...	1	...
Idle and disorderly	M	...	...	...	...	...	...
	F	56	25	7	...	1	1
Accosting and annoying person of the opposite sex	M	38	16	7	...	6	3
	F	...	...	...	...	...	...
Deriving support from the earnings of a prostitute	M	3	2	...	...	...	...
	F	1	1	...	...	...	...
Soliciting for a prostitute	M	1	1	...	...	...	...
	F	...	...	...	...	...	...
TOTAL	M	397	58	83	...	108	11
	F	451	109	86	...	33	8
GRAND TOTAL		848	167	169	...	141	19

[1] Compiled from docket of the Municipal Court of the City of Boston, Second Sessions, 1920.   For discussion of this table, see p. 242.

DISPOSITION OF CASES ARRAIGNED IN THE MUNICIPAL COURT OF THE SECOND SESSIONS, 1920 [1]

| PROBATION | | | | COMMON JAIL | | HOUSE OF CORRECTION | | STATE FARM | | REFORMATORY FOR WOMEN | | PERCENTAGES | |
| Straight | | Suspended Sentence | | | | | | | | | | | |
Convicted	Appealed	Convicted	Appealed	Convicted	Appealed	Convicted	Appealed	Convicted	Appealed	Convicted	Appealed	Convicted (Of those arraigned)	Appealed (Of those convicted)
8	...	19	...	1	1	3	3	...	...	...	...	87.1	11.4
6	...	17	...	4	4	1	1	...	...	...	...	93.5	17.2
33	...	14	...	4	3	7	7	...	...	...	...	91.	14.3
45	...	22	...	18	15	6	6	...	...	1	1	84.7	16.5
20	...	34	...	3	3	10	9	...	...	...	...	84.4	13.7
32	...	31	...	6	6	2	2	...	...	2	2	83.3	11.7
1	...	1	...	...	...	4	4	...	...	...	...	61.5	62.5
3	...	6	...	6	6	1	1	...	...	...	...	79.1	42.1
...	...	...	...	...	...	...	...	...	...	...	...	50.	100.
...	...	1	...	...	...	...	...	...	...	...	...	100.	...
...	...	1	...	...	...	...	...	...	...	...	...	50.	...
...	...	...	...	...	...	...	...	...	...	...	...	50.	33.3
...	...	1	...	...	...	...	...	...	...	...	...	50.	100.
...	...	...	...	...	...	...	...	...	...	...	...	50.	...
13	...	1	...	...	...	1	1	...	...	...	...	88.3	7.6
23	...	6	...	1	1	1	...	...	...	...	...	85.	8.8
3	...	8	...	23	23	...	...	1	1	6	6	77.4	62.5
12	...	12	...	14	14	7	7	...	...	3	3	57.7	44.6
7	...	2	...	2	1	14	12	...	...	...	...	74.5	42.1
...	...	...	...	...	...	...	...	...	...	...	...	...	...
...	...	...	...	1	...	2	1	...	...	...	...	100.	66.6
...	...	...	...	1	1	...	...	...	...	...	...	100.	100.
...	...	...	...	...	...	1	1	...	...	...	...	100.	100.
...	...	...	...	...	...	...	...	...	...	...	...	...	...
82	...	72	...	11	8	41	38	...	...	...	...	85.5	14.6
124	...	104	...	73	70	18	18	1	1	12	12	78.8	24.1
206	...	176	...	84	78	59	56	1	1	12	12	81.8	19 7

[1] For disposition of appealed cases in Superior Court, see Table 19. For correlation of disposition in Municipal Court and Superior Court, see Table 20.

TABLE 7. PLEAS IN RELATION TO OFFENSE AND CONVICTION, MUNICIPAL COURT OF THE CITY OF BOSTON, SECOND SESSIONS, JANUARY 1 TO JUNE 30, 1920

OFFENSE		TOTAL NUMBER ARRAIGNED	BAIL FORFEITURES	PLEAS			CONVICTIONS		
				Guilty	Not guilty	Misc.	Total	Number convicted who plead not guilty	Per cent convicted who plead not guilty
Adultery	M	25	...	11	14	...	23	12	85.7
	F	20	...	9	11	:..	19	10	90.9
Fornication	M	77	2	37	37	1	73	36	97.3
	F	81	8	33	36	4	70	35	97.2
Lewd and lascivious cohabitation	M	46	2	19	25	...	36	19	76.
	F	49	2	21	26	....	41	21	80.7
Nuisance—house of ill-fame	M	8	...	...	8	...	6	6	75.
	F	8	...	1	7	...	7	6	85.7
House of ill-fame	M	1	...	...	1	...	...	...	...
	F	1	...	...	1	...	1	1	100.
Disorderly house	M	...	...	...	...	...	...	...	...
	F	2	1	1	...	...	1	...	...
Permitting premises to be used for immoral purposes	M	4	...	...	4	...	2	2	50.
	F	2	...	1	1	...	1	1	100.
Violating True Name Law	M	43	1	22	19	1	40	17	89.5
	F	40	...	19	20	1	38	18	90.
Common night-walker	M	...	...	...	...	...	...	...	...
	F	24	2	...	22	...	19	19	86.3
Idle and disorderly	M	...	...	...	...	...	...	...	...
	F	58	4	4	50	...	33	29	58.
Accosting and annoying person of opposite sex	M	13	...	...	13	...	9	9	69.2
	F	...	...	...	...	...	...	...	...
Deriving support from the earnings of a prostitute	M	1	...	...	1	...	1	1	100.
	F	1	...	...	1	...	1	1	100.
TOTAL	M	218	5	89	122	2	190	102	83.6
	F	286	17	89	175	5	231	143	81.7
GRAND TOTAL		504	22	178	297	7	421	245	82.5

TABLE 8. DISPOSITION OF FIRST 100 CASES (WOMEN) ARRAIGNED IN
1920 IN THE MUNICIPAL COURT OF THE CITY OF BOSTON, SECOND
SESSIONS, SHOWING NUMBER OF CONTINUANCES PRECEDING FINAL
DISPOSITION [1]

DISPOSITION	TOTAL	NUMBER OF CONTINUANCES					
		0	1	2	3	4	6
Appealed	24	2	5	8	2	6	1
Defaulted	9	6	2	...	1	...	...
Jurisdiction declined	1	...	1	...	...	...	...
Dismissed for want of prosecution	2	...	2	...	...	...	...
Discharged	9	3	2	2	2	...	...
Placed on file	13	5	3	3	...	2	...
Fined	4	1	1	1	...	1	...
Probation	38	9	22	6	1	...	...
TOTAL	100	26	38	20	6	9	1

[1] Compiled from the docket of the Municipal Court of the City of Boston, Second
Sessions, 1920. This table is discussed on p. 243.

TABLE 9. DISPOSITION OF FIRST 100 CASES (WOMEN) ARRAIGNED IN
1920 IN THE MUNICIPAL COURT OF THE CITY OF BOSTON, SECOND
SESSIONS, SHOWING INTERVAL OF TIME BETWEEN ARREST AND
FINAL DISPOSITION [1]

DISPOSITION	DAYS BETWEEN ARRAIGNMENT AND DISPOSITION										
	TOTAL	1 day	2 days	3 days	4 days	5 days	6 days	7 days	8 days	9 days	11-20 days	21-33 days
Appealed	23	1	1	1	2	1	...	3	1	1	12	...
Defaulted	3	...	...	1	1	...	...	...	...	...	1	...
Jurisdiction declined	1	...	...	1	...	...	...	...	...	...	...	...
Dismissed for want of prosecution	2	...	1	...	...	...	1	...	...	...	...	...
Discharged	7	1	1	...	1	1	...	...	...	...	2	1
Placed on file	8	...	1	1	1	...	...	1	1	...	2	1
Fined	1	...	...	...	...	...	...	...	...	...	1	...
Probation	29	1	...	6	5	1	3	7	1	1	3	1
TOTAL	74	3	4	10	10	3	4	11	3	2	21	3

[1] For source of data, see footnote 1, Table 8.

TABLE 10. RELATION BETWEEN NUMBER OF CONTINUANCES OF CASES OF SEVENTY-FOUR WOMEN TO INTERVALS OF TIME BETWEEN ARREST AND FINAL DISPOSITION [1]

TIME INTERVALS	TOTAL	NUMBER OF CONTINUANCES				
		1	2	3	4	6
1 day	3	3	...	...	...	...
2 days	4	3	...	1	...	...
3 days	10	10	...	...	...	...
4 days	10	6	4	...	...	...
5 days	3	3	...	...	...	...
6 days	4	3	1	...	...	...
7 days	11	6	5	...	...	...
8 days	3	2	1	...	...	...
9 days	2	1	1	...	...	...
11–20 days	21	1	6	5	8	1
21–33 days	3	...	2	...	1	...
TOTAL	74	38	20	6	9	1

[1] Based on Tables 8 and 9.

TABLE 11. BAIL FORFEITURES, MUNICIPAL COURT OF THE CITY OF BOSTON, SECOND SESSIONS, JANUARY 1 TO JUNE 30, 1920 [1]

OFFENSE		TOTAL NUMBER OF FORFEITURES	CASH BAIL		REAL ESTATE					PERSONAL RECOGNIZANCE	NOT SPECIFIED	NUMBER OF CASES IN WHICH RECOVERY WAS SOUGHT
			$25	$50	$100	$200	$300	$500	Not Recorded			
Fornication	M	2	...	1	1	...	...	...	...	...	...	...
	F	8	3	...	2	...	...	1	2	...	...	5
Lewd and lascivious cohabitation	M	2	...	...	...	...	...	...	2	...	...	2
	F	2	...	1	...	...	...	...	...	...	1	...
Disorderly house	M	...	...	...	...	...	...	...	...	...	...	...
	F	1	...	...	...	...	...	...	...	1	...	...
Violating True Name Law	M	1	...	...	...	...	...	...	...	1	...	...
	F	...	...	...	...	...	...	...	...	...	...	...
Common nightwalker	M	...	...	...	...	...	...	...	...	...	...	...
	F	2	...	...	...	2	...	...	...	...	...	2
Idle and disorderly	M	...	...	...	...	...	...	...	...	...	...	...
	F	4	...	...	...	2	1	...	1	...	...	4
TOTAL	M	5	...	1	1	...	...	...	2	1	...	2
	F	17	3	1	2	4	1	1	3	1	1	11
GRAND TOTAL		22	3	2	3	4	1	1	5	2	1	13

[1] Compiled from docket of Municipal Court of the City of Boston, Second Sessions, 1920.   This table is discussed on p. 243.

[2] Re disposition in Superior Court of bail forfeiture cases, see Table 13.

TABLE 12. BAIL FORFEITURES, MUNICIPAL COURT OF THE CITY OF BOSTON, SECOND SESSIONS, 1920 [1]

Offense		Total Number of Forfeitures	Cash Bail				Real Estate					Personal Recognizance	Not Specified	Number of Cases in Which Recovery was Sought[2]
			$20	$25	$50	Not recorded	$100	$200	$300	$500	Not recorded			
Fornication	M	8	...	...	3	...	2	...	...	...	1	2	...	2
	F	19	...	5	2	1	3	2	...	1	4	1	...	10
Lewd and lascivious cohabitation	M	5	...	...	...	...	...	...	1	1	2	1	...	4
	F	7	1	...	1	...	...	...	...	...	2	...	3	2
Nuisance—house of ill-fame	M	...	...	...	...	...	...	...	...	...	...	...	...	...
	F	2	...	...	...	...	...	...	...	...	2	...	...	2
Disorderly house	M	...	...	...	...	...	...	...	...	...	...	...	...	...
	F	2	...	...	...	...	...	...	...	...	...	2	...	...
Violating True Name Law	M	1	...	...	...	...	...	...	...	...	...	1	...	...
	F	...	...	...	...	...	...	...	...	...	...	...	...	...
Common night-walker	M	...	...	...	...	...	...	...	...	...	...	...	...	...
	F	5	...	...	...	...	...	5	...	...	...	...	...	5
Idle and disorderly	M	...	...	...	...	...	...	...	...	...	...	...	...	...
	F	8	...	...	...	...	...	4	1	2	...	1	...	7
TOTAL	M	14	...	...	3	...	2	...	1	1	3	4	...	6
	F	43	1	5	3	1	3	11	1	3	8	4	3	26
GRAND TOTAL		57	1	5	6	1	5	11	2	4	11	8	3	32

[1] Compiled from docket of Municipal Court of the City of Boston, Second Sessions, 1920. For discussion of this table, see p. 243.

[2] Re disposition in Superior Court of bail forfeitures, see Table 13.

TABLE 13. DISPOSITION IN SUPERIOR COURT OF REAL ESTATE BAIL FORFEITURE CASES FROM MUNICIPAL COURT OF THE CITY OF BOSTON, SECOND SESSIONS, 1920 [1]

Real Estate	Total	Discontinued on Payment of			Pending July 1, 1921
		$20	$25	$26 to $35	
$100	4	...	1	...	3
200	11	2	...	3	6
300	2	...	...	...	2
400	1	...	...	...	1
500	4	...	1	...	3
Not specified	10	1	5	1	3
TOTAL	32	3	7	4	18

[1] Compiled from court papers filed with Clerk of Superior Court of Suffolk County. For discussion of this table, see p. 243.

TABLE 14. DISPOSITION AT EXPIRATION OF PROBATION OF CASES ARRAIGNED IN THE MUNICIPAL COURT OF THE CITY OF BOSTON, SECOND SESSIONS, 1920 [1]

Offense		Total	Surrendered	Defaulted	Probation Extended	Dismissed from Probation	Warrant Issued before Expiration of Probation	Pending	Unknown
Adultery	M	27	3	7	3	9	...	4	1
	F	23	...	12	5	2	1	3	...
Fornication	M	47	...	9	7	31	...	...	...
	F	67	9	19	15	17	2	4	1
Lewd and lascivious co-habitation	M	54	2	16	15	18	...	3	...
	F	63	5	17	16	21	1	2	1
Nuisance—house of ill-fame	M	3	...	1	...	2	...	...	...
	F	9	1	4	1	2	...	1	...
House of ill-fame	M	...	...	...	...	...	...	...	...
	F	1	1	...	...	...	...	...	...
Disorderly house	M	1	1	...	...	...	...	...	...
	F	...	...	...	...	...	...	...	...
Permitting premises to be used for immoral purposes	M	...	...	...	...	...	...	...	...
	F	1	...	...	...	1	...	...	...
Violating True Name Law	M	14	...	2	1	9	...	1	1
	F	29	1	3	4	20	...	...	1
Common night-walker	M	...	...	...	...	...	...	...	...
	F	11	5	4	2	...	...	...	...
Idle and disorderly	M	...	...	...	...	...	...	...	...
	F	24	3	6	7	7	1	...	...
Accosting and annoying person of opposite sex	M	9	...	...	1	7	...	1	...
	F	...	...	...	...	...	...	...	...
TOTAL	M	155	6	36	27	75	...	9	2
	F	228	25	65	50	70	5	10	3
GRAND TOTAL		383	31	101	77	145	5	19	5

[1] Compiled from the docket of the Municipal Court of the City of Boston, Second Sessions, 1920. For discussion of this table, see p. 232.

TABLE 15. EXTENSIONS ON PROBATION UP TO OCTOBER 1, 1921, OF CASES PLACED UPON PROBATION BY THE MUNICIPAL COURT OF THE CITY OF BOSTON, SECOND SESSIONS, JANUARY 1 TO JUNE 30, 1920 [1]

Offense		Total Number Placed on Probation	Total Number of Probationers Whose Cases Were Extended	Probation Extended			
				Once	Twice	Three Times	Four Times
Adultery	M	18	3	.3	...	...	...
	F	16	7	2	2	3	...
Fornication	M	34	3	2	1	...	...
	F	37	13	11	1	...	1
Lewd and lascivious co-habitation	M	25	10	5	4	...	1
	F	30	10	6	3	1	...
Nuisance—house of ill-fame	M	1	...	...	...	...	...
	F	3	...	...	...	...	...
House of ill-fame	M	...	...	...	...	...	...
	F	1	1	1	...	...	...
Disorderly house	M	...	...	...	...	...	...
	F	...	...	...	...	...	...
Permitting premises to be used for immoral purposes	M	...	...	...	...	...	...
	F	1	...	...	...	...	...
Violating True Name Law	M	4	...	...	...	...	...
	F	17	3	2	1	...	...
Common night-walker	M	...	...	...	...	...	...
	F	4	3	1	2	...	...
Idle and disorderly	M	...	...	...	...	...	...
	F	12	5	4	1	...	...
Accosting and annoying person of opposite sex	M	2	...	...	...	...	...
	F	...	...	...	...	...	...
Deriving support from the earnings of a prostitute	M	...	...	...	...	...	...
	F	...	...	...	...	...	...
TOTAL	M	84	16	10	5	...	1
	F	121	42	27	10	4	1
GRAND TOTAL		205	58	37	15	4	2

[1] Compiled from docket of the Municipal Court of the City of Boston, Second Sessions, 1920. For discussion of this table, see p. 232.

TABLE 16. JUDGES PRESIDING IN SECOND SESSIONS, MUNICIPAL COURT OF THE CITY OF BOSTON, 1920 [1] [2]

1920	JUDGES
JANUARY	Wentworth Bolster
FEBRUARY	Creed Duff
MARCH	Parmenter Sullivan Bolster
APRIL	Parmenter Duff
MAY	Duff Wentworth
JUNE	Parmenter
SEPTEMBER	Wentworth
OCTOBER	Duff Dowd
NOVEMBER	Dowd Murray Sullivan
DECEMBER	Murray Duff Parmenter

[1] Supplied through the courtesy of the Chief Probation Officer of the Municipal Court of the City of Boston.

[2] No regular schedule for July and August.

TABLE 17. DISPOSITION IN SUPERIOR COURT OF SUFFOLK COUNTY OF CASES OF SEX OFFENDERS APPEALED IN THE MUNICIPAL COURT OF THE CITY OF BOSTON, JANUARY 1 TO JUNE 30, 1920 [1] [2]

Offense		Total Number Appealing	Defaulted	Nolle Pros.	On File			Fined	Probation	Common Jail	House of Correction	Pending	Unk own
					On recommendation of District Attorney	By order of the Court	On payment of expenses						
Adultery	M	2		1								1	
	F	3			1				1			1	
Fornication	M	5		1	1		1	2					
	F	15	2	3	3			4	1				2
Lewd and lascivious cohabitation	M	5			4								1
	F	6			2				3	1			
Nuisance—house of ill-fame	M	4				1	1	1			1		
	F	4		1	2				1				
House of ill-fame	M												
	F												
Disorderly house	M												
	F												
Permittng premises to be used for timmoral purposes	M	2					2						
	F												
Violating True Name Law	M	2		1	1								
	F	3			3								
Common night-walker	M												
	F	14	1	4	7	2							
Idle and disorderly	M												
	F	17	2	6	4				5				
Accosting and annoying person of opposite sex	M	2						1					1
	F												
Deriving support from earnings of a prostitute	M	1		1									
	F	1								1			
TOTAL	M	23		4	6	1	4	4			1	1	2
	F	63	5	14	22	2		4	11	2		1	2
GRAND TOTAL		86	5	18	28	3	4	8	11	2	1	2	4

[1] Compiled from docket of the Superior Court of Suffolk County, 1920. For discussion of this table, see pp. 243, 244, 246.

[2] For correlation of disposition in Superior Court with disposition in Municipal Court, see Table 18.

TABLE 18.   CORRELATION OF DISPOSITION OF APPEALED CASES IN THE MUNICIPAL COURT OF THE CITY OF BOSTON AND THE SUPREME COURT OF SUFFOLK COUNTY, JANUARY 1 TO JUNE 30, 1920 [1]

DISPOSITION IN THE SUPERIOR COURT		TOTAL	DISPOSITION IN MUNICIPAL COURT				
			Fined	Common Jail	House of Correction	State Farm	Reformatory for Women
Defaulted	M	...	...	...	...	...	...
	F	5	...	2	1	...	2
Nolle Pros.	M	4	1	1	2	...	...
	F	14	1	5	5	1	2
On file	M	11	5	...	6	...	...
	F	24	2	16	5	...	1
Fined	M	4	...	...	4	...	...
	F	4	...	...	4	...	...
Probation	M	...	...	...	...	...	...
	F	11	...	7	1	...	3
Common jail	M	...	...	...	...	...	...
	F	2	...	2	...	...	...
House of Correction	M	1	...	...	1	...	...
	F	...	...	...	...	...	...
Pending	M	1	...	1	...	...	...
	F	1	...	1	...	...	...
Unknown	M	2	...	1	1	...	...
	F	2	1	...	1	...	...
TOTAL	M	23	6	3	14	...	...
	F	63	4	33	17	1	8
GRAND TOTAL		86	10	36	31	1	8

[1] Compiled from dockets of Municipal Court of the City of Boston, Second Sessions, and Superior Court of Suffolk County, 1920.   For discussion of this table, see pp. 243–245.

TABLE 19. DISPOSITION IN SUPERIOR COURT OF SUFFOLK COUNTY OF CASES OF SEX OFFENDERS APPEALED IN THE MUNICIPAL COURT OF THE CITY OF BOSTON, SECOND SESSIONS, 1920 [1] [2]

Offense		Total	Defaulted	Nolle Pros.	Discharged	On File On recommendation of District Attorney	On File By order of the Court	On File On payment of expenses	Fined	Probation	Common Jail	House of Correction	Pending	Unknown
Adultery	M	4	1	1	...	...	...	...	...	1	...	...	1	...
	F	5	...	...	...	2	...	...	...	1	...	...	2	...
Fornication	M	12	...	3	...	2	...	1	5	1	...	...	...	...
	F	23	2	5	...	5	...	...	5	3	...	...	...	3
Lewd and lascivious cohabitation	M	12	...	1	...	4	...	...	...	3	1	...	...	3
	F	10	...	1	1	2	...	...	...	5	1	...	...	...
Nuisance—house of ill-fame	M	5	...	...	...	...	1	1	2	...	...	1	...	...
	F	8	1	4	...	2	...	...	1	...	...	...	...	...
House of ill-fame	M	1	...	...	...	1	...	...	...	...	...	...	...	...
	F	...	...	...	...	...	...	...	...	...	...	...	...	...
Disorderly house	M	...	...	...	...	...	...	...	...	...	...	...	...	...
	F	1	...	...	...	...	...	...	...	...	...	...	1	...
Permitting premises to be used for immoral purposes	M	2	...	...	...	...	...	2	...	...	...	...	...	...
	F	...	...	...	...	...	...	...	...	...	...	...	...	...
Violating True Name Law	M	3	...	1	...	1	...	...	...	...	...	...	...	1
	F	6	...	...	...	3	...	1	...	1	1	...	...	...
Common night-walker	M	...	...	...	...	...	...	...	...	...	...	...	...	...
	F	30	2	5	...	16	3	...	...	2	2	...	...	...
Idle and disorderly	M	...	...	...	...	...	...	...	...	...	...	...	...	...
	F	25	3	8	...	5	...	...	...	8	...	...	1	...
Accosting and annoying person of opposite sex	M	16	...	8	1	2	...	1	1	...	...	...	...	3
	F	...	...	...	...	...	...	...	...	...	...	...	...	...
Deriving support from earnings of a prostitue	M	2	...	1	...	...	...	...	...	...	...	...	...	1
	F	1	...	...	...	...	...	...	...	...	1	...	...	...
Soliciting for a prostitute	M	1	...	1	...	...	...	...	...	...	...	...	...	...
	F	...	...	...	...	...	...	...	...	...	...	...	...	...
TOTAL	M	58	1	16	1	10	1	5	8	5	1	1	1	8
	F	109	8	23	1	35	3	1	6	20	5	...	4	3
GRAND TOTAL		167	9	39	2	45	4	6	14	25	6	1	5	11

[1] Compiled from docket of Superior Court of Suffolk County, 1920. For discussion of this table, see pp. 243–245.

[2] For correlation of disposition in Superior Court with disposition in Municipal Court, see Table 20.

TABLE 20. CORRELATION OF DISPOSITION OF APPEALED CASES IN THE MUNICIPAL COURT OF THE CITY OF BOSTON, SECOND SESSIONS, AND THE SUPERIOR COURT OF SUFFOLK COUNTY, 1920 [1]

DISPOSITION IN THE SUPERIOR COURT		TOTAL	DISPOSITION IN MUNICIPAL COURT				
			Fined	Common Jail	House of Correction	State Farm	Reformatory for Women
Defaulted	M	1	...	...	1	...	...
	F	8	...	5	1	...	2
Nolle Pros.	M	16	3	3	10	...	...
	F	23	2	12	5	1	3
Discharged	M	1	...	...	1	...	...
	F	1	...	1	...	...	...
On file	M	16	7	1	8	...	...
	F	39	3	28	5	...	3
Fined	M	8	...	1	7	...	...
	F	6	...	2	4	...	...
Probation	M	5	...	1	4	...	...
	F	20	1	13	2	...	4
Common jail	M	1	...	...	1	...	...
	F	5	...	5	...	...	...
House of Correction	M	1	...	...	1	...	...
	F	...	...	...	...	...	...
Pending	M	1	...	1	...	...	...
	F	4	1	3	...	...	...
Unknown	M	8	2	1	5	...	...
	F	3	1	1	1	...	...
TOTAL	M	58	12	8	38	...	...
	F	109	8	70	18	1	12
GRAND TOTAL		167	20	78	56	1	12

[1] Compiled from dockets of Municipal Court of the City of Boston, Second Sessions, and Superior Court of Suffolk County, 1920. For discussion of this table, see pp. 244–246.

TABLE 21. APPEALED CASES PENDING DETERMINATION OF APPEAL IN
THE SUPERIOR COURT OF SUFFOLK COUNTY, 1920 [1]

DISPOSITION		TOTAL	IN JAIL	ON BAIL	UNKNOWN
Defaulted	M	1	1	...	...
	F	8	2	6	...
Nolle Pros.	M	16	1	14	1
	F	23	...	23	...
Discharged	M	1	1	...	...
	F	1	1	...	...
Placed on file	M	16	7	9	...
	F	39	7	32	...
Fined	M	8	4	4	...
	F	6	...	6	...
Probation	M	5	4	1	...
	F	20	6	14	...
Common jail	M	1	1	...	...
	F	5	5	...	...
House of Correction	M	1	1	...	...
	F	...	...	...	...
Pending	M	1	...	1	...
	F	4	2	2	...
Unknown	M	8	...	...	8
	F	3	...	...	3
TOTAL	M	58	20	29	9
	F	109	23	83	3
GRAND TOTAL		167	43	112	12

[1] For source of data and discussion, see footnote 1, Table 22, and p. 244.

TABLE 22. STUDY OF SOCIAL HISTORIES OF FIFTY WOMEN PLACED SECOND

Offense	Total Number of Probationers	COLOR		NATIONALITY								AGE AT TIME OF ARREST							
		White	Colored	American	English	Irish	Canadian	Russian	German	Italian	Spanish	18–19 Years	20–24 Years	25–29 Years	30–34 Years	35–39 Years	40–44 Years	45–49 Years	Over 50 Years
Adultery	8	7	1	5	…	…	1	1	…	1	…	1	5	2	…	…	…	…	…
Fornication	18	15	3	13	1	…	3	1	…	…	…	2	5	3	4	…	3	1	…
Lewd and lascivious cohabitation	12	10	2	5	1	3	…	1	…	1	1	1	4	3	2	1	1	…	…
House of ill-fame	1	1	…	…	…	…	…	…	1	…	…	…	…	…	…	…	1	…	…
Violating True Name Law	4	4	…	1	1	2	…	…	…	…	…	…	…	1	…	2	…	…	1
Common night-walker	1	1	…	…	…	1	…	…	…	…	…	…	…	1	…	…	…	…	…
Idle and disorderly	6	6	…	6	…	…	…	…	…	…	…	2	3	…	…	1	…	…	…
TOTAL	50	44	6	30	3	6	4	3	1	2	1	6	17	8	8	3	6	1	1

[1] For discussion and manner of selecting these cases, see pp. 234–237.
[2] Statements regarding religion are too inadequate to tabulate.

UPON PROBATION BY THE MUNICIPAL COURT OF THE CITY OF BOSTON, SESSIONS, 1920 [1] [2]

OFFENSE	CIVIL CONDITION AT TIME OF ARREST				MANNER OF LIVING AT TIME OF ARREST								CHILDREN					
													None	Legitimacy and Number of Children				
														Legitimate			Illegitimate— 1 child	Legitimacy not established— 1 child
	Single	Married	Widow	Not Stated	With Parents	With Husband	With Relative	Keeping House	In Hotel	In Rooming House	With Lover	Not Stated		1 child	2 children	3 children		
Adultery	...	8	...	...	1	1	...	...	...	...	2	4	4	2[3]	2	...	...	...
Fornication	6	8	3	1	1	...	...	5	1	4	3	4	12	2	...	1	1	2
Lewd and lascivious cohabitation	5	5	2	...	...	...	...	1	...	...	4	7	6	3	...	...	3	...
House of ill-fame	...	1	...	...	...	...	...	...	...	...	...	1	...	1	...	...	...	...
Violating True Name Law	...	3	1	...	...	3	...	1	...	...	...	...	1	...	...	3	...	...
Common night-walker	...	1	...	...	...	...	1	...	...	...	...	...	1	...	...	...	...	...
Idle and disorderly	4	2	...	...	3	1	...	1	...	1	...	...	4	...	1	...	1	...
TOTAL	15	28	6	1	5	5	1	8	1	5	9	16	28	8	3	4	5	2

[3] One probationer had one legitimate child and one child whose legitimacy was not established.

TABLE 23. NUMBER OF PREVIOUS AND SUBSEQUENT ARRAIGNMENTS[1] OF WOMEN PLACED UPON PROBATION IN THE MUNICIPAL COURT OF BOSTON, SECOND SESSIONS, 1920 [2]

Offense	Total Number of Probationers	Number of Previous Arraignments											Number of Subsequent Arraignments in the Municipal Court of the City of Boston, Second Sessions, up to October 1, 1921					
		0	1	2	3	4	5	10	13	14	17	22	0	1	2	3	4	5
Adultery	8	7	...	1	...	...	...	...	...	...	...	...	6	...	2	...	...	...
Fornication	18	11	1	...	1	...	2	1	1	1	...	...	15	...	1	...	1	1
Lewd and lascivious cohabitation	12	10	...	...	...	1	...	...	...	...	1	...	11	1	...	...	...	...
House of ill-fame	1	...	...	1	...	...	...	...	...	...	...	...	1	...	...	...	...	...
Violating True Name Law	4	4	...	...	...	...	...	...	...	...	...	...	4	...	...	...	...	...
Common night-walker	1	...	...	...	...	...	...	...	...	...	...	1	...	...	...	1	...	...
Idle and disorderly	6	4	1	1	...	...	...	...	...	...	...	...	3	3	...	...	...	...
TOTAL	50	36	2	3	1	1	2	1	1	1	1	1	40	4	3	1	1	1

[1] In the absence of a finger-printing system, it is apparent that this record may only partially represent the actual number of recidivists.
[2] For source of data see footnote 1, Table 22.

TABLE 24. FREQUENCY OF CALLS AT HOME OF PROBATIONER IN RELATION TO THE NUMBER OF TIMES PROBATIONER, RELATIVE, OR HOUSEKEEPER WAS FOUND AT HOME [1]

Number of Calls Made at Probationers' Home	Total Number of Probationers[2]	Number of Times Officer Found Probationer					Number of Times Officer Found Relative or Housekeeper in Absence of Probationer				
		0	1	2	3	5	0	1	2	3	4
1	6	5	1	...	...	...	3	3	...	...	...
2	6	3	1	2	...	...	3	2	1	...	...
3	6	2	1	...	2	...	3	3	...	...	...
4	1	...	...	...	1	...	...	1	...	...	...
5	4	...	2	...	1	1	2	...	2	...	...
6	2	...	...	...	1	1	2	...	...	...	...
7	1	1	...	...	...	...	1	...	...	...	...
8	1	...	...	1	...	...	...	...	...	1	...
9	1	...	...	...	...	1	...	...	1	...	...
10	1	...	...	...	1	...	...	...	...	...	1
TOTAL	29	11	5	4	6	3	14	9	4	1	1

[1] For source of data and discussion, see footnote 1, Table 22.
[2] Twenty-one homes were not called upon by probation officer.

TABLE 25. FREQUENCY OF PROBATIONER'S REPORTING BY LETTER IN RELATION TO NUMBER OF CALLS MADE BY PROBATION OFFICER AND TO LENGTH OF PROBATION [1]

Number of Months on Probation	Total Number of Probationers [2]	Number of Times Probationer Reported by Letter								Number of Calls Made by Probation Officer at Probationer's Home										
		0	1	2	3	5	6	7	8	0	1	2	3	4	5	6	7	8	9	10
Up to 3 months	5	4	...	...	1	...	...	...	...	3	1	1	...	...	...	...	...	...	...	...
4–6 months	21	12	5	2	1	1	...	...	...	7	2	5	2	1	2	1	...	1	...	...
7–9 months	6	1	1	1	2	...	1	...	...	...	...	...	2	...	1	1	1	...	1	...
10–12 months	7	4	...	...	...	1	...	1	1	...	3	...	2	...	1	...	...	...	...	1
TOTAL	39	21	6	3	4	2	1	1	1	10	6	6	6	1	4	2	1	1	1	1

[1] For source of data and discussion see footnote 1, Table 22.

[2] The eleven probationers not accounted for in this table were disposed of as follows: one by another department of the court, four returned to their home towns, and four were placed upon inside probation. The records of two probationers could not be found.

[3] Second deputy probation officer informed the writer that girls who were visited by probation officer are not required to write except to inform of change of address.

TABLE 26. DISPOSITION OF PROBATION CASES AT EXPIRATION OF PROBATION [1]

Offense	Total Number of Probationers	Disposition at Expiration of Probation			
		Defaulted	Dismissed	Probation Extended	Still on Probation
Adultery	8	5	...	2	1
Fornication	15	6	4	4	1
Lewd and lascivious cohabitation	11	2	6	3	...
House of ill-fame	1	1	...	...	...
Violating True Name Law	4	...	4	...	...
Common night-walker	...	...	...	...	...
Idle and disorderly	5	2	2	1	...
TOTAL	44	16	16	10	2

[1] For source of data and discussion, see footnote 1, Table 22. For status of probationers October 1, 1921, see p. 237.

[2] Six girls were surrendered before expiration of probation.

CHAPTER IV

THE WOMEN'S DAY COURT OF MANHATTAN AND THE BRONX, NEW YORK CITY

The Women's Court of New York is the first court in the United States to be established as a special court dealing with women sex delinquents. There is doubtless no other court in this country to-day, which is so highly specialized along the lines of sex delinquency, as this court.

There is no court in New York City that corresponds exactly to the Municipal Courts of Chicago, Philadelphia, and Boston.

HISTORY AND COURT ORGANIZATION

Inasmuch as the organization of New York City is so radically different from that of the other cities mentioned, it has been deemed wise to say a word in explanation thereof, before describing further the court with which this study is concerned. The city embraces five counties and five boroughs, the counties being political subdivisions of the state, and the boroughs being subdivisions of the municipality. The borough of Manhattan is coterminous with New York County, the borough of the Bronx with Bronx County, the borough of Brooklyn with Kings County, the borough of Queens with Queens County, and the borough of Richmond with Richmond County. This difference in political organization with the separate county governments, explains the greater lack of uniformity in the courts of New York City than in the other cities studied.

The courts of the borough of Manhattan which have criminal jurisdiction are: the City Magistrates' Courts, the Court of Special Sessions, the Court of General Sessions, and the

Supreme Court. All but the last named court are exclusively criminal courts. In the other counties the jurisdiction of the Court of General Sessions is exercised by the criminal parts of the county courts. In other respects the courts of these boroughs are the same as those of Manhattan. Since the enactment of the Inferior Criminal Courts Act in 1910,[1] the jurisdiction of the City Magistrates' Courts and the Court of Special Sessions has been coterminous with the whole city.

The Magistrates' Court[2] is a court of first instance and is held by a city magistrate who acts as both judge and jury. In these courts are arraigned persons charged with the commission of (1) a felony, or (2) a misdemeanor, or (3) a violation of a law (sometimes spoken of as an "offensé") or ordinance not classified either as a felony or misdemeanor. It is the duty of the magistrate to determine whether he shall discharge or hold to await the action of the grand jury a person charged with committing a felony, or hold for trial at the Court of Special Sessions a person charged with committing a misdemeanor or reduce the degree of the crime upon which the defendant is arraigned. In the third class of cases, he has summary power and jurisdiction to determine guilt or innocence and to sentence those convicted. As already stated, in New York City, crimes are classified into felonies, misdemeanors, and offenses. Persons charged with offenses are tried in the Magistrates' Courts; with misdemeanors, in the Court of Special Sessions; and with felonies, in the Court of General Sessions for the borough of Manhattan and in the County Courts for all other boroughs. Felonies may also be tried in the Supreme Court in all counties. The Magistrates' Courts and the Court of Special Sessions sit without a jury. This later court consists of three judges, determination being by a majority. In these two courts are heard most of the

---

[1] Chap. 659, Laws of New York, 1910. This act was amended in 1912, '13, '14, '15, '17, '18, '19, '21, '22.

[2] Many Special Sessions cases are tried by magistrates sitting as judges of Special Sessions.

cases involving sex delinquency, corresponding to those tried in the courts in other cities previously studied.

The New York laws on the subject of sex delinquency are many and varied:

A prostitute may now be convicted and committed under a bewildering number of statutes, among others, the New York Consolidation Act, Code of Criminal Procedure, the Inferior Criminal Courts Act, State Charities Law, Tenement House Law, Penal Law, and Chap. 353 of the Laws of 1886. Likewise the keeper of a bawdy house makes herself liable to punishment under the Penal Law, Code of Criminal Procedure, Liquor Tax Law, Tenement House Law, Public Health Law, White Slave Traffic Act and the Immigration Laws.[1]

Because of this diversity of statutes, which not infrequently makes one act at the same time an offense, a misdemeanor, and a felony, the crime may be triable in the Magistrates' Courts, in the Court of Special Sessions, or in the Court of General Sessions, depending on the charge upon which the complaint is based. The complainant is generally a police officer, and he determines, frequently without consulting the District Attorney, whether the charge as originally made be a felony, misdemeanor, or offense. The custom seems to be to make most prostitution cases upon charges that can be tried summarily in the Magistrates' Court, so that a speedy disposition may be secured. The Magistrates' Court designated to hear prostitution cases in which women are defendants in the boroughs of Manhattan and the Bronx is the Women's Court. No special Magistrates' Court has been designated to hear prostitution cases in which the defendants are men. In the latter case, the charge is filed and the trial takes place in the court located in the district in which the offense occurred. It will thus be seen that a special study of men's cases is impracticable, because of the fact that they are scattered among eight different courts in Manhattan and the Bronx alone. Furthermore, none of these courts is a

---

[1] Spingarn, *Laws Relating to Sex Morality in New York City,* pp. xi–xii, Introduction.

special court dealing with sex delinquency, to which type of court this study has been limited.

The Women's Court of Manhattan, however, is a specialized court. Cases of women and girls, involving prostitution or incorrigibility (generally coupled with sex delinquency) are the only ones tried. Preliminary hearings of petit larceny cases (shop-lifting only) are held, and these defendants are bound over for trial in Special Sessions. All women arrested in Manhattan and the Bronx for soliciting, streetwalking, offering to commit prostitution, committing prostitution, and knowingly residing in a house of prostitution in a tenement, as well as most women who rent rooms for the purpose of prostitution, who permit a place under their control to be used for such purpose, or who procure another for such purpose are tried in this court. As a matter of fact, the main volume of prostitution in New York passes through this court.[1] Inasmuch as Manhattan contains the "White Lights," the principal theaters and other commercialized amusements, and the principal hotels, cafés, and cabarets, and is constantly thronged with transient visitors and sightseers, this section is chosen by the prostitute for her main *locus operandi*. It is here that she can find the bulk of her customers, and it is also here that the potential customer turns to seek the prostitute. The echoes of this business of prostitution are heard in the Women's Court. A study of this court, therefore, should give a picture of the manner with which prostitution is dealt with in the city of New York. The report of the Committee of Fourteen for 1920 contains the following statement:[2]

With the decrease of disorderly house cases in the Court of Special Sessions to a comparatively inconsiderable number, due to the change

---

[1] In 1920, 882 defendants were convicted for prostitution in the Women's Court of Manhattan and the Bronx; while only 113 were convicted in Brooklyn and one in Queens. The Finger-print Bureau shows no prostitution cases from any of the other boroughs for that year.

[2] Page 19.

of vice conditions and amendments to the law, the Women's Court has become the center of legal proceedings to suppress prostitution in New York City.

The present Women's Day Court is a Magistrates' Court which has been specially designated and set aside, by a resolution of the Board of Magistrates under authority of Sec. 77 of the Inferior Criminal Courts' Act, as amended by Chap. 419 of the Laws of 1918, for prostitution cases in which women only are defendants.   The resolution [1] was enacted on

---

[1] WHEREAS, it is provided by Sec. 77 of the Inferior Criminal Courts' Act, as amended by Chap. 419 of the Laws of 1918, that the sessions of the Separate Court for Women, heretofore held at night, may by a resolution of the Board of Magistrates be held either wholly or partly in the day time, and that said Board shall, if said Separate Court for Women be closed earlier than one o'clock in the morning, make suitable provision for the immediate arraignment of women defendants arrested too late to be arraigned in the day court or said women's Separate Court and before one o'clock in the morning who shall demand an immediate hearing; and

WHEREAS, it is provided by Sec. 70 of said Act, as amended, that the Board of Magistrates may provide for holding in any borough such special City Magistrate Courts or Courts of Special Sessions for the trial of specified classes as they shall determine; and

WHEREAS, it is further provided in said Section 70 that, except as otherwise provided in such act, the territorial jurisdiction of all City Magistrates' Courts other than City Magistrates' District Courts, shall be coterminous with the city, unless the boundaries thereof within the city are otherwise prescribed by the Chief City Magistrate:

THEREFORE, BE IT RESOLVED, that the Separate Court for Women for the Boroughs of Manhattan and the Bronx, known as the Ninth District City Magistrates' Court, be held wholly in the day time on each day of the week, provided that the Chief City Magistrate may dispense with the Sunday sessions of the Court if in his judgment the public interest will not suffer thereby; that said Court shall open at 10:30 o'clock in the morning and shall not close earlier than 5 o'clock in the afternoon; that the City Magistrate assigned thereto shall be in attendance thereat, except during a reasonable recess; and that afternoon sessions may be dispensed with upon Saturdays, Sundays (unless no sessions at all), and legal holidays;

AND BE IT FURTHER RESOLVED, that all women arrested too late to be arraigned in the day court or said Women's Separate Court and before one o'clock in the morning, who shall demand an immediate hearing, shall be arraigned in the Men's Night Court and there detained, released, or paroled pending trial in the Separate Court for Women, and that all women arrested when said Separate Court for

Women shall not be in session but when a district court is sitting shall be June 28, 1918. The present court began its sessions in April, 1919.

This court is a continuation of the Women's Night Court, established in 1910, which itself was an outgrowth of the Night Court for Men and Women begun in 1907. The latter court was located in the Jefferson Market Building and was established so that a speedy trial might be given by the magistrates to those arrested for petty offenses after the close (4 p.m.) of the regular sessions of the district courts.

---

arraigned in the Second District City Magistrate's Court, as at present provided by resolution of the Board of June 30, 1913, adopted pursuant to Section 78 of the said Inferior Criminal Courts' Act;

AND BE IT FURTHER RESOLVED, that pursuant to said Sections 70 and 77 of said act, and in order to carry out the purpose and intent thereof, said Separate Court for Women is hereby declared to be a special court and shall hear and determine all cases and proceedings against women as follows: any violation of Section 150 of the Tenement House Law; any violation of Subdivisions 3 and 4, Section 887 of the Code of Criminal Procedure; any violation of Subdivision 2 of Section 1458 of the Consolidation Act; any violation of Section 1466 of said Consolidation Act, as amended, and commonly known as Chapter 436 of the Laws of 1903, relating to wayward and incorrigible girls or intemperate women; any violation of Section 1146 of the Penal Law (keeping disorderly house); any and all offenses of a prostitutional nature, at present or hereafter defined by law; any violation of the penal law known as petit larceny, where the same shall have been committed in a retail mercantile establishment, commonly known as shoplifting. All cases and proceedings against men and women charged with offenses arising out of the same transactions shall be disposed of as heretofore;

AND BE IT FURTHER RESOLVED, and it is hereby recommended to the Chief City Magistrate, that he continue the territorial jurisdiction of said Women's Separate Court as at present under the powers vested in him by Section 70 of said act;

AND BE IT FURTHER RESOLVED, that said day sessions shall commence as soon as practicable and immediately upon the securing of suitable court room accommodations, and that it be referred to the Chief City Magistrate to select such court room accommodations, which shall be located as near as may conveniently be to the place of detention for women as hereinafter provided;

AND BE IT FURTHER RESOLVED, that the Chief City Magistrate confer with the Police Commissioner and the Commissioner of Corrections to the end that a suitable place of detention for women may be selected and designated by said Police Commissioner pursuant to Sec. 359 of the Greater New York Charter, and that suitable rules and regulations may be adopted relative to the acceptance of bail by the police lieutenant in charge there and to the fixing of responsibility therefor.

The Page Commission Report, Inferior Criminal Courts, 1910, on page 45, says:

The Night Court was established pursuant to the provisions of Chap. 598 of the Laws of 1907. The purpose of the enactment was to put a stop to the evil known as the station-house bond. It was claimed that certain of the police and certain bondsmen were in league, so that by constant arrests of prostitutes these women were compelled to get bail in order to be released until the following morning, and for that bail to pay heavily to the professional bondsmen.

Previously, because of inability to give bail for appearance in court the next morning, many of the defendants spent the night in jail, regardless of innocence or guilt. The giving of an immediate trial was expected to dispense with the necessity of the defendant's seeking to make bail, thus minimizing the bail-bond evil, which was then considered serious.

This court was not established as a special court to deal exclusively with prostitution cases, male and female. Many other types of offenses were also heard. Subd. 4 of Sec. 887 of the Code of Criminal Procedure had not yet been enacted in its present form. There was no law penalizing the male customer, and the prostitute was generally brought in under Sec. 1458 of the Consolidation Act for soliciting or loitering on the streets for the purpose of prostitution. It concentrated the prostitution cases in one court, however, and thereby focused attention upon the problem of prostitution. This no doubt had its influence upon the Page Commission which in 1910 recommended the enactment of the Inferior Criminal Courts Act (Chap. 659, Laws 1910) with its Sec. 77, providing for a separate Night Court for Women,[1] and other

---

[1] Page 48, Page Commission Report on Inferior Criminal Courts, 1910, contains the following statement:

"The establishment of a night court for women only will undoubtedly limit the number of doubtful male characters who are seen from time to time among the spectators at the night court. It will give an opportunity for concentration of effort in relation to cases of women and will enable those philanthropically inclined more effectively to give their assistance to the prisoners as well as to the Magistrates and probation officers."

progressive provisions such as the assignment of magistrates to the court by the Chief City Magistrate, and for the establishment of a Finger-print Bureau in prostitution cases.

Chief Magistrate McAdoo, in Report, Board of Magistrates, New York City, First Division, 1910, on pages 11 and 12, says:

The new law made radical provisions with reference to new courts. It provided for two night courts, one for men and one for women, thus separating the sexes and doing away with the disgraceful conditions which formerly prevailed in a single court where promiscuous throngs of degenerate and wretched unfortunates, professional criminals, and minor offenders of both sexes, sometimes only partly sobered from the effects of alcohol, were herded together nightly.

The law gave to the Chief City Magistrate the right to name magistrates for these courts. In the Night Court for Women, where we deal to a great extent with difficult and delicate questions relating to the social evil, and with the enforcement of the law making for decency and order on the public streets, especially after nightfall, I deemed it best in order that we might get consistency, arising from experience, that three magistrates should be specially assigned for this work, instead of allowing the usual rotation of all the magistrates to this court. This plan has worked admirably. Three conscientious, painstaking, and able magistrates do the work here, and the policy of the court is, while giving every possible opportunity for the defense and conducting the trials with scrupulous fairness, that there shall be coöperation with the police to the extent at least of keeping the streets and thoroughfares of the city free from what would otherwise be an intolerable nuisance. My own idea has been to the effect that fines in these cases are practically useless; that when there is any chance for reformation, probation on commitment to a reformatory is the best course to pursue. But where the defendant, convicted, is an incorrigible professional, the best punishment is a determinate sentence to the Workhouse. This court has practically killed the business of the professional bondsman, and, as the fines were usually paid by the keepers of the assignation houses or the traffickers in "white slaves," to fine them only encouraged the vice than otherwise, and made the city a partner, as it were, with these wretched panders who make out of vice a profitable business.

LAWS RELATING TO SEX DELINQUENCY

In order to present a picture of the limitations as well as the possibilities of the New York court relative to sex delinquency, a brief résumé of the laws is given herewith.

The law which brings most of the offenders to the Women's Court is Subd. 4 of Sec. 887, of the Code of Criminal Procedure. This law reads as follows:

The following persons are vagrants:

4. A person (a) who offers to commit prostitution; or (b) who offers or offers to secure another for the purpose of prostitution, or for any other lewd or indecent act; or (c) who loiters in or near any thoroughfare or public or private place for the purpose of inducing, enticing, or procuring another to commit lewdness, fornication, unlawful sexual intercourse, or any other indecent act; or (d) who in any manner induces, entices, or procures a person who is in any thoroughfare or public or private place, to commit any such acts; or (e) who receives or offers or agrees to receive any person into any place, structure, house, building, or conveyance for the purpose of prostitution, lewdness, or assignation or knowingly permits any person to remain there for such purposes; or (f) who in any way, aids or abets or participates in the doing of any of the acts or things enumerated in subdivision four of section eight hundred and eighty-seven of the code of criminal procedure; or (g) who is a common prostitute who has no lawful employment whereby to maintain herself.

Sec. 889a of the same code provides as follows:

In the trial of any person charged with a violation of subdivision four of section eight hundred and eighty-seven of the code of criminal procedure, testimony concerning the reputation of the place wherein the offense occurred or of persons who frequent or reside therein shall be admissible in evidence in support of the charge.

Careful note should be taken of clause "a" of Subd. 4 of Sec. 887: "Who *offers* to commit prostitution." This embraces a complete offense, and under it, most of the charges are now being brought. This charge can be proved by a minimum of evidence, the following being sufficient to sustain a conviction:

> Prostitute: "Do you want to have a good time?"
> Complainant: "Yes; how much will it cost?"
> Prostitute: "I'll give you a good time for five dollars."
> Complainant: "All right."

The peculiar advantage of this law, from a law enforcement standpoint, is the establishment of the offense without any immoral act on the part of the complaining witness.

The evidence may be analyzed as follows:

The offer, of course, is obvious. The purpose, prostitution, is proved by the mention of money. Prostitution being defined as sexual intercourse for gain, or indiscriminate sexual intercourse without hire, the proof of offering for money establishes the element of indiscriminateness or promiscuity.

Rooming-house landladies who tacitly permit prostitution, and taxi chauffeurs who permit the use of their cars for such purpose are now charged under clause "e" of Subd. 4.

Most of the girl sex offenders under the age of 21 are charged with incorrigibility. The Incorrigibility Statute is known as Chapter 436 of the Laws of 1903 and reads as follows:

1. Whenever any female over the age of twelve years shall be brought by the police or shall voluntarily come before any court or a committing magistrate in the city of New York, and it shall be proved to the satisfaction of such court or magistrate by the confession of such female, or by competent testimony, that such female (first) is found in a reputed house of prostitution or assignation; or in company with, or frequenting the company of thieves or prostitutes, or is found associating with vicious and dissolute persons; or is wilfully disobedient to parent or guardian, and is in danger of becoming morally depraved; or (second) is a prostitute or is of intemperate habits, and has not been an inmate of the penitentiary or (third) is

convicted of petit larceny and is over sixteen years of age and has not been an inmate of the penitentiary, such court or magistrate may judge that it is for the welfare of such female that she be placed in a reformatory, and may thereupon commit such female to one of the following reformatory institutions, namely, the Protestant Episcopal House of Mercy, New York, Roman Catholic House of Good Shepherd (foot of Eighty-ninth Street), in the city of New York, or the New York Magdalen Home, which said institutions are hereby severally authorized to receive and hold females committed under this act.

3. Every commitment made under this act shall state the name and age of the female so committed, together with the cause of her commitment, and shall designate the institution to which she is committed, which institution shall, when practicable, be one which is conducted by persons of the some religious faith as such female, and such commitment shall also state the term of the commitment, which, if the female so committed is an adult, shall be three years; or, if such female is a minor, during her minority, unless sooner discharged by the·trustees or managers of such institution, provided, however, that no commitment made under this act, which shall recite the facts upon which it is based, shall be deemed or held to be invalid by reason of any imperfection or defect in form.

The purpose under which this law was enacted was the protection of the minor girl found associating with vicious or dissolute persons and in danger of becoming morally depraved. The majority of complaints in these cases are made by parents or guardians. However, the police occasionally bring in minor girls who are found under such circumstances as would make them subject to the law.

Prior to 1915 the law most frequently used to bring offenders into the Women's Court was Section 1458 of the Consolidation Act of 1882. However, this law was still being used during the period covered by the tables, viz.: the first six months of 1920. During 1922, Subd. 4, Sec. 887 of the C. C. P., which is a much newer law, was displacing Sec. 1458, for street solicitation. This is due to the fact that much less proof is necessary to convict under Subd. 4.

Sec. 1458, Subd. 2, reads as follows:

Every common prostitute or night-walker loitering or being in any thoroughfare or public place for the purpose of prostitution or solicitation, to the annoyance of inhabitants or passers-by shall be deemed to be guilty of disorderly conduct.

There has been some difference of view as to the proper construction of this section, but the preponderance of judicial and professional opinion leads to this conclusion:

That the cases divide themselves into two classes: (1) where the woman, being a common prostitute or night-walker, loiters in any public place for the purpose stated; or (2) where the woman actually solicits. In practice, nearly all of the cases that come before this court are for actual solicitation, and the evidence divides itself into two forms: (1) where the police officer in plain clothes, or a citizen, gives evidence that he was solicited by the defendant for the purpose named in the act; or (2) where the police officer in plain clothes testifies that he saw the defendant soliciting, in which her actions and the character of the neighborhood are also an evidence. When it is proved that the woman has solicited, *she establishes her character as a common prostitute or night-walker.*[1]

The former is classified as soliciting, and the latter as loitering.

In this class of cases called "loitering" there is circumstantial as well as direct evidence. There is no rule of law that rules out circumstantial evidence in these cases while it allows it for murder and the higher felonies. The Magistrate has before him the complainant, the woman defendant, and all the other circumstances that present themselves to him, sitting as Judge and jury, and this no doubt is the reason that mistakes leading to injustice are so rare as to be practically negligible. The finger-prints, as time goes on, show a professional and determined array of lawbreakers.[2]

---

[1] Annual Report, Board of Magistrates, First Division, New York City, 1911, p. 31.

[2] Loc. cit.

Keepers of disorderly houses, when charged under Sec. 1146 of the Penal Law, are tried in the Court of Special Sessions. A subsequent table will show that the number of disorderly house cases has greatly diminished during the past ten years. This is no doubt due to the extraordinary activity of the New York law enforcement authorities in the repression of prostitution.

Keeping a disorderly house is punishable by Sec. 1146 of the Penal Law, which penalizes the keeping or maintaining of a house of ill-fame or assignation of any description or place for the encouragement or practice, by persons, of lewdness, fornication, unlawful sexual intercourse, or any other indecent or disorderly act. The penalty is imprisonment for not more than one year, or a fine of not more than $500.00, or both, together with the voiding of the lease. Keepers of disorderly or bawdy houses may also be punished as disorderly persons under Sec. 899 of the Code of Criminal Procedure, penalty for which is a determinate sentence of not more than six months to the House of Correction,[1] or under Sec. 150 of the Tenement House Law, if the offense occurs in a tenement, or under clause "e" of Subd. 4, Sec. 887, C. C. P., which have already been quoted. Cases under Section 899 are triable in the Magistrates' Court, female defendants, of course, being tried in the Women's Court. No record can be found of any such cases having been brought.

Many of the offenders who are brought to the Women's Court are charged under Sec. 150 of the Tenement House Law. This law includes five types of offenders: (1) one who solicits another to enter a tenement;[2] (2) one who exposes

---

[1] Or an indeterminate sentence as is provided for other misdemeanors in the Court of Special Sessions.

[2] A "tenement house" is any house or building, or portion thereof, which is either rented, leased, let or hired out, to be occupied, or is occupied, in whole or in part, as the home or residence of three families or more living independently of each other, and doing their cooking upon the premises, and includes apartment houses, flat houses and all other houses so occupied. The Tenement House Law. Chap. 61 Consolidated Laws, Art. I, Sec. 2.

the person for the purpose of prostitution or other indecent act; (3) one who commits prostitution in a tenement; (4) one who knowingly resides in a house of prostitution in a tenement; and (5) one who keeps a house of prostitution in a tenement, or rents rooms therefor:

Sec. 150 reads as follows:

A person who (1) solicits another to enter a house of prostitution or a room in a tenement house or any part thereof for the purpose of prostitution; or (2) indecently exposes the private person for the purpose of prostitution or other indecency; or (3) commits prostitution in a tenement house or any part thereof; or (4) knowingly resides in a house of prostitution or assignation or ill-fame of any description in a tenement house; or (5) keeps or maintains a house of prostitution, assignation, or ill-fame of any description in a tenement house for such purpose, shall be deemed to be a vagrant, and upon conviction thereof shall be committed to the county jail for a term not exceeding six months from the date of commitment, or, if the person convicted is a female she may be placed upon probation except in the following cases: (a) when the offense was that of keeping or maintaining a house of prostitution, assignation, or ill-fame in a tenement house, or (b) when the female has been convicted previously of any offense or crime. The procedure in such case shall be the same as that provided by law for other cases of vagrancy.

The magistrate has jurisdiction to try and to determine finally, cases of this character.

Inasmuch as the male exploiter of prostitution does not pass through the Women's Court, the laws relating to this phase of the subject will not be set forth in full. The male exploiter, the pimp, and the male disorderly house keeper can be punished under Subd. 4 of Sec. 887 of the Code of Criminal Procedure, or as a disorderly person under Subd. 4 of Sec. 899, or under Sec. 150 of the Tenement House Law. All of these offenses are punishable in the Magistrates' Court in the district in which the offense occurred and not before a special court.

Pimps are punishable also, under Sec. 1148 and keepers of disorderly houses under Sec. 1146 of the Penal Law. These are misdemeanors and are triable in the Court of Special Sessions.

White-slavery, the compulsory prostitution of women, and pandering, are punishable under Sec. 2460 of the Penal Law. These are felonies, punishable by imprisonment from two to twenty years, and are triable in the Court of General Sessions in Manhattan, and in the County Court of the other counties, or in the criminal branch of the Supreme Court.

The law which most concerns the Women's Court is, of course, the Inferior Criminal Courts Act.[1] As already stated, it was under the authority of this Act that the Women's Court was created. This Act provides for the organization of both the Court of Special Sessions and the Magistrates' Courts. The provisions relating to the City Magistrates' Courts are contained in Secs. 70–115. These provide, generally, for the organization of the Board of Magistrates, who are the rule-making body, and vest certain administrative duties in the Chief City Magistrate.

The sections that apply particularly to the Women's Court are Secs. 77 and 77a. These read as follows:

Sec. 77. Night Courts; separate court for women. On and after the first day of September, nineteen hundred and ten, the Board of City Magistrates shall provide for the holding of at least two night sessions of the court, one of which shall be exclusively for the hearing of cases and proceedings against men and against men and women charged with offenses arising out of the same transaction, and one exclusively for the hearing of cases and proceedings against women. Said night sessions of court shall be held in different buildings, and each night court shall be open at eight o'clock in the evening, and shall not close earlier than one o'clock in the morning, or at such later hour as the Chief City Magistrate, in his discretion, shall deem best for the public interest. All persons who are arrested after the day

---

[1] Chapter 659, Laws of New York, 1910, as amended by the Laws of 1912, '13, '14, '15, '17, '19, '21, '22.

courts are closed, or at an hour too late to be brought to a day court, for offenses other than felonies, committed within the territorial jurisdiction of the night courts, must be brought to the said night court, and such night courts shall have jurisdiction to hear, try, and determine all cases coming within the summary jurisdiction of a City Magistrate. The Board of City Magistrates may, however, if they deem it best for the public interest, direct that the separate court for women be held either wholly or partly in the day time, anything in this act to the contrary notwithstanding.

The Board of City Magistrates shall, however, if said women's separate court be closed earlier than one o'clock in the morning, make suitable provision for the immediate arraignment of such women defendants arrested too late to be arraigned in a day court or said women's separate court and before one o'clock in the morning who shall demand immediate hearing. The lieutenant or other person in charge of the station-house shall immediately inform all women arrested too late to be tried in the day court or women's separate court and before one o'clock in the morning of such right to immediate arraignment. There shall be established on October first, nineteen hundred and ten, a place of detention, under the jurisdiction of the Commissioner of Correction, convenient to the night court for women, where women may be detained both before and after being heard, and in such detention place the young and less hardened shall be segregated, so far as practicable, from the older and more hardened offenders. Any magistrate, pending adjournment of the trial, or after conviction pending investigation before imposition of sentence, may, in his discretion, parole in the custody of the probation officer any female arraigned in any one of the Magistrates' Courts for any offense other than a felony; or may, subject to release on bail if before conviction, commit her temporarily to such institution for the reception of females as in his judgment is most suitable. Any such institutions are hereby authorized and directed to receive such females upon such short commitments. But no such commitments shall be for a longer period than four days, except with the consent of the defendant.

Pending the completion of a suitable place of detention, young and less hardened offenders arrested when the separate court for women is not in session shall be forthwith conveyed to such institutions for the reception of females as may have been designated by the Chief

City Magistrate as suitable for such purpose, to be there temporarily detained, subject to release on bail, until arraigned, in lieu of detention in a station-house or prison. And such institutions are hereby authorized and directed to receive such females. Any magistrate, pending adjournment of the trial, or after conviction pending investigation before imposition of sentence, may, in his discretion, parole in the custody of the probation officer any female arraigned in any one of the Magistrates' Courts for any offense other than a felony; or may, subject to release on bail if before conviction, commit her temporarily to such institution for the reception of females as in his judgment is most suitable. Any such institutions are hereby authorized and directed to receive such females upon such short commitments. But no such commitments shall be for a longer period than four days, except with the consent of the defendant.

Sec. 77a. Remand of female prisoners for observation and study. Whenever in the city of New York any female is convicted before a Magistrate of violation of section eight hundred and .eighty-seven of the Code of Criminal Procedure except subdivision eight thereof; of violation of subdivision four of section eight hundred and ninety-nine of the Code of Criminal Procedure; of violation of section fourteen hundred and fifty-eight of the New York City Consolidation Act except subdivision one thereof; of violation of section one hundred and fifty of the Tenement House Law; of frequenting disorderly houses or houses of prostitution for the purposes of prostitution; or of vagrancy, or of public intoxication; such Magistrate may, in his discretion, notwithstanding any provisions of the law to the contrary, commit such female to the hospital on Blackwell's Island under the judisdiction of the Commissioner of Correction, or to any suitable public hospital, or to any institution in the city of New York carrying on reformatory work for women in which facilities are available for the physical and mental examination of such female, or to the Waverly House, the home maintained by the New York Probation and Protective Association, or to the Florence Crittenton ·Home, maintained by the Florence Crittenton League, for study and observation, for a period not to exceed fourteen days; and such period may be extended by the Magistrate with the consent of the defendant for an additional period not to exceed fourteen days; and such institutions are hereby authorized to receive such females so committed. Whenever any such female is thus committed, the warden, superintendent, of other officer in charge of such institution shall cause an investigation to be made of the physical and mental condition of the said female and shall certify to the court the result of such study and observation.

APPEALS

Prior to July 1, 1922, appeals from a conviction by the magistrates in Manhattan were heard in Part One of the Court of General Sessions. Under this procedure the hearing on appeal was before only one judge and not by a bench of three or more, as is the case in most appellate courts. These appeals were not trials de novo, but went upon the stenographic record.

This appeal procedure was a survival of the days when magistrates were not necessarily lawyers, and were called police justices. When the qualifications for magistrates were increased, the law relating to appeals was for some reason left unchanged. This resulted in the anomaly of a judge who might not be a specialist in a particular class of cases, reviewing and passing finally upon the decisions of a magistrate who was so qualified.

While there were relatively few appeals from the convictions in the Women's Court, many of them involved points of considerable importance. The appeal procedure was changed by the Legislature in 1922 (Chap. 595, Laws 1922), so that appeals now go to the Court of Special Sessions, where they must be heard by an appellate bench of three judges.[1]

The case still goes up on the stenographic record as in the usual appellate procedure. The Appellate Court may reverse the conviction and discharge the defendant or order a new trial either before itself or in the Magistrates' Court. it also has power to modify the sentence imposed by the magistrate.

---

[1] See Table 3, at the end of this chapter.

PHYSICAL ASPECTS OF THE COURT

The Women's Day Court is located in the Jefferson Market Court Building, at the corner of 10th Street and 6th Avenue, in the borough of Manhattan. The building is of combination brown stone and brick, and of Gothic and Plantagenet architecture. It is connected with the women's temporary detention prison, which is of the same architecture.

The building contains two Magistrates' Courts, the entire second floor being given over to the Women's Day Court and its accessories.

During court hours the main entrance to the building is thronged with women offenders, shyster lawyers, professional bondsmen, men who appear to be pimps, etc. Inasmuch as this entrance serves both courts, the rule of the Women's Court against curiosity seekers does not apply to this entrance.

The Women's Court is approached by a winding stone staircase, which furnishes ingress and egress to the rooms of the Probation Department, as well as to the main court room. The main entrance to the court room is at its rear. On the opposite side is a door leading into the complaint room. The court room is probably large enough to accommodate 150 to 200 people. The room has somewhat the appearance of a church, the windows being ornamented and stained, and the benches resembling church seats. The ceiling is unusually high—probably not less than 40 feet.

A low iron railing separates the spectators from the court proper. Immediately in front of the railing are two rows of benches which during court hours are occupied by members of the vice squad, probation officers, welfare workers, etc. Attorneys are required to occupy the front benches immediately behind the railing. Between the iron railing and the judge's bench is a space about twenty feet wide. On one side is the door leading to the probation rooms and to the judge's chambers, and on the other side is the door leading to the detention rooms, finger-print room, physical examination room, etc., all of which are in turn connected by a corridor with the women's prison.

The judge's bench is on a raised platform, which is set off from the rest of the court room by a solid wooden railing. Immediately in front of the bench and below the platform is a long table with chairs for the defendant, her attorney, and the district attorney. At one end of this table, at the judge's left, is a small table for the court stenographer, and immediately adjoining the court stenographer, on a small platform partially inclosed by the solid railing is the witness chair. This arrangement brings the witness very close both to the stenographer and to the judge. At the judge's right is the desk occupied by the clerk of the court with a table holding the large docket book, etc. Immediately behind the judge, and at the front of the court, is a massive, heavily carved, wooden screen, upon which is the American flag. Behind this screen is a desk for the clerk's assistant, and the steel cases containing the records and files of the Court, the latter objects being entirely hidden from view.

The court room is spacious, well-lighted, and well-ventilated, and would leave nothing to be desired, were it not for its location. It is directly against the elevated railway. Whenever an elevated train passes, the noise is so deafening that it is generally necessary to halt proceedings for several moments, if the front windows are open.

The spectators in the audience are composed mostly of defendants on bail and awaiting trial, witnesses, and lawyers. A uniformed court attendant makes it his practice to question those present, and to ask those unable to show that they have business in the court to leave. The following sign is posted in front of the main entrance:

NOTICE: No person will be allowed in this Court room during the sessions of the Court except persons connected with cases, such as witnesses, defendants, and members of defendants' families, lawyers, newspaper reporters, students of sociology, and persons to whom permission is granted by the presiding Magistrate. No idlers or sightseers are permitted to attend. (Signed) William McAdoo, Chief City Magistrate.

No one is permitted to enter the door leading to the temporary detention room excepting probation officers and women court attendants. This excludes all men excepting the finger-print expert. On this door is a notice to the effect that police officers and male attendants of the court, except the finger-print clerk, are to be excluded from the detention room; that the door is to be kept locked at all times except when the court is in session; and that the key is to be in possession of the warden of the prison.

The place of detention consists of three comfortable rooms, all clean and well-lighted, with easy chairs, settees and tables, having more the appearance of office waiting rooms than of rooms of detention. These rooms replace the old-time bull-pen into which prisoners formerly were herded while awaiting their turn for trial.

The finger-print room contains the facilities for taking finger-prints. The records and files of the department, how-ever, are kept in the record rooms on the floor below, and are carried back and forth by means of a dumb-waiter.

DETENTION HOUSE

For many years plans have been discussed for a proper place of detention for women arrested in New York. Until tried in the Men's Night Court in 1907, arrested women were detained in precinct police stations[1] in charge of a matron. For the past 15 years, with the exception of a brief period discussed elsewhere,[2] women arrested in Manhattan or the Bronx (unless they succeed in making bail) have been taken

---

[1] The bail-bond evil in this connection has been discussed on pp. 278–280.
[2] P. 296.

to the Jefferson Market Prison to await trial. The arresting
officer may take certain young girls, who presumably are first
offenders, to the Florence Crittenton Home, a privately maintained detention home described on page 370. The arrested
woman is allowed to communicate with her friends (through
the matron) by letter, wire or telephone. She may communicate with her lawyer at any time.

Detention quarters in Jefferson Market comprise four
short tiers of 14 cells each, extending in two rows, back to
back, with a corridor running along each side. The barred
door at the end of each row is locked. A row of cells in the
lowest tier is used for colored first offenders and the rows
on the second tier are reserved for white first offenders [1]
and those charged with shop-lifting. The fourth tier is used
for inmates from the Workhouse assigned for duties in the
Detention House; cleaning, washing, serving meals, etc.

The cells, which are about six by seven feet in size, have
recently been fitted out with modern plumbing, although
formerly, as now, each cell had a toilet and a basin with running water. Bedding is changed daily. Meals for all the prison
inmates, men and women, are prepared by a chef and sent
up on the elevator, and the women from the Workhouse serve
the girls in each row, who sit around a table in the corridor.

Four matrons, all of whom are non-resident, are on duty,
three in the day and one at night. Each works 12 hours, the
night matron relieving the others at 7 p.m. The matrons
have for their own use an office and a small kitchen.

The Detention House accommodates 56 individuals, the
count varying from 20 to 40. On the day the house was
visited, the count was 22. Women are said to be held there·
seldom longer than a week.

Detained women await the call of their case in rooms and
corridors opening off the Women's Court. Supposed first

---

[1] The matron in charge has been there for four years, having served as a
workhouse matron for 13 years. She says that she readily recognizes the new
and old offenders, and classifies them accordingly.

offenders occupy one room; those charged with shop-lifting or petit larceny, an adjoining room. Each room receives plenty of light and air from an open window, and each has a toilet. Those awaiting trial for incorrigibility sit on a bench in the corridor running past these two rooms. At the end of a long corridor leading to the examining room, stands a large cell where old offenders are held while waiting for their call.

Defendants convicted in the court are turned over by a court attendant to the matron, who leads them to the finger-print room. She then records the woman's name and other pertinent facts. On the following day she takes her to the doctor's room for examination.

On July 1, 1921, the use of the Jefferson Market Prison as as place of detention was discontinued and not resumed until March 23, 1922. During the intervening months, women were detained in special quarters at the Workhouse. Usually they had to make at least six trips between the Court and the Workhouse before receiving sentence.

COURT PERSONNEL

The personnel of the Women's Court is comprised of the following:

1. A Judge, who is appointed by the Mayor for a term of ten years as a City Magistrate[1] and is assigned to the Women's Court by the Chief City Magistrate. Three Magistrates are specially assigned to this Court during the period of a year, and they serve interchangeably.

2. A Deputy Assistant District Attorney, appointed by the District Attorney of New York County.

3. The official court stenographer, who is a male.

4. Three male bailiffs, called court attendants, who are civilian appointees. They are clad in blue uniforms with brass buttons. One

---

[1] The annual salary of a Magistrate is at present $8000.

of them is known as captain, and wears two bars as an insignia of that office.

5. Five women Probation Officers, one of whom acts as Probation Officer in charge for that Court. They are all appointed by the Board of Magistrates, and are assigned by the Chief Probation Officer to this Court.

6. A male clerk and two assistants, who are appointed by the Board of Magistrates and are assigned by the Chief Clerk of the Magistrates' Court to this Court.

7. One male finger-print expert.

8. One interpreter.

9. One stenographer for Probation Department.

10. Four social workers, furnished by private organizations, Catholic, Protestant, Jewish and Colored.

All of the above are selected from the eligible list of the City Civil Service, excepting the Judge and the District Attorney.

The Report of the Committee of Fourteen for 1920 contains the following statement relative to the assignment of magistrates:[1]

Shortly after his appointment as Chief City Magistrate in 1910, Judge McAdoo assigned four of his associates—Magistrates Barlow, Corrigan, Herbert, and Murphy—to sit in rotation in the Women's Night Court. The assignments of Magistrates Herbert and Murphy were continued until their appointment to the Court of Special Sessions in 1914 and 1915. Magistrate Barlow[2] would still be rendering great service in the Court if ill health did not prevent. Changes of assignment to the Women's Court have been made from time to time, and have included, in addition to those mentioned and those now serving, Magistrate Cobb, assigned 1916–1919, Magistrate Frothingham, 1915–1918, and Magistrate Marsh, 1915–1919.

The appointment of special magistrates to the Women's Court has proved most satisfactory, for not only were those who accepted the appointment interested in the peculiar problems of that Court, but

---

[1] Report of the Committee of Fourteen, 1920, p. 22.
[2] Since deceased.

they speedily became experts in the special problems of the Court and in the increasingly technical procedure of the cases.

*   *   *   *   *   *

Judge McAdoo, for 1920, designated Magistrates McGeehan, Mancuso, and Norris to preside in the Women's Court; thus breaking for the first time his custom of so designating four magistrates. Judge McGeehan had twice previously been designated, but it was the first regular assignment of his two associates. Judge Norris had been appointed but recently a magistrate, and is the first woman to hold judicial office in New York City.[1]

In 1921 Judges McGeehan, Norris, and Silberman were designated, and in 1922 Judges Hatting, Norris, and Silberman.

PROCEDURE

The usual procedure followed in non-jury criminal courts is observed in the Women's Court. Inasmuch as the court is not a court of record, all pleadings are oral. The charges tried summarily in this court, as before stated, are neither misdemeanors nor felonies but are minor contraventions of the law known as "Offenses." All offenses tried in this court are prosecuted on a written complaint which is sworn to before the magistrate by the complainant.

1. *Arrest.* All cases observed by the writer had been initiated by the police and arrest had been made either with or without a warrant except in charges of incorrigibility.[2] Inasmuch as practically all cases are brought in through police initiative it might be well to say a word about the organization of the police department relative to this kind of work. A special squad of plain-clothes men known as the Special Service Division operates from the central police headquarters and its territory covers the entire city. As a matter of fact,

---

[1] Loc. cit., p. 37.

[2] The use of warrants in this class of cases was declared illegal in the case of People *vs.* Olin, Inf. Cts. Green Supp.

the bulk of its work is done in the "white-light district" of Manhattan which extends approximately from 30th Street to Columbus Circle, with Broadway as the center. This squad is composed of between 50 to 60 plain-clothes men. There is also a squad attached to headquarters known as the Headquarters Squad, of which about a half-dozen men are assigned to vice work, and operate directly under the Chief Inspector of Police. In addition there are squads of plain-clothes men assigned to each inspector, their territory being limited to the particular district assigned to the inspector. The number of men assigned to vice work on these squads varies in Manhattan from 10 to 20, depending on the district. The police very often base their action upon evidence in the form of complaints furnished by private organizations and private citizens. The plain-clothes police are so well organized and their machinery for vice work is so well developed that every class of prostitute, high or low, eventually finds its way into the Women's Court.

Recent vice surveys by the American Social Hygiene Association have shown that at the present time there is probably not one open house of prostitution in the city of New York. It further shows that the bulk of prostitution which now remains, takes place in tenement houses, rooming houses, cheaper hotels, and taxicabs. Tables published in the reports of the Board of Magistrates indicate that the volume of prostitution in New York, judging from arrests and convictions, has probably decreased more than 70 per cent in the last ten years. Prostitution as it is now practiced in New York, therefore, is no longer open but is almost entirely clandestine. Therefore, the prostitute most frequently seen in the Women's Court is clandestine. The women arrested upon the street comprise two classes: (1) Those who are seen to accost other men and who are arrested for loitering, under Sec. 1458 of the Consolidation Act; and (2) those who directly solicit the police officer. In the former case it is customary for the police to observe the prostitute accost two men before they stop her when the third man is accosted. When she has stopped the third man it is customary for the police to question the man in her presence and hearing as to the nature of the conversation between the woman and himself. If the man states that she asked him to have a good time and the price was stated, and if this statement is not denied by the prostitute, or is expressly admitted by her, the woman is arrested, charged with loitering. Inasmuch as no offense has been committed by the man, under the statute as at present construed, he is allowed to proceed on his way. Examples of the evidence requisite to sustain a conviction will be given in another place. If the woman is arrested for soliciting an officer, she was likewise charged in 1920, the period of this study, under Sec. 1458, though she might have been charged under Subd. 4a of Sec. 887 of the Code of Criminal Procedure for offering to commit prostitution, the mere offer being sufficient to constitute an offense.

When police officers observe a woman appearing to be a prostitute pick up a man on the street, they follow the couple to the room to which they may go, which they enter after sufficient time has elapsed for incriminating evidence to be obtained. This is called a "jump-raid."[1] The jump-raid is also used where a definite complaint has been lodged against an apartment or room and where the police have had the premises under observation for some time. When they have seen what they believe to be a couple going into the room and apartment for the purpose of prostitution, a jump-raid is made ten or fifteen minutes later. The object of the jump-raid is to secure evidence as well as to make an arrest. The

---

[1] "In these cases (jump-raids), the officers, having good reason to believe that a crime is being committed, enter private places without a warrant and from what is admitted by those found there, make the arrests. The conviction in these cases, therefore, depends upon the conditions found and upon the admissions made by defendants. A conflict of testimony is therefore more likely in these cases . . . Because of these conflicts, the magistrates are more hesitant to find the defendant guilty." Report, Committee of Fourteen, 1920, p. 30.

justification for the entering of the premises, however, is based upon the theory that a crime is being committed and that a portion of the crime has been committed in the view of the officer; namely, the solicitation, or the taking of a person into a place for an unlawful, immoral purpose. When the entry is made, the first question asked of the man and woman is whether or not they are husband and wife. If the police are satisfied that they are not, the man is questioned in the presence and hearing of the woman and the following colloquy generally ensues:

Officer addressing the man: "What did you come here for?"
Man: "For a good time."
Officer: "Were you going to pay any money?"
Man: "Yes, the woman said it would cost $10."
Officer: "Did you pay her the money?"
Man: "Yes."
Officer, turning to the woman: "Did you hear what the man said?"
Woman: "Yes."
Officer: "Is it true?"
Woman: "Yes."
Officer: "Return the man his money."

Whereupon the woman surrenders a ten-dollar bill which the officer takes, giving the man another in its place. The officer takes the bill for the purpose of offering it in evidence at the trial. Observations are also made of the attire of the man or woman; of the condition of the bed, the character of the room. These facts may establish the offense by circumstantial evidence. In order to minimize perjury and corruption on the part of the police and to prevent them from changing their testimony between the time of arrest and the trial of a case, it is required that the arresting officer immediately fill out a statement on a form giving the material facts of the case which must be subscribed by the desk lieutenant and immediately forwarded to the presiding magistrate of the Women's Court. The following statement is a copy of an actual case which was sent in on the blank referred to with the names and addresses, of course, left blank:

POLICE DEPARTMENT

City of New York

STATEMENT OF ARRESTING OFFICER IN PROSTITUTION CASE

To Presiding Magistrate, 9th District Court

Time, 1: 20 A.M.   Date, July 28, 1922.

1. Name and address of defendant: xx Manhattan Ave.
2. Name and address of man with whom found: John Doe, xx Boulevard.
3. Location of offense: xx Manhattan Ave.
4. Character of room in which found: Bedroom.
5. Condition of clothing: (a) Woman: Shirt and stockings; (b) Man: Underwear.
6. Where found in room: (a) Man: At bed; (b) Woman: On bed.
7. Condition of bed: Disturbed.
8. Statement of man: Woman offered to commit prostitution with him for the sum of $15.
9. Purpose of visit: Prostitution.
10. Consideration paid: $15.
11. Statement of woman in response to statement of man, if any: ''Please let me go. I won't do it again.''
12. Was money returned: Yes.

. . . .
Desk Lieutenant   Precinct   Arresting Officer   Shield No.   Command

The male customer of the prostitute is rarely arrested because of the difference of opinion as to whether or not he is guilty of a violation of any law. Fornication is not an offense in the state of New York. The customer if guilty of any offense must be guilty of some offense under Subd. 4 of Sec. 887 of the Code of Criminal Procedure or else under Sec. 150 of the Tenement House Law. Under Subd. 4 the only clauses applicable to the customer would be clauses ''d,'' ''e,'' or ''f'' (see Subd. 4, page 401). A test case of a customer charged with violating clauses ''d'' and ''f'' was brought during 1921, in which one of the writers, Mr. Worthington, appeared as *amicus curiae*. In this case, known as the Breitung case, the facts were as follows.

The complainants and only witnesses were the two arresting officers. The complaint charged that at a certain hour at certain premises in the city of New York the defendant did induce, entice, and procure certain named women to commit lewd and indecent acts and did aid and abet and participate in such acts in violation of Subd. 4, Sec. 887 of the Code of Criminal Procedure. The officers testified that they observed the defendant enter the premises at about 3 p.m. and that at about 4.45 p.m. they went to the apartment in question and knocked on the door; that it was opened by a Mrs. K. who tried to push them out; that they walked into the bedroom and found the defendant lying in bed between two girls who were entirely nude and that the defendant was in his union suit. The witnesses disagreed as to whether such union suit consisted of B. V. D.'s or underwear of another make. There was no other conflict of testimony. Witnesses further testified that they had a conversation with the defendant and the two women in the presence and hearing of the defendant and that he had stated that he came "to get cooled off" and that he "had come for a good time." The defendant when asked if he had paid the girls any money, replied, "Yes, I gave them $25 apiece." One officer also testified that when he entered the two girls arose from the bed and put on their clothes and the defendant sat on the edge of the bed and said, "I am guilty of all this. This is all my fault."

The defendant's attorney did not put the defendant upon the stand but at the close of the case moved to dismiss the complaint and discharge the defendant upon the ground that the evidence adduced by the People was insufficient to constitute a crime under Sec. 887. Briefs were furnished by the District Attorney and by Mr. Worthington in behalf of the People, and by attorney for the defendant. The magistrate in a long opinion followed a decision of the Iowa Supreme Court which held that a statute which made it a crime to resort to a house of ill-fame for the purpose of prostitution did not apply to a man who went there as a customer but only to the actual female prostitute, because prostitution in the opinion of that Court was a practice of women only. On the point raised by the prosecution that the defendant, being an accomplice of the prostitute, was therefore a principal within the purview of the penal law, the magistrate has the following to say: "A man participating therein cannot be held as a principal because the nature of the act is such that he cannot in fact be a principal under any circumstances and, therefore, cannot be made a principal by Sec. 2 of the Penal Law.''

The magistrate also cited an old New York case which holds that the person who purchases liquor is not an accomplice of the seller. His conclusion is as follows: ''Only those who are connected with her (prostitute's) business and are, therefore, engaged in commercialized vice can properly be said to participate in and to aid and abet her in her prostitution.''

As to the other clause, namely, inducing, enticing, and procuring, the opinion of the magistrate reads as follows: ''The words 'induce, entice, and procure' read in connection with the word 'procuring' refers to the business of procuring, and the word 'procure' has nothing to do with the seeking of a prostitute as a personal companion. It relates to the business of obtaining a prostitute as a companion for a man; it refers to the business of a pander or procurer.''

One or two other magistrates have taken a different view in their interpretation of the foregoing clauses and have convicted the male customer in uncontested cases. These have been so few, however, as to discourage the police from making arrests under charges of that character for fear of civil suits for false arrest, in case the defendant is discharged.

Subd. 2, Sec. 150, of the Tenement House Law, reads as follows: ''A person who indecently exposes the private person for the purpose of prostitution or other indecency.'' It would seem that an opening is left in this clause for the prosecution of the male customer, but up to the present time a test case has not been made thereunder, and no arrests, therefore, are being made of the customer under this section. Men are not infrequently convicted under Sec. 4 of the Tenement House Law for knowingly residing in a house of prostitution or assignation in a tenement house but the latter are generally pimps rather than customers of a prostitute.

2. *Detention and Bail.* Immediately after arrest the woman is taken to the nearest precinct station where she is booked under the charge made by the arresting officers. She

is thereupon given an opportunity to secure bail. Bail fixed at the station-house is never under $500 and is very frequently in the form of cash or liberty bonds. If the woman desires an immediate arraignment and the Women's Court is closed, she may be taken to the Men's Night Court on 54th Street, and arraigned there.

If she does not demand an immediate arraignment and if she fails to put up bail, she is taken from the precinct station-house to the Women's Detention Prison in connection with the Women's Court. She is not taken to this prison by the arresting officers but by a regular patrolman especially detailed for that purpose. The purpose of this is further to minimize police corruption. When taken to the Women's Prison the defendant is kept separate and apart from the women who have already been convicted. Her arraignment will then take place the following morning in the Women's Day Court. If the defendant appears to be very young, after being booked at the police station, she is taken either to the Florence Crittenton Home or to Waverly House for temporary detention until arraignment. After arraignment she will continue to be detained at either one of the temporary detention homes until after her case is disposed of.

3. *Complaint and Trial.* In connection with the Women's Court there is a complaint room under the supervision of a deputy clerk of court. In this room are kept very carefully prepared blanks with a different form for each offense. The complaint room has a window opening into the detention rooms and the morning following the arrest the defendant is shown the complaint against her, which has been filled out by the arresting officer, and she is given an opportunity to fill out the statement attached to the complaint. This statement is not made under oath and in it she states whether or not she is guilty, what her nationality is, date of birth, date of arrival in United States, etc. The complaint is sworn to before the magistrate at the time of the original arraignment. A sample of a complaint charging the offense of offering to

commit prostitution is given herewith to illustrate the procedure outlined:

CITY MAGISTRATES' COURT OF THE CITY OF NEW YORK

Ninth District, Borough of *Manhattan*

STATE OF NEW YORK, } *ss.:*
County of New York.

JOHN JONES, of *the Fourth* Police Inspection District-Squad, being duly sworn, deposes and says, that on the *9th* day of *December, 1922,* at the City of New York, in the County of *New York, MARY DOE* (now here), was in a *hallway* at No. 22 *Black Avenue,* and did offer to commit prostitution with deponent, demanding and receiving the sum of $2 therefor, and did thereupon offer to expose her person to deponent for said purpose.

Whereupon, deponent prays that said defendant be adjudged a vagrant, pursuant to the provision of Sec. 887, Subd. 4, Clause ''a,'' of the Code of Criminal Procedure.

Sworn to before me, this 10*th* }
    day of *December,* 1922.

JOHN JONES.

RICHARD ROE,
City Magistrate.

STATE OF NEW YORK, } *ss.:*
County of New York.

MARY DOE, being examined according to law, on the charge above mentioned, says that she was born in *Russia, June* 1, 1890, is 32 years of age, is married, and has 3 children living. Examinant further says, I *am not guilty.*
....
....
Date of arrival in the United States? *July,* 1920. How long in the United States? 2 *years.*
Arrived at (Port) New York.
Arrived under name of *MARY DOE.*
Taken before me, this 10*th* }
    day of *December,* 1922.

MARY DOE.

RICHARD ROE,
City Magistrate.

When the defendant is called before the court for arraignment she may proceed to trial at once or she may secure an adjournment of at least two days for the purpose of getting in touch with friends and relatives, and for securing counsel. At the time of her arraignment the court captain states to her in open court as follows:

Your case may be heard at once or you are entitled to an adjournment for the purpose of securing counsel and getting in touch with relatives and friends. You may have the use of a telephone for that purpose free of charge. Which do you wish to do, have your trial now or secure an adjournment and if so, to what day?

One of the magistrates now sitting in the Women's Court explains to the defendant at great length that she may have ample time to get in touch with friends to secure counsel and to prepare her defense. He impresses upon the defendant the fact that she does not have to have her case tried at once. Frequently the defendant if not represented by counsel will insist upon an immediate trial. This is more often true if she is a recidivist. At this time the plea of the defendant is received. If her plea is "guilty" she is remanded for forty-eight hours for sentence. This period is necessary for the purpose of investigation, identification, and examination.

If she pleads not guilty and requests an immediate trial, the case is tried forthwith. During the year 1920, 23 per cent of the defendants pleaded guilty, according to statistics of the Committee of Fourteen.

If the plea is "not guilty" and an adjournment is desired, bail is fixed by the court, as the station-house bail under which the defendant was released after arrest is good only until the defendant is arraigned. The minimum amount of bail fixed by magistrates in the Women's Court for defendants charged with an offense involving prostitution is $500. If the District Attorney or Judge, or some other court official, recognizes the defendant as having been convicted before, the bail is usually fixed at a larger sum than $500. Cases were noted by the writer in which the bail had been fixed at $1000, $1500, and $2000 respectively. The magistrate frequently increases bail when subsequent adjournments are requested by the defendant, almost invariably in denominations of $500. The following statement appears on page 39 of the Report of the Committee of Fourteen for 1920:

Of the 1308 cases in the Women's Court in 1920 bail was given by 46 per cent of the defendants. Of those bailed 75, or 12 per cent, failed to appear for trial. The bonds given by these defendants were, with few exceptions, for $500 each, so that the total sum collected from these forfeitures was $37,500, an amount approximating the total collected in 1907 for fines in prostitution and disorderly house cases, Manhattan and the Bronx. There has been no difficulty in collecting these bonds since the security was generally cash or Liberty Bonds or a surety company was on the bond.

Table 5, at the end of this chapter shows the bail forfeitures in the Women's Court from January 1 to June 30, 1920, giving the total number of cases, the nature of the offense, and the character of the bond received. It will be noted that out of 28 bail bonds only five were real estate bonds, the rest being cash, liberty bonds, or commercial surety bonds. These bonds with the exception of one real estate bond were collected for the full amount.

Probably not less than one hundred trials were observed by Mr. Worthington. One thing which particularly impressed him was the manner in which the trials were conducted. The greatest care was exercised by the court to preserve for the defendant all the rights to which she might be entitled under the constitution and statutes. Indeed the trial seemed to be "summary" in name only, as the trials were as carefully conducted as if they had been before a jury. Incompetent evidence was either not admitted or else invariably stricken from the record. In the words of Judge McAdoo, the cases are conducted "with that degree of patient investigation which many of them require and with those protracted hearings which are often necessary in important matters." The defendants are very frequently represented by attorney and many of the attorneys who appear in the Women's Court seem to be of the shyster lawyer type who are a disgrace to the profession. (Court rules require the attorney to file a written notice of appearance.) Of the trials observed in which defendants were represented by counsel, it was noted that two attorneys apparently had a monopoly of the cases. It would seem that here would be a fruitful field for investigation by the Grievance Committee of the Bar Association, to ascertain how it is that these two attorneys secure such a monopoly. It was noted that directly across the street from the Jefferson Market Building in which the court is housed were several law officers with the lawyers' names in large letters and that in the same offices with the lawyers were the shingles of professional bondsmen who appear in the Women's Court. This would seem to indicate a very close connection between the bondsmen and the attorneys who practice in this court.

Only a general statement of the procedure of the trial will be made at this time inasmuch as specific cases in illustration will be given in another place. The People's case generally consists of the testimony of the arresting officer corroborated by his brother officer. If the defendant is represented by an attorney it is frequently conceded that the testimony of the arresting officer will be corroborated in all material facts by that of the brother officer and in this way the time necessary for the giving of his testimony is saved. It would almost seem that the defendant who is not represented by counsel is better off than the one who has an attorney, inasmuch as the defendant's attorney on cross-examination frequently brings out facts in favor of the People which would be inadmissible on direct examination. At the close of the People's case, the usual motion is made for the dismissal of the case and the discharge of the defendant on the ground of insufficient evidence to sustain the charge. The judge may withhold decision in this motion until the close of the case, or deny the motion, or grant it. If the motion is granted, the defendant, of course, is discharged and the case is ended. It not infrequently happens that the defendant convicts herself by her own testimony or else tells a story which is so improbable as seriously to affect her credibility in the eyes of the court. Crafty counsel who are assured of the guilt of their clients will refuse to place the defendant upon the stand. It sometimes happens, however, that the defendant insists on taking the stand even when her attorney wishes to plead her guilty. This is frequently the case when the charge is that of an offer to commit prostitution. In such a case the defendant frequently labors under the impression that an act of sexual intercourse is necessary before she can be convicted of an offense. It is hard for her to understand that her offer to commit prostitution constitutes a complete offense without any other act upon her part. It, therefore, not infrequently happens that when the defendant takes the stand she admits that the offer to commit prostitution was made, but insists that nothing else was done. She, therefore, honestly believes herself innocent. Judge Foster, of the Court of General Sessions, in the case of the People vs. Rosie Klein has aptly stated the following with reference to this kind of offense:

> The appellant's contention appears to result from a confusion between prostitution and rape. To constitute rape, sexual penetration must be proved, while an offer of her body to indiscriminate sexual intercourse for hire is sufficient to establish an act of prostitution. While it is true that there was no actual sexual intercourse, there assuredly was an offer thereto by the defendant and plainly such an offer is an "act of prostitution."

In the Women's Court all cases are prosecuted by a deputy assistant district attorney and the writer cannot refrain from saying that he has nowhere else observed a prosecutor who prosecutes cases with such a degree of fairness mingled at the same time with thoroughness, as in this court. He seems to be seeking not merely convictions, but also ultimate just results.

SPECIALIZATION

The Women's Court is the most highly specialized court of the series studied. Three magistrates are assigned by the chief city magistrate, who sit alternately in this court. The selection of magistrates has been most carefully made and is indeed fortunate. The magistrates sitting in this court have a happy combination of judicial fairness, kindliness, and courage. By frequently sitting in the same court they become thoroughly experienced in the class of cases tried there and can, therefore, be regarded as experts in dealing with sexually delinquent women. They are progressive, sympathetic, and at the same time scientific. They are not only well trained in the law but they possess the happy faculty of being socially-minded as well. It must, of course, be taken into consideration that the legal machinery which the magistrates administer is very highly developed. The methods of treatment which may be given the defendant and the methods of disposition are numerous. After the defendant is convicted she is finger-printed, which thereupon makes it possible for the magistrate to know absolutely whether or not the defendant is a previous offender in the City of New York.[1] The magistrate also has before him, before sentence, the report by the excellent probation department, in case the defendant is a first offender. A detailed account of the workings of the probation department is given in another section. There is also placed before the judge after conviction and before sentence a certificate from the health department stating whether or not the defendant has a venereal disease in an infectious stage. With these guides, the judge has available the following possible dispositions:

1. Probation: If the defendant is a first offender, this is a frequent disposition. If diseased, she is frequently permitted to go to Kingston Avenue Hospital for treatment. After her release from that institution by the health department she is returned to court for sentence.

2. Commitment to reformative institution. If she is under 30 she may be sent to the State Reformatory for Women at Bedford Hills. If a Catholic, commitment is frequently made to the Roman Catholic

---

[1] Finger-print records of prostitutes were provided for in the Inferior Criminal Courts Act and hence are complete since September, 1910.

House of the Good Shepherd; if a Protestant, to the Protestant Episcopal House of Mercy or to Inwood House.

3. A definite sentence of from one day to six months to the Workhouse on Blackwells Island (now called Welfare Island).

4. An indeterminate sentence of two years to the Workhouse under the Parole Commission Law, if the defendant has been convicted at least twice prior to the present conviction within the past two years, or has at least three prior convictions during any period. This is discussed more fully on pages 372–377.

5. Suspended sentence.

"The fine as a penalty in prostitution cases was discontinued in the Women's Court in 1912 by agreement between the magistrates assigned there, and in 1913 the provision for fines in such cases was abolished by law." [1]

This is a very wise provision indeed. Fining drives a woman to renewed exertions in breaking the law, or places her under obligations to those unspeakable male creatures who live on such women, whether as pimps or disorderly house keepers. Fining makes the city a partner in the business in that it becomes a sharer in the proceeds. It has been well stated that such a system makes of the city a "super-pimp."

In order to give a picture of the procedure in the Women's Court it is believed wise to describe a sample daily program. The first cases called after court has been convened are of those who are ready for sentence. There probably will be several who have been released from Kingston Avenue Hospital where they have been under treatment after conviction and prior to sentence. Of each of these defendants the probation officer makes a report directly to the court. This report not only gives the social history of the defendant, but also states how she has demeaned herself at the hospital. Most of the defendants in this group are thereupon placed upon probation with the exception of those who have shown by their actions at the hospital that they require closer supervision. In that case, the defendant may be sent to a reformatory or to the Workhouse. The next group of cases will be defend-

---

[1] Annual Report, Committee of Fourteen, 1920, p. 25.

ants who have been convicted and remanded for forty-eight hours for finger-printing, social investigation, and physical examination. If a finger-print record shows no previous conviction and the report of the health department shows that the defendant is not suffering from a venereal disease in an infectious stage, the defendant, upon recommendation of the probation officer, may be put upon probation. If there is no previous conviction and she has a venereal disease, the defendant is asked whether she consents to go to Kingston Avenue Hospital for treatment. If she agrees to go to Kingston Avenue Hospital, sentence is deferred frequently with a note on the papers by the judge: "Recommended for probation." Rarely does the defendant refuse to go to the hospital. In the few cases observed in which the defendant did refuse, she was thereupon sentenced to Bedford Reformatory. This is, of course, an indeterminate sentence of not more than three years with release on parole at the discretion of the Board of Managers of that institution. If the defendant has more than one conviction, whether diseased or not, if she appears to be under 30 years of age, she may be sent to Bedford or one of the other reformatory institutions previously mentioned. If the defendant has a sufficient number of convictions to warrant sentencing her under the Parole Commission Law she may receive such a sentence. However, the Parole Commission Law is not used very frequently at the present time because of the fact that it is interpreted by the magistrates as not being mandatory. A discussion of the Parole Commission Law is given on pages 372–377. If the defendant appears to be too old for a reformatory sentence and yet has more than one prior conviction, and is diseased, she is generally sent to the Workhouse for one hundred days. The one hundred day term is fixed because the magistrates have been informed by the health department that such detention and treatment are sufficient to render the ordinary case of venereal disease non-infectious. However, if the defendant has several prior convictions, it may be that she will receive a definite sentence of six months in the Workhouse whether diseased or not. On the other hand, it was noted that a few defendants who were not diseased but who had many previous convictions, were given a short Workhouse sentence of from ten to thirty days. This indicates that there are other considerations entering into the sentence of the defendant besides the prior number of convictions and the question of disease. For instance, it may be that the defendant pleaded not guilty to the charge, or that she had seemed to be "more sinned against than sinning," or that the magistrate believed that her case contained some of the elements of police persecution. The magistrate also considers the honesty or dishonesty of the defendant on the stand, and also her demeanor, her lack of defiance, her apparent state of intelligence, and the character of the offense committed.

After the cases of those awaiting sentence have been disposed of, the cases of defendants awaiting arraignment are called. In these cases, as explained before, the defendant is given the opportunity of adjournment, for the purpose of securing counsel or communicating with friends or relatives, or of having an immediate trial. Frequently the defendant pleads guilty upon arraignment.

After the arraignments, come the cases which have been definitely set for trial on that day. It occasionally happens that the defendant does not appear when her case is called, and bail is thereupon declared forfeited. It not infrequently happens that the defendant will ask for an adjournment. It may be that her counsel believes that the magistrate sitting at that time is more severe than the other two magistrates and she may attempt to secure an adjournment for that reason. The magistrates, however, are loath to grant adjournments and frequently the bail is raised when the adjournment is granted. Table 8, at the end of this chapter, indicates that very few adjournments are granted after the third time, probably because by that time the defendant has run out of excuses which seem valid to the magistrate. Adjournments are most frequently requested when a defendant is represented by counsel, and generally are for the sole purpose of securing a delay. Because of the difficulty in securing adjournments many subterfuges and excuses are resorted to, such as the failure of counsel to appear when the case is called, or the production of an affidavit from a physician that the defendant is not physically able to be present in court. Occasionally the magistrate requires the physician to appear in person and in some of such cases it was noted that upon cross-examination the physician admitted that he had not seen the defendant immediately prior thereto. Needless to say, adjournment was refused.

ILLUSTRATIVE CASES

The procedure of the trials themselves will be better illustrated by the actual cases which follow:

E. G., white, about 30 years old. Charge—offering to commit prostitution, Sudb. 4a, Sec. 887, C. C. P. Officer testified that defendant stopped him on the street during afternoon, and invited him to come to her room that evening for the purpose of prostitution, stating that the price would be $10.

Officer accompanied by brother officer, kept the appointment, the other officer remaining outside of room. Witness testified that defendant was in room when he entered; that she greeted him warmly, and after a few words of conversation, asked him if he were ready. He replied in the affirmative, and she asked for the money. He paid her with a $10 bill which she put in her right top bureau drawer. She then disrobed, exposing her person and exclaimed "Come on!" Witness stated that he thereupon went to the door and summoned his brother officer who asked witness in presence and hearing of defendant what he was there for. The reply was, "For a good time." When asked if he had paid defendant any money for the good time he replied that he had given her $10. The brother officer was said to have thereupon asked defendant "to give him back his money," referring to witness. Defendant in response to this, went to the right bureau drawer and extracted therefrom a $10 bill which witness kept, placing his initials thereupon in defendant's presence. This he offered in evidence.

The foregoing testimony was corroborated by the brother officer. Defendant thereupon took the stand. In a strong cockney accent, she denied meeting the officer in the street, earlier in the day. She stated that she was in her room when the officer forced his way in stating, "You're under arrest. I've got to make a case, and it might as well be you as any one else."

She said she was the daughter of a sea-captain and was supported by him. She couldn't recall when she had last received any money from him, and also admitted that she was not working. Her testimony was unconvincing and her demeanor was defiant. Found guilty and remanded for sentence. Defendant admitted her guilt to probation officer, after conviction.

White, about 28 years old. Charge—offering to commit prostitution in a tenement, Subd. 3, Sec. 150, Tenement House Law. Officer stated that he visited room of defendant at about 5 o'clock in afternoon, saying to defendant that he had been sent there by Sam; that defendant stated that if he had been sent by Sam he must be all right but she first insisted on searching his person for a gun or shield. After these preliminaries she said, "Are you ready for your good time?" Officer testified that he replied, "Well, how much will it cost?" She said $5. Officer stated that he thereupon gave defendant $5 which she placed in her right leg stocking, and removed her kimono and lay down upon the bed, exposing her person. The officer stated that he thereupon put her under arrest and called in his brother officer. Brother officer in corroboration testified that he entered room finding defendant clad only in a "teddy" and sitting on the edge of the bed; that complaining officer stated to him in the presence of the defendant that he had paid defendant $5 for a good time and that she had exposed her person. The corroborating officer then told defendant to return to the officer his money and that she removed the $5 bill from her right leg stocking and handed it to the officer. This money was placed in evidence by the officer on his statement that he had kept it separate and apart from his own money and had marked it in the presence of defendant. The defendant was represented by a young lawyer who upon cross-examination of the officers drew out facts which would have been inadmissible under their direct testimony. He forgot to make his motion for a dismissal and put defendant upon the stand at the close of the People's case. His questions of defendant on direct examination were so unskillful that defendant corroborated the officers in practically every material fact. The district attorney thereupon waived cross-examination and defendant was found guilty and remanded.

A., colored, about twenty years old. Charge—offering to commit prostitution. Subd. 3, Sec. 150, Tenement House Law.

B., colored, past 40 years old. Charge—keeping a house of prostitution, assignation, or ill-fame in a tenement house. Subd. 5, Sec. 150, Tenement House Law.

C., colored, about 20 years old. Charge—knowingly residing in a house of prostitution or assignation in a tenement house. Subd. 4, Sec. 150, Tenement House Law.

The complaining officer was a colored man attached to a vice squad. Officer testified that he had had apartment under observation for some time. That upon entering apartment he found Defendant A. in bed entirely nude, in company with a colored man with his trousers removed. He asked the man if he was married to defendant and he said no, in the presence and hearing of defendant; that he had come there to have a good time with defendant and had paid her $6; that the arrangements were made in the presence of Defendants B. and C., and that after Defendant A. had collected the $6 she gave $2 in his presence to Defendant B., stating that it was for the use of the room. Officer stated that he called in A. and B. and asked them for the money which had been paid by the unknown man, and that A. produced four one-dollar bills and B. produced two one-dollar bills which were returned to the man and that the officer took this money from the man and replaced it by money of his own, which money was offered in evidence. The officer then testified that he called in his brother officer who made a search with him of other rooms in the apartment and found in another room Defendant C. who testified that she lived in the apartment. The defendants then took the stand and each one told conflicting stories. Defendant A. said that the man was a friend of hers, but when asked on cross-examination what his name was, she stated that she could not recall. She said that she had met him at some dance, although on direct examination she had testified that she had known him for more than two years. She stated that the money that he paid her was for a pawn ticket which she had received for pawning a bird of paradise. When asked where she got the bird of paradise she stated that it had been smuggled in by a sailor friend and given to her. She could not recall, however, where she had pawned the bird and also contradicted herself on the amount that she had received from the pawnbroker. The landlady stated that she had collected $2 from A. but that it was money which the defendant owed her. She also stated that she knew about the bird of paradise being pawned and stated that the unknown man was a friend of A. She contradicted A., however, on the place of meeting and as to the length of time the man was known. Defendant C. testified that she was present when the man came in and that he had stated that he did not want to see her but wanted to see her friend and, therefore, she had gone to her own room. Defendants were found guilty and remanded. When the three defendants came up for sentence two days later, the finger-print records showed that defendants B. and C. had previous records for prostitution. A. was investigated by the probation officer who stated that the apartment in question was a regular dive and that all three defendants admitted that prostitution had been practiced there. B. and C. being diseased and having previous records were given sentences of six months at the Workhouse, and A. was sent to Kingston Avenue Hospital for treatment.

Defendants, white, 28 and 30 years of age, respectively, tried together by consent of counsel. Charge—offering to commit prostitution, Subd. 3, Sec. 150, Tenement House Law. Officer testified that he and his brother officer had the two women under observation on the street; that he saw them address two men and walk away with them; that he and his brother officer followed defendants to an apartment which they entered about ten or fifteen minutes later, finding both defendants in bed with the unknown men, all being clad in their underwear. Officer testified that he questioned both the men in the presence and hearing of both defendants and asked them whether they were married to defendants. The men replied no, that the women had picked them up on the street and had taken them to the apartment for a good time. They testified that each of them had paid the women $5 for that purpose. The officers gave the names of the unknown men. The officer testified that after the defendants had heard what the unknown men had said they were asked whether or not the statement was true; that the women said, "Yes, but please give us a chance." The money paid by the men was returned in the usual way and offered by the officer in evidence. The brother officer also testified after having been excluded by the court, and corroborated the complaining officer in all the essentials. The defendants were then placed on the stand by their attorneys and on direct examination denied the testimony of the officers. Upon cross-examination they made many conflicting and contradictory statements. The attorneys for defendants then produced two men who in turn took the stand as witnesses for defendants and who testified that they were the men who were in the room with defendants at the time of the arrest. The men had all the appearance of being pimps. One testified that he worked in a pool hall and the other said that he was a chauffeur for a judge. He stated that he had frequently taken one of the defendants out riding and knew her very well. When asked if he had taken her out in his employer's car, he said no, he had taken her out in a friend's car. When suddenly asked by the district attorney to give the name of that friend he was unable to remember his name. The man who had stated on direct examination that he was a cook, stated on cross-examination, when asked where he worked, that his place of employment was a pool hall. The district attorney stated, "I thought you said that you were a cook?" Witness answered, "Yes, I am a cook in a pool hall." The officers when recalled to the stand for rebuttal denied that the two men produced by the defendants were the unknown men whom they had questioned in defendants' apartment. Defendants were found guilty and remanded for sentence.

White, about 30 years old. Charge—offering to commit prostitution, Subd. 3, Sec. 150, Tenement House Law. Represented by one of the shyster lawyers who has almost a monopoly of business in Women's Court. Officer testified he had apartment under observation and saw a man enter; that a few minutes later he and his brother officer entered and found defendant undressed in bed and the man with his coat off, who was in the act of buttoning up his clothes. The man, when questioned in the presence and hearing of the defendant, was reputed to have said that he was a stranger to defendant and that he had paid her $2 for the purpose of prostitution; that the defendant when questioned by the officer as to the truth of the man's statement, said it was true and gave the officer the money alleged to have been paid her by the man. The complaining officer's testimony was corroborated by the brother officer. The defendant then took the stand and denied categorically each and every one of the allegations of the officers. She further stated that there was no man at all in the apartment and that the supposed man was an absolute fiction on the part of the officers. She proved to be a very difficult witness to shake. On cross-examination she did contradict herself on several particulars. The attorney for defendant then made the charge that there was no unknown man in this case and that it was purely a fabrication and frame-up on the part of the officers. Much to the defendant's surprise after she had rested her case the district attorney produced three witnesses who were residents of the apartment building in question. One was a woman of about 45, housewife, apparently reputable, who stated that she had seen the officers watching the apartment, one from the stairway above and one from the stairway below; that her attention being attracted to the apartment by this, she watched proceedings from her doorway almost directly across the hall from defendant's apartment; that she saw a man enter while the officers were watching the apartment; that after the officers entered the apartment she came to the door to listen as she had been suspicious of the place for some time; and that she heard some of the conversation from the open door. She stated that one of the officers then came to the door and seeing her and two other residents of the apartment building nearby, asked all of them to come in, and that while there, they saw defendant and the man described by the officers; that this man had not yet put his coat on. Defendant was found guilty and remanded.

White, 35 years old. Charge—receiving a person into a place for the purpose of prostitution, Subd. 4e, Sec. 887, C. C. P. Officer testified that he entered and found defendant and man in bedroom in underwear and also found another couple in another bedroom. That the other woman had already been convicted under another charge. That the man had stated, in the presence and hearing of the defendant, that the defendant had accosted him on the street and brought him up to the apartment for a good time. The man is alleged further to have stated that he had paid the defendant $5 for a good time and $5 more for the use of her room. Officer stated that he had asked defendant if that were true and she had replied yes and had returned the money. After the conclusion of the People's case, the defendant asked to change her plea from not guilty to guilty, which was received.

White, 45 years old. Charge—knowingly permitting a person to remain in a place for the purpose of prostitution, Subd. 4e, Sec. 887, C. C. P. The officer testified that defendant was a proprietress of a rooming house. That he entered rooming house and found a couple in bed together and that the girl had subsequently pleaded guilty to a charge of offering to commit prostitution. He stated that the girl had told him, in the presence and hearing of defendant, that she and the man had rented the room for just a little while, and that they had come there without baggage. This was all of the testimony on behalf of the People. The defendant took the stand and testified that the couple had engaged the room for a week and had paid her $2 down and had stated that their baggage was in the Pennsylvania Station and that they were going to send for it immediately. She stated that she believed that they had hardly had time to send for the baggage when the officers entered and made the arrest. She stated that she fully believed that defendants were a young married couple. She produced a witness to corroborate her testimony. The case was thereupon dismissed and defendant discharged on the ground that the evidence was insufficient to constitute the offense alleged.

White, about 21 years old. Charge—committing prostitution in a tenement house, Subd. 3, Sec. 150, Tenement House Law. Complaining officer testified that he observed defendant and an unknown man through an open window, engaged in an act of sexual intercourse; that he and his brother officer thereupon entered the apartment which was on the ground floor, and questioned the unknown man who stated, in the presence and hearing of defendant; that he was a stranger to her and that he had paid her $2 for a good time. The defendant was alleged to have admitted that she had received the $2 and returned it to the man. The officers took the money, replacing it for some of their own, marked it in defendant's presence, and offered it in evidence. Defendant was represented by attorney. She took the stand and denied the testimony of the officer which had been corroborated by brother officer by stipulation of the defendant's attorney. Defendant stated that she had come to the man's room to collect some money that he owed her husband and that she had just collected it when the officers rushed in. She denied that she or the man were in bed, and denied that they were undressed. She also denied that the man had made the statements to which the officers had testified, and stated that he actually had said that he had paid the money that he had owed her husband. On cross-examination, however, the woman could not give the circumstances under which she could have known that the man owed her husband money or any circumstances by which she would know where he lived and she admitted that she had met him on the street and said that she would come up to his apartment later to collect the money. She could give no reason why she did not collect the money when she saw the man on the street. She was thereupon found guilty and remanded for sentence. After conviction, her attorney announced that he had advised her to plead guilty but that she had refused to do it.

White, 25 and 30 years old, respectively. Charge—aiding or abetting or participating in prostitution, Subd. 4f, Sec. 887, C. C. P. Younger defendant charged with violating Subd. 4a of same section, offering to commit prostitution. Officer testified that he and his brother officer entered room of younger defendant and found her in bed with unknown man; that upon questioning man in her presence and in the presence of the other defendant, the man stated that he was a stranger to both of them, that they had picked him up on the street and taken him to the room for the purpose of prostitution and that he had paid the younger defendant $20. The officer testified that he had then turned to the younger defendant and had asked if the statement of the man was true and she said yes. Officer then asked her to return the $20. She said, "I haven't got it." Officer asked where it was and she said that the other defendant had it. The other defendant then produced the $20 which was taken by the officer in substitution for money of his own, and it was offered as evidence at the trial. The statements of the complaining officer were corroborated by his brother officer. The defendants were represented by an attorney who moved at the close of the People's case to dismiss as to the older defendant who had been charged with aiding, abetting, and participating, on the ground that there was no evidence relative to her participation. The court reserved decision on the motion. The younger defendant thereupon took the stand, admitted that she had met the man in question, that he was a stranger to her, but that he had stopped the other defendant and herself and asked them if they did not want a drink, saying that he had some liquor on his hip; that they said yes, and that they had therefore gone up to the room in which the older defendant lived. On cross-examination she practically admitted that she had offered to commit prostitution with the man. The other defendant then took the stand and admitted that she had received the money from the other woman but denied that she had any knowledge of what they did in the room. She stated that after she had gone up with the other girl and the man to the apartment, that her friend had given her $20 to keep for her and she had gone into another room and did not know what they were doing. Both defendants were convicted and remanded for sentence. When their cases came up for sentence two days later the medical examination showed both of them to have venereal disease but showed that they were first offenders. The older defendant's husband appeared in court and the probation officer recommended probation for her so that she might return to her husband, and for the other defendant so that she might return to her home in Philadelphia. Both defendants consented to go to Kingston Avenue Hospital for treatment.

Many other cases were observed in which the testimony was substantially the same as that illustrated in the foregoing cases. The testimony of the officers on the statement of the unknown man to the police officers, is stricken from the record if the officer testifies that the woman denied the statement of the man. The theory on which such statements are admissible is that they are admissions by the defendant of the offense charged. Therefore, when she denied the statement of the man or remained silent when asked by the officer whether the statement was true, there would be no evidence before the court, of admissions on her part and she would, therefore, be acquitted. The trials were conducted very carefully and there were so many checks on the police that the writer believes that there is practically no possibility of an innocent woman being convicted of prostitution in this court.

It may occasionally happen, however, that a woman has been arrested by the police who is not guilty of the offense charged. When this appears from the testimony of the officer, the district attorney is very careful to move at once for a dismissal of the case. One case was observed in which the defendants were discharged at the end of the entire case after the defendants had produced reputable character witnesses and had put up a very good appearance upon the stand. In this case, the court made the statement which went into record, that he had observed the testimony of the complaining officer on two previous occasions which, upon being checked up, had been found to be untrue and that on the two prior occasions the defendants had been acquitted. He said further, that taking the two previous occasions with the present one into consideration, he was notifying the Police Commissioner that he would never again believe the testimony of this officer and should this officer appear again in court while he was sitting as judge, he would immediately discharge the defendants against whom this officer appeared as complainant.

Many cases were gone over after trial and investigation with the probation officer, and it was found that after conviction the defendant almost invariably admitted the truth of the charge against her. On this subject Chief Justice McAdoo has the following to say:[1]

In each of these cases the defendant generally goes on the stand and tells a story which is repeated over and over again by defendants and which is unreasonable on the face of it. The Magistrate has also to note her appearance, her manners, her language, and cross-examines her. In most cases she admits she has no regular employment or settled home, has not worked for a long time. Her excuse given for being on the street at the time of the arrest is unreasonable and often absurd. In more than half the cases the finger-prints show she has been previously convicted for the same offense.

I was two years Police Commissioner and I have been nearly six years in this office and I can say without reservation that I have never known of a single case of an honest, decent, and virtuous woman being arrested by the police mistakenly for street-walking.

---

[1] Annual Report, City Magistrates' Court, 1915.

The following are some other types of cases dealt with by the court:

White, about 21 years old. Charge—disorderly conduct, loitering, Subd. 2, Sec. 1458, Consolidation Act. Officer testified he saw defendant accost two men. He stated he did not know what she said to them. Then he saw her stop a third man who, after a conversation with her, ordered a taxi. The officer then stepped up and asked the man if he knew the defendant. He stated that he had never seen her before; that she had stopped him and invited him to go to her room for a good time. The officer testified that the man stated that defendant told him it would cost him $5 with $2 additional for the room. Corroborating officer was not called. Defendant was represented by attorney who refused to put her on the stand. Defendant was found guilty and remanded for sentence.

This defendant at the end of the remand period came before another judge for sentence. Probation officer reported that defendant lived in a very poor house with an Italian woman; that she could not see that the girl had any means of making a living and did not believe that the old Italian lady was in a position to support her. She stated further that there was no basis for probation and recommended that defendant be not placed upon probation. The girl seemed to be rather young and innocent looking and was represented by a young attorney who stated that she was innocent and had been the victim of police persecution. He also stated that the Italian woman was in court and was willing to take care of the girl if she was placed on probation. The judge called the Italian woman to the bench and asked her how she had become acquainted with the defendant. She stated that the girl's mother was a friend of hers in Connecticut and that the girl had come down on a visit and was now working for her in her second-hand store. She stated that she could pay the girl $12 a week and that she could take care of her. The girl was thereupon placed on probation in custody of the Italian woman. The next morning the same defendant reappeared in court charged with offering to commit prostitution under Subd. 4a. This time she appeared in an expensive mink coat and could hardly be recognized through her finery as the poor and innocent-looking girl of the day before. She asked for adjournment to secure counsel and her bail was fixed by the court at $1500 which was furnished by a surety company. When her case was called two days later she forfeited bail. Apparently the girl was being exploited by some one who had means.

White, about 34 years old. Charge—disorderly conduct, loitering, Subd. 2, Sec. 1458, Consolidation Act. Officer testified he saw her accost three men in less than half hour and that she boarded a cross-town 23rd Street car with the third man. Officer also boarded car and followed defendant. He observed defendant and man go to a dark corner near the 23rd Street ferry-house, whereupon he approached the man and asked him if he knew defendant. Man stated, in presence and hearing of defendant, that he did not know her, that she had asked him if he wanted to spend $2 for a good time, that he had accepted but had not yet paid her the money. The officer then stated that he had asked defendant if that was true and that she had said yes. The defendant took the stand and testified that she had no home and no place to sleep. She had the appearance of a derelict. She testified that she had merely asked the man to pay her car fare on the 23rd Street line and that she was talking with him near the ferry-house when the officer approached. She admitted that she had not seen the man before. She stated that she had been married ten years and had had several children, none of whom was living and that she was not living with her husband at present. Found guilty and remanded.

White, 20 years old. Charge—offering to commit prostitution, Subd. 4a, Sec. 887, C. C. P. Officer testified that he observed defendant accost a man in front of a restaurant and thereafter she entered restaurant with man during which time he had them both under observation; that he followed them from the restaurant to a room which he kept under observation for about ten minutes before entering; that upon entering he found the girl in bed and the man was sitting on the edge of the bed in his underwear; that he questioned the defendant and man as to whether or not they were married and that man stated, in presence and hearing of defendant, that he had never seen the girl previous to that evening and that she had agreed to give him a good time for the price of $5 but that the money had not yet been paid; that when the girl had been asked by the officer if the statement by the man were true, she had remained silent. Motion was made by defendant's attorney for dismissal and discharge of defendant on ground that there were insufficient facts to constitute an offense. The attorney had previously conceded that the officer's testimony would be corroborated in every material fact by the brother officer. Decision was reserved by the judge. Defendant thereupon took the stand and on direct examination denied statements of the officer. After a very rigid cross-examination by the district attorney she admitted that she did not know the man's name although she said that he was a friend of hers. She further admitted that man had accompanied her to her room. When asked what she went there for she said, "Well, you did not expect us to go there to say our prayers." When further cross-examined as to whether or not any price had been mentioned she stated that the man said he would take care of her. She also stated, "Why didn't you arrest the man? If I'm guilty of anything, he is too." Defendant found guilty and remanded.

White, about 25 years old. Charge—offering to commit prostitution, Subd. 4a; Sec. 887, C. C. P. Officer testified that he had had defendant's apartment under observation for some time, that he saw a man enter the apartment and that he entered about a half an hour later; that he found defendant in her kimono and the man in her bedroom in his stocking-feet and with his outer shirt off. The officer asked the man, in the presence and hearing of the defendant, whether he was her husband, to which he replied that he had never seen defendant before that day; that he had been sent up there by a chauffeur by the name of "Shorty"; that he had told the defendant that "Shorty" had sent him; and that she had admitted him. He stated that he had paid her $25 for a good time which had already been completed. The officer testified that he thereupon turned to the defendant and asked her if the statement of the man were true; that defendant had stated no; that the man was her friend; and that he had owed her the $25 and had come up that evening to pay it back. The officer then asked her where the $25 was, and she turned to her right leg stocking from which she extracted two ten-dollar and one five-dollar bills which were returned to the man and which the officer took and replaced with money of his own. This money was marked by the officer and was offered in evidence by the district attorney. It was accepted as evidence after the officer had stated that he had marked it in the defendant's presence and had kept it separate and apart from any other money since that time. Defendant's attorney conceded that the testimony would be corroborated by the other officer and moved for the dismissal of the defendant. The motion was denied by the court. He thereupon refused to put the defendant upon the stand and she was found guilty and remanded.

White, about 16 years old. Charge—incorrigibility, Chap. 436 of the Laws of 1903. Complaint was made by mother who took the stand and testified against her daughter. She stated that the defendant remained out late every night and ran around with a man whom she did not know; that frequently the girl would not return until 3 or 4 o'clock in the morning. The defendant then took the stand and admitted that she stayed out late and when questioned as to the identity of the man, stated that he was a friend. She was found guilty and remanded to Waverly House for investigation.

White, each apparently under 21 years old. Charge—incorrigibility, Chap. 436 of the Laws of 1903. Officer testified that he visited room occupied by defendants and found them fully dressed with two sailors who were in their underwear; that one sailor had stated that one of the defendants was his sweetheart and that they were soon to be married, and that the other girl was a friend of hers. Officer testified that neither the girls nor the sailors could explain satisfactorily why the sailors were in their underwear but inasmuch as the girls were very apparently under 21 years of age he had arrested them under an incorrigibility charge. Attorney for the defendants conceded the corroboration by brother officer and made the usual motion of dismissal which was taken under advisement by the judge, and decision reserved. Defendants thereupon took the stand and each testified that she was 21 years of age. Under cross-examination by the district attorney, however, the defendants gave the dates of their birth, each being approximately 17 years of age. They admitted that the sailors were in their underwear, that it was a rainy night, and that the sailors had gotten their uniforms wet and had taken them off to dry. One girl stated that one of the sailors was to be discharged very shortly from the navy and was going to marry her. Defendants were convicted and remanded. Two days later when the defendants appeared for sentence, the probation officer brought in the husband of the girl who stated she was to marry the sailor soon, together with the marriage certificate which showed that this same girl had been married less than six months previous. Both girls were found to be suffering from an infectious venereal disease, one of them with both gonorrhea and syphilis, and upon their consent were sent to Kingston Avenue Hospital for treatment. The sailors who appeared in court at the time of sentence were notified of the condition of the girls and the one who was the "would-be husband" was notified that his reported fiancée was already married and they were also told that their commanding officer would be notified of the circumstances. During the period of remand both girls were detained in the Florence Crittenton Home.

White, apparently 25 years old. Charge—offering to commit prostitution in taxicab, Subd. 4a, Sec. 887, C. C. P. Officer testified that defendant solicited him on the corner of 42d Street and Sixth Avenue about 1 A.M. for the purpose of prostitution. He stated that the conversation between himself and defendant was as follows:

When he passed defendant, she smiled and the defendant then said, "Hello, bad boy, where are you going?"

Officer replied, "No place in particular."

Defendant: "What do you want to do?"

Officer: "I don't care."

Defendant: "Want to spend a little money for a good time?"

Officer: "I don't care, how much would it cost?"

Defendant: "It will only cost you $5 and the price of the room."

Officer: "Do you know where to go?"

Defendant: "Haven't you got any place?"

Officer: "No."

Defendant: "Then let's take a taxicab."

Officer: "All right."

Officer then testified that defendant led him to a taxicab which was standing near-by, which they entered; that she thereupon asked him for the money which he paid her and which she placed in her right leg stocking; that defendant thereupon exposed her person, and he placed her under arrest and took her to the police station. The officer's testimony was not corroborated. The defendant then took the stand and stated that she met the officer on the corner mentioned, that she did not know that he was a police officer and that they got into the taxicab just to take a ride; that upon entering the taxicab she went into hysterics and fainted and could not remember what happened. When asked if the story the officer told about the $5 was true she replied that she had fainted so that she did not remember. After a long cross-examination defendant contradicted herself in so many particulars that the court disregarded her testimony and found her guilty and remanded her for sentence. Defendant when she appeared for sentence was found to be suffering from a venereal disease and the probation officer stated that the girl had admitted the truth of the officer's story and that the girl further admitted that she had just come to New York from the south where she had been an inmate of a house of prostitution. Probation officer stated that defendant had no friends or relatives in the city and she recommended that the girl be sent to Bedford Reformatory. The defendant was thereupon so sentenced.

FINGER-PRINT SYSTEM

The Inferior Criminal Courts Act provides for the general use of finger-prints as a mode of identifying those convicted in these courts. Consequently a finger-print system has been in operation in connection with the Women's Court since 1910, for the taking of finger-prints of defendants after conviction.

Section 78, contains the following provisions:

In the Night Court for Women and such courts as the boards of magistrates may designate, there shall be established and maintained the method of identification of prisoners known as the finger-print system. The finger-prints of all females convicted for any of the offenses enumerated in Sec. 89 of this act shall be taken by officers or employees of the police department detailed for that purpose or by such officers or employees as may be designated by the chief city magistrate. One impression or duplicate shall be classified and preserved in the court where the same was made; a second shall be promptly delivered to and classified and preserved in the office of the chief clerk of the division; and the third shall be forthwith delivered to the police commissioner. The board of city magistrates of each division is empowered to make and from time to time to amend rules and regulations prescribing the courts in which females arrested after the closing of the night court for any of the offenses enumerated in Sec. 89 of this act shall be arraigned and the court where such females shall be tried, and to provide for their detention, release, or parole pending trial.[1]

The value of the finger-print system has been very well set forth by Chief Magistrate McAdoo, who has the following to say:[2]

The magistrates who preside in that court all bear testimony that it is not only advantageous to them in a just disposition of a case, but is of benefit to the defendant herself. It establishes, beyond question, whether or not she has a record in these courts. Most defendants, on conviction, will deny at once that they have ever been arrested or convicted before. The finger-print answers the question beyond doubt. If a woman has never been convicted before in that court, it is so established to her credit, and helps the magistrate to determine what should be done with her. If otherwise, and she has been frequently finger-printed, he knows he is dealing with an incorrigible case. All concerned are of the opinion that this is of the greatest benefit to the proper, just, humane, and effective disposition of these cases, and that it would be disastrous to go back to the old way . . . Every conscientious and right-thinking magistrate, however experienced, will, I think, admit how difficult it is, in many cases, to satisfy his conscience and his intelligence in fixing the measure of punishment without investigation and identification of the defendant. With the use and services of the probation officers, properly applied, and the taking of finger-prints, the whole status of the defendant can be definitely and conclusively ascertained before judgment is pronounced. . . . There is nothing humiliating nor disgraceful in having the finger-prints taken. Such means of identification are now used in banks and in the Army and Navy of the United States, and they will be invaluable to us in sorting out the different classes of offenders and give the people of the city, through the statistics which will later appear, a better idea than they can possibly have now as to what the forces of law have to contend with.

---

[1] As amended by Chap. 372, Laws of 1913.
[2] Report of the Board of Magistrates, New York City, 1912, pp. 20–21.

In the report for 1911, the following statement appears:[1]

The finger-print system . . . has given good results. It protects the woman who is convicted for the first time, and it enables the judge to deal properly with the woman who has been convicted a number of times. Some of these women have been up as many as ten times; a majority at least once before; quite a number, four, five, six, and seven times. It shows that we are dealing with a regular army of street-walkers, numbering within certain districts alone, about 3000, who engage in this work as a business and who take the chances of imprisonment as a part of their profession . . . The finger-prints, as time goes on, show a professional and determined array of law-breakers.

The report for 1914 says:[2]

The results of the finger-printing have been astonishingly gratifying and effective. Defendants of both sexes will stand before the magistrate and solemnly state that they have never been in court before, and within a few minutes afterwards the finger-prints will show, two, three, four, five or even more convictions. This shows the magistrate at once what kind of a case he is dealing with and it is often better than a report made after investigation . . . The results already achieved by finger-printing certain classes of offenders in these courts indicate that the system can be extended, with great public benefit, in the suppression of crimes generally . . . In every case printed in these courts two impressions are taken. The extra copy is supplied to the Department of Correction, so that it accompanies the prisoner to the place of detention, thus furnishing a sure means of identification, and prevents any substitution or change in their names by prisoners. This step has been made necessary by the discovery recently of a thriving trade among prisoners by which a short-term man for a consideration would take the name of a long-term man and personate him at the institution.

Magistrate Cobb in the case of the People vs. Sadie Blum, said:[3]

---

[1] Report of the Board of Magistrates, New York City, 1911, pp. 28, 31.

[2] Report of the Board of Magistrates, New York City, 1914, p. 23.

[3] Magistrate Cobb in People, etc., of N. Y. *vs.* Sadie Blum, Inferior Criminal Courts *Supplement*, pp. 54, 56, 58.

Science has furnished society with what is to all intents and purposes an absolutely accurate medium of personal identification, viz., the finger-print system. When once generally established it promises to solve problems in criminology with results of far-reaching importance to society . . . The system is spreading over the entire civilized world and has already proved of untold value . . . Its statistical value with respect to "repeaters" is of the utmost importance; it enables the court to recognize and properly to deal with the previous offender as well as more readily to extend leniency to the first offender; it makes for uniformity of treatment and sentence among the magistrates so far as consistent with the needs of the individual; it is doubtless a deterrent to those whose cases have been finger-printed to know that they will be recognized in any Magistrate's Court in the entire City of New York into which they may come again.

The variety of cases to which it is applied, makes the Finger-print Bureau of the Magistrates' Courts of particular value.

PROFESSIONAL BONDSMEN

An act that may do much to diminish the professional bail-bond evil was enacted by the 1922 legislature (Chap. 303, Laws 1922).

This act provides that any person, firm or corporation, who deposits money or property as bail, or executes as surety any bail-bond more than twice in a month, and who charges a fee therefor, shall be regarded as a professional bondsman.

Such professional bondsmen are no longer permitted to give bonds without a license, which is to be granted by the Superintendent of Insurance of the State of New York.

The act provides that no premium or compensation which is greater than three per cent of the amount of the bond or deposit shall be charged. Those who violate this provision are guilty of a misdemeanor, and are also liable civilly to the client to treble damages for any overcharge.

This act went into effect September 1, 1922.

PHYSICAL EXAMINATION

The authority under which the Women's Court and the Health Department Act is found in Secs. 343m and n of the Public Health Law as amended by Chap. 40 of the Laws of 1919, which read as follows:

Sec. 343m. *Suspected Persons.* Whenever the board of health or health officer of a health district shall have reasonable ground to believe that any person within the jurisdiction of such board or health officer is suffering from, or infected with, any infectious venereal disease and is likely to infect or to be the source of infection of any other person, such board of health or health officer shall cause a medical examination to be made of such person, for the purpose of ascertaining whether or not such person is in fact suffering from, or infected with, such disease, and every such person shall submit to such examination and permit such specimens of blood or bodily discharges to be taken for laboratory examinations as may be necessary to establish the presence or absence of such disease or infection, and such person may be detained until the results of such examinations are known, provided, that the required examination shall be made by the health officer, or, at the option of the person to be examined, by a licensed physician who, in the opinion of the health officer, is qualified for this work and is approved by him, and such licensed physician making such examination shall report thereon to the board of health, health department, or health officer, but shall not issue a certificate of freedom from venereal disease to or for the person examined. Such suspected person may apply to a magistrate for an order restraining such examination and no examination shall then be made except upon order of such magistrate. Before such examination each suspected person shall be informed of this right and be given an opportunity to avail himself or herself thereof.[1]

Sec. 343n. *Persons under Arrest.* Every person arrested for vagrancy as defined under Subdivisions three or four of Sec. 887 of the Code of Criminal Procedure or under Sec. 150 of the Tenement House Law or under any statute or ordinance for any offense of the nature specified in Subdivision four of Sec. 887 of the Code of Crim-

---

[1] Amended by Chap. 40, Laws of 1919; in effect March 12, 1919.

inal Procedure, or arrested charged with a violation of Sec. 1146 or
1148 of the Penal Law, or any person arrested for frequenting disorderly houses or houses of prostitution, shall be reported within 24
hours by the court or magistrate before whom such person is arraigned, to the board of health or health officer of the health district
in which the alleged offense occurred, and shall be examined in accordance with the provisions of the preceding section. For purpose of
examination and diagnosis as provided in the preceding section, such
person may be detained until the results of such examination are
known. No such person if convicted shall be released from the jurisdiction of such court or magistrate until the person so convicted has
been examined as provided for in the preceding section.[1]

The section which particularly influences the procedure at
present followed in the Women's Court is Sec. 343n. It will
be seen that under this, defendants who are arrested for
offenses over which the Women's Court has exclusive jurisdiction are to be reported within 24 hours by the court or
magistrate before whom such person is arraigned to the City
Board of Health, for examination in accordance with the provision of 343m. This part of the section is not observed by
the New York City Health Department for the reason that
there is some doubt as to its constitutionality. Therefore,
defendants are not at this time detained until after conviction. The discretion for the release of the defendant on bail
after conviction is limited by this section until such time as a
person so convicted has been examined as provided in
Sec. 343m.

Convicted defendants, with a few exceptions noted elsewhere, are given this physical examination by the Bureau of
Preventable Diseases of the Department of Health to determine whether they have a venereal disease in an infectious
stage. Blood specimens and smears are taken in the Detention Prison by a woman physician assigned by the Bureau
for such service. Within twenty-four hours, the Bureau of
Laboratories of the Department of Health examines these

---

[1] Amended by Chap. 40, Laws of 1919; in effect March 12, 1919.

specimens and submits a report to the Bureau of Preventable Diseases which furnishes the court with a statement certifying the presence or absence of venereal disease in an infectious stage. A diagnosis of syphilis is made on the basis of a positive Wassermann of two plus or over, and of gonorrhea on positive laboratory findings, or on definite clinical findings, or both.

In 1920, it was the practice to send convicted women found to be suffering from a venereal disease to the Workhouse or to one of the three private institutions empowered by law to receive commitments from the Women's Court.[1] Or, if the woman seemed a suitable case to place on probation, she was given an opportunity to enter Kingston Avenue Hospital in Brooklyn, of her own free will, to remain there voluntarily until rendered non-infectious. If, at the termination of a Workhouse sentence, the woman still had a venereal disease in an infectious stage, she was transferred to Kingston Avenue Hospital, there to complete her treatment. Frequently, before full coöperation between the Department of Correction and the Health Department was established in the latter part of 1920, inmates of the Workhouse refused to take treatment from the staff physicians, claiming that they would be sent to Kingston Avenue Hospital anyway at the expiration of sentence. In this way, many Workhouse cases received no treatment whatever during the period studied. Such cases naturally had to be transferred to Kingston Avenue Hospital at the expiration of sentence, so needlessly prolonging their period of confinement. These practices threw first and old offenders together indiscriminately at the hospital, besides offering serious disciplinary problems with which it was not equipped to cope. Health officials contended that theirs was a hospital, not a jail or reformatory. The situation called forth much criticism. Finally, magistrates ascertaining that three months usually sufficed to render a

---

[1] House of Good Shepherd, House of Mercy, and Inwood House.

case of venereal disease non-infectious,[1] began in September, 1920, to commit to the Workhouse for 100 days, certain offenders who were found to be diseased.

That this period of time usually suffices to render the case non-infectious seems to be evidenced by the fact that during the present year[2] not one of the 129 cases sentenced to the Workhouse for 100 days was transferred to Kingston Avenue Hospital. In fact, throughout this period, only three Workhouse cases were transferred to the hospital. Two of these had served a 20- and one a 30-day sentence. One of the magistrates has stated:

Whereas it is no doubt true that in theory the 100-day sentence is not proper because it requires a consideration of the physical condition of the defendant rather than her delinquency, yet as practiced at the present time, it appears that this sentence is applied to the class of defendants to whom the magistrate might well be justified in giving a sentence of that length.

From the three tables which follow, it will be noted that 67 of the 129 cases with a venereal disease, sentenced to the Workhouse were first offenders. It should be stated that none of the 67 cases was considered suitable for probation. Only six of the 129 were under 21; more than half, between 21 and 30; while ten were over 40. Correlating the facts shown in the first two tables, we find from the third table that the six cases under 21 years of age were all first offenders; of the 80 cases between 21 and 30, 40 were first offenders and 22, second offenders; seven had had four or more previous convictions.

---

[1] Of 113 court cases treated wholly at Kingston Avenue Hospital during the first six months of 1920, seven were treated 100 days or over.

[2] Up to June 30, 1922.

Offense and Age of Cases with a Venereal Disease, Sentenced to 100 Days in the Workhouse, January 1 to June 30, 1922[1]

OFFENSE	TOTAL	AGE AT TIME OF ARREST						
		19–20	21–25	26–30	31–35	36–40	41–45	Over 45
Soliciting[2]	99	4	23	35	15	12	6	4
Offering to secure a prostitute (C. C. P. Sec. 887-4b)	4	...	...	3	...	1	...	...
Permitting premises to be used for immoral purposes (C. C. P. Sec. 887-4e)	6	...	...	2	4	...	...	...
Violating Tenement House Laws (T. H. L. 150 Sub. 3, 4, 5)	20	2	15	2	1	...	...	...
TOTAL	129	6	38	42	20	13	6	4

[1] Compiled from original papers in the Women's Court and from records of the Finger-print Bureau.
[2] For offenses included under this grouping, see Table 1, footnote 3, at the end of this chapter.

Relation of Offense to Number of Previous Convictions of Cases with a Venereal Disease, Sentenced to 100 Days in the Workhouse, January 1 to June 30, 1922[1]

OFFENSE	TOTAL	NUMBER OF PREVIOUS CONVICTIONS								
		0	1	2	3	4	5	6	7	10
Soliciting[2]	99	47	26	9	7	4	1	2	2	1
Offering to secure a prostitute (C. C. P. Sec. 887-4b)	4	2	1	1	...	...	...	...	...	...
Permitting premises to be used for immoral purposes (C. C. P. Sec. 887-4e)	6	6	...	...	...	...	...	...	...	...
Violating the Tenement House Laws (T. H. L. 150 Sub. 3, 4, 5)	20	12	4	2	1	...	1	...	...	...
TOTAL	129	67	31	12	8	4	2	2	2	1

[1] Compiled from original court papers in the Women's Court and from records of the Finger-print Bureau.
[2] For offenses included under this grouping, see Table 1, footnote 13, at the end of this chapter.

Correlation of Age and Previous Convictions of Cases with a Venereal Disease, Sentenced to 100 Days in the Workhouse, January 1 to June 30, 1922.[1]

NUMBER OF PREVIOUS CONVICTIONS	TOTAL	AGE AT TIME OF ARREST						
		19-20	21-25	26-30	31-35	36-40	41-45	Over 45
0	67	6	20	20	10	8	...	3
1	31	...	10	12	4	3	1	1
2	12	...	3	3	3	1	2	...
3	8	...	2	3	2	...	1	...
4	4	...	2	1	...	...	1	...
5	2	...	1	...	1	...	...	...
6	2	...	...	2	...	...	...	...
7	2	...	...	...	...	1	1	...
10	1	...	...	1	...	...	...	...
TOTAL	129	6	38	42	20	13	6	4

[1] Based upon two preceding tables.

The nature of the treatment for venereal disease given by Kingston Avenue Hospital and by private institutions, during the first six months of 1920, is discussed in connection with those institutions.

At present,[1] after a girl convicted in the Women's Court and treated in Kingston Avenue Hospital has been rendered noninfectious, she is returned to the court for sentence. Usually, if her conduct while under treatment at the hospital has been good, she is placed upon probation. If, however, her conduct is unfavorably reported upon, or the investigations of the Probation Department do not seem to warrant it, she is committed to a private institution, the State Reformatory, or the Workhouse. Of 118 women with a venereal disease, convicted in the Women's Court during the first six

[1] August, 1922.

months of 1920, and treated at Kingston Avenue Hospital
before sentence, 25 were still in the hospital on June 30, 1920;
89 were placed upon probation; one was committed to the
House of Good Shepherd; and three to the Workhouse.[1]

Treatment for Venereal Disease. Certain factors must be
taken into consideration in discussing the treatment of the
230 women found, after conviction in the Women's Court
during the first six months of 1920, to have a venereal disease
in an infectious stage: First, place of treatment. Some received treatment wholly at Kingston Avenue Hospital; some,
wholly at the Workhouse; and some partly at the Workhouse
and partly at Kingston, owing to the practice prevailing at
that time of transferring infectious cases of venereal disease
from the Workhouse to Kingston at the expiration of sentence. Still other cases, as indicated in Table 10, were treated
in private institutions. Second, length of treatment. This
can be stated definitely only in regard to those who received
their treatment wholly at Kingston Avenue Hospital. For,
although the date of admission to the Workhouse hospital and
the date of discharge therefrom to the prison proper is duly
recorded, these dates do not necessarily indicate the length
of treatment at the Workhouse, because, owing to limited
hospital accommodations at that time, it was the practice to
place in the prison those women who were thought least liable
to spread contagion. Their treatment, however, was continued.

The length of treatment of the 118 cases entering Kingston Avenue Hospital direct from the court during the first
six months of 1920 was ascertained with respect to 113. The
range of treatment in days was from five to 70 for syphilis,
from 22 to 119 for gonorrhea, and from 43 to 115 for syphilis
and gonorrhea. The average length of treatment for these
diseases was as follows: 46.3 days for syphilis; 65.4 days for
gonorrhea; and 69.9 days for syphilis and gonorrhea. Eighty-

---

[1] See Table 13 at the end of this chapter.

eight cases with a venereal disease were sentenced to the Workhouse, 33 of whom completed the necessary treatment there; the remaining 55 being transferred to Kingston Avenue Hospital.

Venereal-Disease Tables. Table 9, at the end of this chapter, shows the incidence of venereal disease in cases of women convicted in the Women's Court, New York, January 1 to June 30, 1920. Of 465 women convicted during this period, all but 30 (6.4 per cent) were physically examined. Twenty-six of those not examined were incorrigibles, who are examined only at the request of parent, guardian, or probation officer. Of the 379 women examined, who were convicted of offenses involving prostitution, 193, or 50.9 per cent, were found to have a venereal disease in an infectious stage: 62, gonorrhea; 101, syphilis; and 30, both diseases. Of the 81 convicted of incorrigibility, 55 (68 per cent) were examined, of whom 67.2 per cent were infected. This high percentage is not surprising, however, in view of the fact that only those who presumably have exposed themselves to infection are examined.

Table 10 shows the immediate disposition by offense of cases with a venereal disease, convicted in the Women's Court, New York, January 1 to June 30, 1920. Of the 230 venereal-disease cases, 118 were treated at Kingston Avenue Hospital; one was placed upon probation; one received a suspended sentence; one, a drug case, was sent to Riverside Hospital; 21 were committed to private institutions; and 88, to the Workhouse. In this period, therefore, over half of the diseased, convicted women were treated at Kingston Avenue Hospital, while more than a third were committed to the Workhouse, receiving treatment there.

From Table 11, cases of women with a venereal disease, convicted in the Women's Court, New York, January 1 to June 30, 1920, who received treatment at Kingston Avenue Hospital, it will be seen that in addition to the 118 women who agreed to enter Kingston, 55 were transferred from the Workhouse to Kingston at the completion of their sentences. These 173 women received treatment for the periods indicated in Table 12 which with the one following, has already been discussed. Table 14 shows the cases of women with a venereal disease, sentenced to the Workhouse by the Women's Court, New York, January 1 to June 30, 1920, and admitted to Kingston Avenue Hospital at the expiration of sentence, showing relation between length of detention in Workhouse and length of subsequent treatment in Kingston Avenue Hospital.

KINGSTON AVENUE HOSPITAL

Pavilion No. 3 of Kingston Avenue Hospital in Brooklyn, one of four hospitals maintained by the Department of Health for the treatment of contagious diseases, has been used for the treatment of women with venereal disease, since August, 1919. Prior to that time, such cases were treated at Riverside Hospital. Since September, 1920, the hospital has admitted voluntary cases from the city as a whole or from the Women's Court, provided that they are not under 16, or hardened offenders. Pregnant cases on the onset of labor are transferred to Kings County Hospital, a block away, being returned to Kingston Avenue Hospital shortly after confinement, for continued treatment.

Of the 303 cases admitted to the hospital from January 1 to June 30, 1920, 118 came from the Women's Court and 55 from the Workhouse. The remaining 130 applied voluntarily for treatment. The superintendent pointed out that former patients sometimes returned for treatment or advised friends to take treatment there.

The hospital records show:

Number of patients in hospital, Jan. 1, 1920.................... 85
Number of patients admitted to hospital, Jan. 1 to June 30, 1920.. 303

388

Number of patients admitted to hospital, Jan. 1 to June 30, 1920, for
Syphilis 136
Gonorrhea 112
Syphilis and Gonorrhea.............................. 55

303

Number of patients admitted to hospital, 1920, for
Syphilis 199
Gonorrhea 250
Syphilis and Gonorrhea.............................. 113

562

Pavilion No. 3, comprising ten wards divided into glass cubicles, has 120 beds. This pavilion was designed for the treatment of diphtheria cases. When it became necessary, however, to move venereal-disease cases from Riverside Hospital, it seemed well adapted to their treatment, particularly as the arrangement of the wards afforded proper segregation for cases of active syphilis and gonorrhea. White girls occupy the lower- and colored, the upper-floor wards. A well-equipped operating room is used also for administering salvarsan and mercury. Another room provides for douche treatment of gonorrheal cases. A report of the Department of Health says:[1]

Through the courtesy of the Public Health Service, there were presented to the hospital three irrigating tables. The principal feature of these tables is represented by a holding device for hot water, or chemical irrigation solution, whereby it is possible to begin irrigation with a solution of as high a temperature as the patient can bear in the initial injection, and change, without discontinuing irrigation, to

---

[1] Annual Report of the Department of Health, 1919, p. 222.

a temperature several degrees higher. The patient, herself, can manipulate the device and one nurse can direct treatment for several patients at one time. This method of treatment lessens the length of the infection and permits discharge of cases much earlier than was the case before it was installed.

Upon entering the hospital, the girl is interviewed and examined by the woman hospital physician in charge of venereal service. A card record is kept for each case, showing name, address, date, manner of admission, diagnosis, a brief social history, entries of the precise nature of each treatment administered, date of discharge, and other pertinent facts. On the day of our visit in June, 1922, the pavilion count was 87. The superintendent stated that recently it had varied from 85 to 100.

While under treatment in the hospital, the patients are assigned definite duties. Each one cares for her own cubicle; some wait upon bed cases, others serve meals and assist the matrons in various ways. They enjoy the use of a room furnished with piano, pianola, books, and easy chairs. An original and thoroughly worthwhile activity is afforded through the coöperation of the Board of Education, which, on November 1, 1920, assigned two teachers to the hospital. One instructs a group, organized as an ungraded class, in English, arithmetic, music, drawing, and other rudimentary subjects, while the other teacher gives sewing lessons. A practical feature of her instruction to pregnant girls is showing them how to make a layettes in accordance with certain specified requirements. Thus, before leaving the hospital, the girl has usually made for herself a complete layette of approved style. Materials are furnished partly by the Board of Education and partly by private agencies. Six hours and twenty minutes daily, exclusive of Saturday and Sunday, are supposed to be devoted to educational work, but as this is secondary to medical treatment and duties around the hospital, the time spent in this way is usually less.

Before discharging a case of syphilis which is not actively infectious, the Department of Health, in 1920, and at the present time [1] administers at least six salvarsan and twelve mercurial injections. Clinical symptoms of the disease must, of course, be absent. An attempt is always made to hold the case until negative, the Wassermann test being made once a week. Even though negative, however, on one or more tests, the patient is not released until the prescribed dosages have been administered. Before discharging a case of gonorrhea, "an approved course of treatment" must be given. The condition of release is phrased in this way, according to the Bureau of Preventable Diseases, because many different types of dosage are given. In addition to the required treatment, the case must show two consecutive negative smears from the urethra, vagina, and cervix, respectively, taken a week apart.

Although these women are not discharged by the hospital until they are no longer infectious, it is frequently desirable that clinical treatment be continued. However, no follow-up system was in force in 1920, and at present such a system remains incomplete. The Bureau of Preventable Diseases estimates that five per cent of the cases discharged by the hospital, continue treatment.

PROBATION

Probation has been applied to women sex offenders convicted in the Magistrates' Courts of New York City, since 1901. Under Sec. 98 and 98a of the Inferior Criminal Courts' Act, as amended by Chap. 516, Laws of 1918

... An adult convicted of an offense of which a magistrate has summary jurisdiction may be placed on probation for such time as the magistrate may deem proper, not longer, however, than one year. ...

---

[1] June, 1922.

After a conviction or a plea of guilty, a magistrate sitting as such
. . . may remand the defendant . . . for a period not to exceed
three days for investigation before pronouncing sentence . . .

In the same act, provision is made for the appointment of
probation officers, their powers and duties being broadly specified. When the two divisions of the City Magistrates' Courts
were combined into one, by Chap. 531 of the Laws of 1915,
a corresponding consolidation was effected by legal enactment in the probation departments of the two divisions. Thus,
Sec. 96 of the Inferior Criminal Courts Act, as amended by
Chap. 531 of the Laws of 1915, provides, with respect to the
City Magistrates' Courts, as follows:

96. Probation Officers; appointment and removal. . . . The chief
probation officer and each of the probation officers of the City Magistrates' Courts in office on the said day shall be continued as probation
officers until removed in accordance with provisions of this act. On
or before the first day of August, nineteen hundred and fifteen, the
chief city magistrate shall appoint one or more deputy probation
officers. The duties of the chief and deputy chief probation officers
and of the probation officers shall be prescribed by the chief city
magistrate and he shall assign them for service to the courts herein
provided for subject to the provisions of this act. No police officer
shall be designated or act as probation officer. The chief justice or
the chief city magistrate, as the case may be, or a majority of the
justices or a majority of the board of magistrates, may at pleasure
remove the chief probation officer or any probation officer. The suc-
cessors of the chief probation officer, deputy chief probation officers,
and probation officers of the Magistrates' Court shall be appointed
by the chief city magistrate. The chief city magistrate may from
time to time appoint such additional probation officers as the board
of aldermen, upon the recommendation of the board of estimate and
apportionment, may authorize.

97. Powers and duties of probation officers. Each probation officer
shall have all the powers and duties conferred upon probation officers
by the Code of Criminal Procedure. Probation officers shall keep
such records and conform to such rules and regulations as may be

established by a majority of the justices or of the magistrates, as the case may be. It shall be the duty of the chief justices and each city magistrate, respectively, to see that such rules and regulations are observed and that such records are properly kept.

By these broad powers, enumerated in Subd. 234 of Sec. 11a of the Code of Criminal Procedure, the work of the Probation Department of the City Magistrates' Court, under the direction of the chief probation officer, is divided into five or six different bureaus or districts. These are supervised by deputy chiefs and probation officers in charge. The probation work of the Women's Court is directed by Miss Alice C. Smith, who for 20 years has labored unremittingly in behalf of wayward girls.[1] Her department comprises four women probation officers who investigate and supervise cases residing in their respective districts. In this task the municipal officers receive substantial aid from certain private organizations supported by Catholics, Protestants, and Jews. The Catholic Charities, the Church Mission of Help (an Episcopal organization which looks after any Protestant girl), and the Jewish Board of Guardians [2] each maintains a worker in the court, the Church Mission of Help furnishing in addition a colored worker. Each of these privately appointed agents is directly responsible to the municipal probation officer in whose district her case may reside. Thus, if two Catholic girls living in different probation districts were assigned to the Catholic worker, she would report with respect to one girl to the municipal officer in charge of that girl's district and with respect to the other to the municipal officer in charge of the other district. In this way a municipal dis-

---

[1] Miss Smith began her services under private auspices in the Fourth District City Magistrates' Court on East 57th Street in 1902, as the majority of arrested women were arraigned there before the Women's Court was established. She responded, however, to calls from any of the other Magistrates' Courts. In 1907 she was placed upon the Civil Service list and in 1910 was appointed first probation officer of the Women's Court.

[2] Formerly, Central Committee for Friendly Aid to Jewish Girls.

trict probation officer in addition to her own probationers, is supervising whatever Catholic, Protestant, or Jewish cases she may have assigned to the private agencies already mentioned. This system furnishes an excellent example of how coöperation between public and private organizations may be effected, giving as it does free rein to the private bodies and yet in no way impairing the official character of the probation service. Miss Smith finds the generous assistance given by private agencies of inestimable value.

In the Women's Court, with few exceptions, only incorrigibles [1] and those not previously convicted are investigated by the probation department. Because of inadequate clerical help during the period covered by our study, the records of the department were very limited at that time. There are none from which the proportion of investigated cases placed upon probation could be determined. The chief probation officer of the City Magistrates' Courts estimates that it was then about 30 per cent. He reports for the period January 1 to August 1, 1922, that 829 defendants in the Women's Court were investigated, of whom 384 (46 per cent) were placed on probation. Of these, 197 (51 per cent) were first treated for a venereal disease in Kingston Avenue Hospital. When a girl or woman arraigned in this court pleads guilty or is convicted, her case is remanded for finger-printing and for a report from the Health Department on her physical condition as to venereal disease. First offenders and certain other cases are investigated by the probation department to determine their fitness for probation. As the City Magistrates' Courts file prints only of those convicted of certain offenses in their own courts, it is necessary to inspect also the finger-print files of the Police Department, for convictions of offenses over which the Magistrates' Courts do not have summary jurisdiction, and of the Department of Correction

---

[1] As incorrigibles are not finger-printed, it cannot be stated whether they are first offenders.

for conviction of those minor offenses under the designation "disorderly conduct" which are not finger-printed in the Magistrates' Courts. One probation officer usually looks up these records for the day. A preliminary social investigation of first offenders is then made by the municipal probation officers—rarely by the private workers. When the case is called for sentence, the investigating officer communicates orally to the judge in court the result of her inquiries.

If probation is recommended, the girl's mother, father, or guardian (if such can be found) [1] is taken before the judge in order that the conditions of probation imposed by the court may be heard and fully understood. The judge invariably stipulates that the girl shall behave, work, and report as directed, sometimes specifying also with whom she shall live. After the judge has designated her probation officer, the work of supervision begins. In this, as has been pointed out, the municipal officer receives substantial assistance from the workers representing certain private agencies. The girl is visited in her home and required to report regularly at court to her probation officer, who seeks to find suitable employment and wholesome recreation for her. Records at the Central Probation Bureau show that the municipal officers usually have about 61 cases at a time under supervision.

Six months is the usual period of probation, although occasionally a year is given. The Women's Court requires the probationer to appear informally before one of its magistrates for a brief review of her case before discharge. This became a practice without formal resolution or process of law, early in 1920. At first, one of the judges had these hearings in chambers in the Jefferson Market Building on alternate Monday nights. Later, an associate shared this voluntary service. The writers, who were present on one of these evenings, were impressed by the thoroughness with which

---

[1] Compare manner of living at time of arrest, Table 15, at the end of this chapter.

pertinent facts were reported by the officers and the kindliness with which the probationer herself was drawn out and questioned by the judge. Relatively few cases have their period of probation extended, although it may be continued for an additional three months if the judge sees fit. Before dismissing a case, the judge considers the probationer's reported behavior and work records, forming in addition his own estimate of her general attitude.

During the first six months of 1920, 186 cases, constituting 40 per cent of the 465 cases convicted in the Women's Court in that time, were placed upon probation. Of these, 89 (47.8 per cent) were first treated in Kingston Avenue Hospital for a venereal disease. In order to determine the extent to which defendants in the Women's Court had ever been placed upon probation previously, a special study of convictions in the first three months of 1920 was undertaken. This revealed 379 arraigned cases, of whom 245 were convicted. Of the latter, 42 cases were incorrigibles and therefore not finger-printed. It was found that 21 of the 203 convicted of offenses involving prostitution had been placed upon probation once prior to conviction in 1920 and one of these was again given probation at the 1920 hearing. Two of the 203 convicted women had been placed upon probation twice prior to 1920, of whom one again received probation at that time.

Of the 69 cases placed upon probation during the first three months of 1920 (exclusive of incorrigibles) 61 were first offenders; six had been previously convicted once; one, three; and one, five times. Thus, 11.9 per cent of finger-printed probationers were not first offenders. As no special study of their histories was attempted, these exceptions to the general policy of the court are not explained. Of these 69 cases (up to October 1, 1921) [1] seven were subsequently convicted once; one for intoxication and six for violating the Tenement House Law. They were sentenced as follows: one to Bed-

---

[1] For comparative purposes the study was not carried beyond the period studied in Philadelphia and Boston.

ford; four to the Workhouse for 2, 20, 30, and 100 days respectively. One received an indeterminate sentence to the Workhouse. Eight of the same group of 69 violated their probation and warrants for their arrest were issued. Three had absconded; one, however, was found five months later and sent to Bedford; one was committed to the Workhouse; three, to private institutions; and in one case, probation was continued. In five cases, the violations were failure to report and to live where directed, and in three cases, disorderly conduct at Kingston Avenue Hospital.

In New York as elsewhere, through the courtesy of the Probation Department, we were permitted to examine 50 records. The object was to note definitely the practices of the department and to secure data for statistical purposes. Two sets of consecutive records were studied, one of the first 25 cases placed upon probation in 1920 and one of the last 25 in the period ending June 30, 1920. In this way, as in other cities, allowance was made for possible seasonal influence upon conduct. These 50 cases constitute 26.8 per cent of the 186 cases placed upon probation during the first six months of 1920 and should, therefore, be considered a fair sampling. The period covered extends from the date when the probationer first became known to the court, that is, from September, 1910, when finger-prints were first taken, to October 1, 1921.[1] In Tables 15 through 18, at the end of this chapter, we have summarized the results of our study.

DISCUSSION OF PROBATION TABLES

Table 15, a statistical analysis of the social history of our 50 cases, shows that 40 probationers were convicted of prostitution, loitering, or soliciting; only seven are incorrigibles. The remaining three offered to secure a prostitute or permitted permises to be used for immoral purposes. Thirty-six of the probationers are white and 14 colored. Eleven are

---

[1] See footnote 1, p. 350.

of foreign birth. Nine are under 20 years of age; 24 are less than 25 years old. Four are over 50. Seventeen are single. Fifteen are Catholic, 27 Protestant, and eight Jewish. In four instances, the school record is not stated, and in nine it is miscellaneous in character. Of the 37 whose schooling is definitely recorded, nine attended high school (two completing the course); 14 completed the eight grade; six, the seventh; two, the sixth, and the remaining five went no farther than the third, fourth, or fifth grades. At the time of arrest, 20 were living with parents, husband, or other relative; six were living with lover; the others were keeping house or boarding.

The number of convictions prior and subsequent to the one in 1920 at which the 50 women received probation, is indicated in Table 16. Of the four who are not first offenders, three are credited with one previous, and one with three previous convictions. These, like the cases cited on pages 350–351, constitute, apparently, an exception to the general rule. Up to October 1, 1921, only four of the 50 probationers were again convicted in a magistrates' court, each once.

Table 17, relating to the incidence of venereal disease in the group, shows that 45 were examined for both gonorrhea and syphilis. The five not examined are incorrigibles, who are examined only at the request of parent, guardian, or probation officer. Of the 45 examined, 20 were found to have a venereal disease in an infectious stage, 12 being infected with syphilis, six with gonorrhea, and two with syphilis and gonorrhea. All were treated at Kingston Avenue Hospital. No psychologist or psychiatrist is attached to this court at present. In January, 1920, Dr. John S. Richards was detailed by the Department of Charities to make a preliminary examination of convicted women who were thought by the court or probation department to be mentally defective. On his recommendation, magistrates committed suspected cases to Bellevue for observation. According to monthly bulletins issued by the Committee of Fourteen, less than 100 cases were examined in our six-month period. Of these, one was sent to Bellevue for observation.[1] [2]

The records of the Probation Department do not state systematically who, if any one, was seen by the officer when she called at the girl's home. It is possible, therefore, merely to indicate the number of calls made and the number of times the probationer reported to her officer. These facts are shown in relationship in Table 18. Twelve girls were never visited. Of these, ten had returned to their homes in other cities. The homes of 27 were visited from one to three times; and of 11, from four to eight times. Twelve never reported to their officer; six reported from one to three times; 13, from four to ten times; and the remaining 19, from 11 to 18 times.

Correlating visits and reporting, we find that seven were not visited and did not report. Of these, four lived in other cities. Of the 27 who were not visited more than three times, 16 reported ten or more times; of the six who did not report more than three times, four were never visited; the other two were visited two or three times.

The report on these cases on October 1, 1921,[3] was as follows:[2]

Finished with improvement and not re-arrested..................... 38
Finished without improvement and not re-arrested................. 3
Finished with improvement and re-arrested once................... 2
Finished without improvement and re-arrested once................ 1
Probation revoked and sent to House of Good Shepherd............. 1
Absconded 4
Absconded and later re-arrested for a new offense................ 1

---

[1] These are classed as follows: Three, high grade moron; two, border line; one, mental age of ten.

[2] On October 17, 1920, the New York Probation and Protective Association gave to the Women's Court, the part-time services of a psychiatrist who for ten months examined women convicted there. The results of these examinations, made by Dr. Augusta Scott, are published in *Mental Hygiene*, vol. vi, no. 2, April, 1922, in an article entitled: Three Hundred Psychiatric Examinations Made at the Women's Day Court, New York City.

[3] This date corresponds to the one concluding the study of subsequent records in Philadelphia.

[4] This summary is based upon the records of the Finger-print Bureau and the probation officers' records covering estimated result of probation.

Thus three-fourths of the cases made good, so far as known.

As already pointed out in this series of reports on specialized courts, too great importance must not be attached to bare records. They are broadly indicative of practices obtaining in each court. In the very nature of the case, they are more definite on the negative than on the positive side. So long as probation officers are overburdened with cases, actual work must take precedence over detailed entries regarding the officer's activities and observations.

Records. Data relating to probationers are filed in individual, numbered folders, indexed by name. Each folder contains a preliminary investigation sheet and a sheet showing record of supervision. The obverse of the former sheet contains essential identification, police and court information, a record of previous court and institutional experiences, and the reverse calls for certain social facts. The record sheet contains a blank schedule showing dates of visiting and reporting by officer and probationer respectively; employment record; date of expiration or continuance of probation, with results. Each month, the probation officer fills out a schedule showing time spent daily on duty, whether in court attendance or on investigation, supervision, or clerical work; the number of home visits and the number of investigations.

At the central Probation Bureau, cards which briefly summarize the court and social history of each probationer are filed. Owing to the Bureau's limited staff, practically no compilations of the valuable social data recorded are made. The Annual Report of the City Magistrates' Courts for 1920 contains only the statistics of the Probation Department of the Women's Court presented below:

WOMEN'S COURT—BOROUGHS OF MANHATTAN AND THE BRONX

Probationers received during year	467
Probation officers	4
Average number pending at any one time	60

RESULTS OF PROBATION

	Number	Per cent
Discharged with improvement	344	77.3
Discharged without improvement	41	9.2
Revoked and committed	24	5.4
Absconded and lost from oversight	36	8.1
Total	445	100.

HOME VISITS

Total visits	797
Probation officers	4
Average per officer	199
Average per case	3

INVESTIGATIONS

Total investigations	792
Probation officers	4
Average per officer	198

PUBLIC INSTITUTIONS

Bedford Reformatory

This is the New York State Reformatory for Women.

Sec. 89 of the Inferior Criminal Courts Act provides that women, convicted of offenses over which the Women's Court has exclusive jurisdiction, may be sentenced as follows:

2. The magistrate may commit such female for the term of three years to the State Reformatory for Women at Bedford, pursuant to the provisions of Sec. 226 of the State Charities Law, Chap. 55 of the Consolidated Laws as amended, to be there confined as provided by such law . . .

Such sentences are indeterminate, and the person so sentenced may be released upon parole at any time before the expiration of the sentence by the parole board of Bedford.

A recent publication of the Board of Control of Bedford Reformatory contains the following statement:

The State Reformatory for Women at Bedford Hills, New York,

was founded by an Act of Legislature of the State of New York in the year 1892, for the reformation and training of delinquent women between the ages of sixteen and thirty.

The institution, which covers nearly 200 acres of farming country, is located among the picturesque hills of Westchester County. It is built on the cottage system with all modern facilities and is ideally adapted for the physical, mental, and moral reformation of delinquent young women.

On their admission to the institution, inmates are received in the reception house. Here they undergo quarantine as well as observation for physical and mental disorders, are classified according to their physical and mental health and previous record of delinquency, prior to their transfer to an appropriate cottage in the main colony.

This admission building is one of the group which was built and equipped by Mr. John D. Rockefeller, Jr., and leased to the state at a nominal cost of one dollar per year.

After a period of quarantine, classification, and opportunity for adaptation to the general life of the institution, the inmates receive training in the following departments: Academic and Commercial Training, Cooking, Industrial, Farming, Music, Athletics.

In the training of the inmates—mental, physical, and industrial— the aim is to avoid routine, group, and haphazard methods. Each individual is carefully studied from a psychiatric and psychologic standpoint, in the endeavor to discover, not only the natural ability and aptitude for certain work, but also the individual's desire and inclination, which are so essential to ultimate success.

The work is not meted out to the inmates as a species of discipline or punishment. On the contrary, they are made to feel that their occupation and training is intended to develop their latent energies and talents, thus insuring economic independence and future welfare upon their return to community life.

Catholic, Protestant, and Jewish religious services are held weekly and every effort is made to awaken the spiritual consciousness of the inmates.

A rational parole system is one of the most important factors in reformatory work.

To-day there are scattered throughout the state girls who have passed through the institution. Some are happily married, mothers of our future citizens; others are in trades and gainful occupations, a number occupying positions of trust in their various communities.

To carry on the policy of helping the girl to help herself, a parole committee has recently been organized and developed. The object of the committee is to visit and keep in touch with the inmates shortly after they enter the institution and to do intensive case work in furnishing aftercare to those who are paroled or discharged, with a view of rehabilitating them.

The Board of Managers, the Superintendent, and the Parole Officers of the institution hold monthly conferences in which the private agencies, Catholic Protective Society, Church Mission of Help, and Jewish Board of Guardians, also take part, and extend their valuable coöperation. At these conferences, each individual inmate to be paroled is carefully considered so that she may be restored to the environment best suited to her needs. A monthly report of each girl's status is submitted to the Board of Managers by the various agencies, and difficult cases are discussed.

Following is a report of the Parole Committee from Nov. 1, 1920, to Jan. 1, 1922:

Number placed on parole	114
Re-arrested on new charge and returned	3
Violated parole and returned to institution	7
Violated parole, whereabouts unknown	27
Discharged from parole	23
Remaining on parole and conditions satisfactory	54
Total	114

These figures indicate that 67 per cent of the girls who have been paroled during this period and placed in various occupations and vocations in the community are doing satisfactorily.

Workhouse

The Workhouse, a gray, granite structure erected early in the last century, is one of the institutions maintained by the Department of Correction. It stands on Welfare Island,[1] one of a group of islands lying in the East River used for city charges. The Workhouse receives commitments from the

---

[1] Formerly Blackwell's Island.

Magistrates' Courts and the Court of Special Sessions. A central building, containing kitchen, dining room, chapel, sewing and other rooms for general use, connects the north and south wings, formerly used for women and men prisoners, respectively. In 1920, the Workhouse was in process of change. The men prisoners had been removed to other institutions of the Department of Correction and the south wing, in which they had been formerly confined, was being remodeled as a clearing house for women prisoners. It was planned to use the entire building exclusively for women. The women prisoners, meantime, were still housed in the three-tier north wing, with fairly large outside cells. The tiers extend around a large, oblong, central space. At that time, Penitentiary cases (women) committed by the Court of General Sessions, the Court of Special Sessions, the County Court, and the Supreme Court, were kept in this same wing. It was the practice then, as now, to place white and colored Penitentiary and Workhouse cases in separate cell blocks. Such segregation is little more than a form, however, as the women roam around more or less freely when not confined to their cells. On the ground floor are seven or eight "coolers," all empty when the Workhouse was visited in March, 1920. On that day, there were 100 Workhouse and 35 Penitentiary women in the wing. This count was said to be low—the usual number being about 200. The remodeled south wing, formerly used for the men, now serves as a hosiptal for the women. In 1920, the women inmates were doing practically all of the work about the building. The chef, storekeeper, carpenters, and plumbers constituted the main exceptions. The superintendent stated that most of the women put in an eight-hour day, cleaning, laundering, sewing, and other housework. Visitors were allowed once in two weeks. Interviews took place in the presence of a matron and police-officer, one on each side of a heavy screen with an exceedingly fine mesh. Prisoner and visitor were compelled to hold their hands behind their backs while talking, because formerly visitors had been detected slipping drugs through. While talking, they would lean against the screen and pry the meshes apart with a knife. The Workhouse had in 1920 a well-equipped operating room, and medical and surgical wards of 10 or 12 beds each. At that time, however, as has been pointed out in the section on venereal disease, relatively few took treatment. According to the Acting Medical Director, these numbered scarcely more than a dozen women out of 100 to 150. Records, which were kept by the inmates, are considered unreliable. Many were actually destroyed. Thus, little knowledge of practices in 1920 can be gleaned from those still available. Inmates were examined at expiration of sentence by a doctor from the Board of Health and if found to be diseased were transferred to Kingston Avenue Hospital.

The use of a portion of the Workhouse as a place of detention for women awaiting trial is discussed on page 296. The tiers used in 1920 for the Workhouse and Penitentiary women remain practically unchanged.[1] Changes effected in the past two years relate chiefly to hospital facilities and methods of treating venereal-disease cases. Five rooms are reserved for the reception and examination of the committed women. On entering the Workhouse, her valuables are checked, she is stripped, bathed and given an enema. On the next day she receives a general and local examination. Very few psychiatric examinations have been given. The woman is isolated for 24 to 48 hours for these preliminaries. After close coöperation was established between the Department of Correction and the Department of Health, in the latter part of 1920, diseased women rarely refused to take treatment. They were given a minimum standard treatment differing only in method from that followed at Kingston Avenue Hospital.[2] The treatment was intensively administered over three successive days, the patient resting for the balance of the week. Further, the patients do not douche themselves, as at

---

[1] August, 1922.
[2] Described on p. 342 ff.

Kingston Avenue Hospital.   The treatments are rapidly given by two men doctors and two nurses, assisted by two inmates who drape the patients.   While two patients are on the table taking treatment, two stand ready to replace them and two wait their turn in the doorway.   Treatments for gonorrhea take from three to five minutes.   About 100 cases are treated at each clinic.   Of 321 women in the Workhouse and Penitentiary on August 15, 1922, 167 were under treatment in the hospital wing, which was opened in June, 1921. The hospital has separate wards for general medical cases, surgical cases, tuberculosis, drug addicts, gonorrhea and syphilis, with a total capacity of 190 beds.   In August, 1922, the Workhouse hospital was designated a hospital of the Department of Health.   This means that women still having a venereal disease at the expiration of sentence may be transferred to the hospital adjoining and thus assume the status of "patients."   A portion of the central building connecting the two wings, is used as a place of detention for arrested women known to be in immediate need of medical treatment. These women mingle in no way with convicted women in either wing.

PRIVATE INSTITUTIONS [1]

Subd. 1 of Sec. 89 of the Inferior Criminal Courts Act refers to women convicted in the Women's Court, using the following language:

The magistrate may commit such female for the term of three years in the Boroughs of Manhattan and the Bronx to the Roman Catholic House of the Good Shepherd, the Protestant Episcopal House of Mercy, or the New York Magdalen Benevolent Society [2] . . .

---

[1] Because of the difference of the laws of procedure in New York from those of the other cities, which laws provide that commitments from the Magistrates' Courts may be made to certain designated private institutions, it has been found advisable to describe these institutions in connection with the New York report. This was not done in the reports of the other cities because of the absence of laws of this character.

[2] Now called "Inwood House."

House of the Good Shepherd

The Good Shepherd, one of the cloistered orders of the Roman Catholic Church, began its mission in New York on Fourteenth Street shortly before the Civil War. Within a few years, outgrowing these quarters, it moved into a cottage on the site of its present extensive property, covering the city block bounded by 89th and 90th Streets, the East River, and Avenue A. The present buildings of red brick with granite trimmings were completed in 1862.

Prior to the passage of the Inferior Criminal Courts Act in 1910, the charges of the Good Shepherd entered voluntarily or were brought in by parents or private agencies. The Page Law, quoted in part above, designated the Roman Catholic House of the Good Shepherd, among others, as an institution to which magistrates may commit "females convicted of certain offenses," for a term not to exceed three years.

The city pays a nominal sum for each girl committed by the court, and usually such cases comprise half the population. The expenses of the institution are said to be met by city and county appropriations, by donations, and by earnings from "activities," as the commercial work of the institution is termed.

Through the courtesy of the Mother Provincial, Miss Topping was conducted over the House of the Good Shepherd and informed concerning the scope of its work. The House ministers to two main classes of delinquents, the voluntarily committed and those committed by the court. With the exception of a few colored girls committed on remand by the Juvenile Court, no girl under 16 years of age is received.[1] No limitations are imposed as to the girl's religion, although the majority are Catholics, or as to the number of offenses she may have committed. Unmarried mothers are received. Pregnant girls who are sent there are transferred to the City

---

[1] White girls under 16 years of age are cared for by this order at St. Germaine's Home at Peekskill.

or Metropolitan Hospital, usually in the sixth month of
pregnancy.

Inmates of the House of the Good Shepherd are divided
according to age into two groups, housed in separate buildings. The younger, comprising girls from 16 to 21 years of
age, is termed "St. Mary's Class"; and the older, comprising those over 21, "St. Michael's." Within these classes still
other divisions exist, for shortly after admission the girl is
assigned to a group of six or eight judged to be of her own
"moral status."

Admission. Girls brought by their families or sent by the
courts are detained for two or three weeks in the Reception
House (in which there is dormitory for this purpose) where
they are observed in order to determine where they can best
be fitted into the life of the institution. Their family name
is then replaced by that of a saint and they are assigned to
their class and group. The mental tests previously made by
a psychologist are now given by a sister trained for this purpose. Each girl is given a general and local examination.

Physical Examination. On admission, all girls are examined for venereal disease. The street floor of the reception
building contains a clinic with two operating tables and facilities for giving douches.

Infirmary. This three-story building to which girls may
be sent for any kind of illness, is in charge of a sister who
is a trained nurse. The building has isolation rooms for
infectious diseases. One floor, which is used as a dormitory
for those assigned to work in the building, may be used wholly
for patients, if necessary.

Visitors. Each class has a week assigned for visits, although, for special reasons, a girl may at any time see her
lawyer or other interested persons or agencies.

St. Mary's Class. This class numbered 120 on the day of
the visit.[1] It occupies a five-story building with accommoda-

---

[1] August, 1922.

tions for 150. A refectory is on the main floor and a recreation hall on the second. The third floor is used as an industrial shop-room, while the fourth and fifth floors are devoted to dormitories with 60 beds each, ranged in four or five rows. A chair stands by each bed, over the foot of which are hung the girl's towel and wash-cloth. Four or five toilets and baths are installed at the end of each floor. The girls retire at eight and rise at six. At night "grand silence" is observed by all and the girls are under surveillance while they sleep. The industrial room on the third floor used for sewing, embroidery, beading, and millinery, is equipped with 60 power machines.

The entire class receives instruction in grade subjects, and those qualified take commercial courses. Still others are trained in domestic science in a modernly equipped school-kitchen. This program is carried on by the Board of Education of New York City, which in November, 1921, assigned two teachers to the House of the Good Shepherd. The number has since been increased to five. On the day the institution was visited, Board of Education diplomas issued to inmates, were on exhibition. These certified to satisfactory completion of grammar-school studies in accordance with the standards of required public schools in the city. Teachers from the Board of Education instruct the class from one to three in the "school building" in the subjects already mentioned. In the morning and after three in the afternoon, they are trained in certain industrial arts; sewing, embroidery, beading, and millinery. Several New York firms supply the convent with the necessary materials and pay for the finished products. The factory which provides the material for aprons, shirts, and similar merchandise, installed the power machines already referred to. In addition, it assigns one of its women to instruct the girls and to supervise their work. The power plant is shut down in the afternoon, but the hand work is carried on from three to five by those employed at the machines in the morning. After five, the class has recreation. The convent aims to have the girls learn to make articles for which there is a large, steady demand. At the rear of the industrial room, the girls are taught by a trained sister to make beading and embroidery in the manner carried on in commercial establishments. On the day of the visit, the girls were embroidering and beading flounces for evening gowns. These were held securely in large frames on which the girls worked rapidly and well. It was said that in periods of slack work, the Good Shepherd workroom was given preference. The girls were observed to be under close surveillance by a sister who was seated on a high platform commanding a view of the entire room.

It is said that these girls are paid a certain sum weekly, which is banked for them in a nearby institution under their individual names. On leaving, the girls are given the accumulated earnings.

St. Michael's Class. This class, housed in a separate building, numbered 140 on the day visited. Like St. Mary's, it has a refectory on the main floor and two floors used as dormitories corresponding to St. Mary's in capacity. A laundry in a separate building occupies two floors—one for the work of the sisters and inmates, and one for work from the outside. Both have the complete, modern equipment of commercial laundries. The heavy weight machines are operated by men, who are separated from the women by heavy partitions. Outside work is received mostly from private families, colleges, etc. Laundry work is the only industrial occupation carried on by St. Michael's Class. They are instructed, however, in grade subjects from 9 to 11, in the school building. Or, if they are foreigners, they are admitted to the Americanization class. Their hours are so arranged, however, that they do not come in contact with the members of St. Mary's Class. Among the older women were observed many wearing the black dress and silver cross of the "consecrated" as those are called who, at expiration of their sentence, elect to remain there another year. This promise may be renewed from year to year. Indeed, many wearing the garb of the consecrated were gray-haired women. Answers in response to the sister's queries as to how long they had been there, varied from 20 to 40 years.

Parole and Follow-up. Girls are not paroled from the institution. On discharge, they are referred for follow-up work to the Catholic Protective Society. Later, this work was taken over by the Catholic Charities. A full-time social worker is said to attend to all the after-care work.

Records. In the record room is a file containing a card for each girl admitted to the institution, and a bound book in which is entered the chronological record of admissions showing name, age, offense, dates of admission and discharge, and other pertinent data. Another book records transfers to hospital, length of treatment there, and other medical information. These records were consulted for the purpose of finding out how long the girls committed from the Women's Court during the first six months of 1920 had been kept at the House of the Good Shepherd.

Although only 35 cases were committed to the House of the Good Shepherd by the Women's Court during the first six months of 1920, the four who were sent there in July, after treatment at Kingston Avenue Hospital, have been included in our analysis because of the small number of cases available for study.

The 39 girls and women were convicted of the following offenses: soliciting,[1] 12; permitting premises to be used for immoral purposes, 1; prostitution in tenements, 6; incorrigibility, 20. Nineteen were under 21 and therefore in St. Mary's Class; and 19 over 21, in St. Michael's Class.[2] In St. Mary's, 17 were incorrigibles and two prostitutes. In St. Michael's, the majority were committed for offenses involving prostitution, although three, aged, 22, 23, and 25, respectively, were charged with incorrigibility. While most of those in

---

[1] For offenses included under this heading, see Table 1, footnote 13, at the end of this chapter.

[2] The age of one girl is not stated.

St. Michael's Class were between 21 and 30, four were over 40.

All committed for offenses involving prostitution were examined for venereal disease at the court: eleven were not infected; four had syphilis; three, gonorrhea; and one, syphilis and gonorrhea. Twelve of the 20 incorrigibles were examined by the court: two were not infected; one had syphilis; seven, gonorrhea; and two, syphilis and gonorrhea. When the remaining eight incorrigibles were examined at the House of the Good Shepherd, one, a pregnant girl, was found to have gonorrhea; of the seven not infected, three were pregnant. Of the entire 39 women, seven were pregnant, of whom two had gonorrhea. Of the 24 women requiring hospital care because diseased or pregnant, five were first treated at Kingston Avenue Hospital, nine received treatment at the City or Metropolitan Hospital, and ten were treated in the institution itself.

While nothing could be learned of the previous and subsequent convictions of the incorrigibles, as they are not finger-printed, records of the 19 women convicted of offenses involving prostitution were looked up, with the following result: seven were found to have no previous or subsequent [1] convictions; eight, who had had from one to 17 previous convictions, were not subsequently convicted in the Women's Court; one, with eight previous convictions, was subsequently convicted once; two, with seven and nine previous convictions, respectively, were subsequently convicted twice; and one, with 17 previous convictions was subsequently convicted five times.

The girls in St. Mary's Class are said to remain in the institution a year. Twelve of the 20 in that class remained a year or more.[2] Nine of these 12 girls were neither infected nor pregnant when admitted.[3] Of the remaining seven members of the class who were kept less than a year, all were

---

[1] Up to July 1, 1922.

[2] One has been in the institution two years and four months and is still there.

[3] Four had been treated at Kingston Avenue Hospital prior to admission.

infected with a venereal disease or pregnant. Five of these were in the institution less than six months.

Women in St. Michael's Class are said to remain in the institution about six months. Of the 19 in that class, five were kept six months and ten, from ten months to a year. Nine of these 15 women were free from infection. The four who were detained less than six months [1] were pregnant or infected.

The fact that in both classes only pregnant or diseased women are kept less than the time usually prescribed, taken in conjunction with the large proportion of noninfected or nonpregnant girls and women among those detained the full time or longer, would seem to establish a definite connection between health and the period of detention.

House of Mercy

The House of Mercy, a Protestant-Episcopal home to which girls may be committed from the court under the section of the Page Law that applies to the House of the Good Shepherd and Inwood House, received but two commitments from the Women's Court during the first six months of 1920. About two years ago, the institution closed temporarily and moved to Valhalla, New York.

Inwood House [2]

Inwood House, organized in 1833 and incorporated in 1851, has for its purpose "the promotion of moral purity in the City of New York in a way both preventive and corrective." The work is nonsectarian. Until 1920, it provided a reformatory on Bolton Road, Inwood, overlooking the Hudson, for unfortunate and wayward girls (immoral and intemperate) from 16 to 30 years of age. They were committed from the

---

[1] The time varied from one to four months.
[2] Formerly the New York Magdalen Home.

Women's Court in accordance with the provisions of Sec. 89 of the Inferior Criminal Courts Act, which designates the New York Magdalen Benevolent Society as a place of commitment for females convicted of certain offenses. Girls were also received at the request of parents or private agencies or they could enter voluntarily.

From January 1 to May 28, 1920,[1] 43 girls and 14 babies were admitted to Inwood House. Twenty-four of the girls were committed from the Women's Court. At that time they were taught certain school subjects, domestic science, sewing, and laundry work. Special provisions were made for unmarried mothers, who were instructed in the care of their babies. Efforts were made to find positions where they might have their babies with them.

For many years, the institution has been giving douche and mercury treatments for venereal diseases. In 1916, more intensive work was started. Cases of gonorrhea were given packing about three times a week and douches every day. When they showed three negative smears, they rested for a time, after which treatment was renewed. Treatments were continued until there was no discharge whatever, and three negative smears were secured over a period of two weeks. Smears on these cases were taken at monthly intervals until the time of the girl's discharge. Cases of syphilis received a course of ten treatments with salvarsan administered once a week, or twice if the case was very active. At the same time, hypodermics of mercury were given twice a week until twenty had been received by the patient. A two-weeks' rest followed this course of treatment, at the end of which time a blood test was given. If the result was still positive a similar course of treatment followed. This plan was continued until a negative Wassermann resulted. Three negative Wassermanns obtained over a period of three months were usually considered evidence that the disease was held in check. Wasser-

---

[1] After this date, for reasons which will be explained later, Inwood received no further court commitments until August, 1922.

manns on each of these cases were, however, taken monthly during the first year and later, at stated intervals, until her discharge from the institution. Girls were also mentally examined in 1920.

Before discussing the change of policy adopted by the Board of Managers in 1921, it may be well to comment briefly upon the 24 cases referred to. Eight were committed for soliciting; two for violating the Tenement House Law; and 14 for incorrigibility. Fifteen were under 21; six, between 21 and 25; and three, between 26 and 30. Three, convicted of soliciting, had syphilis, and two incorrigibles had gonorrhea. One incorrigible was pregnant. Previous and subsequent convictions of incorrigibles cannot be stated, as they are not finger-printed. Of the ten convicted of offenses involving prostitution, three had been convicted formerly once, and two, twice. Two others were subsequently re-arrested while on parole, convicted, and sent to Bedford. One had spent six and one nine months in Inwood House. Another was re-sentenced to the Workhouse.[1] With the exception of these three cases, all are still[2] out on parole after having spent from three to nine months in the institution. Three were in the institution three months; four, seven months; ten, eight months; and four, nine months.

After the Board of Managers of Inwood House had transferred its girls to other institutions or paroled them, it sold its property, in June, 1920, to the Jewish Memorial Hospital, and rented a house on East 54th Street for headquarters and for any paroled cases requiring special care.

In March, 1921, after carefully studying the needs of delinquent and pre-delinquent girls in New York City, "the Board of Managers decided to continue its policy of caring for the girl committed from the court, to be received regard-

---

[1] This girl was sent to Bellevue for observation five days after admission, and returned to Inwood where she remained for nearly three weeks before re-sentence to the Workhouse.

[2] August, 1922.

less of religion, but the age limit to be from 16 to 21 years."[1]

At present,[2] Inwood maintains a reception home and clearing house for girls committed by the Women's Court or referred by individuals or agencies. There they attempt to appraise the girl scientifically by means of physical and mental examinations as well as by observation of her conduct and attitude while in the home. Twenty girls may be accommodated here. The house staff now comprises an executive secretary, four matrons (two day, one night, and one kitchen), and a visiting woman physician. The Board of Managers plans to open small boarding homes from time to time, where ten or twelve girls may live while they continue their education or work in the community. Inwood House will seek to place in charge of these homes a matron whose influence may prove more potent than rules or precepts. After the girl has been thoroughly studied in the central clearing house, the work will be decentralized, community facilities being employed to the utmost. They aim not to institutionalize the girl, rather to develop and adjust her in the outside world. Their plan represents an intermediate stage between probation and an institution, with all the freedom of the former minus the unnatural environment of the latter. As an experiment designed to meet the needs of the problem or delinquent girl, it is bound to be observed with deep interest.

FLORENCE CRITTENTON LEAGUE, INC.[3]

No provision has been made in New York for a municipal temporary house of detention for girls who have been

---

[1] Annual Report, Inwood House, 1921, p. 8.

[2] August, 1922.

[3] Section 77a of the Inferior Criminal Courts Act designates the Florence Crittenton Home and Waverly House as places to which defendants convicted in the Women's Court may be detained for observation and study for a period not to exceed four days unless such period is extended with the consent of the defendant for an additional period of the same length.

arrested, pending their disposition. It was early demonstrated that such an institution was necessary and the needs have been largely filled by two private institutions, namely, Florence Crittenton Home and Waverly House.[1]

The home of the Florence Crittenton League was opened in 1914 as a place of detention for girls 16 or over, brought in by the police or private agencies or sent temporarily from the Women's Court. Although the work of this branch of the National Florence Crittenton Mission differs considerably from that carried on elsewhere in the United States, the national organization allows it to use a four-story and basement house on West 21st Street, rent and tax free. For its running expenses, however, the League depends entirely upon voluntary contributions.

The only sentenced cases received are a few probationers brought there by their officers until a suitable plan can be made for them or until they are returned to their homes out of town.

The house has a capacity of 25, although, at need, as many as 39 have been cared for. Its staff comprises a non-resident house physician, five resident, and two non-resident matrons. One of the matrons, a trained nurse, acts as superintendent of the League, and another, as dietitian. Under the direction of the matrons, the girls do all the housework, except the laundering.

On entering the Home, the girls are bathed and their scalps cleansed. A record is then taken showing name, age, how referred, family history, and other important facts. Later, this record is verified by one of the matrons who makes also a social investigation. Each admitted girl is examined by the house physician and, if it seems desirable, referred

---

[1] A very few of the incorrigibles are detained at Waverly House, a private institution maintained by the New York Probation and Protective Association. The principal function of the Society is not to serve the Women's Court but the needs of the pre-delinquent girl. For this reason it is not deemed advisable to describe its activities.

to a psychiatrist for a mental examination.[1] No seriously infected girl is allowed to remain in the Home.

On the first floor is a large, attractive room used for conferences and similar activities. At the rear is the office. Dining room, kitchen, and laundry are in the basement. Two large rooms on the second floor are set aside for sewing and recreation. Opening from the latter is a small room with three beds used for unmarried mothers and their babies. The two upper floors serve as dormitories, one with nine, and one with twelve beds. The doctor's examining room is on the top floor.

THE PAROLE COMMISSION LAW

The following authoritative statement relating to the history and origin of the Parole Commission Law was prepared by Dr. Katharine Bement Davis,[2] who was Commissioner of Corrections of New York City at the time the law was enacted:

The Indeterminate Sentence and Parole Law, Chap. 579 of the Laws of 1915, amended by Chap. 287 of the Laws of 1916, was passed at the 1915 session of the Legislature of the State of New York.

The Department of Correction of New York City was directly responsible for the enactment of this law.

The law was framed only after many consultations with the chief magistrate, other representative magistrates and judges of superior courts, and persons interested in prison reform.

A rough draft of the bill had been prepared by the Department of Correction. This was submitted to the Bill Drafting Bureau of Columbia University, redrafted by them, and submitted to the bill Drafting Bureau at Albany, who modified it only as to forms of expression, not as to content.

With reference to that portion of the law which refers to the Workhouse, the considerations leading to the special provisions in the law were these: To the Workhouse, prisoners were sentenced from the magistrates' courts for definite terms not to exceed six months.

---

[1] The New York Probation and Protective Association and Inwood House have both made available for this purpose the services of their psychiatrists.

[2] General Secretary of the Bureau of Social Hygiene.

In the Workhouse were prisoners who had anywhere from one to ten terms annually and who over a period of years had sentences varying in number from half a dozen to two hundred (an extreme case). In many instances this type of prisoner remained in the Workhouse for a few days only, was discharged and reëntered the institution within a month. Obviously this was futile so far as any help for the prisoner was concerned and expensive for the public who pay for the repeated rearrests and trials, especially as in many instances the individual prisoner preyed upon the public between sentences. With this in mind the law was framed to provide an indeterminate sentence not to exceed two years and administered by a parole commission with the power of parole and parole supervision.

1. It provided that only those prisoners were to be affected who had had two previous convictions during the preceding twenty-four months, or three previous convictions within any period. The two and the three convictions it will be noted are *preceding* convictions—not the conviction on which the indeterminate sentence is given, which will be at *least* the third or fourth conviction.

2. It would thus give a prisoner who was capable of improvement in place of the short definite term, insufficient for physical rehabilitation, for the formation of new habits, or for any industrial training, a term of sufficient length to accomplish actual rehabilitation.

It was the purpose of the Department of Correction to develop Riker's Island as a farm colony and Hart's Island as an industrial colony for the men prisoners, and to establish at Greycourt a farm colony for women. The old Workhouse would be used as a clearing house.

By the parole provisions of the law, these hopeful prisoners could be released according to the discretion of the Parole Commission and would be under the supervision of parole officers in the community until the expiration of the two years.

3. For the recidivist for whom there was little hope of rehabilitation there would be custodial care for at least two years. Where the indeterminate sentence had been applied and the time served and where the prisoner in a very brief space again committed an offense, it would practically mean permanent custodial care. In our judgment this was desirable, both from the point of view of the prisoner and of the community.

4. It was our intention that the law should be mandatory so far as the imposition of an indeterminate sentence upon Workhouse prisoners was concerned provided they had the requisite preliminary number of convictions (two or three). We believe that the law should be interpreted as mandatory in this particular.

It will be noted that the wording of Section IV of this law bears out this interpretation. It reads: "Then the court *shall* sentence such offenders."

5. The law does not mean that the magistrate has no discretion in the sentencing of such offender. It is mandatory only *if he desires to commit such offender to the Workhouse*. He retains his power of suspended sentence, probation, or sentence to some other institution. In the case of women offenders he has the choice of commitment to a private or a state institution.

The law provides for the creation of a parole commission in cities of the first class, wherein there is a Department of Correction having jurisdiction over a workhouse, penitentiary, and a reformatory. A parole commission is provided for by resolution of the Board of Estimate and Apportionment and is appointed by the mayor. The commission includes the commissioner of correction, the commissioner of police, and three other members appointed by the mayor. The act provides that any magistrate or judge who shall make commitments under indeterminate sentences to the Workhouse may sit as a member of the parole commission during the consideration of the eligibility for parole of any person committed by him, with authority to vote. The section with which this study is particularly concerned is section 4, which reads as follows:

After the creation of a parole commission in any of the said cities as hereinbefore provided, any person convicted of any crime or offense upon conviction for which the court may sentence to a penitentiary, workhouse, city prison, county jail, or other institution under the jurisdiction of the Department of Correction of said city, who shall not be committed in default of payment of a fine imposed, or for failure to furnish surety or sureties upon a conviction of disorderly conduct tending to a breach of the peace or of abandonment, and who is not insane or mentally or physically incapable of being substantially benefited by the correctional and reformatory purposes of any such institution, shall, if sentenced to any institution under the jurisdiction of the Department of Correction in said city, be sentenced and committed to a penitentiary or a workhouse or a reformatory under the jurisdiction of the said Department of Correction. No person shall be committed to a penitentiary under the jurisdiction of a Department of Correction in any such city because of failure to pay any fine or fines imposed, or for failure to furnish surety or sureties, or to a penitentiary, reformatory, or workhouse under the jurisdiction of a Department of Correction in any such city for a term of imprisonment with a fine imposed in addition to the term of imprisonment. The term of imprisonment of any person sentenced to any such penitentiary shall not be fixed or limited by the court in imposing sentence. The term of such imprisonment shall be terminated in the manner prescribed in section five of this act and not otherwise, and shall not exceed three years. The term of imprisonment of any person sentenced to any such workhouse shall be fixed by the court in imposing sentence which term shall be for a definite period and shall not exceed six months; provided, however, that no person convicted in any of said cities of vagrancy, disorderly conduct tending to a breach of the peace, public prostitution, soliciting on streets or public places for the purpose of prostitution, or of violation of section one hundred and fifty of chapter ninety-nine of the laws of nineteen hundred and nine, as amended, shall be sentenced to any such workhouse for a definite term until the finger-print records of the City Magistrates' Courts of said city, are officially searched with reference to the particular defendant and the results thereof duly certified to the court; and provided, further, that if it shall appear to the court at any stage of the proceeding prior to the imposition of sentence and after due notice and opportunity to the defendant to be heard in opposition to such accusation of prior convictions that any person convicted of any or each of these offenses last enumerated has been convicted of any or each of these offenses two or more times during the twenty-four months just previous, or three or more times previous to that conviction, then the court shall sentence such offender to a workhouse of the said Department of Correction in said city for an indeterminate period. The term of imprisonment of any person convicted and sentenced to any such workhouse for an indeterminate period shall not exceed two years and shall be terminated by the parole commission in the manner prescribed in section five of this act and not otherwise. Commitment to reformatories for male misdemeanants under the jurisdiction of a Department of Correction in any of the cities as aforesaid shall be made in conformity with laws providing for such institutions and commitments thereto. The term of imprisonment of persons so convicted and sentenced to reformatories shall be terminated by the parole commission in the manner prescribed in section five of this act and not otherwise.

Nothing in this section shall be deemed to interfere with or prevent the commitment of any person in accordance with law to a state institution not under the jurisdiction of a Department of Correction in any of the said cities which was on May tenth, nineteen hundred and fifteen, or now is or may hereafter be authorized by law to receive persons convicted in the courts in any of said cities.

A study of the records for the first six months of 1920 discloses 97 cases in which the Parole Commission Law was applicable. Only 41, however, were given sentences under this law. The following table indicates that during this period the law was not applied in the majority of eligible cases:

41 Cases in Which Law Was Applied		56 Cases in Which Law Was Not Applied	
No. of Cases	No. of Previous Convictions	No. of Cases	No. of Previous Convictions
1	18	1	20
1	13	2	18
3	12	1	17
1	10	1	16
3	9	1	14
7	8	1	10
3	7	3	8
8	6	2	7
6	5	6	6
8	4	7	5
		21	4
		10	3

The reason for this lies in the fact that many of the magistrates believe that the law is discretionary in Workhouse sentences. They, therefore, do not apply it in all cases in which it was intended to be applied, and in pronouncing sentence they take into consideration other circumstances besides those of the number of previous convictions.

The law reads:

> If it shall appear to the court . . . that any person convicted of any or each of these offenses last enumerated has been convicted of any or each of these offenses . . . two or more times during the twenty-four months just previous, or three or more times previous to that conviction, *then the court shall sentence such offender to a workhouse . . . for an indeterminate period.*

In the opinion of the writers, this section of the law is mandatory as to persons sentenced to the Workhouse. The law, if discretionary, seems to be so only in that it apparently still leaves with the magistrates the power to impose sentences to Bedford or private institutions or to place upon probation or suspend sentence.

CONCLUSION

The study was facilitated through the access given by the Committee of Fourteen [1] to its card records of prostitution cases in the Women's Court. These cards are prepared monthly by the Committee in the preparation of the Committee's monthly bulletin and study of court proceedings. This bulletin is an intensive study of the court's proceedings for the month, and is distributed to the Chief City Magistrate, the judges especially assigned to the court, and the various agencies interested in and working with the court.

---

[1] This Committee, a voluntary organization formed in 1905 to suppress commercialized vice, follows most carefully the proceedings in the Women's Court, which, with the decrease of disorderly house cases in the Court of Special Sessions to a comparatively inconsiderable number, due to the change of vice conditions and amendments of the law, has become the center of legal proceedings to suppress prostitution in New York City.

TABLE 1. DISPOSITION OF CASES OF SEX OFFENDERS ARRAIGNED IN

OFFENSE	TOTAL NUMBER ARRAIGNED	DEFAULTED[3]	DISCHARGED[4]	SUSPENDED SENTENCE	PAROLED TO WAVERLY HOUSE	KINGSTON AVENUE HOSPITAL[5]	
						Sentenced prior to June 30, 1920[7]	Sentence pending June 30, 1920[8]
Soliciting[13]	272	10	56	1[14]	...	37	13
Offering to secure a prostitute (C. C. P. Sec. 887-4b)	11	2	6	...	...	...	...
Permitting premises to be used for immoral purposes (C. C. P. Sec. 887-4e)	44	...	20	...	...	5	...
Prostitution in tenements (T. H. L. 150–Sub. 3, 4, 5)	235	16	68	...	...	37	4
Incorrigibility[15]	122	...	41	1	1	18	8
TOTAL	684	28	191	2	1	97	25

[1] Compiled from the card records of the Committee of Fourteen, which were transcribed from the original court papers.

[2] This table, like the corresponding tables for Chicago, Philadelphia, and Boston, includes only those cases receiving sentence prior to July 1, 1920 and excludes cases still pending June 30, 1920.

[3] For amount of bail forfeiture, see Table 5.

[4] " Discharged " includes, in addition to those acquitted·

Discharged on technicality............................ 2
Discharged on motion of District Attorney............. 3
Discharged to Letchworth Village..................... 2
Discharged to Bellevue for observation................ 2
Discharged, insane.................................. 4

[5] Sentence deferred and on defendant's consent she was sent to Kingston Avenue Hospital for treatment for infectious venereal disease. Two drug cases were sent to Riverside Hospital, and four to Bellevue, for in this period drug cases were tried in Women's Court.

[6] This column includes cases placed on probation at the time of sending to the hospital. Table 13 shows the disposition of cases after discharge from the hospital.

THE WOMEN'S COURT, NEW YORK CITY, JANUARY 1 TO JUNE 30, 1920 [1] [2]

OFFENSE	CONVICTED						TOTAL NUMBER CONVICTED	PER CENT CONVICTED (OF THE TOTAL NUMBER ARRAIGNED)
	INSTITUTIONS							
	Private				Public[10]			
	PROBATION[9]	Inwood House	House of Mercy	House of Good Shepherd	Workhouse[11]	Workhouse Parole Commission[12]		
Soliciting[13]	59	8	2	12	99	12	206	75.
Offering to secure a prostitute. (C. C. P. Sec. 887-4b)	1	...	...	...	2	...	3	27.2
Permitting premises to be used for immoral purposes (C. C. P. Sec. 887-4e)	11	...	...	1	10	2	24	54.5
Prostitution in tenements (T. H. L. 150 Sub. 3, 4, 5)	74	2	...	6	60	5	151	64.2
Incorrigibility[15]	41	14	...	16	...	...	81	67.5
TOTAL	186	24	2	35	171	19	465	67.9

[7] This disposition, being of a temporary nature, does not affect the total number arraigned and convicted, the 97 being distributed throughout the table.

[8] The 25 cases in this column are included in the total number arraigned and convicted because, although their sentence was pending on June 30, 1920, they had been convicted.

[9] This column includes cases receiving treatment at Kingston Avenue Hospital. Table 13 shows the number of probationers receiving such treatment, classified by offense.

[10] During this period no cases were committed to the New York State Reformatory for Women at Bedford Hills.

[11] For length of term, see Table 2.

[12] Sentence indeterminate.

[13] The following offenses are included under the heading " soliciting ": loitering, soliciting under Sec. 1458, Sub. 2 of the Consolidation Act, committing prostitution, and offering to commit prostitution, the last named charges being for violation of Section 887-4a and 4g of the Criminal Code, respectively.

[14] Sentence suspended because of Parole Commission Warrant.

[15] An incorrigible may or may not be a sex offender.

TABLE 2. LENGTH OF SENTENCE TO WORKHOUSE OF SEX OFFENDERS COMMITTED BY THE WOMEN'S COURT, NEW YORK CITY, JANUARY 1 TO JUNE 30, 1920 [1]

OFFENSE	TOTAL	1 day	5 days	10 days	15 days	20 days	30 days	60 days	90 days	2 mos.	3 mos.	4 mos.	6 mos.
Soliciting[2]	99	2	10	16	4	1	25	19	3	3	10	2	4
Offering to secure a prostitute (C. C. P. Sec. 887-4b)	2	...	1	1	...	...	...	...	...	...	...	...	...
Permitting premises to be used for immoral purposes (C. C. P. Sec. 887-4e)	10	...	4	...	1	...	2	2	...	...	...	...	1
Prostitution in tenements (T. H. L. 150- Sub. 3, 4, 5)	60	1	14	6	1	1	21	7	3	...	5	...	1
TOTAL	171	3	29	23	6	2	48	28	6	3	15	2	6

[1] Compiled from card records of the Committee of Fourteen, which were transcribed from the original court papers. For discussion, see p. 357ff.

[2] For offenses included under this heading, see Table 1, footnote 13.

TABLE 3. APPEALS FROM THE WOMEN'S COURT, NEW YORK CITY, JANUARY 1 TO JUNE 30, 1920 [1] [2]

OFFENSE	TOTAL	DISMISSED[3]	AFFIRMED[4]	REVERSED
Soliciting[5]	1	...	1	...
Permitting premises to be used for immoral purposes (C. C. P. Sec. 887-4e)	1	...	1	...
Prostitution in tenements (T. H. L. 150-Sub. 3, 4, 5)	3	2[6]	...	1[7]
TOTAL	5[8]	2	2	1

[1] Data secured from card records of the Committee of Fourteen, which were transcribed from the original court papers.

[2] For correlation of disposition in General Sessions with disposition in the Women's Court, see Table 4.

[3] Appeal dismissed on the ground that defendant failed to perfect appeal.

[4] Both cases were sentenced to the Workhouse by the Women's Court, for 15 and 30 days respectively; and in both judgment was affirmed without modification.

[5] For offenses included under this heading, see Table 1, footnote 13.

[6] Sentence in the Women's Court, for one, probation; for the other, 30 days in the Workhouse.

[7] Reversed, with new trial in General Sessions if desired.

[8] During the whole year 1920, 10 appeals were determined; during 1921, 19 were determined.

TABLE 4. CORRELATION OF DISPOSITION OF APPEALED CASES IN THE
WOMEN'S COURT,[1] AND GENERAL SESSIONS, JANUARY 1 TO JUNE 30,
1920 [2]

DISPOSITION IN GENERAL SESSIONS	TOTAL	DISPOSITION IN WOMEN'S COURT	
		Probation	Workhouse
Dismissed[3]	2	1	1[4]
Affirmed	2	...	2[5]
Reversed	1[6]	1	...
TOTAL	5[7]	2	3

[1] Appeals go to General Sessions on the record; there are no trials *de novo*.
[2] Data secured from card records of the Committee of Fourteen which were transcribed from the original court papers.
[3] Cases did not reach General Sessions because appeals were dismissed on the ground of defendant's failures to perfect appeal.
[4] Sentenced for 30 days.
[5] One sentenced for 15 and one for 30 days. In both cases, judgment affirmed without modification.
[6] Reversed, with new trial in General Sessions, if desired.
[7] During the whole year 1920, 10 appeals were determined; during 1921, 19 were determined.

TABLE 5. BAIL FORFEITURES, WOMEN'S COURT, NEW YORK CITY,
JANUARY 1 TO JUNE 30, 1920 [1]

OFFENSE	TOTAL	$500 BAIL[2]			
		Cash	Liberty Bonds	Real Estate	Surety Bonds
Soliciting[3]	10	...	7	3	...
Offering to secure a prostitute (C. C. P. Sec. 887-4b)	2	...	2	...	...
Prostitution in tenements (T. H. L. 150-Sub. 3, 4, 5)	16	1	12	2	1
TOTAL	28	1	21	5	1

[1] Data secured from Bail Forfeiture Record in District Attorney's office. For discussion, see p. 308.
[2] These bonds, with the single exception of a real estate bond, were collected for the full amount.
[3] For offenses included under this heading, see Table 1, footnote 13.

TABLE 6.   DISPOSITION OF FIRST ONE HUNDRED CASES ARRAIGNED IN 1920 IN THE WOMEN'S COURT, NEW YORK CITY, SHOWING NUMBER OF ADJOURNMENTS PRECEDING FINAL DISPOSITION [1]

DISPOSITION	TOTAL	No AD- JOURN- MENTS[2]	AD- JOURN- ED ONCE	AD- JOURN- ED TWICE	AD- JOURN- ED THREE TIMES	AD- JOURN- ED FOUR TIMES	AD- JOURN- ED FIVE TIMES	AD- JOURN- ED SEVEN- TEEN TIMES
Defaulted	2	2	...	...	...	...	...	...
Discharged	25	3	9	8	4	...	...	1
Suspended Sentence— Parole Commission Warrant	1	...	1	...	...	...	...	...
Committed to River- side Hospital	1	...	1	...	...	...	...	...
Probation[3]	27	3.	12	8	3	1	...	...
Inwood House	10	7	2	1	...	...	...	...
House of Good Shepherd	6	3	2	1	...	...	...	...
Workhouse	25	3	6	12	3	...	1	...
Workhouse—Parole Commission	3	1	2	...	...	...	...	...
TOTAL	100	22	35	30	10	1	1	1

[1] Compiled from card records of the Committee of Fourteen and the original court papers.   For discussion, see pp. 314–315.

[2] The practice of remanding convicted cases is described on p. 307.   This type of continuance is not counted as an adjournment.

[3] Includes cases receiving treatment at Kingston Avenue Hospital.

TABLE 7. DISPOSITION OF THE FIRST ONE HUNDRED CASES ARRAIGNED IN 1920 IN THE WOMEN'S COURT, NEW YORK CITY, SHOWING INTERVAL OF TIME BETWEEN ARREST AND FINAL DISPOSITION [1] [2]

DISPOSITION	TOTAL	0 days	2 days[3]	3 days	4 days	5 days	6 days	7 days	8 days	9 days	10 days	12 days	13 days	14 days	15 days	Over 15 days[4]
Defaulted	2	2	...	...	...	...	...	...	...	...	...	...	...	...	...	...
Discharged	25	3	...	...	2	...	4	2	1	2	3	1	2	...	1	4
Suspended Sentence— Parole Commission Warrant	1	...	...	...	1	...	...	...	...	...	...	...	...	...	...	...
Committed to Riverside Hospital	1	...	...	...	...	...	...	...	...	...	...	...	...	...	...	1
Probation[5]	27	...	3	2	4	6	1	4	1	1	1	...	...	1	...	3
Inwood House	10	...	7	1	1	...	...	...	...	...	...	...	...	...	...	1
House of Good Shepherd	6	...	3	1	...	1	1	...	...	...	...	...	...	...	...	...
Workhouse	25	...	3	2	2	...	2	3	...	1	2	2	...	...	1	7
Workhouse Parole Commission	3	...	1	1	...	...	...	...	...	...	...	...	...	...	...	1
TOTAL	100	5	17	7	10	7	8	9	2	4	6	3	2	1	2	17

[1] Compiled from card records of the Committe of Fourteen and the original court papers. For discussion see pp. 314–315.

[2] This time interval includes the 48 hours granted for examination after conviction and before sentence is pronounced.

[3] For investigation only.

[4] Of these, ten were in the hospital. The seventeen cases were continued as follows: three, for 17 days; three, for 21 days; one, for 23 days; one, for 24 days; one, for 31 days; one, for 35 days; two, for 39 days; one, for 40 days; one, for 41 days; one, for 57 days; one, for 76 days; and one, for 265 days.

[5] Includes cases receiving treatment at Kingston Avenue Hospital.

TABLE 8.   RELATION OF NUMBER OF ADJOURNMENTS OF CASES OF SEVENTY-EIGHT WOMEN TO INTERVALS OF TIME BETWEEN ARREST AND FINAL DISPOSITION [1]

TIME INTERVALS	TOTAL	NUMBER OF ADJOURNMENTS					
		1	2	3	4	5	17
3 days	7	7	...	...	...	...	...
4 days	10	10	...	...	...	...	...
5 days	7	5	2	...	...	...	...
6 days	8	3	4	1	...	...	...
7 days	9	2	6	1	...	...	...
8 days	2	1	1	...	...	...	...
9 days	4	1	1	2	...	...	...
10 days	6	2	4	...	...	...	...
12 days	3	...	2	1	...	...	...
13 days	2	...	2	...	...	...	...
14 days	1	...	...	1	...	...	...
15 days	2	...	2	...	...	...	...
Over 15 days	17	4	6	4	1	1	1
TOTAL	78	35	30	10	1	1	1

[1] Based on Tables 6 and 7.

TABLE 9. INCIDENCE OF VENEREAL DISEASE IN CASES OF WOMEN CONVICTED IN THE WOMEN'S COURT, NEW YORK, JANUARY 1 TO JUNE 30, 1920 [1]

| OFFENSE | TOTAL NUMBER AR-RAIGNED | TOTAL NUMBER CON-VICTED | TOTAL NUMBER EXAM-INED (of those con-victed)[2] | NOT IN-FECTED | INFECTED | | | | |
					Total	Per cent of those ex-amined	Gonor-rhea	Syph-ilis	Gonor-rhea and syphilis
Soliciting[3]	272	206	203	95	108	53.2	30	59	19
Offering to secure a prostitute (C. C. P. Sec. 887-4b)	11	3	3	2	1	33.3	...	...	1
Permitting premises to be used for immoral purposes (C. C. P. Sec. 887-4e)	44	24	24	13	11	45.8	4	7	...
Prostitution in tene-ments (T. H. L. 150-Sub. 3, 4, 5)	235	151	149	76	73	48.9	28	35	10
Incor-rigibility	122	81	55	18	37	67.2	27	6	4
TOTAL	684	465	434	204	230	52.9	89	107	34

[1] Compiled from card records of the Committee of Fourteen, which were transcribed from the original court papers, and from the records of the Bureau of Preventable Diseases. For discussion of this table, see p. 341.

[2] As a rule, all convicted women, except incorrigibles, are examined as a matter of routine. Girls convicted of incorrigibility may also be examined upon request of relative or probation officer.

[3] For offenses included under this heading, see Table 1, footnote 13.

TABLE 10. IMMEDIATE DISPOSITION BY OFFENSE OF CASES OF WOMEN
WITH A VENEREAL DISEASE CONVICTED IN THE WOMEN'S COURT,
NEW YORK, JANUARY 1 TO JUNE 30, 1920 [1]

OFFENSE	TOTAL NUMBER OF VENE-REALLY DIS-EASED WOMEN	HOS-PITAL[2][3]	PRO-BATION	SUS-PENDED SEN-TENCE	INWOOD HOUSE	HOUSE OF MERCY	HOUSE OF GOOD SHEP-HERD	WORK-HOUSE	WORK-HOUSE PAROLE COMMIS-SION
Soliciting[4]	108	47	1	...	2	1	8	45	4
Offering to secure a prostitute (C. C. P. Sec. 887-4b)	1	...	...	...	...	...	...	1	...
Permitting premises to be used for immoral purposes (C. C. P. Sec. 887-4e)	11	5	...	...	...	...	...	4	2
Prostitution in tenements (T. H. L. 150-Sub. 3, 4, 5)	73	41	...	...	...	...	1	29	2
Incorrigibility	37	26	...	1	4	...	5	...	1
TOTAL	230	119	1	1	6	1	14	79	9

[1] Compiled from card records of the Committee of Fourteen and from records in
Kingston Avenue Hospital.   For discussion of this table, see pp. 340–341.
[2] Kingston Avenue Hospital, with the exception of one drug case sent to Riverside Hospital.
[3] For disposition after discharge from hospital, see Table 13.
[4] For offenses included under this heading, see Table 1, footnote 13.

TABLE 11. CASES OF WOMEN WITH A VENEREAL DISEASE CONVICTED IN THE WOMEN'S COURT, NEW YORK, JANUARY 1 TO JUNE 30, 1920, WHO RECEIVED TREATMENT AT KINGSTON AVENUE HOSPITAL [1]

OFFENSE	TOTAL	ADMITTED FROM	
		Jefferson Market Court	Workhouse [2]
Soliciting[3]	70	46	24
Offering to secure a prostitute (C. C. P. Sec. 887-4b)	1	. . .	1
Permitting premises to be used for immoral purposes (C. C. P. Sec. 887-4e)	8	5	3
Prostitution in tenements (T. H. L. 150-Sub. 3, 4, 5)	68	41	27
Incorrigibility	26	26	. . .
TOTAL	173	118	55

[1] Compiled from card records of the Committee of Fourteen and records in the Kingston Avenue Hospital. For discussion of this table, see pp. 341–342.

[2] In 1920 it was the practice to continue treatment in Kingston Avenue Hospital of cases whose sentences in the Workhouse had expired before they were rendered noninfectious.

[3] For offenses inluded under this heading, see Table 1, footnote 13.

TABLE 12. RELATION BETWEEN THE VENEREAL DISEASES AND LENGTH OF TREATMENT, IN KINGSTON AVENUE HOSPITAL [1]

DISEASE	TOTAL	LENGTH OF TREATMENT					
		5-30 days[2]	31-60 days[3]	61-70 days	71-80 days	81-119 days	Unknown
Gonorrhea	63	1	30	8	8	11	5
Syphilis	78	9	63	3	. . .	. . .	3
Gonorrhea and syphilis	32	1	16	6	4	5	. . .
TOTAL	173	11	109	17	12	16	8

[1] Compiled from records in Kingston Avenue Hospital.

[2] Of those detained from fiye to 30 days, three escaped.

[3] Of those detained from 31 to 60 days, two were returned to court; one for stealing and one for disorderly conduct.

TABLE 13. DISPOSITION MADE IN THE WOMEN'S COURT, NEW YORK, OF CASES OF WOMEN WITH A VENEREAL DISEASE FIRST TREATED AT KINGSTON AVENUE HOSPITAL, JANUARY 1 TO JUNE 30, 1920 [1]

OFFENSE	TOTAL	STILL IN HOSPITAL JUNE 30, 1920	PRO-BATION	HOUSE OF GOOD SHEPHERD	WORK-HOUSE
Soliciting[2]	46	13	32	...	1
Permitting premises to be used for immoral purposes (C. C. P. Sec. 887-4e)	5	...	4	...	1
Prostitution in tenements (T. H. L. 150–Sub. 3, 4, 5)	41	4	36	...	1
Incorrigibility	26	8	17	1	...
TOTAL	118	25	89	1	3

[1] Compiled from card records of the Committee of Fourteen and records in the Kingston Avenue Hospital.
[2] For offenses included under this heading, see Table 1, Footnote 13.

TABLE 14. CASES OF WOMEN WITH A VENEREAL DISEASE SENTENCED
TO THE WORKHOUSE BY THE WOMEN'S COURT, NEW YORK,
JANUARY 1 TO JUNE 30, 1920, AND ADMITTED TO KINGSTON AVENUE
HOSPITAL AT THE EXPIRATION OF SENTENCE, SHOWING RELATION
BETWEEN LENGTH OF DETENTION IN WORKHOUSE AND LENGTH
OF SUBSEQUENT TREATMENT IN KINGSTON AVENUE HOSPITAL[1]

LENGTH OF DETENTION IN THE WORKHOUSE	TOTAL	LENGTH OF TREATMENT IN KINGSTON AVENUE HOSPITAL					
		5-30 days	31-60 days	61-70 days	71-80 days	81-119 days	Unknown
5 days	7	...	6	...	...	1	...
10 days	9	1[2]	4	3	...	1	...
15 days	1	...	1	...	...	...	...
20 days	1	...	1	...	...	...	...
30 days	13	1	12	...	...	...	...
60 days	7	...	7	...	...	...	2
90 days	3	1	2	...	...	...	...
2 mos.	2	...	1	...	1	...	...
3 mos.	9	3	4	2	...	...	...
4 mos.	1	...	1	...	...	...	...
TOTAL	55	6	39	5	1	2	2

[1] Compiled from card records of the Committee of Fourteen and records in Kingston Avenue Hospital.
[2] Escaped from hospital at end of fourteen days.

TABLE 15.   STUDY OF SOCIAL HISTORIES OF FIFTY WOMEN PLACED UPON PROBATION DURING THE FIRST SIX MONTHS OF 1920 [1]—Concluded

OFFENSE	AGE AT LEAVING SCHOOL										SCHOOLING									MANNER OF LIVING AT TIME OF ARREST							CHILDREN					
	10 Years	12 Years	13 Years	14 Years	15 Years	16 Years	17 Years	18 Years	19 Years	Not Stated	Third Grade	Fourth Grade	Fifth Grade	Sixth Grade	Seventh Grade	Eighth Grade	High School[3]	Miscellaneous[4]	Not Stated	Parents	Husband[2]	Relative	Keeping House	Boarding House	Hotel	Lover	None	Legitimate 1 child	Legitimate 2 children	Legitimate 4 children	Illegitimate 1 child	Illegitimate 2 children
Soliciting[5]			1	2	3	1		2	3	4			2	1	1	2	6	2	2	4	1	2		5	2	2	14	1	1			
Offering to secure a prostitute (C. C. P. Sec. 887-4b)						1									1								1						1			
Permitting premises to be used for immoral purposes (C. C. P. Sec. 887-4e)			1					1								1	1				1		1				1				1	
Prostitution in tenements (T.H.L. 150-Sub. 3, 4, 5)	1	1	4	2	6	4	2		1	3	1	2	1	1	3	8	1	6	1	1	4	3	7	6		3	14	3	4	1	1	1
Incorrigibility				3	1	1			1	1					1	3	1	1	1	1	2	1		2		1	6				1	
TOTAL	1	1	6	7	10	7	2	3	5	8	1	2	3	2	6	14	9	9	4	6	8	6	9	13	2	6	35	4	6	1	3	1

[1] Based upon the study of fifty case histories, a fair sampling. For method of selection and discussion see pp. 351–354.

[2] One woman was separated from her husband and one divorced.

[3] Only two of these girls completed their high school courses.

[4] Includes art school, boarding school, business school, convent and nurses' training.

[5] For offenses included under this heading, see Table 1, Footnote 13.

TABLE 15. STUDY OF SOCIAL HISTORIES OF FIFTY WOMEN PLACED UPON PROBATION DURING THE FIRST SIX MONTHS OF 1920 [1]

OFFENSE	TOTAL NUMBER OF PROBATIONERS	COLOR		NATIONALITY					AGE AT TIME OF ARREST						CIVIL CONDITION AT TIME OF ARREST				RELIGION		
		WHITE	COLORED	AMERICAN	ENGLISH	IRISH	SWEDISH	RUSSIAN	15–19 YEARS	20–24 YEARS	25–29 YEARS	30–34 YEARS	35–39 YEARS	OVER 50 YEARS	SINGLE	MARRIED[2]	WIDOW	COM'LAW MARRIAGE	CATHOLIC	PROTESTANT	JEWISH
Soliciting[5]	16	14	2	12	1	..	1	2	..	7	6	1	2	..	8	5	2	1	7	7	2
Offering to secure a prostitute (C. C. P. Sec. 887-4b)	1	1	..	1	..	..	..	..	..	..	..	..	..	1	..	1	..	..	..	1	..
Permitting premises to be used for immoral purposes (C. C. P. Sec. 887-4e)	2	2	..	1	..	..	..	1	..	..	1	..	..	1	..	2	..	..	..	1	1
Prostitution in tenements (T. H. L. 150–Sub. 3, 4, 5)	24	14	10	18	2	2	..	2	4	7	5	3	3	2	4	17	3	..	4	16	4
Incorrigibility	7	5	2	7	..	..	..	..	5	1	1	..	..	..	5	2	..	..	4	2	1
TOTAL	50	36	14	39	3	2	1	3	9	15	13	4	5	4	17	27	5	1	15	27	8

[1] Based upon the study of fifty case histories, a fair sampling. For method of selection and discussion see pp. 351–354.
[2] One woman was separated from her husband and one divorced.
[3] Only two of these girls completed their high school courses.
[4] Includes art school, boarding school, business school, convent and nurses' training.
[5] For offenses included under this heading, see Table 1, Footnote 13.

TABLE 16.   PREVIOUS AND SUBSEQUENT CONVICTIONS IN THE WOMEN'S
COURT, NEW YORK [1]

OFFENSE	TOTAL NUMBER OF PROBATIONERS	NUMBER OF PREVIOUS CONVICTIONS			NUMBER OF SUBSEQUENT CONVICTIONS UP TO OCTOBER 1, .1921	
		0	1	3	0	1
Soliciting[2]	16	15	1	...	15	1
Offering to secure a prostitute (C. C. P. Sec. 887-4b)	1	1	...	...	1	...
Permitting premises to be used for immoral purposes (C. C..P. Sec. 887-4e)	2	2	...	...	1	1
Prostitution in tenements (T. H. L. 150-Sub. 3, 4, 5)	24	23	1	...	22	2
Incorrigibility	7[3]	5	1	1	7	...
TOTAL	50	46	3	1	46	4

[1] Based upon the study of fifty case histories.   For discussion see p 352.
[2] For offenses included under this heading see Table 1, Footnote 13.
[3] Because incorrigibles are not finger-printed, the number of previous and subsequent convictions can be stated only where the defendant was recognized.

TABLE 17. INCIDENCE OF VENEREAL DISEASE AMONG FIFTY WOMEN PLACED UPON PROBATION DURING THE FIRST SIX MONTHS OF 1920 [1]

OFFENSE	TOTAL NUMBER OF PROBATIONERS	NOT EXAMINED	EXAMINED FOR GONORRHEA AND SYPHILIS	RESULTS			
				Not Infected	Infected[2]		
					Gonorrhea	Syphilis	Gonorrhea and Syphilis
Soliciting[4]	16	...	16	8	1	4	3
Offering to secure a prostitute (C. C. P. Sec. 887-4b)	1	...	1	1	...	...	...
Permitting premises to be used for immoral purposes (C. C. P. Sec. 887-4e)	2	...	2	1	...	...	1
Prostitution in tenements (T. H. L. 150-Sub. 3, 4, 5)	24	...	24	15	1	2	6
Incorrigibility	7	5	2	...	...	...	2
TOTAL	50	5	45	25	2	6	12

[1] Based upon the study of fifty case histories and records of the Bureau of Venereal Diseases. For discussion of this table, see p. 353.

[2] One girl was examined for syphilis only.

[3] Twenty girls were sent to Kingston Avenue Hospital for treatment.

[4] For offenses included under this heading see Table 1, Footnote 13.

TABLE 18. FREQUENCY OF CALLS MADE BY PROBATION OFFICER IN RELATION TO PROBATIONER'S REPORTING IN PERSON [1] [2]

Number of Calls Made by Officer at Probationer's Home	Total Number of Probationers	Number of Times Probationer Reported in Person																
		0	1	2	3	4	5	6	8	9	10	11	12	13	14	16	17	18
0	12	7		2	2			1										
1	5	3									1						1	
2	11				1	1			1	1	3	1	2		1			
3	11	1						1			1	2	1		1	2		2
4	3	1	1									1						
5	2									1						1		
6	2											1		1				
7	2						1							1				
8	2									1				1				
TOTAL	50	12	1	2	3	1	1	2	1	3	5	5	3	2	2	4	1	2

[1] Based upon the study of fifty case histories. For discussion see p. 353.
[2] Visits made by private agencies coöperating with the city probation officer are counted as officials' visits.

CHAPTER V

SUMMARY AND COMPARATIVE STUDY OF THE SPECIAL COURTS IN CHICAGO, PHILADEL-PHIA, BOSTON, AND NEW YORK

In the treatment accorded women sex offenders in the Chicago, Philadelphia, Boston, and New York courts, marked differences as well as similarities appear. Each city finds itself burdened with prostitutes and their customers, incorrigible and runaway girls—with their concomitant problems of defective heredity, vicious environment, mental abnormality, disease, drug addiction. To handle these common problems, special machinery has been devised and set in motion in each city—simple or intricate in regard not only to the number of parts but in the relation of these parts one to another. Parts obviously common to these machines are laws to define offenses and fix penalties, police to apprehend violators, courts to administer justice, and agencies or institutions, whether punitive or reformative, to deal with the offender after she has passed through the machinery of the police and courts. Special parts, designed to aid in effective functioning, are added from time to time. Thus, we find the unified court with the jury waiver system in Chicago; the centralized court with its socio-medical departments in Philadelphia; and the Women's Court in New York with specialists on the bench as well as in its socialized departments; fingerprinting, social investigations, case work, and physical examinations—all valuable cogs. Coördinated with these legal machines are the health departments in each city.

THE COMMON PROBLEM, PROSTITUTION

All four of the cities find themselves burdened with the problems arising from the institution of prostitution. For convenience, we may subdivide the general subject of prostitution into those aspects related to exploitation and those individual aspects which are not commercialized by a third party. Exploitation has to do with the keeping of bawdy houses, disorderly hotels, apartments, and rooming houses, and the furnishing of recruits therefor; also with the activities of the go-between and of the pimp, which are especially directed toward the securing of male customers. The individual aspects are those which have to do with the activities of the prostitute and her customer, and these exist even where there is no exploitation by a third party. They cover the measures adopted by the prostitute herself to sell and those of the man to purchase sexual gratification.

These studies have had more to do with the activities of the individual, namely the prostitute and her customer, for two reasons: first, because the jurisdiction of most of the courts does not cover the activities of the exploiter, which are usually felonies; and second, because the exploiter is not the type of offender for which, at present, there is any particular need of a specialized court. The keepers of disorderly houses, procurers, pimps, etc., who constitute the majority of the exploiters, belong to the hardened or more unregenerate type of offender. The laws relating to exploiters have been made so severe in most of the cities, with penalties so extreme, that the backbone of this aspect of prostitution may be said to have been broken. Very few cases of this kind are now finding their way into the courts.

With prostitution are its concomitants, venereal disease, mental deficiency, and moral wreckage.

METHODS AIMING AT SOLUTION

Steps aiming at the solution of this common problem have been taken in all of the cities. Unlike European methods of regulation or abolition,[1] the methods adopted in this country are based on the theory of repression. Each city or state seeks to solve the problem by enacting laws making prostitution a crime, and by setting up administrative and judicial machinery to carry the laws into effect. These laws vary widely, especially in the dispositions provided.

Laws. In the case of Chicago, the city and the state have attempted to legislate on all aspects of prostitution, with reference both to exploitation and to the activities of the individual. However, the kinds of disposition which have been provided are very meager, and the penalties are for the most part inadequate. The study of the Chicago Court shows that the majority of defendants, whether male or female, were given merely nominal fines. In the first six months of 1920, out of a total of 507 convicted defendants, male and female, 393 were fined. The report of the Committee of Fifteen shows that in the month of October, 1921, in the same court, out of a total of 241 defendants convicted, 182 were fined a total of $1342; and in October, 1922, out of a total of 719 defendants convicted, 612 were fined a total of $5833.

A curious discrimination against the prostitute and in favor of the exploiter exists in the Illinois laws. Whereas it is possible, under the Kate Adams Law, to commit both the male and female inmates of houses of prostitution and street-walkers to the House of Correction for a year, the greatest penalty that is provided against the keeper of the bawdy house is a fine of $200. The great State of Illinois and the City of Chicago, have thus elected to become sharers in the proceeds of prostitution.

We find in the City of New York, on the other hand, the opposite extreme, in that all fines for prostitution have been

[1] By this is meant the abolition of a system of state regulation of prostitution.

abolished by law; and between these two, we find Philadelphia and Boston, in which fining has been almost entirely abandoned in practice. (Only four sex offenders were fined in Philadelphia in 1921.)

By way of disposition outside of fines, we find like difference in the laws. Illinois has provided no adult women's reformatory, and the only commitment possible is that to the House of Correction, which is purely a penal institution. All of the other three states now have reformatories where women sex offenders may be sent for indeterminate periods of not more than three years. We find few if any commitments made from the Boston Court, because of the escape from justice by the offender provided by the trial *de novo*. In Philadelphia we find that very few offenders of this type are sent to the adult reformatory, perhaps because the judges have not yet developed a habit of making such commitments, due, possibly, to the newness of this institution. But in New York we find large numbers of defendants are committed to a long-established state reformatory institution and also to several semi-private institutions for reformation and rehabilitation.

We have pointed out that the State of Illinois and the City of Chicago have legislated on virtually all of the aspects of prostitution, but inadequately as to the penalties and dispositions. The reverse holds true in Philadelphia, where more or less adequate penalties and dispositions are found, but where the laws are inadequate as to their inclusiveness. Thus the chief prostitution law, as far as the individuals are concerned, is the law which permits the punishment of streetwalkers and disorderly persons. However, those activities of prostitution which take place in hotels, rooming houses, cafés, cabarets, apartments, etc., that are not *per se* disorderly or bawdy houses are not covered by any legislation. Therefore, Philadelphia is not attempting to solve the problem as to this large class, and thus her expensive and valuable court machinery is used for a very limited group.

In Boston we find the laws more adequate as to inclusiveness than in Philadelphia, but we find the court there constantly confronted by the loophole provided by the trial *de novo* system, a peculiarly American development in the criminal court system, now largely used by defendants as a means to thwart justice.

In New York we find the nearest approach to adequacy, as far as legislation is concerned, of all of the cities studied. The only doubt that exists is whether all of the activities of the customer of the prostitute have been provided against.[1] That New York is approaching the solution of the problem seems to be indicated by the fact that the number of cases passing through the Women's Court in 1921 had been reduced to 1668 as compared with 5365 cases handled by the same court in 1911, with no marked diminution of police activities. Indeed, there perhaps was a marked improvement in police methods and technique during this period, which should have increased the number of arrests had not the total volume of prostitution been greatly diminished. This is further borne out by the fact that only 39 per cent of defendants reappeared in 1921 as compared with 44 per cent in 1911.

Law Enforcement. The existence of laws obviously implies agencies for their enforcement. The chief agencies are the police and the courts, which represent the administrative and the judicial branches of the government. No especial attempt was made in any of the cities to check up the relative efficiency of the police departments. The authors did find, however, that New York and Philadelphia were the only cities which possessed centrally organized vice squads. Because of the lack of inclusiveness of the prostitution laws in Philadelphia, and because of the recent upheaval in the police department in Boston resulting from the general police strike there, we shall not attempt to compare their administration by the police in those cities. Perhaps not an entirely perfect means

---

[1] See discussion on page 302.

of comparing efficiency, and yet one which should have some bearing on their relative efficiency, is a comparison of percentages of convictions secured upon police evidence. In 1920 in Chicago only 19.4 per cent were convicted; whereas for the same period in New York the evidence was regarded strong enough to convict 68 per cent.[1]

The judicial machinery for carrying out these laws has been largely centralized (in each of the four cities) in one special court the sex delinquency cases are tried.

The Boston Court is not exclusively for sex delinquency cases, but hears all cases in which the Municipal Court has jurisdiction where a woman is the defendant. The dispositions provided by statute are largely rendered nugatory by the trial *de novo* system before referred to. As pointed out in the special report on Boston a large number of appeals were taken, which automatically carried the case to the Superior Court for a new trial before a jury without any reference whatsoever to what had gone before in the Municipal Court, and due to the congestion of the docket of the Superior Court with felonies, very few of the sex delinquency cases ever came to trial at all, most of them being settled through some bargain between the defendant's attorney and the District Attorney, the usual disposition being to "place the case on file."

In Philadelphia we find a court with excellent social machinery but with limited jurisdiction. The present status of the law requires inmates and keepers of disorderly houses to be tried before a jury so that these cases must be taken before the criminal branch of the Municipal Court or the Court of Quarter Sessions, neither of which is specialized. The

---

[1] "Anywhere from 40,000 to 80,000 citizens of Chicago or strangers within her gates are arrested every year either without cause or on such trifling charges that they get no further than the threshold of the Municipal Court. On the basis of accuracy of police work, these figures seem to indicate a record of efficiency of from 38 to 50 per cent during the last dozen years." *The Survey of the Cook County Jail,* 1922, p. 41.

defendants who are tried in the misdemeanants' branch are incorrigible and runaway children, street-walkers, and disorderly persons. Pennsylvania has not yet enacted laws which provide for the punishment of the prostitute or her customer where their activities take place in connection with automobiles, hotels, rooming houses, apartments, etc., which are not known as bawdy houses. A peculiar advantage of the Philadelphia court from the legal standpoint is its centralization, viz., the dedication of one building exclusively to all cases over which the court has jurisdiction, for the entire city. Both Philadelphia and New York possess finger-print bureaus. In the latter, all persons are finger-printed after conviction; and in the former, all defendants, except runaway children are finger-printed immediately after arrest. Both of these courts have stenographers to record the testimony and appeals are made upon the record without a trial *de novo*.

In New York we find the most highly specialized court of all, a court that is given over exclusively to the trial of women defendants. No trials are had in this court of any other class of offenders than sex delinquents, but arraignments are held of women arrested under the charge of shop-lifting. The latter are bound over for trial in the Court of Special Sessions. The New York court is specially notable for its well-conducted trials, for the careful winnowing of the evidence, for the checks placed upon the possibilities of perjury by the police, by the high bail that is demanded of the defendant which insures her appearance for trial, care being taken not only to affix a large sum, but also to accept only such surety as will assure the collection of the bond in case of forfeit. It was found that no difficulty has been experienced in collecting the few bonds in which a forfeit was made.

There are public prosecutors in both the New York and Chicago courts in contrast to the Boston and Philadelphia courts where the case must be prosecuted by the arresting officer. New York has what appears to be a very practicable machinery for the disposition of the defendant. This has been set up by the Inferior Criminal Courts Act. After conviction defendants are remanded for forty-eight hours for medical and social investigation. When the day arrives for sentence, there are several alternatives awaiting the defendant:

1. She may be hospitalized.
2. She may be placed on probation.
3. Sentence may be suspended without condition.
4. She may be given an indeterminate sentence (not exceeding three years) to the State Reformatory at Bedford, or to a semi-private reformative institution.
5. She may be given a definite sentence to the Workhouse (not to exceed six months). This is purely punitive in character, however.

Under the Parole Commission Law the defendant may also be sentenced to the Workhouse for an indeterminate period not exceeding two years, in which case she comes under the jurisdiction of the Parole Commission and may be paroled under such conditions as the commission may desire to impose. The Parole Commission sentence may not be given unless the defendant has been convicted of certain enumerated offenses twice within two years immediately prior to the present conviction, or if convicted three times previously during any period. A curb has also been placed by law on the professional bondsman, but it was noted that no curb has yet been placed in any of the four courts on the activities of the shyster lawyer.

The method of dealing with the male customer differs somewhat in the four cities. In the cities of Chicago, Philadelphia, and Boston we are perhaps safe in saying that in many cases, if not in a large majority of the cases, the customer is arrested in raids in which the prostitute is apprehended. In Chicago and Philadelpiha the practice observed was either to acquit the male customer or let him off with a small fine. In Boston he could find a comparatively easy method of escape through the trial *de novo*. Whether the customer of the prostitute may be punished in New York has not yet been judicially determined by the Appellate Court and the practice with reference to the customer varies in the different boroughs of the city. Evidences were found of a practice in Brooklyn on the part of the police to arrest and on the part of the courts to convict customers of the prostitute whereas in Manhattan the police are not at present making any such arrests, although records of arrests, and both convictions and acquittals in Manhattan were found. There is a legal barrier at present, however, to establishing a specialized court in New York in which both men and women may be tried, inasmuch as the men under the present law must be tried in the district in which the offense occurs and the city is divided into a vast number of districts. Because of the practice in New York of designating only three judges for a period of a year to the Women's Court, the judges have become more nearly expert in their subject than in the other cities studied. These judges have become to a considerable extent specialists on the subject of sex delinquency. The defendant in all of the cities except in Chicago was given a speedy trial, but in the latter city the peculiar system of confusing delinquency and disease, has been the cause of a number of protracted delays, where if a real trial for delinquency were given, the facts would have become stale long before the time for trial arrived. However, the treatment rendered the defendant by the health department is there considered the equivalent of trial and punishment so that the trials rarely amount to more than a combination of arraignment and preliminary hearing.

Chicago seems to have a solution of the unsatisfactory system of jury trials, in its jury waiver system, a system borrowed from a practice that has been in use for some time in civil courts in many jurisdictions.

Under the constitutions of New York and Pennsylvania the defendants are not entitled to a jury trial in the class of cases over which the particular courts studied have jurisdiction. This arises from the theory that the right to a jury trial did not exist in minor offenses summarily tried, at the time the constitution was adopted.

In Philadelphia the jurisdiction of the courts should be increased, but to do so the jury waiver system probably will be necessary. For instance, as before stated, inmates of disorderly houses must be tried in the jury court. With the jury waiver system all defendants who waived the jury would be tried in the special court and judging from the Chicago figures, the majority would thus waive a jury.

In Boston the underlying theory of the pernicious trial *de novo* is the constitutional right of the defendant to a trial by jury. He should be permitted by law to waive this right.

Detention. Insanitary conditions in the remodeled police stations of Chicago where common drinking cups and unchanged bed linen are matched only by the indiscriminate mingling of all classes of offender—from runaway girls and lost children of both sexes to prostitutes and felons, stand in sharp contrast to Philadelphia's Detention House for women, with its excellent sanitation and separate floors for younger and older offenders. Between these extremes lie Boston and New York—the former housing its detained women in feebly lighted, wretchedly ventilated cells in the basement of the court house and the latter using well-lighted, well-ventilated cells in the top-story tiers of the court building. In New York, however, two private institutions offer especially desirable facilities for arrested young women.

METHODS OF HANDLING DISEASED WOMEN IN SPECIAL COURTS

As methods of treating venereally diseased women in the four specialized courts studied have been described at length in separate reports, our observations will be limited to a comparison of certain outstanding features in the four cities. In the main, we shall want to know what women are examined; the proportion found to be diseased; the disposition made, both before and after conviction; facilities for treatment—

hospital, institutional, clinical. As Boston examines but a negligible number our comments must be confined for the most part to Chicago, Philadelphia and New York.

1. *Who are Examined.* Chicago and Philadelphia, unlike Boston and New York, make physical examinations of almost all women arrested for sex offenses, for the purpose of detecting venereal disease. While New York examines nearly all convicted women, Boston follows this practice with respect to a very limited number of those convicted. The Chief Justice of the Boston court holds that any attempt to legalize routine compulsory examinations, even of convicted women, would arouse strenuous opposition.

2. *Incidence of Venereal Disease.* Of those examined in Philadelphia and New York, over one-half were found to be infected with gonorrhea, syphilis, or with both diseases. In passing it should be noted that the incidence of venereal disease is 2.3 per cent higher in Philadelphia, which examines arrested women, than in New York, which examines only convicted women.[1] Figures showing the incidence of venereal disease among cases examined in Chicago in 1920 were not available.

3. *Disposition Before Conviction of Cases Found to be Venereally Diseased.* Chicago invariably sets forward on the calendar, cases reported by the health officer to have a venereal disease in an infectious stage. Such cases are at once sent to a special hospital for treatment and only tried as to their innocence or guilt after the hospital pronounces them no longer infectious. Philadelphia follows the same procedure with respect to about one-fourth of its venereal-disease cases. While it is claimed that only first offenders are sent to its special hospital, it was found in 1920 that over one-third of the cases committed there were old offenders.[2]

4. *Disposition After Conviction of Cases Found to be*

---

[1] See Table 3 at the end of this chapter.

[2] Seventh Annual Report of the Municipal Court of Philadelphia, Table 8, pp. 158-159.

Venereally Diseased. Diseased women, after they have been rendered noninfectious at the special hospital in Chicago, are returned to court for trial. This usually is perfunctory in character, the prevailing attitude being that "they have suffered enough" in loss of freedom for six or eight weeks. Their "discharge" follows as a matter of course. Although clinical treatment is frequently recommended, no follow-up system has as yet been devised for seeing that it is actually taken.

Philadelphia proceeds differently. All cases returned from its special hospital as noninfectious receive the customary court trial. Of 166 cases so returned in the last six months of 1920, 124 (more than two-thirds) were placed upon probation. Of these, over half were required to report regularly to the State Dispensary for further treatment. To a special nurse has been assigned the task of following up such cases. Of the diseased women who were given an immediate trial the greater proportion were sent to the House of Correction. Some were placed upon probation "with medical supervision," still others on "straight" probation, without medical supervision, while some were discharged outright.

New York adheres to a fairly well-defined policy with respect to the disposition of convicted women found to be venereally diseased. If the delinquent seems a suitable case to place on probation she is given an opportunity to enter a special hospital, of her own free will, to remain there voluntarily until rendered noninfectious. Unless her conduct at the hospital has been objectionable, she is placed upon probation upon the completion of her treatment there. Frequently such cases are instructed to continue treatment at a clinic but a system of follow-up still remains incomplete. Cases apparently unsuitable for probation are sent to the Workhouse, the State Reformatory, or to a semi-private reformative institution. Since the fall of 1920, magistrates have frequently given diseased offenders a sentence of 100 days in the Workhouse on the ground that three months usually suffice to render a case noninfectious. With reference to this policy one of the magistrates of the Women's Court has stated:

Whereas it is no doubt true that in theory the 100-day sentence is not proper because it requires a consideration of the physical condition of the defendant rather than her delinquency, yet as practiced at the present time, it appears that this sentence is applied to the class of defendants to whom the magistrate might well be justified in giving a sentence of that length.

The legality of the systems outlined in the three cities has not yet been tested in a higher court. While there may be a shadow of doubt as to the constitutionality of the procedure in Philadelphia and Chicago of making a compulsory examination after arrest and before conviction, the system followed in New York probably would not be open to challenge.

PROBATION

Probation merits careful consideration not only as the major disposition accorded convicted women sex delinquents in the four specialized courts studied, but because at this writing it is assailed from many quarters. In a report of the Special Committee on Law Enforcement of the American Bar Association, it is stated:

It is our united opinion that the means provided in the United States for coping with crime and criminals are to-day neither adequate nor efficient, for example:

First we find that the probation and parole laws, as administered, very generally fail to accomplish the purposes for which the laws were designed and weaken the administration of criminal justice. We recommend that first offenders, and first offenders only, should be eligible for probation.[1]

Papers throughout the country have declared probation largely responsible for the so-called crime-wave. Advocates of probation, on the other hand, hotly contest these allega-

---

[1] Report of the Forty-fifth Annual Meeting of the American Bar Association, August, 1922, pp. 424-432.

tions. Recently, in reply to the statement of a New York City magistrate, to the effect that probation in many cases is a failure, Mr. E. R. Cass, General Secretary of the Prison Association of New York, clarifies this controversy by pointing out that if probation is a failure, as alleged, the fault may not lie in the theory of probation, but rather in its administration. Mr. Cass points out further that until a careful analysis of the results of probation is made, it cannot be soundly and statistically shown that probation is an absolute success or failure. "Too frequently," he writes, "the successes are computed on the basis of the offender's conduct during the period of probation. . . . However, the ultimate test . . . must be determined wholly on the basis of the offender's standing and conduct five or ten or more years subsequent to release from probation." While our partial investigation of the results of probation does not meet this requirement, and although no case-work study of individual probationers was attempted, the facts gleaned with respect to the administration of probation in the four cities and with respect to a representative group of probationers in Philadelphia, Boston, and New York [1] throw valuable light on the question.

1. *Selection.* That court practices in the administration of probation vary widely is evidenced in methods of determining the defendants' eligibility for probation. All arrested women sex delinquents in Boston and Philadelphia are interviewed by probation officers before trial and the information secured verified as far as possible. In New York, however, as a rule, only convicted young women charged with incorrigibility [2] or found by the Finger-Printing Department to be first offenders, are considered even tentatively eligible for probation. Although Philadelphia finger-prints arrested women,[3] the results are not made the basis of a weeding-out

---

[1] Access was not afforded to probation records in Chicago.
[2] Incorrigibles are not finger-printed in New York.
[3] The Department may use its discretion in finger-printing those under 21 regardless of offense.

process so far as eligibility for probation is concerned.[1] In Boston, if the defendant is convicted, the probation officer tells the judge what she has learned respecting her court and social history. For the former, of course, in the absence of a finger-print system, she must rely upon card records and her memory.[3] This procedure is practically meaningless, however, because of the system of trial *de novo,* for old offenders frequently are placed upon probation, frankly as a compromise measure, when in the judgment of the court they merit a penal sentence or are in need of reformative treatment in an institution.

Thus, the advantage which Boston undoubtedly has over the other cities in its trained probation staff (many of whom are college women or lawyers) is almost wholly nullified. In Philadelphia, the judge is given before trial a brief written statement regarding the court record, and physical condition of each defendant. A marked divergence from the practices in these two cities is seen in the Women's Court of New York, where, as pointed out, the Probation Department strictly delimits its field. Rarely are those beyond the pale of a first offense presumed eligible for probation. To only a third of · these, possibly, is probation granted. Chicago has no definable method for determining eligibility for probation. Arrested women, while awaiting the call of their cases, may be interviewed by two or three different women court officials, but, curiously, not by a member of the probation department itself unless, later, the judge contemplates placing the defendant on probation. In that event she is referred to the probation officer attending the court, who, on the basis of a hurried interview, makes her recommendation. Inadequate as the probation service of the Chicago Morals Court unquestionably is, one might suppose its deficiencies would be supplied

---

[1] Out of the 50 representative case records studied in each of the three cities, it was found that 22 persons placed on probation in Philadelphia had been convicted previously from one to ten times; 14, in Boston, from one to 22 times; and four in New York, from one to three times.

by its social service secretary. For this title implies the existence of a special department of the court concerned with the welfare of arraigned persons. It might well be supposed that the secretary would direct and supervise such activities as are commonly embraced by the term, "social service." What, actually, is she accomplishing? The social service secretary interviews detained women, partly for the purpose of determining their eligibility for probation. Frequently, as a result of these interviews she is able to summon relatives or friends to the court or to get in touch with families of girls from other towns in order to send certain ones home.

She is almost hopelessly handicapped, however, not only by the lack of a staff and facilities for carrying out any systematic well-developed policy, but by the unorganized state of the court and the divided authority under which its personnel operates. The social service secretary (who deals with women defendants only) is appointed by the Chief Clerk of the Municipal Court; the probation officers, by the Chief of the Adult Probation Department; the policewomen, by the Chief of Police; the women bailiffs, by the Chief Bailiff; the woman physician and the man psychiatrist, by the Chief Justice. The activities of many of these court officials merge and overlap in a manner that defies untangling. We see a woman physician taking social histories, while a man physician in the health department makes physical examinations, and a woman probation officer supervises men burglars; the social service secretary is largely occupied with the keeping of statistics although two men clerks, also appointees of the Chief Clerk, might reasonably be expected to discharge that function; and almost anyone except the psychiatrist passing upon mentality. Of some value, however, are the social service secretary's individual card records showing the court and social history of arraigned women. Even though the absence of a finger-print system impairs the accuracy of the former and lack of verification the significance of the latter, the information recorded frequently enables the court to detect old offenders and to review somewhat the previous history of the case. While certain bulk statistics are built up from the records, they are rarely correlated, and form, therefore, scant basis for analysis besides being unreliable with respect to the important problem of recidivism.

2. *Investigation.* Probation officers in the four courts enter upon their task of supervision with varying degrees of knowledge concerning the probationer. In Philadelphia, Boston, and New York, where alleged addresses are verified, the officer is at least sure of finding the probationer. Philadelphia and New York, through their finger-print bureaus, know whether they are dealing with first, occasional, or frequent offenders. Philadelphia, New York and Chicago, know whether the probationer is venereally diseased. Philadelphia alone knows the probationer's general physical and mental condition. Philadelphia and New York have fairly complete knowledge of the woman's social and economic status; Boston, slight knowledge. From the foregoing, it is evident that Chicago knows only that the probationer is or is not venereally diseased; Boston, for the most part, only that she lives at a certain place; New York, her court and social history, her address, and whether she is venereally diseased; Philadelphia, her court and social history, address, whether venereally diseased, and her general physical and mental condition.

3. *Supervision.* Whatever minimum standards of selection and investigation may be advocated by the proponents of probation, it is evident that practices vary widely. Shall we find greater uniformity in methods of supervision? To what extent are probation officers making concrete plans for each probationer, suited to her individual needs?

It is surprising to find in the Misdemeanants' Division of Philadelphia—the one court where departments have been created for studying the individual from practically every angle, and where each department writes out elaborate reports concerning cases brought to it—a general absence of constructive planning for probationers. What purpose is served in finger-printing the defendant if five or more previous convictions are no bar to placing her on probation? What value is there in a general medical examination or in recording that the defendant has "lost the tip of her index finger," "denies use of drug," has "a wide skull and small features," "generalized adenopathy," or "one carious tooth," when only occasionally recommendations for medical or dental treatment are carried out? Why should the medical department inquire into defendant's social history when the probation department not only interviews each case but verifies the statements made as well? Or why should the neuropsychiatric department attempt to interview every woman arrested, when, even though mental abnormality is detected in the preliminary interview and a mental test ordered, it is made, probably, in only half the cases; or why should this department submit written statements of the girl's mentality with recommendations as to her special needs, only to have them utterly ignored? The one department to whose findings weight is given is the branch of the medical service which makes pelvic examinations. Philadelphia, like Chicago and New York, definitely recognizes the importance of venereal disease as a problem of sex delinquency, although, curiously enough, out of 993 women found to be infected in 1920, 77 were discharged outright. Of these, 38 had gonorrhea; 22, syphilis in an active stage; and 7, gonorrhea and syphilis.

4. *Visiting.* How frequently do the officer and probationer see each other? The study of 50 cases referred to shows that officers in Philadelphia and Boston saw less than half their probationers in their own homes. Although officers in New York visit their probationers more frequently than in the other cities, they fail to record how often they actually find and talk with the girl herself.

5. *Results.* Where methods of selecting probationers are so diverse and degrees of knowledge and manner of approach

so varied, almost any outcome might reasonably be expected. In Philadelphia, Boston, and New York, where 50 representative case records of probationers were examined and the subsequent history up to a given period ascertained, it was found that approximately half of the cases in Philadelphia and Boston terminated unsatisfactorily, while in New York about one-fourth were unsatisfactory. Of the 50 cases in each city, 24 either absconded or were re-arrested in Philadelphia; 23, in Boston; and nine in New York. The relatively favorable result in New York indicates that discriminating selection is an important factor in proper probation. To what extent, however, this is due to selection, to coöperation with private agencies and institutions, to intelligent supervision, or to a combination of these and other factors, it would be difficult to determine. Where careful selection, diagnosis, planning, and supervision, are so notably absent in other cities, one feels warranted in the inference that favorable results occur in spite, rather than because, of the probation methods practiced.

Until some Binet in the realm of ethics devises tests for determining moral levels, for gauging degrees of reformability in units of moral responsibility, judges and probation officers must continue to grope among probabilities and content themselves with "sizing up" delinquents. A pinch of science and a dash of common sense must still remain the formula for a verdict. Hence, the practices of different courts probably will continue for some time to vary as widely as the individuals comprising them.

The following charts indicate graphically how the procedure, with respect to women arrested for sex offenses, varies in the four cities studied.

CHART I. CHICAGO

Procedure in dealing with women charged with sex offenses in the Morals Court of Chicago.

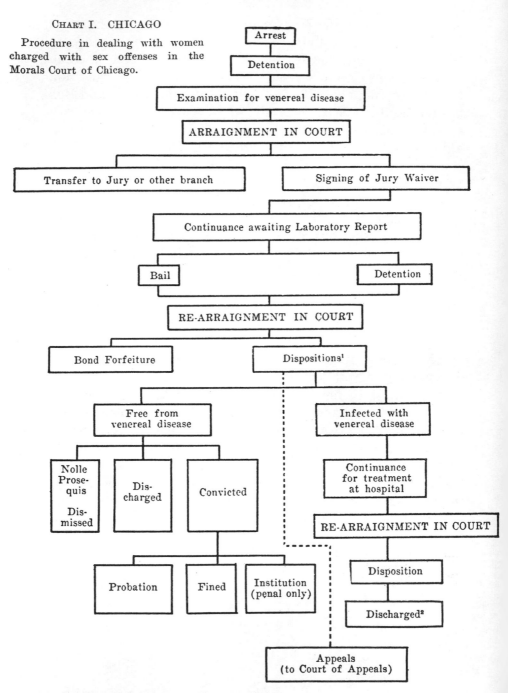

[1] A formal sentence is not always pronounced.
[2] Practically all cases are discharged.

CHART II.

PHILADELPHIA

Procedure in dealing with women charged with sex offenses in the Misdemeanants' Division of the Philadelphia Municipal Court.

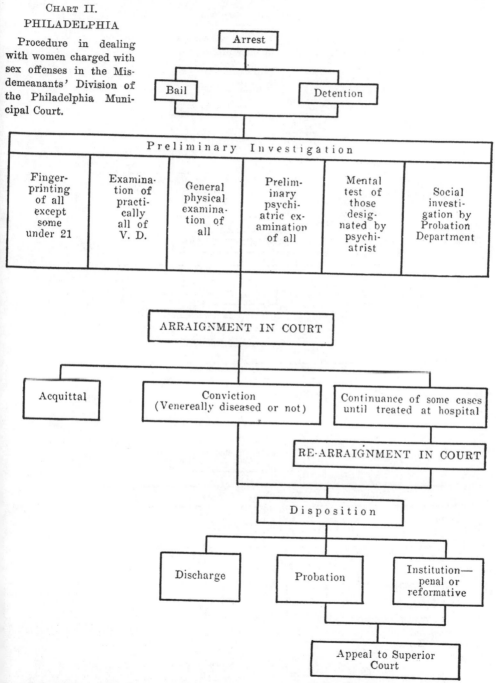

| Arrest |

| Bail | | Detention |

Preliminary Investigation

| Finger-printing of all except some under 21 | Examination of practically all of V. D. | General physical examination of all | Preliminary psychiatric examination of all | Mental test of those designated by psychiatrist | Social investigation by Probation Department |

| ARRAIGNMENT IN COURT |

| Acquittal | | Conviction (Venereally diseased or not) | | Continuance of some cases until treated at hospital |

| RE-ARRAIGNMENT IN COURT |

| Disposition |

| Discharge | | Probation | | Institution—penal or reformative |

| Appeal to Superior Court |

1 Information regarding bond forfeiture could not be obtained from the Philadelphia Court.

CHART III. BOSTON

Procedure in dealing with women charged with sex offenses in the Second Sessions of the Municipal Court of the City of Boston.

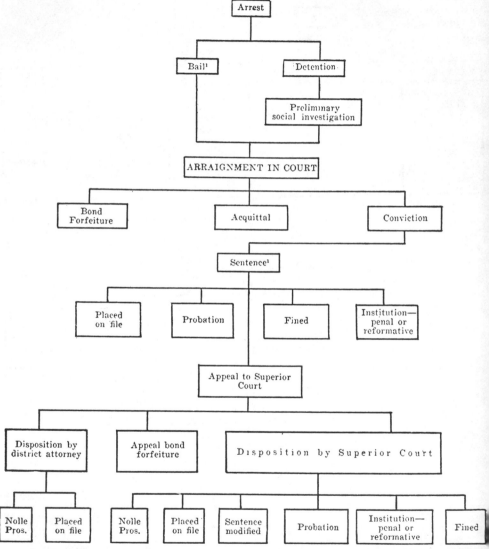

[1] Occasionally convicted women are given a mental examination or a physical examination for venereal disease.

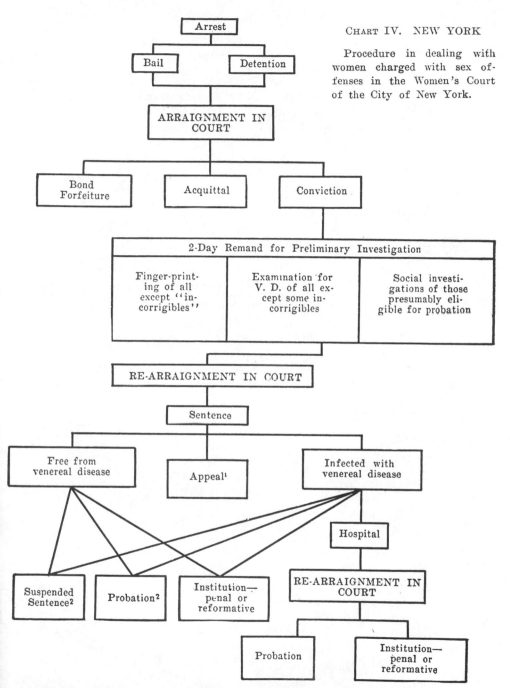

CHART IV. NEW YORK

Procedure in dealing with women charged with sex offenses in the Women's Court of the City of New York.

1 Very few cases appeal. Appeals are now made to a special appellate court.
2 Rarely given if infected with a venereal disease.

TABLE 1. HISTORY OF CASES OF WOMEN SEX OFFENDERS ARRAIGNED
IN FOUR SPECIALIZED COURTS, JANUARY 1 TO JUNE 30, 1920 [1] [2]

COURT	TOTAL NUMBER ARRAIGNED	CONVICTED[3]		DISCHARGED		OTHER DISPOSITION (No sentence)	
		Number	Per Cent	Number	Per Cent	Number	Per Cent
Chicago	1003	195	19.4	687	68.4	121[4]	12.1
Philadelphia	864	548	63.4	153	17.7	163[5]	18.8
Boston	286	231	80.7	33	11.5	22[6]	7.6
New York	684	465	67.9	191	27.9	28[7]	4.0

[1] As it was practically impossible to secure adequate comparative statistical data on the male customer (who corresponds to the prostitute) the few available figures relative to the court disposition are omitted. These may be consulted, however, in the separate reports for each city.

[2] While the offenses for which these cases are arraigned vary from city to city, a general comparison is, nevertheless, possible. Incorrigibles are tried in the specialized courts of New York and Philadelphia only.

[3] For disposition of convicted persons, see Table 2.

[4] This number includes 4, who were nolle prossed; 12, dismissed for want of prosecution; 24 dismissed for want of jurisdiction; 35 who defaulted; and 46 who were transferred to the Jury Branch.

[5] Of these, 27 were listed under "Other Dispositions" and 136 were under treatment in the hospital.

[6] These were disposed of as follows: 2 declined jurisdiction; 2 were dismissed for want of prosecution; 17 defaulted; and the disposition of one was unknown.

[7] All defaulted

SUMMARY AND COMPARISON OF COURTS

TABLE 2. DISPOSITION OF CASES OF WOMEN SEX OFFENDERS CONVICTED IN FOUR SPECIALIZED COURTS, JANUARY 1 TO JUNE 30, 1920

COURT	TOTAL NUMBER CONVICTED	COMMITTED TO INSTITUTIONS				PLACED ON PROBATION WITH OR WITHOUT SUSPENDED SENTENCE		FINED		OTHER DISPOSITION	
		Penal		Reformative							
		Number	Per Cent	Number	Per Cent	Number	Per Cent	Number	Per Cent	Number	Per Cent
Chicago	195	5	2.3	...	...	69	35.3	121	62.0	...	...
Philadelphia	548	198	36.1	43	7.8	306	55.8	1	.1	...	...
Boston	231	51	22.0	8	3.4	121	52.3	13	5.6	38[1]	16.4
New York	465	190	40.0	61	13.1	186	40.0	...	...	28[2]	6.0

[1] Placed on file.
[2] Suspended sentence without probation.

TABLE 3. INCIDENCE OF VENEREAL DISEASE IN CASES OF WOMEN EXAMINED IN PHILADELPHIA AND NEW YORK, JANUARY 1 TO JUNE 30, 1920 [1]

CITIES	TOTAL NUMBER ARRAIGNED	TOTAL NUMBER CONVICTED	TOTAL EXAMINED[2]	NOT INFECTED	TOTAL INFECTED	GONORRHEA	SYPHILIS	GONORRHEA AND SYPHILIS	PER CENT INFECTED OF THOSE EXAMINED	NOT EXAMINED OR RESULTS UNSATISFACTORY
Philadelphia	868	548	824	369	455	193	163	99	55.2	44
New York	684	465	434	204	230	89	107	34	52.9	31[3]

[1] Information for this period was refused in Chicago. No system of routine physical examination exists in Boston.
[2] In Philadelphia, arrested women are examined, while in New York only convicted women may be examined.
[3] As a rule, all convicted women, except incorrigibles, are examined as a matter of routine. Girls convicted of incorrigibility may also be examined upon request of relative or probation officer.

TABLE 4. RELATIVE SPEED IN ADMINISTRATION OF JUSTICE—LAPSE OF TIME BETWEEN ARREST AND FINAL DISPOSITION IN ONE HUNDRED CONSECUTIVE CASES (WOMEN) IN FOUR COURTS, JANUARY 1 TO JUNE 30, 1920

COURT	LESS THAN ONE WEEK	1–2 WEEKS	2–3 WEEKS	3–4 WEEKS	4–5 WEEKS	5–6 WEEKS	6–7 WEEKS	7–8 WEEKS	8–9 WEEKS	9–10 WEEKS	10–11 WEEKS	11–12 WEEKS	12 WEEKS OR OVER
Chicago	4	12	19	13	3	7	11	6	2	3	6	3	11[1]
Philadelphia	79	14	3	1	...	...	...	...	1	1	...	...	1[2]
Boston	60	24	13	1	2	...	...	...	1	...	...	...	...
New York	54	26	6	5	1	5	...	...	...	...	1	...	1[3]

[1] The lapse of time in each of these cases was (in days) as follows: one, 88; one, 89; two, 91; two, 95; one, 100; one, 101; one, 103; one, 153; and one, 167.
[2] Ninety-two days.
[3] Two hundred and sixty-five days.

TABLE 5. PREVIOUS AND SUBSEQUENT CONVICTIONS (FIFTY CASES PLACED UPON PROBATION IN EACH OF THREE CITIES, 1920)[1]

Court	Number of Previous Convictions											Number of Subsequent Convictions up to October 1, 1921					
	0	1	2	3	4	5	10	13	14	17	22	0	1	2	3	4	5
Philadelphia[2]	28	13	6	1	1	..	1	..	..	..	..	32	14	2	1	1	..
Boston[3]	36	2	3	1	1	2	1	1	1	1	1	40	4	3	1	1	1
New York[2]	46	3	..	1	..	..	..	..	..	..	..	46	4	..	..	..	1

[1] Information not available for Chicago.
[2] Based upon finger-print records.
[3] Based upon memories of court officials.

TABLE 6. INCIDENCE OF VENEREAL DISEASE (FIFTY CASES PLACED UPON PROBATION IN EACH OF THREE CITIES, 1920)[1]

Court	Examined					Results					
	Not Examined	For gonorrhea and syphilis	For gonorrhea	For syphilis	Indecisive	Not Infected			Infected		
						Of those examined for gonorrhea and syphilis	Of those examined for gonorrhea	Of those examined for syphilis	Both gonorrhea and syphilis	Gonorrhea	Syphilis
Philadelphia	3	42	1	4	2	17	1	2	6	6	13
Boston	31	19[2]	..	..	..	16[2]	..	..	1	2	..
New York	5	45	..	..	..	25	..	..	12	2	6

[1] Information not available for Chicago.
[2] Records do not state whether complete examination is made.

TABLE 7. FREQUENCY OF CALLS AT HOME OF PROBATIONER (FIFTY CASES PLACED UPON PROBATION IN EACH OF THREE CITIES, 1920)[1] [2]

COURT	NUMBER OF CALLS MADE AT PROBATIONER'S HOME											
	0	1	2	3	4	5	6	7	8	9	10	11
Philadelphia	11[3]	15	10	5	1	3	1	2	...	...	1	1
Boston	21[4]	6	6	6	1	4	2	1	1	1	1	...
New York	12	5	11	11	3	2	2	2	2	...	...	...

[1] In considering the frequency of calls, one naturally must bear in mind the length of the probation term. This varied, in the Philadelphia and Boston cases studied, from three to fifteen months, as follows: In Philadelphia, nine cases were on probation three months or less; fourteen from 4 to 6 months; eleven, from 7 to 9; eleven, from 10 to 12; and five, from 13 to 15 months. In Boston, five were on probation 3 months or less; twenty-one, from 4 to 6 months; six, from 7 to 9; and seven, from 10 to 12 months. In New York, the cases studied were all placed on probation for six months.
[2] Information not available for Chicago.
[3] Three had returned to their homes in other cities.
[4] Four had returned to their homes in other cities.
[5] Ten had returned to their homes in other cities.

TABLE 8   STATUS ON OCTOBER 1, 1921, OF FIFTY CASES PLACED ON PROBATION IN EACH OF THREE CITIES, IN 1920[1]

COURT	ABSCONDED	DIED	STILL ON PROBATION AND NOT REARRESTED	NOT RE-ARRESTED	DISMISSED FROM PROBATION—REARRESTED				PROBATION REVOKED AND SENT TO INSTITUTION
					Once	Twice	Three Times	Four Times	
Philadelphia	6	1	6	19	14	2	1	1	...
Boston	13	...	3[2]	24[2]	5	2	2	1	...
New York	5[3]	...	...	41	3	...	...	...	1

[1] Information not available for Chicago.
[2] Not rearrested so far as known. Sex offenders are not finger-printed in Boston.
[3] One later rearrested.

CHAPTER VI

STANDARDS FOR A SOCIALIZED COURT FOR DEAL-ING WITH SEX DELINQUENTS

Before discussing standards for a socialized court dealing with sex delinquents it may be well to outline some of the essential features of such a court.

OUTLINE

I. THE COURT

    A. Court Having Jurisdiction.

    Either a specially designated branch of a central-ized court, such as a municipal court, or a court specially created to handle sex delinquents. Laws re disposition of defendants and jurisdiction should be adequate.

    B. Nature of Proceeding.

    A summary quasi-criminal action without a jury if possible. General public should be excluded.

    C. The Judge and Other Personnel.

    Judge should be carefully selected and should have a knowledge of social problems with a social point of view and an understanding of psychology, in addition to the usual legal qualifications. Court should have its own personnel, such as bailiffs, court attendants and probation officers.

II. PROCESS AND POLICE COÖPERATION

    Cases should not go before Grand Jury but should be brought either upon information or complaint. Close coöperation between court and police im-portant.

III. DETENTION

Temporary house of detention a requisite for women defendants awaiting trial. There should be facilities for segregating different classes of offenders. Preferable to house very young girls in separate building. Arrested women should be taken to detention house rather than to police station. Facilities should there be available for fixing adequate bail.

IV. TRIAL

Small court-room. District Attorney should assist. Liberal procedure and human emphasis. Few adjournments.

V. STUDY OF CONVICTED DEFENDANTS

A. Remand Period.
Remand after conviction for at least 48 hours for study and investigation.

B. Investigation.
Finger-print record. General physical and mental examination. Social and personal study and investigation.

C. Coöperation with Health Department.
Coöperation between the Court and Health Department recommended.

VI. DISPOSITION OF CASES

A. Suspended Sentence.
B. Probation.
C. Reformative Sentence.
D. Punitive Sentence.
(Fallacy of fines in prostitution cases.)
E. Indeterminate Sentence.

VII. PROBATION AND SUPERVISION

VIII. RECORDS AND STATISTICS

Uniformity.

SEX DELINQUENTS. DEFINITIONS

Who are sex delinquents? In this final article we shall delimit this expression to the man or woman who has been guilty of some minor sex dereliction, such as the individual activities of the prostitute, or the male who pays her for her unlawful acts. We thus exclude the exploiter of the prostitute whether male or female, or the man who lives off the earnings of a prostitute. We shall also exclude the sex criminal, such as the rapist, pervert, or the one guilty of such unnatural relations as incest. We shall limit the use of the term to a class of men and women who may be said to be quasi-criminal, rather than criminal, a class whose treatment by the court might be said to be of a reformative and rehabilitative character, rather than punitive or penal.

The length of the foregoing definition indicates a difficulty that is now being experienced in the matter of legal terminology. The law does not recognize any such special group as the adult delinquent, corresponding to the juvenile delinquent, and development of socialized treatment has been too rapid in the last two decades for the law to keep pace as to terminology. A person who is proceeded against by an action in court in the name of the government or of the people or the sovereign, for the determination of his guilt, is known only as a criminal if convicted, and such action is designated a criminal proceeding,[1] and whatever disposition is made of such person if convicted, is punishment, under the legal terminology employed. The purpose of this punishment may be to prevent the offender from further offending, as by killing or imprisoning him, or to deter others from similarly offending, or for public defense or retribution, or for the reformation of the offender.[2]

Of the last purpose, Wharton says:[3] "Undoubtedly the

---

[1] See Wharton, *Criminal Law*, p. 19.

[2] See Wharton, *Criminal Law*, Chap. 1.

[3] See Wharton, *Criminal Law*, p. 5, Sec. 5.

reformation of the offender is one of the objects which a humane judge will have in view in the adjustment of his sentences; but it cannot be viewed as the primary object, or as supplying the sole standard. The protection of the unoffending, if we reduce the question to a mere personal balance, is at least as important an object of humanitarian consideration as is the reform of the offender. And, again, if we examine the theory critically, we find we are reduced to this absurdity—that we can punish only when we can reform, and hence that the desperate and irreclaimable offender cannot be punished at all.''

The term juvenile delinquent, of course, is well known to the law, and connotes a special treatment of the individual, which for the most part is not opposed to constitutional guarantees, inasmuch as the judge, in such a case, is construed to be *in loco parentis*. The relation of the state to the adult, however, is not synonymous with that of the parent toward the child.

The studies of the four courts make it apparent, however, that there now is a type of treatment which is being applied to the adult sex delinquent which is not vindictive. This treatment is based upon a study of the defendant, against whom a determination has been had, which is known in legal phraseology as a ''conviction'' or a finding of guilty—his history, including court record, his associates, his environment, and his physical and mental equipment; the purpose of such investigation being to provide the basis for an intelligent disposition of the case by the court in the way of probation, or reformative, indeterminate, or punitive sentences. It must be further remembered, that the particular type of lawbreaker with whom this study is concerned, is not, in the main, an offender against a private individual as well as the state, as in the case of one who assaults or robs another, but his offense is against society collectively.

I. THE COURT [1]

A. Court Having Jurisdiction and Extent Thereof.

It is essential that the court dealing with sex delinquents have ample jurisdiction. Whether it is a part or a division of a court of general jurisdiction or whether it is a court specially established, its powers should be broad enough to make such disposition as the nature of the case requires. Two courts have been observed by Mr. Worthington in which a very practical and simple arrangement has been worked out, namely, Chicago and Detroit. The Chicago court, which was described in the first report, has jurisdiction of all misdemeanors. There a centralized municipal court has been established by law, presided over by a chief justice which court and justice has power to establish as many special parts as may be necessary. The part that has been designated for the trial of sex delinquents is known as the Morals Court. In Detroit, there is a Consolidated Criminal Court, having jurisdiction over all crimes committed within the city, felonies, and misdemeanors alike, and it would be possible to set aside a part of this court which could be devoted exclusively to sex delinquency cases, where the judge would have power to make any disposition permitted by law, without the case having to be referred to another or higher court. Very few cities have a centralized or unified criminal court system. It will be found that crimes may be triable in Magistrates, Special Sessions, General Sessions, County or Supreme Court, as in New York, or in the Quarter Sessions or Municipal, as in Philadelphia, or the Municipal or Superior Court, as in Boston. It will probably be generally found, however, that there is no constitutional obstacle to the establishment by the legislature

---

[1] Mr. Worthington has observed the municipal, recorder's, and police courts in the following twenty-one cities: Spokane, Seattle, Wash.; San Francisco, Los Angeles, Cal.; El Paso, San Antonio, Houston, Dallas, Tex.; St. Louis, Mo.; Chicago, Ill.; Milwaukee, Wis.; Detroit, Mich.; Rochester, New York City, N. Y.; Boston, Mass.; Philadelphia, Pa.; Atlanta, Ga.; New Orleans, La.; Oklahoma City, Okla.; and Denver, Colo.

of an approximately centralized or unified court system. The reason for the existence of courts of different jurisdiction in this country is largely historical, due to the desirability of the disposing of minor causes promptly in inferior courts without waiting for the "terms" of the higher courts. This has resulted in the gradual increase in jurisdiction of such inferior courts until many of them are no longer "inferior" except in name, although inheriting still the procedure and traditions of the police and justice of the peace court.

In only one of the courts studied, viz., New York, was the court exclusively a woman's court. While this seems to be very successful, it would seem that there is an economic waste as well as a social loss in having defendants who are arrested in the same transaction, tried in different courts to say nothing of the different results and treatment that might be recorded in two separate courts. It is essential, of course, that the sexes be segregated in separate detention rooms, but surely there should be no objection to trying the prostitute and her patron in the same court, especially when only those persons connected with the particular case are present.[1]

While obviously no obstacle should be placed in the way of appeal to a higher court, yet a case which, by its nature, requires a trial in a specialized court, should not be permitted to go to another court of original jurisdiction for a trial *de novo* under the guise of an appeal.[2] In Boston, we found that the trial *de novo* not only defeated the purpose of the socialized court, but actually resulted in the thwarting of justice.

B. Nature of Proceeding.

The practice of Juvenile Courts in providing for a chancery proceeding probably cannot be followed. The only alter-

---

[1] In New York, where a special woman's court has been established, it has been suggested that two parts be established. Part I for women defendants arrested singly and Part II for those arrested jointly with men.

[2] For a discussion of the pernicious system of trial *de novo*, see pp. 217-221.

native at the present time is a criminal law proceeding, perhaps quasi-criminal in character, to be more accurate. If possible under the constitution, as in New York, it is preferable
that there be no recourse to a jury trial, the case being heard
by the judge sitting as judge and jury. If the constitution
has been construed to require a jury trial for this type of case,
nevertheless, a procedure probably can be established for the
waiving of a jury, as is done in Chicago. Chicago's experience has been that the majority of defendants will waive a
jury trial. For cases in which a trial by jury is required
under the law, it is suggested that they be tried in the same
court by the same judge and that certain days of the week be
set aside by this court for the trial of jury cases. These might
be designated as "jury days." Trials of this kind are designated "summary," but this does not mean that they should
be unnecessarily hurried. The attitude should not prevail
in the court that, because of an unfortunate legal classification, it is "inferior"; on the contrary, the attitude that
these cases are important should be encouraged, and they
should be conducted with the same degree of care as prevails
in the so-called superior courts, even though this may involve,
in some cases, very protracted hearings. One who is accused
of a crime has a constitutional right to a public trial. However, as to what a public trial is, the courts have differed.
In the type of case with which we are concerned, much discretion is vested in the judge in the matter of excluding idle
on-lookers in the interest of public decency or the good order
of the court proceedings.

C. The Judge and Other Personnel.

One of the essentials to a successful socialized court is
the selection of a proper type of judge. It is, of course,
important that the entire personnel be adequate. However,
the most progressive social machinery can be upset and
rendered practically nugatory by a hostile or unintelligent
judge; for example, it would be useless for the court to have

a probation department, no matter how splendidly equipped and no matter how efficient, if the judge refused to place anyone on probation. There is some difference of opinion as to the preferable method of selection of judges. Many authorities, including Dean Roscoe Pound,[1] advocate the appointive method of selection. In large cities, such as Chicago, where a Central Municipal Court has been established, a modification is possible; that is, the presiding judge may be empowered to select from the entire bench of the Municipal Court the judges who are best suited for each of the specialized branches. Where the bench comprises a large number of judges, a fairly good selection may be made in this manner, regardless of whether the judges are elected or appointed in the first instance. The judge should, in addition to his legal qualifications, have some knowledge of social problems and an understanding of psychology. The term should be at least ten years. Where the assignment to the court is of considerable length, a person of ordinary adaptability can ultimately become an expert in the problems of sex delinquency.

The court should have its own personnel. The court should not be dependent upon the police department or some other branch of government for its bailiffs, court attendants, or other similar personnel. The social service department, the probation requirements, as well as facilities for investigation, such as mental and physical examination, etc., will be discussed in detail in another section.

II. PROCESS AND POLICE COÖPERATION

Under present conditions practically all sex delinquents are brought to court by the police. There should therefore be very close coöperation between the police and the court. In all four cities studied, arrests were made by the police both with and without warrants. The majority of such arrests

---

[1] *Criminal Justice in Cleveland*, p. 276.

were made by members of the special plain-clothes division of the police department. Attention is called especially to the procedure followed in the New York department, which is found on pages 298–310 of the New York study. This is a combination of the centralized-decentralized [1] system, and appeared to be the most effective of the four cities studied. Attention is also directed to the care observed by that department in the matter of securing evidence and of the checks which are provided against perjury on the part of the police or any of those other corrupt practices which are prone to occur in connection with prostitution. From the very nature of the *modus operandi* of the sex delinquent, it is not always pratical to secure a warrant prior to the making of an arrest, and for this reason special care should be exercised against any possible injustice.

Crime commissions are beginning to question the wisdom or necessity of the grand jury system. Observations have been made by the writer in states where the practice of indicting by grand jury has been abandoned even in felony cases, which are prosecuted upon an information by the district or prosecuting attorney. Certainly it should not be necessary to bring sex delinquency cases before a grand jury. A procedure should be inaugurated whereby they may be prosecuted either upon information of the prosecuting attorney or upon complaint of a private individual, or a police officer.

III. DETENTION [2]

An adequate detention house should be provided for the temporary .detention of women delinquents prior to trial.

---

[1] This was the system in existence in New York at the time of the study.

[2] Special reference is made to women offenders, because facilities for women in the average police station are notoriously inadequate. Better accommodations are generally possible for men in police stations than for women offenders. The detention house can well be used for the temporary detention of all arrested women, regardless of offense, pending trial, providing proper segregation is made.

Facilities should be provided in this detention house for the segregation of the apparently hardened offenders from the less hardened ones. Very young girls, who are yet over the juvenile age, should be housed, if possible, in a special building, or at least on a separate floor, as in Philadelphia. Special attention should be given in these buildings to sanitation, heat, light, and air. It is obvious, of course, that they should be in charge of women. An excellent procedure is followed in Philadelphia whereby the police, immediately after the arrest of the woman sex delinquent, take her directly to the central house of detention, without subjecting her to the necessity of first appearing at a police station. It is demonstrated in Philadelphia that the woman may be slated or booked by the police at such detention house without greatly interfering with police routine.

Arrangements can also be made whereby the officer in charge of slating or booking the defendant may be empowered to fix bail. Where this is done, however, adequate safeguards should be provided, such as a rule fixing the amount of bail for different types of offense, such amounts being sufficiently large to guarantee the appearance of the defendant at the trial. A rule which seems to work very well in New York does not permit the desk lieutenant, charged with the fixing of the bail, to accept anything but cash collateral or liberty bonds in prostitution cases in the sum of $500. Safeguards should also be taken to prevent defendants from getting into the clutches of bond sharks. This has been done in New York by requiring all persons engaged in bonding for gain to be licensed, and fixing a maximum commission which they may charge for bonding service. Adequate detention facilities and an immediate trial, also do much to minimize the bond-shark evil.

IV. TRIAL

Observations in the various cities indicate that the best results seem to be obtained where a district or prosecuting attorney is present in court. He not only is of great assistance to the police in properly presenting the evidence and in bringing out the facts of the case, but he may also serve as a check upon over-zealousness or possible oppression on the part of the police. For instance, if upon questioning the police, he finds they have no legal evidence against the defendant or that their evidence is extremely weak, he will promptly move for a dismissal of the case.

A small court is preferable for several reasons: It permits a certain amount of informality which tends to encourage the bringing out of the real facts of the case, and also it makes more easily possible the exclusion of the general public, who can have no other interest in a court of this kind than that of morbid curiosity.

Judge Edward F. Waite, of Minneapolis, has well said, in speaking of a socialized court, that its aim should be not so much the adjudication of private rights as the performance of what are conceived to be community obligations. It would seem therefore in carrying out this idea that a more liberal procedure and a more human emphasis is possible than is observed where the adjudication of private rights is involved.

It is very important that an immediate trial be not only possible but that it be encouraged by the judge. The dilatory tactics of shyster lawyers in requesting adjournments and delays, usually for the sole purpose of tiring out or discouraging witnesses or in some other way to thwart justice, should be strongly discountenanced.

The trial of a case of the kind with which we are here concerned, involves the determination of facts which predicate the right of the government to interfere with the defendant. Such determination should be particularly careful because it involves the fixing of the status of the defendant, which may or may not be that of a person with whom public interference is warranted. Until the present laws with reference to the swearing of witnesses, the methods of taking testimony in conformity with the rules of evidence, the question of the weight of evidence, etc., have been modified, strict adherence to them is, of course, necessary.[1] After conviction, however, when the status of the defendant has been fixed, the door is open for a much broader social treatment than exists before the finding of guilty.

V. STUDY OF CONVICTED DEFENDANTS

A. Remand Period.

It will be remembered from the New York study that the practice is there followed, immediately after conviction, of remanding the defendant for study and observation for a minimum period of 48 hours. This period may be extended if necessary. This practice seems to be the most effectual of that observed in any of the courts enumerated. It is obvious that in order to permit the judge to make an intelligent disposition of the case, a thorough study should be made of the social case history of the defendant. The most practicable period from all angles (constitutional rights being considered) seems to be that space of time which intervenes between conviction and sentence. The purpose of such a study is to determine whether or not the defendant should be placed upon probation or sent to a reformatory or receive a corrective or punitive sentence.

B. Investigation.

One of the first things which should be done is to secure the finger-print record of defendant for the purpose of determining his previous court record. For instance, the record, as kept in New York, can show, within five minutes, the

---

[1] The chief aim, in fact as well as in theory, should be the simple ascertainment of the truth.

offense, the date of previous sentence, the judge rendering it, its duration and nature, whether probation, reformatory, or workhouse. This record informs the investigator whether or not the defendant is a recidivist,[1] and furnishes several clues upon which he may work.✓ During the remand period a general physical and mental examination of the defendant is essential, because it is now pretty generally believed that crime and delinquency are medical and mental as well as legal problems.| It is urged by some that courts should be clinics in charge of medical men, by others that they should be psychopathic laboratories in charge of psychiatrists and psychologists, and however this may be, there is no longer any denying that our criminal court system needs reconstruction to keep pace with modern science, business efficiency, psychology, psychiatry, and sociology.

It is important that facilities be provided for the court for a complete mental and physical examination. A precedent for this is found in the Philadelphia court, which has its own psychopathic laboratory and its medical department. ✓This will permit the court to have full and complete information, physical and mental, as well as social. These all have a very important bearing on the disposition of the case; for example, the mental examination may disclose that defendant is suffering from a mental disease or that he is a defective, requiring a special type of custodial care. On the other hand, the physical examination may indicate that defendant's criminal propensities may be due indirectly to causes which may be removed by medical or surgical treatment, or that defendant may be infected with communicable diseases transmissible to other persons with whom he may be brought into contact by the court's disposition if this knowledge is not available. |

It is obvious, of course, that a complete investigation should be made of the personal and social history of the defendant. It has been said that probation is really case

---

[1] One who repeatedly relapses into prior criminal habits.

work in court. The preliminary investigation, which is the beginning of the case work with the defendant, logically falls within the province of the probation department of the court. This preliminary investigation should be made of all convicted defendants, regardless of their previous record. A fuller discussion will be found under the topic "Probation and Supervision."

C. Coöperation With Health Department.

Another coördinate arm of the government, namely, the health department, is charged with the conservation and protection of public health just as the court is charged with the protection of public morals. Obviously there should be coöperation between them. If the physical examination of the defendant discloses the existence of a communicable disease, there is a duty in the court to report that fact to the health department, under the same logic that there is such a duty devolving upon every individual who has knowledge of similar facts. The question of whether or not the defendant has a communicable disease should not of course enter in the question of the guilt or innocence of defendant. Inasmuch as the defendant's condition, where he has a communicable disease, has been reported to the health department, the court may rightfully assume that the health officer, being a responsible public officer, will take such action as he may deem necessary in the premises. The health officer, on his part, may be satisfied that sufficient protection is given the individual and the public, where the defendant, if committed, goes to an institution where treatment is provided. The duty has already been established in the governing boards and heads of public institutions to provide treatment facilities. Where the defendant is placed on probation if the health officer believes that defendant should be hospitalized, any action on his part with reference thereto, need not interfere with the terms of probation.

VI. DISPOSITION OF CASES

The usual dispositions possible are: suspended sentence, probation, reformative sentence, indeterminate sentence, and punitive sentence (including fines).

A. Suspended Sentence.

Where other dispositions are possible, including probation, there would seem to be little if any justification for the suspended sentence. An instance where it might properly be used would be where defendant is an escape from an institution outside the state or has violated parole under a commitment to a reformative institution in another state, and where the parole or other officer from such institution is present in court so that the court may deliver the defendant over to such officer after suspending sentence in the case in which the immediate conviction has occurred.

B. Probation.

Various practices with reference to probation were observed in the different cities. In New York, where the selection seemed to be most careful, a rule is generally followed of placing only first offenders on probation. Whether this should be made an invariable rule will be more fully described in the section on probation. The studies have confirmed our belief that probation should not be made a "catch all" for cases for which there seems to be no other disposition possible, but probation should be given only to those whom the careful preliminary study indicates as persons likely to be benefited by such a procedure.

C. Reformative Sentence.

Almost as great care in selecting defendants for this type of disposition should be exercised as that in case of probation. This should be given to the younger delinquent who requires closer supervision than is possible in probation, and for whom there seems to be a prospect of rehabilitation, and with whom probation has either been unsuccessfully tried, or for whom it does not seem to be practicable.

D. Punitive Sentence.

The protection of the unoffending should, of course, be an object of humanitarian consideration as well as the reform of the offender. It is true of sex delinquents as it is of confirmed criminals that they are of vastly different types and some may be found for whom punishment seems to be the only alternative.[1] In New York, many defendants receive sentences in the workhouse for periods varying from one day to six months. These might be roughly classified in two categories:

(1) Those receiving sentences of less than 30 days, for which sentence there seems to be little justification other than a frank admission that the court does not know what else to do with them and uses this as a catch-all.

(2) Those receiving sentences from 30 days to six months, who the judge probably believes are in need of punishment.

The fine as a punishment or deterrent in prostitution cases should be completely discarded.

The following excellent statement with reference to fines is contained in the resolutions of the All-America Conference on Venereal Diseases, which convened in Washington in December, 1920:

"Whereas a woman who prostitutes herself for hire, alone of all prostitutes, derives her livelihood thereby; and

"Whereas the occasional imposition of petty fines against prostitutes is not a deterrent, but results in stimulating them to greater activity in practicing their business to pay their fines and further makes the community a sharer in the proceeds of prostitution; and

"Whereas the majority of States have no reformative

---

[1] All sentences should be, however, for an indeterminate period.

institutions for adult women, and the personnel and funds for intelligent supervision of women under probation are inadequate:

"Resolved, That the only justification for the imposition of fines as punishments in this class of cases is where the court has no power to impose any other punishment, and that in such cases the most appropriate procedure is to impose so large a fine that the delinquent will be unable to pay and will upon default in payment automatically go to an institution. The imposition of a fine should not be permitted by the police to operate under any circumstances as a license; and

"It is further Resolved, That the All-America Conference on Venereal Diseases is opposed to the fining system in prostitution cases and recommends the immediate repeal of all laws permitting fines in communities having adequate reformative or penal institutions and probation systems, and a similar repeal of laws permitting such fines in other communities as fast as such communities establish such adequate institutions and probationary machinery."

E. Indeterminate Sentence.

This classification is given to that type of delinquents for whom is provided in New York the so-called Parole Commission sentence. Under the Parole Commission Law, this sentence may be given to those defendants who have had two previous convictions during the preceding 24 months or three previous convictions within any period. It is an indeterminate sentence not exceeding two years. This permits of a long period of observation of persons who have perhaps been tried under probation or in reformatories with apparent failure, and of whom a longer study is necessary than could be made during the remand period. An administrative board, such as the Parole Commission, after a sufficiently long observation and supervision, can determine whether or not something may be done towards the reclaiming of the offender or whether or not an indefinite period of detention is desirable, both in the interests of the individual and of society.

VII. PROBATION

Probation has been defined as "a system used by courts in suitable instances to discipline or improve the conduct or conditions of adult offenders or children without commitment to an institution, by releasing them conditionally under the authoritative, helpful oversight of an official known as the probation officer."[1] The executive secretary of the National Probation Association characterizes this system as "nothing more nor less than social case work in the courts, organized and legalized."

To determine, therefore, what offenders are suitable for probation, what manner of discipline or improvement may be applied, and what kind of supervision should be exercised, constitutes the essential problem of this method of treatment.

Standards. Standards for effective probation work were formulated a few years ago at one of the annual conferences of the National Probation Association.[2] These standards, 31 in number, stress among others, the importance of:

1. Limiting the number of cases supervised by one officer at any one time, to fifty.

2. Inducing the judges not to place on probation the definitely feeble-minded, confirmed inebriates, or habitual offenders.

3. Making a preliminary investigation.

4. Securing the services of physicians, psychiatrists, and psychologists to examine delinquents before sentence.

---

[1] *Methods of Supervising Persons on Probation.* Report of a committee appointed by the New York State Probation Commission to investigate and make recommendations concerning methods of supervising probationers. Albany, 1922, p. 3.

[2] *Social Courts and Probation.* Proceedings of the 13th Annual Conference of the National Probation Association, Atlantic City, 1919.

5. Individualizing treatment.   Points of concentration should be health, education, employment, recreation and spiritual development.

6. Receiving reports and making home visits systematically.

7. Making a definite constructive effort to help probationers by means of kindly guidance, home visiting, and practical service.

8. Requiring definite qualifications as to character, ability, and training on the part of probation officers..

In spite of the fact that organizations have so clearly recognized the essential elements of their task, one still finds serious discrepancies between theory and practice.   On the basis of special studies of probation, the writers feel impelled to raise this query: "How many officers in the United States are able to limit cases to fifty or less—cases assigned after a careful preliminary investigation on the part of a trained social worker—cases among which no feeble-minded, inebriate, or habitual offender may be found?   How many probation officers in the country are finding it possible to individualize treatment to the extent of making a definite, constructive plan for each probationer based upon a report that deals even with the outstanding factors of the social, physical, mental, and emotional needs of the delinquent?"

After much discussion with probation officials, one is able to formulate from their statements a composite point of view relative to their difficulties, which might read somewhat as follows:

"Because we are too few in number, it is frequently necessary for a single officer to carry from one to two hundred active cases at a time.   Many of these are unsuitable subjects for probation.   Some might profit by training and discipline in the state reformatory or some private institution, but the judges don't like to take two or three years out of a young girl's life.   If they are sent to the Workhouse they will mix with the old, hardened offender. Some of these unsuitable types are mentally deficient, but our institutions for the feeble-minded have long waiting lists. While probation is, in a great many instances, applied to women who undoubtedly will derive little benefit from it, because of the factors indicated, by a process of elimination it frequently seems to be the best available disposition. Burdened with these practically hopeless cases, we are hampered in exercising constructive supervision on behalf of those cases to whom probation has been wisely applied. As it is, our officers frequently are unable to visit many of their cases more than once or twice during the probation period; sometimes, in fact, not at all. Instead, the probationer reports at the court. Only too often, in such cases, the officer is absent, with the result that a purely perfunctory report is made to a clerk or stenographer. Another reason why our officers cannot adequately supervise cases is that most of their time is taken up in investigating new cases. Furthermore, it is impossible to get trained officers for the salaries offered.''

In attempting, therefore, to indicate the requisites of a model probation department, one is immediately conscious of the fact that they have been stated repeatedly by those best informed about the matter, namely, court officials and probation associations. With equal clearness, those dealing with delinquents have defined their difficulties in realizing even approximately the desired standards. It becomes apparent that a model probation department is compatible only with a model court. As such a court is not likely to spring fully equipped into being, suggestions for improved probation methods, even where the department works under some of the handicaps indicated, may not be out of place.

Preliminary Investigation and Supervision. The activities of a probation department are marked by two well-defined stages, namely, preliminary investigation and supervision. for only a portion of those investigated are actually placed upon probation. In fact, it is generally held that the purpose of the preliminary investigation is to determine which cases are presumably eligible for probation.[1]

Preliminary Investigation. The Probation Department of the Women's Misdemeanants' Division in Philadelphia makes a preliminary investigation of all defendants. In New York, on the other hand, usually only first offenders are investigated. And of these, only a portion are placed on probation. Thus it is apparent that the Probation Department, in order to determine which cases are eligible for probation, must make an investigation of many court cases. Naturally, no court would think of inviting the superintendent of a reformatory or of a private institution receiving commitments from the court, to make an investigation of all convicted persons in order to determine the fitness of some for their particular institutions. Nor should those directing any form of supervision or control, study all in order to treat a few. Yet this is what the Probation Department does whenever it investigates all cases in order to select probationers. Such an incongruous procedure would be obviated if the original purpose and scope of the department were broadened to include a social investigation of every case for the purpose of determining the best possible disposition. In this way the Probation Department would become an important part of the social service of the court. Gradually our courts are realizing that every sentence meted out should be based on social as well as legal considerations; that it is impossible to make a suitable disposition of any case without adequate insight into the social, physical, mental, and emotional history of the defendant.[2] To secure such information the court will need

---

[1] The first probation law, passed in Massachusetts in 1878, authorizes the appointment of ''a suitable person, whose duty it shall be . . . to investigate the cases of persons charged with or convicted of crimes and misdemeanors, and to recommend . . . the placing on probation of such persons as may reasonably be expected to be reformed without punishment.''

[2] That a preliminary investigation is of value to the judge in determining what sentence to impose is the experience of the Probation Department of the

the services of a physician, psychiatrist, psychologist, a case supervisor and a sufficient number of trained social workers. The first three might be attached to the court or to community clinics. The case supervisor and the social workers would naturally be the chief probation officer and her staff.

Those who may object to the investigation of recidivists need only to be reminded that the records concerning such persons when they entered the court for the first time are still available. The new investigation need cover only the period of time which has elapsed since the last conviction. If in the meantime, the delinquent had received custodial care, the results of any studies made in the institution may be made a part of the court records. Whether the recidivist should be placed upon probation is a matter to be determined only after a thorough study of all aspects of the case. One cannot say that no recidivist should be placed upon probation any more than one can assert that all first offenders should be placed on probation.

First of all, the court will wish to know whether the person awaiting sentence is a first, occasional, or habitual offender; whether she is free from infectious disease, of whatever nature; whether she is of sound mentality. It will then need to know something of her social and economic status and her outstanding characteristics. It will wish also to learn whether the girl or her family is known to welfare agencies or institutions. A brief summary of the outstanding results of the investigation, with recommendations as to disposition, would follow as an obvious corollary of the preliminary studies made. The recommendations, which should be specific in character and made in writing, might well comprise two sets: First, those within the range of facilities available; second, those that might presumably meet the requirements of the

---

Recorder's Court in Detroit, where "the percentage of investigations is gradually growing, as judges prefer to know social factors before sentencing." *Report on Probation for Women*, by Elva M. Forncrook, Director, Women's Division, 1924, ms.

case. Then, by recording the steps taken, the outcome of the case, and a brief analysis of the important factors contributing to success or failure, the court would gradually develop an insight into the needs of its charges and could in turn make the community aware of those needs. Instead of standing on an apologetic defensive, reiterating the handicaps under which it is laboring, the court should be able to assume an intelligent offensive that would enlist public support.

The court, of all social institutions, is perhaps the most in need of enlightened support from the community in which it operates. Specialists in any field often find themselves occupying a lonely outpost and are apt to feel exasperated, when the cause which they espouse is not accorded whole-hearted public support. Legislatures do not appropriate the needed thousands. The public is ignorant and apathetic. Specialists rather easily overlook the fact that their distinction as such would disappear if the general public possessed their knowledge. And to-day, those who advocate treating delinquency as a malady to be cured, rather than a crime to be punished, are prone to forget that they hold such a view only as a result of intimate contact with offenders and close, extended, scientific study of their needs. When they come forward with requests for modern institutions for the feeble-minded, reformatories constructed on the cottage plan, appropriations for better trained probation officers in order that the delinquent may be "adjusted" while continuing to live in the community, they must remember that the public in its innocence, supposes that the courts exist for the protection of society and the punishment of those who threaten its peace and safety. Is not this the tradition, centuries old, in which it has been wrapped? If the awakening be too rude, is it strange that the public talks of "coddling" prisoners, or of probation as responsible for the so-called crime wave? The courts, as laboratories for the study and treatment of the law-breaker, with the view of reclaiming him, is a conception so far removed from the old one of punishment, that it calls for careful intelligent interpretation on the part of those charged with the task. Such a work has been undertaken by a group of women in Connecticut who are seeking to interest the women of the state concerning their responsibilities on behalf of delinquent women. If the courts need public funds, they need, still more, public understanding.

Certain cities may very properly inquire: "Of what practical value is such a study if we have no state training school, no adequately developed probation system, or insufficient accommodations for the custodial treatment of the feeble-minded?" This will be discussed elsewhere. The probation officer, when the selection of certain apparently unsuitable types for probation has been criticized, is wont to reply plausibly: "In deciding whether the case is suitable for probation, one must bear in mind what alternatives are open to the judge. For he must ask himself, not whether the delinquent is ideally suitable for probation, but whether probation would not be better than a jail sentence or commitment to a reformatory." So long as such a system of probation by elimination is adhered to, so long as we cling to the belief that we must put up with what we have, so long as we conceive of probation as a catch-all disposition, rapid advance in a truly socialized treatment of the offender need hardly be expected. The danger of such a complacent attitude lies in the fact that the whole probation system is brought into disrepute, and its genuine merits obscured by the inevitable failures.

Who shall make the preliminary investigation? Some would have special officers undertake this work, reserving for the supervision of cases placed upon probation those officers who show special aptitude in dealing with individuals. Others feel it is unfortunate, in case the delinquent is placed upon probation, for a new officer to start afresh. Such a procedure, they hold, practically discards the friendly confidential relations established between the investigator, the girl, and her family. This latter point of view apparently overlooks the fact that only a portion of those investigated will be placed under the supervision of a probation officer. Apparently, also, those holding this view do not concede that a competent investigator may not be equally successful in winning the confidence and affection of those she is seeking to influence.

Supervision. After the delinquent has been placed upon probation and assigned to the care of a probation officer, the first step of the officer should be to review the reports and recommendations contained in the preliminary investigation, in order to develop a suitable plan for the girl's rehabilitation. A careful analysis of the various reports would show her assets and liabilities. The latter could be listed in the order of their importance. A change of environment, medical treatment, training for some special work, better recreational facilities, might be matters for immediate consideration. The objectives, of whatever nature, should be listed and plans for their attainment tentatively worked out. Probation departments in Detroit and Buffalo are said to follow plans somewhat similar to the one outlined. Such a procedure enables the officer to check up on what she actually accomplishes with respect to each case. From time to time, it would be well for the officers, the psychiatrist and the psychologist to discuss progress in their treatment of the girl, so that needed modifications of their plan might be effected. Thus, it is seen the period of supervision is marked by three distinct stages:

1. Remedial and constructive measures.

2. Observation of the effect of those measures.

3. Modification or development of plans in accordance with observations made.

Only too frequently, in the writer's observation, supervision apparently implies policing the probationers. Visiting on the part of the probation officer and reporting on the part of the girl may indicate somewhat "how she is getting along." It leaves open the question whether her good behavior may be ascribed to the efforts of the probation department, or her bad behavior to the inadequacy of those efforts. It may fairly raise the question whether, under a suspended sentence without probation, the offender might not have done as well or as poorly.[1] For if probation is indeed "nothing more nor less than social case work in the courts" it must undertake constructive measures on behalf of the delinquent, and not merely note the outcome of the case.

VIII. RECORDS AND STATISTICS

Adequate records and statistics should be maintained by the specialized court. These are important, not only with relation to the individual delinquent, but as a basis for evaluating the methods employed by the court. It is highly desirable that the courts adopt, where practicable, a uniform system of records. Such a system should preserve the outstanding facts relative to arrest, detention, trial, and disposition of the delinquent. It should also include the written recommendations to the court, the findings of the Probation Department, and the various specialists who examine the girl. If the girl is placed upon probation, a record should be kept by the Probation Department, showing its plan of supervision and treatment. After the case is closed, a summary and discussion of the main features of the case, with a statement as to the outcome, and a brief analysis of the factors contributing to success or failure, should be added. If the delinquent is committed to an institution, a duplicate copy of her institutional history should be filed with the papers in the Statistical Department of the specialized court.[2]

---

[1] This does not mean that the writers advocate a suspended sentence. They merely wish to point out that the condition described has been frequently observed.

[2] In New York a committee has been formed representing the Women's Court, all organizations coöperating with it, and the different institutions to which the court makes commitments, for the purpose of providing a uniform system of classification, terminology, and records.

ADDENDA

Since the making of the studies in the four courts, certain statutory changes have been made by the legislatures of Illinois, New York, and Pennsylvania, in laws with which the courts dealing with sex delinquents are concerned. These changes are as follows:

Illinois. Amendment of the Kate Adams Law, Sec. 57, a-1, by page 403 of the laws of 1921, to provide for the commitment of both male and female of a house of ill-fame or assignment.

Sec. 57 of the Criminal Code was amended by the Laws of 1923 to provide for the commitment of keepers and patrons of houses of ill-fame.

New York. Amendment of the incorrigibility statute known as The Wayward Minor Law. This was amended by Chap. 868 of the Laws of 1923 to enlarge the powers of the court to deal with females between the ages of sixteen and twenty-one.

Pennsylvania. The Legislature in 1923 enacted a new statute known as Public Law 982, Sec. 1–5, which defines prostitution as the offering or using of the body for sexual intercourse for hire, and which penalizes such acts as well as solicitation, assignment, and the keeping or using of any place, structure, building, or conveyance for the purpose of prostitution. The act provides for commitment in case of conviction.

INDEX

A

Addenda, 450
Additon, Henrietta, vi
Adult delinquents, 427
American Institute of Criminal Law and Criminology; minimum requirements for criminal court records, 60, 61, 140
American Social Hygiene Association, v, vi
Appeals: Chicago court, 68; Boston court, 220; trial de novo not an appeal as the terms is commonly understood, 245; tables, 256, 265, 266, 267, 268, 269; New York court, 291; tables, 380, 381
Arrest: Chicago court, 11, 12; Philadelphia court, 89, 90; New York court, 289, 298, 304; arrests and convictions compared, 67

B

Bail: Chicago court, 12, 13, 61, 62, 68: table showing number and amount of cash bonds accepted January 1 to July 1, 1920, 81; discussed, 13; rules governing in Municipal Court, Chicago, 12; Boston court tables of forfeitures, 260, 261; Real estate forfeiture table, 261; discussion of tables, 243; New York court, 304, 305, 307, 308; table of forfeitures, 381; discussed, 308; night court to stop evil of station-house bond, 280; bail to be fixed at detention house, 433; safeguards in fixing bail, 433
Barlow, Peter T., 297
Bedford Reformatory: The New York State Reformatory for Women described, 355–357: Commitment to, 311; probation cases to, 350, 351; rearrested on parole sent to, 357, 369; report of parole committee, 357; sentenced to when refused to go to hospital for treatment, 313
Bellevue Hospital mentally defective cases to, 352

Big Sisters, Chicago, 57
Bill drafting bureau, 372
Binet and Simon direct method testing and attempt to do the same for the psychoses, 33
Board of Education: teaching in hospital, 344; instruction at House of Good Shepherd, 363
Bondsmen, professional, 281, 333
Boston court, see Municipal Court, Boston
Bridewell, The House of Correction, Chicago, 52–54
Bureau of Laboratories, New York, 335
Bureau of Missing Persons, Philadelphia, 131
Bureau of Personal Service, Chicago, 57
Bureau of Preventable Diseases, New York, 335
Bureau of Social Hygiene, v

C

Catholic charities: follow-up work on girls discharged from House of Good Shepherd, 365; maintain a worker in the court, 347
Catholic Protective Society, follow-up work, 365
Case on file, Boston, 218, 219, 244, 400
Cases cited: Ben Zellern, change of venue, 16; Breitung, male customer not guilty, 302, 303, 304; Sadie Blum, Cobb on identification by finger-printing, 332; Rice, Kate Adams law held to apply only to women, 10, 18; Olin, warrants illegal under incorrigibility statute, 298; Rosie Klein, offer is act of prostitution, 310; disorderly conduct, Pennsylvania, 87; In re alderman and justices of the peace, 87; streetwalking, Pinkerton, Galloway, Stalcup, 86
Cases illustrative: Philadelphia court, 93–97; Chicago court, 21–24; Boston court, 224, 225; New York court, 315–330

451

I

Identification bureau, Philadelphia, 103

Illinois Vigilance Association, 55

Illustrative cases: New York court, 315–330; Boston, 224, 225; Chicago, 21–24; Philadelphia, 93–97

Incorrigibility statute, 283

Incorrigibles and runaways, Philadelphia, 129–134; table, 130

Indeterminate sentence, standards for, 440

Indiscriminateness, sexual, proof of, 283

Inferior Criminal Courts, Page Commission Report, 280

Inferior Criminal Courts act, New York, 275, 278, 280, 288, 401, 402; sections that apply to New York Women's Court, 288, 289, 290; provides for use of finger-prints, 330; referring to private institutions, 360, 368, 370; probation under, 345, 346; provides for sentence, 355

Institutions: public, New York, 355–360; private, New York, 360–372

Instruction in New York institutions: at Bedford Reformatory, 356; at House of Good Shepherd, 363, 364; at Inwood House, 368

Interdepartmental Social Hygiene Board, 57

Investigation, standards for, 435

Inwood House, 312; described, 367–370; organized, incorporated, purpose, 367; instruction, 368; venereal disease, 368; annual report 1921, 370; formerly New York Magdalen Benevolent Society, or New York Magdalen Home, 360, 367

Iroquois Hospital, Chicago: examination at, 12, 29; probation department can obtain statement of physical condition from, 48

J

Jefferson Market prison, New York, 295

Jewish Board of Guardians, New York, maintains worker in court and aids probation officers, 347

Journal of Social Hygiene, vi

Judges: Chicago court, 3; Municipal Court, Chicago, 3; desirable to have permanent assignments, 19; presiding in the Chicago court, 67; table, 76; Philadelphia court, 145; New York court, 296, 297; system of rotation permits judges to become expert, 145; standards for, and other personnel, 424, 430

Judicature commission, report of, 216, 217

Jump-raid, defined, 96; New York, 300

Jurisdiction: Municipal Court, Chicago, 3; Chicago court, 4, 6; Philadelphia court, 83; Boston court, 215, 216; New York court, 275–282

Jury: not provided in New York Inferior Courts, 275; jury demands, number, Chicago, 21

Jury trial waiver: Chicago court, 14, 16, 20, 64; Philadelphia does not have waiver system, if jury trial required must go before grand jury, 85; trial in Boston court does not constitute jury waiver, 217; compared in the courts studied, 403, 404; procedure probably can be established for 430

Juvenile Court, Boston, 216

Juvenile delinquent, 427

K

Kate Adams law, Illinois, 8, 52; amended, 10; only women punishable under, 10, 18; commitment under, 18

Kings county hospital, New York, 342

Kingston avenue hospital, New York, 311, 312, 313, 336, 340, 341, 348, 351, 352, 359, 365; described, 342–345; routine in, 344

L

Lee, Captain, 87, 89, 90

Law Enforcement: methods compared, 399–404; report on probation by special committee on, 407

Lawndale hospital, 23, 30–31, 54, 56, 60

Laws: adult probation, 38–40; adultery, 9, 10, 23, 87, 221; age of consent, 221; appeal, 291; consolidation act, 280, 284; detaining in house of prostitution, 88, 221; disorderly conduct, 6, 285; disorderly persons, 286; creating Philadelphia court, 84; Chicago court, 4; Boston court, 215; New York court, 278; concerning Philadelphia court, 86–88; Chicago court, 6–11; Boston court, 221–222; New York court, 282–291; enticing for prostitution, 221; failure to keep